Political

The Prolife Cause after 25 Years of *Roe v. Wade*

By
Kenneth D. Whitehead

With the new prospects opened up by scientific and technological progress there arise new forms of attacks on the dignity of the human being. At the same time a new cultural climate is developing and taking hold, which gives crimes against life a new and — if possible — even more sinister character, giving rise to further grave concern: broad sectors of public opinion justify certain crimes against life in the name of the rights of individual freedom, and on this basis they claim not only exemption from punishment but even authorization by the state, so that these things can be done with total freedom and indeed with the free assistance of health-care systems.

—Pope John Paul II, Encyclical *Evangelium Vitae* (#4)

They even offered their own sons
And their daughters in sacrifice to demons
They shed the blood of the innocent
The blood of their sons and daughters

—Psalm 106

ISBN 1-892875-02-0

Published by New Hope Publications/CUL
New Hope, Kentucky 40052

Printed in the United States by
St. Martin de Porres Lay Dominican Community

TO

Rev. Msgr. Michael J. Wrenn

Priest, Counselor, Collaborator, Friend

"I have fought the good fight...

I have kept the faith..."

—II Timothy 4:7

Table of Contents

Introduction

Who could possibly want to read a book about abortion?

It is a singularly distasteful and depressing subject by anybody's standards, and so perhaps it should really not be too surprising that most people generally try to avoid the subject if they possibly can. Nevertheless, legalized abortion in our society has become one of the most important moral issues of our time; if we care about what our country is doing and where it is going, we cannot avoid the subject no matter how much we might like to; we have to inform ourselves about abortion whether we like it or not, and we have to be prepared and willing to do whatever is given to us to do about it. We cannot be indifferent: "The voice of your brother's blood is crying to me from the ground" (Gen 4:10).

Moreover, abortion is more than merely a moral issue; it is inescapably a political issue as well, for no society can really survive as a cohesive and civilized human society as long as it allows and tolerates the elective killing of some of its own members. The very thought of democracy or of a just society is nothing but a mockery under such circumstances. We can see this with increasing clarity now that such evils as assisted suicide and mercy killing have also come upon us — as prolifers were almost alone in predicting that they eventually *would* come upon us back when abortion was first legalized.

Prolifers were often impatiently and condescendingly laughed to scorn when they first talked about "slippery slopes" and insisted that the legalization of abortion would lead not only to additional forms of legalized killing but to yet other moral horrors as well. In the event, though, prolifers have already been proved absolutely right. Once society itself, via the United States Supreme Court, granted that legalized killing was permissible in the case of abortion, not a few others among us, including especially the federal courts, have not been at all slow to extend quite broadly this newly permissible area of willful human control over human life — exercised without regard to the moral law of God.

Essential elements of the moral law of God — specifically, the commandment, "Thou shalt not kill" — were, in fact, simply dropped by our society when abortion was legalized. For more than a few practical purposes the ancient commandment not to kill is now virtually a dead letter in America today; nobody ever imagined in advance that it could or would come about so easily and so fast, but come about it has; and we have now reverted back to the law of the jungle, where at least under certain circumstances the strong now arbitrarily dispose of the weak as they wish.

And it all began with legalized abortion. Nor can it end before the current social acquiescence in allowing the taking of the lives of the unborn has been reversed and placed back outside the pale of what can legally be done in a civilized society. Thus, abortion is inescapably a political as well as a moral problem, and it therefore requires concrete political action and solutions as well as the changes of hearts which indubitably also have to be brought about.

We cannot evade our political responsibility by deciding that abortion is distasteful or merely a "private" moral responsibility, and the main thing is therefore to be compassionate to women who find themselves with "problem pregnancies." Prolifers are the first to agree that we should be compassionate to women with problem pregnancies; but the problems posed by legalized abortion go far beyond that. The fact is that there is no way that we maintain any consistent line (except perhaps temporarily) against any other form of private and elective killing, as long as we continue to permit private and elective killing by abortion: we need think in that connection of the juries in Michigan who now regularly acquit a grisly serial killer such as Dr. Jack Kevorkian in spite of what the law plainly says, and in spite of what was plainly understood by everybody only yesterday, namely, that "Thou shalt not kill." All Dr. Kevorkian has had to do in the present climate is to claim to be "assisting" people to die in the name of compassion, and the laws against killing by private individuals that have stood for thousands of years suddenly go by the boards and are no longer seen as applicable by juries composed of average people.

This book is about the political dimensions of the abortion question in the mid-1990s — during the five years between 1993 and 1998, roughly the principal years of the Clinton Administration. While the Clinton Administration has been more consistently proabortion than anything else at all, the prolife movement, during the same years, has also both grown and matured, and now represents a comparatively strong force in American political life by comparison with what it represented when abortion was first legalized by the Supreme Court's *Roe v. Wade* decision in 1973. At that time the prolife movement did not exist at all; it has obviously come a very long way since then — although, as will be seen in these pages, it still has a long way to go.

In some ways, though, the prolife movement has come to be influential beyond anything anyone imagined in the beginning. During the Clinton years in particular, the prolife movement can point to many undoubted successes achieved in the face of a cynical national administration which both believes in and openly promotes abortion, an equally supportive media which also believes in and promotes abortion, and a public opinion which, even where it can be shown to oppose abortion — which isn't exactly always the case — is nevertheless almost wholly passive about it and tends to evade the issue whenever it can.

Yet much, very much urgently remains to be done on the prolife front: indeed the essential remains to be done: recognizing again as a society the heinous crime that abortion in fact is; and moving by appropriate political means to place it out of bounds again, where, prior to the year 1966, it was officially and rightly consigned in the laws of all fifty of our states.

This book, then, focuses on the current political aspects and implications of legalized abortion. The chapters which comprise it were all written for periodical publication over approximately the past momentous — but also very troublesome — few years represented roughly by the time the Clinton Administration has been in office.

Most of the chapters in the book originally appeared in either *Culture Wars* or *Fidelity* magazines, where editor E. Michael Jones has admirably maintained a strong and consistent interest in the unfolding developments on the political front related to legalized abortion. But there are also included chapters which first appeared in *Catalyst: the Journal of the Catholic League for Religious and Civil Rights, The Catholic World Report, Crisis* magazine, and the *New Oxford Review*.

Because each chapter was written separately as an article, addressing related but usually somewhat different points, and recording new developments as they occurred, it has not been possible to eliminate some points and even some language which are repetitive or duplicative. Nevertheless, all the chapters together should converge to provide a timely broad-brush picture, with considerable detail included, about where the issue of legalized abortion stands after 25 years of *Roe v. Wade*, and what the prolife movement needs to be doing about it.

Kenneth D. Whitehead

Is the Prolife Movement a Political Orphan?

I

Abortion is the political issue everybody wishes would go away. It is widely believed that it cannot be allowed to go on confusing our national life and our national priorities; it must at all costs be "settled," many assert. So firmly is this believed by some that it regularly keeps being decided — prematurely it always turns out — that prolifers, in particular, must "face reality" and recognize that their cause cannot be allowed to stand in the way of what is held to be this or that tolerable "settlement" or "compromise" that supposedly will end all the turmoil and rancor and confusion that has steadily accompanied abortion as a political issue.

Prolifers are given this same message by their enemies, by many who profess to stand "in the middle" on the abortion issue, and even by some who describe themselves as their "friends." While it is understandable that those who favor abortion would like to see the issue settled on the basis of the status quo, namely, Supreme Court decreed legal abortion considered to be a "woman's right" and available virtually on demand at any stage of a pregnancy, with only a few minor restrictions in a few states; but it is not quite so easy to see why so many who say they are prepared to concede that the prolifers may have a point or two are nevertheless also so quick to advise prolifers that their "absolutist" idea that the unborn child should have a right to life under our legal and constitutional system is unrealizable and that prolifers must therefore reconcile themselves to a "compromise."

This may sound to many like a reasonable position, but the fact is that no compromise is being offered anywhere that takes any of the prolifers' real points into consideration. Logically, the opposing side cannot offer any compromise, that is, if abortion truly is a woman's

---

Originally published in *Fidelity* magazine, December, 1993.

constitutional "right," as a vocal and apparently sizeable feminist movement strongly favored by the media keeps on relentlessly insisting.

When something is repeated often enough, it unfortunately too often comes to be widely believed, even if it is in fact not true. And when it thus comes to be widely believed, it also quickly comes to be the conventional wisdom in society at large that the prolifers are the ones who must compromise if we are ever going to be able to put the messy and intractable abortion issue behind us and move on to presumably more important things.

Many today reach this practical conclusion who do not necessarily believe that abortion is an absolute constitutional right of a woman; they may even think it is an evil; but as a practical matter they have decided that it either cannot be effectively fought against or that they themselves do not wish to join the prolifers in fighting against it. Unfortunately, even many who continue to call themselves "prolife" fall into one or the other of these two defeatist categories. The unhappy result of this is that a fairly large number of people end up holding that, whatever the evil of abortion, failure to find a prompt and tolerable accommodation to it represents a greater evil yet.

From here it is but a short step to declaring that a tolerable accommodation to it *has* been found. Scarcely were the 1992 elections over, for example, before syndicated columnist Charles Krauthammer rushed into print to declare with finality that the abortion debate was "over." "With the court's overturning a Guam law criminalizing abortion, and with the election of a down the line prochoice president," pundit Krauthammer wrote, "November, 1992, mark[ed] the end of the 20-year abortion wars. The principle has been settled. . ."

"One can declare a great national debate over," Krauthammer went on, "when all three independently (s)elected branches come to the same position. The Supreme Court, a court that has had not a single Democratic appointment in 25 years, declared unequivocally in the Pennsylvania ruling last summer that it would not permit the criminalization of abortion. With Clinton pledged to appoint abortion rights judges, the already remote possibility of a Supreme Court majority to overthrow *Roe v. Wade* has vanished."

"The other branches are equally secure," Krauthammer averred. "The new president is rigidly prochoice, and there are majorities in both houses of Congress for the Freedom of Choice Act, the legislative equivalent of — and safety net for — *Roe*." It was in fact fairly reliably estimated that the proabortion ranks had gained around ten additional new votes in the House of Representatives in the 1992 elections.

Nevertheless, the 1992 elections were far from a referendum on the abortion issue; the issue had become almost invisible during the campaign, in fact, with the Clinton forces themselves insisting that "It's the economy, stupid!" The Republican "family values" thrust had also quickly beat a rather undignified retreat when pressed by an all-out media assault against "bigotry." The far reaching conclusions of a Charles Krauthammer about the implications of the 1992 elections as regards abortion may thus merely represent how quick and eager commentators on the abortion issue generally are to decide that, where abortion is concerned, "it's all over." This same conclusion, of course, has been announced a number of times before, notably when the *Roe v. Wade* decision itself was first handed down by the Supreme Court.

However that may be, President Clinton certainly acted as if he thought it was all over; and that abortion was henceforth to be considered an established "woman's right." On his third day in office, he removed all restrictions on abortion which were within his legal power as chief executive to remove. By executive order he rescinded a ban on elective abortions in military hospitals; he dissolved the so-called "gag rule" forbidding abortion counseling by non-physicians in federally supported family planning clinics; he ended a moratorium on federal funding of research involving the transplantation of fetal tissue from aborted babies in attempts to cure various diseases; he instructed the Food and Drug Administration to study the lifting of a ban on the importation and commercial availability of the deadly RU-486 "morning after" abortifacient pill; and he reversed the 1984 Reagan Administration restrictions on U.S. aid to international population programs that include abortion as a method of family planning.

In demonstrating these proabortion priorities, President Clinton chose the very day when up to 100,000 prolife demonstrators were physically present on the Mall outside his White House window for what was perhaps the largest March for Life ever on the anniversary of the Supreme Court's *Roe v. Wade* decision. For going on twenty years prolifers had annually braved subfreezing temperatures and even blizzards to turn each January 22 in Washington into a beacon light to the whole country signaling that the slaughter of America's unborn children by abortion cannot be allowed to continue.

Few movements in American history — or none — have ever consistently mustered so many demonstrators, year after year for over two decades, in the service of a single cause; and in this regard the annual March for Life has merely been symbolic of the increasing numbers and heightened convictions of dedicated prolifers all around the country generally.

Yet this massive and sustained prolife effort over two decades somehow seemed to leave the nation little moved. President Clinton's executive orders seemed to cause scarcely a ripple on the surface of the nation's public life — especially by comparison with the widespread and vehement protests immediately aroused by the same president's proposal to allow active homosexuals to serve openly in the military services. This issue quickly proved that Americans were still capable of rising up in a body out of a sense of moral outrage; and, although the prolife cause too has been driven by a broad and justified moral outrage, it has unhappily not been able, over the course of over twenty years, to achieve the same critical mass of apparent public support which the anti-homosexuals-in-the-military cause achieved almost overnight.

The reasons for America's comparative quiescence in the face of mass abortion on demand are no doubt multiple and complex. For one thing, the opposition early won the "public image" battle as to how the whole issue was going to be framed — as a woman's issue and not as a child's issue. And the fact is that it *is* hard to get across to many people the truth that the "embryo" or "fetus" is really a developing child, and that this child is killed by abortion. It is particularly hard to get this across when the media generally refuse to present — often even as paid advertising — the truth concerning fetal development and what an abortion does to the developing child in the womb.

Moreover, sadly, it may well be that, even understanding some or much of this, too many Americans are still prepared to allow the permissive taking of this developing human life anyway — for utilitarian purposes perceived to be "benefits." There is almost always a strong question of perceived "self interest" in people's opinions concerning abortion; however morally wrong abortion might be conceded to be in the abstract, an insidious question always remains: what if *I* (or a loved one) ever *needed* an abortion?

Few stop to analyze the concept of "need" here; and hence many fail to realize that, in the case of abortion, the idea of someone "needing" one means roughly the same thing as the same word means in the sentence, "Hitler's Germany 'needed' *Lebensraum* ("living space") and did not hesitate to by-pass morality in fulfilling this 'need.'"

Various polls and studies have shown that while a majority of Americans (one poll gives 57 per cent) believes that abortion is indeed the taking of a life, an even larger percentage (74 per cent according to the same poll) nevertheless believes a woman should have a right to take that life if she so decides. Few stop to think what it means for our law and jurisprudence generally once we have conceded the principle that individuals have the right to make life and death decisions concerning other individuals.

And whatever the inconsistencies of public opinion on the abortion issue generally, one other hugely important factor which has characterized the era of legal abortion over the past two decades has been the *consistency* of the hostility of the media to the prolife cause. The media have been consistently hostile to prolifers and their cause, both in the way the cause has been presented to the public (as a fringe cause promoted by violence-prone, right-wing kooks and religious fanatics); and also in the fact that significant aspects of the issue, such as the massive total numbers of abortions performed, the numbers performed late in pregnancy, the grisly and brutal methods involved in most of the abortion "procedures," and the further fact that there are no "medical" reasons whatsoever for nearly all of these abortions — these things are never brought out at all, any more than is ever brought out the fact that our Constitution nowhere provides, nor consistently could provide, any such thing as a "right" to an abortion.

For years on end, for example, the media scarcely even reported at all on the — always non-violent — annual March for Life. *Roe v. Wade* was supposed to have "settled" the abortion issue once and for all, and for the media and other cognoscenti the expectation always was that each successive March was always going to be the prolife movement's last gasp. When the Marches kept recurring anyway, year after year, and the numbers joining the Marches even increased, so that they could no longer be ignored, the media simply took to reporting the event "even-handedly," that is, by giving equal time to many thousands of marchers on the Mall and to, say, a "vigil" of a dozen feminists holding up contrary signs before the Supreme Court. If anything, the feminists always got the longer interview time before the TV cameras to state their case.

Similarly, the media have long since taken to using the term "abortion rights" whenever they report on the issue at all, thus not so subtly pre-judging the issue in favor of the woman's supposed "right," while the very existence of the child is pretty consistently left out of the discussion entirely.

In spite of all this drearily regular tendentious public treatment of the abortion issue, though, enough members of Congress have always gotten the message from the grass roots — just as the Reagan and Bush Administrations too always publicly professed to be officially prolife — so that, in spite of the Supreme Court, there were nevertheless in place some restrictions on wide open abortion: the ones which President Clinton moved to rescind when he took office.

The fact is too that, whenever the issue has been clearly posed for a straight up or down vote or its equivalent, the prolife movement has usually not fared too badly. Prolife efforts in many of the states, in particular, have often been quite impressive and have sometimes even been crowned with remarkable success, especially considering the narrow limits within which any prolife political action has even been possible as long as *Roe v. Wade* has been considered "the law of the land."

And finally, the growing incidence and visibility of such direct action prolife manifestations as the picketing of hospitals and abortion clinics by Operation Rescue and others have pointed to the continuing existence, not only of a strong and motivated prolife movement, but also to one that is growing. Similarly, the growth and proliferation of such entirely peaceful, symbolic demonstrations as the Life Chains that have been organized around the country have pointed to exactly the same thing, namely, that "it is *not* over"; it is far from over. In fact, it may have barely even gotten started.

II

None of this has prevented a Charles Krauthammer from trying to declare it over, of course. The Democratic National Convention earlier in the summer of 1992 similarly seemed to be acting on that same assumption when it refused to allow prolife Pennsylvania

Democratic Governor Robert P. Casey even to bring up the issue of abortion at the Democratic convention.

President Clinton, for his part, certainly acted as if he intended to put a quick end to the debate, if indeed the debate was not over yet; for besides his executive orders, his Administration has also been aggressively promoting priority federal legislation such as the Freedom of Choice Act (FOCA), about which more presently, and yet other draft legislation that would make it a felony under federal law to block access to abortion clinics; this latter bill was drafted after a Supreme Court decision in January, 1993, ruled that a Reconstruction-era federal civil rights law could not be used to guarantee women access to abortion clinics.

Both of these anti-life legislative initiatives seemingly received added impetus when, in March, 1993, the murder of an abortionist in Florida by an isolated individual brought such a wave of media censure of prolife violence (while the news of the forthright and unqualified condemnation of this action by *all* the major pro-life organizations, including especially the National Right to Life Committee, was generally blacked out) that people relying only on media reports could perhaps have been pardoned for thinking that the days of the prolife movement really were finally numbered.

The same media phenomenon was repeated later in the summer when a prolife woman shot another "abortion doctor" in Kansas, and the clinic access bill received yet another shot in the arm when even some "prolife" legislators announced support for it in order to stop the "violence."

Already by May, 1993, the *Washington Post* was editorializing that "the country seems to be reaching a consensus on abortion in the light of the Supreme Court's reaffirmation of *Roe* last year and the election victory of abortion rights supporters. There is no longer real fear that the protections afforded by *Roe* are in jeopardy or that hard core opponents, law-breaking as some of them are, will prevail in the court or Congress." It was in the light of this supposed new "consensus" that the same *Post* editorial saw "both houses of Congress. . . moving towards consideration of freedom of choice legislation, and if all goes well, passage can be expected by summer. . ."

The legislation referred to by the *Post* here was the so-called Freedom of Choice Act (FOCA), already mentioned above, surely one of the most radical and far reaching proposals ever put before any human legislature for consideration. The bill specified that "a state may not restrict the right of a woman to choose to terminate a pregnancy. . .before viability; or, at any time, if such termination is necessary to protect the life or health of the woman."

The only exceptions to this sweeping prohibition of virtually *any* restrictions whatsoever on the performance of abortions in the bill as drafted were clauses allowing states, if they wished, to require minors to "involve" a parent, guardian or responsible adult" in an abortion decision; and providing a "conscience clause" for those unwilling to participate in the performance of abortions on grounds of conscience. But even these seeming exceptions to the absolutely wide open legal abortion the bill would have mandated were mostly cosmetic, since "viability" was not defined, and hence an abortion could be performed at any time simply by stating that the woman's "health" was being affected.

Moreover, to "involve" a "responsible adult" in the abortion of a minor could simply mean, for example, involving the Planned Parenthood abortion counselor. Similarly, the "conscience clause" failed to exempt institutions such as, for example, Catholic hospitals, from possible requirements to perform abortions; such exemptions, currently found in the laws of 37 states, would be among the things that would have been invalidated at one stroke by the passage of FOCA.

An identical FOCA bill had been introduced into Congress a year earlier, in 1992, but was never brought forward for a vote in spite of promises to do so by the Democratic congressional leadership at the time of the Democratic National Convention which nominated Bill Clinton. At that time, the Bush Administration's Attorney General, William P. Barr, had written to the Democratic leadership expressing doubt that Congress possessed the constitutional authority to enact such a statute.

And indeed the "finding" in the Senate version of FOCA to the effect that Congress does possess this authority, both under the "interstate commerce" clause of the Constitution, and under the power given to Congress by the Fourteenth Amendment to enforce its own provisions, would indeed seem to be highly dubious. In fact, such a finding would amount to saying that Congress can forbid the states from enacting laws on subjects which do not even come under the jurisdiction of Congress itself, as far as the Constitution is concerned!

If the subject were not so serious, and the stakes so high, an idea such as this would probably have been considered almost laughably absurd in any era before the present era — who would ever have imagined, for example, invoking the "interstate commerce" clause as the justification for killing unborn children? Unhappily, however, the present era has proved to be one where both courts and legislatures have taken to declaring by fiat the existence of new "rights" which nobody afterwards ever apparently dares to question; and in this climate FOCA was taken very, very seriously indeed.

When *Roe v. Wade* was decided by the Supreme Court in 1973, overturning the abortion laws of all fifty states, though, it was generally understood that a constitutional amendment would be required in order to reverse it and to restore the protection of the law to unborn children. Numerous efforts were in fact made to draft and enact various constitutional amendments. The prolife plank of the Republican Party continues to call for the enactment of such an amendment today.

Some twenty years after *Roe*, however, it suddenly seems to have been discovered that Congress can now accomplish by a simple statute, the FOCA bill, what before only the laws of fifty different states managed under the Constitution. When this remarkable discovery of new and apparently unlimited congressional powers was announced, nobody reacted; and soon the *Washington Post* was calmly observing that "passage can be expected."

That FOCA could even be seriously considered as a possible statute under our Constitution is really an indication of how radically the abortion issue distorts and twists out of shape everything it touches, including especially the previous common understanding of the meaning and limits of our Constitution. Why, following the precedent of FOCA itself, could not prolife legislators respond to FOCA by introducing a Right to Life Act, forbidding by simple statute any state from "abridging" the right of life of anyone within its jurisdiction from conception through natural death? Why not indeed? But we better not hold our breaths.

Quite apart from its highly dubious constitutionality on any truly rational grounds, then, FOCA would in any case seem to represent a sharp slap administered directly in the face of current U.S. public opinion. FOCA would forbid state "informed consent" laws (favored by 85 per cent of Americans, according to a 1992 Gallup Poll); laws requiring parental consent for a minor's abortion (favored by 75 per cent); laws forbidding abortions on the basis of sex selection (favored by 91 per cent); laws requiring waiting periods before abortions (favored by 74 per cent); laws forbidding elective abortions after three months (favored by 72 per cent); or laws requiring spousal notification before an abortion (favored by 73 per cent).

That the passage of any such bill as this could actually have been "expected," even by the *Washington Post*, surely bespeaks a situation where there is no longer any normal relationship between public opinion on an issue and what is considered to be politically viable. In fact, the frequently expressed and confident expectations of normally knowledgeable people that FOCA was not only enactable but would be enacted are probably only explicable at all on the doctrinaire hypothesis that the abortion issue must and will be "settled," once and for all, and cannot be allowed to drag on and divert our attention from supposedly more important priorities. Customarily delivered in peremptory and, indeed, often in "absolutist," tones, this conviction that the abortion issue must be brought to a conclusion forthwith is normally addressed only to the prolife side of the controversy — in order to make clear once again that prolifers are the ones standing in the way of a "settlement."

In the event, though, the first recorded vote on the abortion issue in the new House of Representatives issuing from the 1992 elections — with its supposed ten additional proabortion votes — settled nothing. Rather, this vote, on June 30, 1993, saw *upheld* the sixteen year old prohibition of federal funding of abortions under Medicaid. Known as the Hyde Amendment after its perennial sponsor, Republican Representative Henry J. Hyde of Illinois, this measure was upheld in a recorded House vote by a margin of 255 to 178; in other words, the victory turned out to be on the prolife side against all expectations and predictions.

The proabortion forces had confidently expected to be able to keep this amendment from even coming to the House floor for a vote when the appropriations bill for the Department of Health and Human Services was being voted on. But they were out-maneuvered on procedural grounds, and once there was a recorded vote, the House was ultimately unwilling, as it almost always has been in the past, to require taxpayer funded abortions, regardless of whether or not there really exists a "woman's right" to have them.

Congressman Hyde and his allies were constrained this time to accept rape and incest, along with danger to a mother's life, as exceptions to the general ban on government funded abortions; despite the fact that pregnancies brought about as a result of rape or incest amount to less than one per cent of all aborted pregnancies, some politicians irrationally continue to believe that these exceptions are "necessary."

What was largely hidden from public view in the case of this unexpected House vote upholding the Hyde Amendment, though, was the fact that many members of Congress have never stopped getting the message from very large numbers of their constituents that abortion continues to be seen as unacceptable, in spite of what public opinion about it is supposed to be — and also in spite of what the media regularly continue to say about it. Few causes — or, again, none — have ever generated as much congressional mail. Since the summer before, nearly all the prolife organizations, including especially the National Right to Life Committee with all its state affiliates, had been concentrating on defeating the FOCA bill, and had evidently generated a simply enormous number of letters and calls to members of Congress about it.

These calls and letters actually intensified after the 1992 elections when, for example, more than five million anti-FOCA postcards to be sent to Congress were distributed by the prolife arm of the National Conference of Catholic Bishops alone. How many of these postcards actually ended up in congressional offices is never likely to be known; but there were a couple of tantalizing references in the press to the effect that shortly after the 103rd Congress had convened, the members were informed by the House Post Office that it temporarily *could not deliver the mail*, so back-logged was it by over a million still undelivered prolife missives addressed to individual members of Congress.

Contrary to the general expectations, then, the summer in which the passage of the Freedom of Choice Act had been confidently predicted in order to "settle" the "emotional" abortion issue once and for all instead saw FOCA placed indefinitely on hold while the Hyde Amendment, though modified, was re-enacted. In September, 1993, the Senate duplicated the House action and re-enacted the same modified Hyde Amendment by a surprisingly decisive majority of 59 to 40. These really crucial votes against government funding of abortion immediately raised the question of whether President Clinton could even get approved the health care plan which he had been trying to make the centerpiece of his whole program, if this plan continued to include coverage for abortions — as both the president and his wife continued to indicate that it must, while his most fervent supporters also strongly insisted that it must.

With the re-enactment of the Hyde Amendment, though, some observers were speculating whether the abortion issue might not actually be the thing to kill the Clinton health care plan itself — a surprising reversal from January, 1993, when Clinton had gone along with the conventional wisdom assuming that the abortion issue had been "settled" for good.

The picture was nevertheless still far from rosy, of course, since a couple of other bills allowing federal abortion funding in the District of Columbia and in the Federal Employees Health Benefit Program did manage to slip through. Besides, how far along is a prolife movement that can only more or less prevent public funding of abortion but cannot succeed in outlawing legal abortion itself?

Nevertheless, whatever the future of abortion as a political issue in the United States, it seemed pretty clear during the 1993 legislative session expected to "settle" the issue for good on the other side's terms that the debate about it was in fact *not* "over," after all; *no* tolerable "settlement" that would finally put the issue behind us was apparently even in sight.

III

Even if the reports of the death of the prolife movement, like the quondam report of the death of Mark Twain, proved to be highly exaggerated, the fact remains that abortion is still the political issue that practically everybody wishes would go away. The cry — or is it, as often, a sigh? — is insistent for no more "one-issue" campaigns! No more "litmus tests"! No more signs reminding us about child killers! No more fetuses in jars! No more "intolerance" and "bigotry"!

For some of us it is hard to understand why such things as these should be considered so undesirable and even unsavory if abortion itself is not so considered. Over the past couple of decades there have been around 4400 abortions every day in America, that is, 1.6 million every year, or over 30 million since *Roe v. Wade* was handed down.

Each one of these abortions represents a death, often a bloody and painful death for the victim. In all the wars of American history, by contrast, there have been around 1.2 million fatalities in all, according to the *World Almanac* — fewer than we destroy every year by abortion.

The fact that such appalling statistics as these can be put aside and passed over while alleged prolife "extremism" and "violence" are made the issues over which respectable heads shake surely indicates that Americans are "into denial," as psychologists say, in a very big way; it is just one more indication of how the abortion issue distorts everything it touches, especially rational judgments about itself.

In a world where the elective killing of a significant percentage of the next generation of Americans has, for the moment, been successfully represented not only as normal, but in a weird way as somehow desirable, it has to be admitted that things have been turned a bit topsy turvy generally. The wonder is perhaps that the prolife movement is not twice or more as large and active as it is, on the one hand; and, on the other, that mere expressions of dislike or irritability with prolife tactics or anxious and fretful appeals to "consensus" are all that generally do come out in our public discourse on the subject. Abortion represents a major national, moral, and social crisis which — strangely — is rarely substantively discussed if at all.

One thing has become very clear, however: America heartily dislikes being reminded about how the least visible and most vulnerable of her children are being treated; America is very uneasy about abortion in spite of everything.

Another thing is equally clear: while the majority of Americans almost certainly do not concede that abortion is the absolute constitutional right of a woman, large numbers of Americans, if not a majority, are at the same time apparently not at the moment prepared to take a principled stand in favor of the child's right to life.

Nevertheless this situation in no way points to any possible "compromise" settlement, as so many who would like to see the issue "settled" once and for all appear to believe; it simply points to the fact that America is confused and inconsistent at the same time that she is, understandably, very uneasy about abortion. Public opinion on the issue is not only fluid; it is mercurial. The abortion issue *cannot*, precisely, be settled on the basis of such movable and changeable positions among the people at large, swayed as they are by each successive wind of doctrine or new public opinion poll.

This has been true since the abortion issue first became a political and legal issue at the end of the 1960s and especially during the 1970s. The states which liberalized abortion to any extent before *Roe v. Wade* did so on the basis of certain so-called "indications" which supposedly justified abortion: danger to the life or health of the mother; possible fetal defects or deformities; or pregnancies brought about by rape or incest. Nearly all these indications, even at the time, were mostly pretexts for elective abortion, as the abortion statistics since *Roe* have overwhelmingly demonstrated; nevertheless they have continued to seem plausible to enough people so that they continue to be thought of as important factors in any possible abortion legislation and perhaps even as the basis of the fervently desired compromise settlement. Even Henry Hyde, as we saw, felt compelled to agree to the rape and incest exceptions to the new Hyde Amendment because, as he remarked, "I didn't think the votes were there anymore for a straight ban on abortion funding."

However, to include "health" as a justifiable indication for abortion results in something very close to abortion on demand anyway. This was amply verified in some of the states with liberalized abortion laws even prior to *Roe*; and in any case *Roe*'s companion Supreme Court decision, *Doe v. Bolton*, came along and defined "health" to mean "all factors — physical, emotional, psychological, familial, and the woman's age — relevant to the well-being of the patient." Under this definition, "health" can obviously mean any reason whatsoever why the woman might not want to bear a child, and this understanding of the term has been abundantly verified in practice. For those who imagine that the ultimate solution to the abortion issue lies in somehow "balancing" the mother's rights against the child's, there is no way the child's very life can ever be "balanced" against such a definition of maternal "health" or "well-being" as this.

The *Roe v. Wade* decision itself simply by-passed the question of the child's right to life entirely by observing in a footnote that the unborn had never been considered legal persons in the full sense; and then the court applied the Fourteenth Amendment, which should have served to guarantee the child's right to life and to the equal protection of the laws, to the case of the woman instead, creating out of nothing thereby her alleged right to decide whether or not to have a child.

Obviously, in strict logic, such a right of a woman could only obtain *before* she is pregnant; after she is pregnant, she already *has* a child, and so it is impossible to speak logically about her "deciding" whether or not to have one. But then nobody ever found logic to be the strong suit of the *Roe v. Wade* decision.

Nevertheless, the whole abortion issue has been considered and debated almost entirely in terms of *Roe* ever since that decision was handed down. What this means is that the fundamental issue of whether or not there *is* actually a *right* to life under our legal and constitutional system has never really been joined and debated. In other words, as has already been remarked, there has not yet really ever been any substantive abortion debate in our society in the true sense of the word; instead the abortion question has regularly been posed and answered on the basis of pure falsehood.

For the issue has been publicly treated almost entirely in terms of what restrictions, if any, the *state* might properly place on the practice of abortion. But this is to turn the whole issue on its head, as if the practice of abortion were the norm (instead of childbirth). In point of fact, this is not far from how the issue *has* regularly been treated in our public discourse.

One of the results of this way of treating the issue is that even prolife lawyers, judges, and justices are constrained to argue against abortion from the standpoint of a narrow constitutionalism or federalism rather than from the standpoint of protecting innocent life against willed, pre-meditated, and often highly sophisticated deadly assaults upon it.

In this perspective, since the Constitution, in so many words, guarantees neither the child's right to life nor the woman's alleged right to kill her child, the legislative arm(s) under our system presumably have to decide these questions for themselves in conformity with general constitutional principles. This, in fact, would seem to be the predominant "conservative" view on abortion today. It is not necessarily a prolife view as such. For as Justice Antonin Scalia, considered a "friend" of the prolife movement on the Supreme Court, says in his dissent in the 1992 *Planned Parenthood v. Casey* decision: "The states may, if they wish, permit abortion on demand, but the Constitution does not require them to do so." Clearly there is no hint here that the Fifth and Fourteenth Amendments ought to *prevent* the child from being deprived of life without due process of law.

This *Casey* decision, thought before it was decided to be the vehicle that might possibly overturn *Roe*, did little or nothing to advance the prolife cause. In many ways it set it back. The decision did affirm the legitimacy of certain state restrictions on abortion which had been enacted into law in Pennsylvania: 1) a requirement that a woman receive information pertinent to abortion 24 hours before undergoing one; 2) that one parent consent to the abortion of a minor; and 3) a requirement that those performing abortions must maintain and report certain data to the state department of health. Provision for exceptions even to these minor restrictions, though, were also included in the law in the case of "medical emergencies" (thus, again, anyone who "needs" an abortion only has to find an abortionist who will define her need as a "medical emergency").

It should be fairly evident from all this that prolife "victories" of the *Casey* type represent pretty small potatoes in comparison with the enormity of the abortion problem. The *Casey* decision actually struck down a provision of the Pennsylvania law requiring a wife to notify her husband before aborting their child — so much for the right of a father to protect or have an interest in the well-being of his own child! Some rights are more equal than other rights, apparently, like the animals on George Orwell's Animal Farm. It is perhaps no wonder that so many men in our society are taking no responsibility for the children they father, either!

Indeed *Planned Parenthood v. Casey* has probably moved us further away from any consideration of the right of the child to life under our Constitution. *Roe v. Wade* had based the woman's alleged right to kill the child she had conceived on a supposed right of "privacy" of hers, a right not only mentioned nowhere in the Constitution but logically nowhere derivative from it; nevertheless the court found such a right of privacy anyway. *Casey*, however, located this right in the "liberty" guaranteed by the Fourteenth Amendment. "At the heart of liberty," the court said, "is the right to decide one's concept of existence, of meaning, of the universe, of the mystery of human life" — in other words, a "right" to decide to do as one pleases, an idea that, if taken seriously in other areas and consistently applied, could quickly unravel the whole fabric of human rights and responsibilities, law and morality, in our society as a whole (it's happening!).

Unfortunately, this idea, however absurdly false, *is* taken seriously by the U.S. Supreme Court, at least where abortion is concerned; it supposedly grants to a woman in positive law the "liberty" to kill her child. The conclusion of the *Casey* decision is that the state may place no "undue burden" on the woman's exercise of this liberty of hers. In his concurring opinion in the *Casey* decision, Justice John Paul Stevens even went out of his way to remind everybody that "an abortion is not the termination of life entitled to 14th Amendment protection."

This overall conclusion of the Supreme Court in the *Casey* decision was, in effect, ratified by a majority of the court in December, 1992, when the court declined to review an appeals court ruling overturning a Guam abortion statute which had declared that "the life of every human being begins at conception, and that unborn children have protectible interests in life, health, and well-being."

Now this, of course, is a plain statement of *fact* — and a rather refreshing one, it would seem, after some twenty years of steady reiteration of the claim that women have a right to "terminate" pregnancies they have begun. Surely a society which has no trouble concluding that it can ban smoking by law but which, after many years of distortions and contortions, cannot see any way to ban abortions by law, must itself be a society that is more than a little bit disoriented if not actually crazy. We should therefore be grateful to the islanders of Guam for bringing the abortion issue back into the sunshine and fresh air once again — and out of the artificial atmosphere of the ideological hothouse where we have been forced to live for the past two decades, courtesy of *Roe v. Wade.*

The Guam abortion law made it a felony to perform abortions and allowed exceptions only to save a woman's life or prevent "grave impairment" to her health. What could possibly make more sense, considering what abortion really is? This, however, contradicted the basic principles already supposedly established forever by the Supreme Court, and so the Ninth U.S. Circuit Court of Appeals in San Francisco said that it would be "wrong and presumptuous" to allow the Guam law to stand.

How there could even be any notion of "wrong" on the basis of the current logic of the Supreme Court is not immediately evident; but given its "logic," it can surely be no surprise that the court declined to review the Guam case, and that is where we stand on abortion at the moment: we remain where we have been since 1973.

IV

Abortion on demand, then, with no significant restrictions, remains the law of the land in the United States. Meanwhile, many people, while perhaps disliking or even deploring this state of affairs, have concluded that little or nothing can be done about it as a practical matter — just as many of (roughly) the same people conclude that nothing can really be done about rampant street crime, drug addiction, teenage pregnancies out of wedlock, child abuse and similar pathological manifestations of our determinedly permissive society.

Indeed it may well be that nothing *can* be done about many of these phenomena, at least in the absence of any socially agreed upon moral code applying to personal and, especially, to sexual behavior. For one of the principal reasons why all of these phenomena have come about on the scale we are now experiencing them is that our society, by a largely tacit but nevertheless very real series of decisions, has over the past generation simply stopped attempting to uphold the traditional moral code of the West based on the Ten Commandments, at least with regard to personal and, especially, to sexual behavior.

The current moral code with regard to these matters in our society is: anything goes. The individual makes up his own mind; nobody tells him how to live his life. Law, custom, or morality are no longer even invoked; nor is any attempt made to require certain kinds of social behavior. In fact, the law has now moved over to *justifying* the new moral permissiveness, in spite of its deleterious social consequences, as when the Supreme Court in its *Casey* decision included among its justifications for continuing legalized abortion the fact that "for two decades of economic and social developments, people have organized intimate relationships and made choices that define their views of themselves and their places in society in reliance on the availability of abortion in the event that contraception should fail." This represents a simple abdication on the part of the highest court in the land that the law has anything to do with upholding a moral code. The consequences to our society as a whole will surely not be minimal when this wholly permissive principle comes to be applied to larger areas extending beyond personal and sexual morality, as is steadily happening.

For the historical fact of the matter is that one of the functions of law in society has always been to uphold society's moral code, at least on a minimal, external level, in order that human beings might be enabled to live together in society at all. The law may not be able to look into people's hearts but it nevertheless should play a considerable and very large role in keeping people on the straight and narrow as regards behavior of theirs that affects other people. To assume that society *cannot* attempt to require certain kinds of social behavior by means of law, custom, morality and the various types of social sanctions which have traditionally attached to them — as many people apparently seem to take for granted today in the case of legalized abortion — is, historically, really an idea as novel and untrue as the idea that people simply ought to be allowed to engage in unfettered sexual self expression.

For it would seem to be the case that every human society known to history and anthropology before our own has had — and has steadily and unself-consciously "imposed" on its members — a moral code relating to sexual behavior and to the consequences of sexual behavior. The single exception to this rule would seem to be the society of the modern Western world over the past generation. Many of the social ills we are suffering at present are precisely the consequences of our unwise tacit decision over the past generation to allow the jettisoning of the old personal moral code based on the Ten Commandments.

In practice, though, our society is currently trying very hard not to admit that anything much has really gone amiss. As a society the last thing we can now imagine is trying to "impose" morality on anyone; look how the Republicans got clobbered when they tried to run the flag of "family values" up the political flagpole! So we try not to notice the consequences of today's massive immorality — or else we try to pretend that these consequences do not stem from immoral behavior. This has not been easy, and it is not getting easier; indeed it is not a situation that can be contemplated with equanimity, and so when it can no longer be ignored, equanimity is usually the first thing to go.

As regards abortion, this is one of the reasons for the frequent high-pitched judgment, again usually addressed almost exclusively to prolifers, that the abortion issue must imperatively be "settled" and disposed of, and prolifers must be the ones to accept whatever "compromise" is thought necessary to accomplish this. Prolifers regularly hear this argument, as we have noted, not only from their enemies and those who describe themselves as being in the middle on the abortion issue but, increasingly, from their "friends" as well.

Following the 1992 elections, for example, a solid prolife politician such as retiring Republican Representative from Minnesota Vin

Weber told an audience of prolifers that "abortion is going to be a less volatile issue. For the time being, [the nation] has resolved the issue — not to my liking — but we have to face the facts." Missouri Republican Senator John Danforth, also a strong prolife voter in the upper house, similarly declared: "I'm prolife. But I don't think it should be a plank in a political platform." A number of other voices have been heard, and more than a few stories have appeared in the press, to this same effect: the prolife plank in the Republican Party platform has to be dropped or changed. Many "country club" Republicans have apparently been particularly vehement about this since the Bush defeat, and some big party contributors are said to be threatening to cut off financial support unless abortion and other social issues are de-emphasized by the Republicans.

Prominent proabortion Republicans like Pennsylvania Senator Arlen Specter and Kansas Republican Nancy Landon Kassebaum have been diligently trying to oblige these same elements within the party. These two senators launched what they called the Republican Majority Coalition shortly after the 1992 elections precisely in order to de-emphasize the party's stand on abortion and on the social issues. Six months later, a similar group calling itself the Conference for a Republican Majority was organized for a similar purpose. The claim of these groups that they constitute a "majority" in the party is not lost on even the dullest of Republicans.

Meanwhile, certain Republican "friends" of the prolife movement — in this case, Jack Kemp, William Bennett, and Jeane Kirkpatrick — were organizing something called Empower America, which, while in no way antilife, initially planned quite deliberately to de-emphasize the social issues; subsequently, each of these three leaders has evidently found it necessary to reaffirm a prolife commitment; but the initial plan to proceed without reference to the prolife issue was only too indicative of the way many people were thinking. In particular, many Republicans have expressed apprehension about the rise of the so-called Christian right within the party; it has not been a trend universally welcomed by old line Republicans, in spite of the many new voters who have entered the Republican ranks thereby.

All in all, Republicans seemed to be almost as impressed by the results of the 1992 elections as pundit Charles Krauthammer was. In his column declaring the abortion debate "over," Krauthammer had also written that "it is important for Republicans to recognize that the battle is over. Years ago Republicans suicidally carried on against the New Deal long after it had been accepted by most citizens as part of the fabric of American political life. Republicans had better not do the same with legal abortion now; for better or for worse, it is also now part of the fabric of American life."

This logic has apparently seemed compelling to many Republicans, in spite of the solid and loyal support which the Republican Party's prolife component had provided both for the Bush-Quayle ticket and for Republican candidates in general. The prolifers were said to have provided the winning margins in such states as Texas, Florida, Virginia, and the Carolinas, if not elsewhere (just as they did later in special elections in Georgia and Texas, and for candidates who were not even prolife but only anti-FOCA). Nevertheless prolifers would have been unrealistic to expect any credit, much less gratitude; the anti-prolife *Zeitgeist*, even in the Republican Party, irrational though it is, has just been too pronounced.

The most dramatic instance of the actual bitterness that is harbored against prolifers in some Republican quarters, in spite of all that prolifers have sincerely tried to do for the party, probably came at the meeting of the Republican National Committee convened in late January, 1993, to select a new Republican National Chairman. On that occasion, the outgoing chairman, Bush operative Rich Bond, informed the meeting — and through media reports the whole world — that "America is getting more diverse, not more look-alike. Our job is to recognize this change and offer platforms and candidates and policies that reflect changing times and do not cling to zealotry masquerading as principle and to the stale ideas of the dead and dying past."

"Zealotry masquerading as principle. . ." It would be hard to think of a more calculating, deliberate, and insulting put-down of one of the major components of what in the Reagan and Bush years was a winning Republican majority coalition. Bond's gesture would have been comparable to, say, an outgoing Democratic National Chairman going out the door loudly and offensively proclaiming that the blacks who support the Democratic party in such elevated numbers really exert way too much influence in the Democratic Party.

We can be pretty confident that no Democrat would ever be quite that dumb (not to speak about the other objections that could be made about somebody expressing such views). On the evidence, though, we apparently cannot credit some fairly prominent Republicans with even that minimum amount of savvy — but, again, where abortion is concerned, the normal rules never seem to apply.

Probably because the media were so especially eager to report any Republican attack on the prolife cause, most of the reports on Rich Bond's ungracious exit from the party leadership failed to note the irony of this architect of the failed Bush presidential campaign presuming to explain to the party the formula for winning elections.

Bond's successor as Republican National Chairman, Haley Barbour, promptly announced upon his selection: "I am prolife. . . but if you make abortion the threshold issue of Republicanism, you need your heads examined." Barbour must have liked this phrase, since he repeated it almost word for word in a later newspaper interview — as if anyone were making abortion "the threshold issue of Republicanism."

Rather, the question was whether a major constituency of the Republican Party would be snubbed and asked to swallow a major change in a party platform position which had helped the party win three presidential elections — and for no reason, apparently, beyond uneasiness about the growing numbers of prolifers and of the "Christian right" in the Republican ranks. How could anyone interested in winning elections possibly object to *greater numbers* of people coming into the party? For some Republicans, apparently, distaste for these new elements in the old party outweighs the patent fact that the increasing numbers of these new elements are what make Republican victories possible on a national scale.

Prior to the 1992 elections, the Republican Party prolife platform position had already undergone a major challenge, accompanied by another media blitz, mounted by the egregious Republican conservative prochoice direct-mail fund raiser, Ann Stone; yet in accordance with all regular party platform procedures, the challenged prolife plank was nevertheless strongly reaffirmed. Nor has any serious analyst even remotely suggested that George Bush lost the election primarily because of his prolife stand; rather, the evidence suggests that this stand was a net benefit for him. Nevertheless, more than somewhat surprisingly, prolife Republicans have been the most frequent targets of the sharpest post-election resentments within the Republican Party.

We can only wonder, therefore, why anyone would think prolifers should continue to be active or even to take much of an interest in a party showing itself to be so capable of reproaching or repudiating *them*, in spite of their consistent loyalty and their significant contributions. Maybe the idea that the loyalty of a political party's own people should actually deserve the party's support has proved to be too complex an idea for some of the party's political professionals to grasp. Six months after their installation at their meeting in Chicago, Mr. Haley Barbour and his friends were still to be found pressing doggedly on, trying to please every element of the party except its strong profamily and prolife component. As one press story in July, 1993, expressed it: "Republican Party officials from 50 states wound up their third day of meetings here with almost no mention of traditional or family values by any of the scheduled speakers" — this *after* the failure of the Democrats to eliminate the Hyde Amendment and the even more spectacular failure of President Clinton to gain acceptance of his plan to admit homosexuals openly into the military services!

It does sometimes seem, then, as if there are out there among all those supposedly hard-nosed Republican politicians a fair number who apparently *want* their party to go the way of the old Whig Party — which went out of existence back in the 1850s because of its unwillingness to deal with a national, social, and moral crisis on a principled basis. Who ever heard of or even imagined a political party apparently willing to sacrifice one of its largest and fastest growing constituencies to such vague notions as Rich Bond's code-language assertion that "America is getting more diverse"? What Bond was expressing, of course, was the conviction apparently shared by many Republicans, in spite of the party's official prolife position on the issue, that legalized abortion is here to stay, that nothing can or should be done about it regardless of how incompatible with our system it manifestly is, and that the Republican Party does not want or need a prolife "albatross" around its neck.

There is considerable evidence that Rich Bond's position on this issue is indeed shared by many Republicans and conservatives (less and less, apparently, can "conservative" be equated with "prolife," by the way); they believe that abortion is a losing issue, and hence the party must at all costs work for a tolerable "settlement" of it and move on to things imagined to be more important.

Does all this mean that the prolife movement is in the process of being rejected by the only one of the two political parties that has accepted it up to now? That, as our title suggests, the prolife movement is in the process of becoming a political orphan? Some strong signs certainly point that way, although the process is far from complete — and it is surely not irreversible either. But the signs are nevertheless ominous. No prolifer can afford to be complacent; the political future of the movement is at stake, at the same time that the political dimension of the abortion issue continues to form one absolutely essential element in the ultimate solution of the problem of abortion in America. Yes, hearts do have to be changed; but votes count too.

V

What should prolifers do then? First, prolifers should remain confident that they are *right* on the basic issue, no matter how fainthearted and short-sighted politicians and other self interested people turn out to be — and no matter how often such people try to put prolifers down. No serious and knowledgeable American can accept the present American situation of wide open abortion. If the Republican Party leadership, for example, cannot see that legalized abortion is something that has to be actively and vigorously opposed, then the party will have failed a historic test and at a certain point some other means will have to be sought and found to oppose the evil of abortion by political action. This is inescapable. A country that can acquiesce in the idea that allowing a huge percentage of its children to be killed before birth does not even qualify as a civilized nation, much less as the beacon light of freedom to the whole world which so many Republicans and conservatives, in particular, like to fancy that we still are.

If it is replied that, civilized or not, abortion is now permitted practically everywhere else in the world today, so why not here? — the answer has to be that this has not been true in the past; abortion represents a *corruption* of our civilization which, until very recent times, did afford legal protection to the unborn by the simple expedient of making abortion illegal. This is the situation that has to be restored. The moral and legal corruption we have recently suffered is not necessarily permanent; it is reversible, and it can and must be reversed.

Secondly, because they are right on the basic issue, prolifers are obliged to take a *principled stand on the right of a child to life* under our system. This is necessary not only for the sake of the child but also for the sake of our system. Anyone who has seriously contemplated the current state of our public morality knows that abortion is just one of a number of areas where the currently dominant "culture" *is determined to abolish the traditional moral code of the West based on the Ten Commandments.*

How anyone imagines we are going to have any freedom or democracy left after the moral code is gone for good ought to go back at least as far as the American founding to discover how morality and virtue were considered by the Founding Fathers to be the *indispensable* foundation stones for the American system then in the process of formation. Prolifers must understand that they are working not merely on behalf of the unborn but also on behalf of the entire moral tradition of the West, without which civilization as we have known it — and hence justice — will be impossible.

Thirdly, prolifers should *not*, for the moment at least, abandon the Republican Party. *It seems better for the moment to stay with the Republican party* and to try to shape its policy and to keep it on its current official prolife path than it does to try to influence the political process without a specific party base. Even though the current Republican leadership, with its shortsightedness, waffling, double-talk, backpedaling, lack of principle, and even sometimes active hostility to the prolife cause represents a very defective instrument indeed for attempting to carry on the prolife fight in the political arena, the prospects of attempting to start a third party or attempting to operate as an independent movement surely pose even greater difficulties.

It may be that the current Republican leadership will actually prove to be obtuse enough in the end to drive the prolifers away (while stalwart prolifers of the type Pennsylvania Governor Casey has proved to be might sometime open the Democratic Party back up!). It may even be that too many mainstream Republicans really "don't get it," in which case the party probably is doomed. But all these things will become apparent soon enough, if they are destined to happen, and if and when such things do happen, the consequences will extend beyond the issue of abortion alone, so that prolifers will have a better idea of whom they can ally with and where they have to go in order to pursue their necessary objectives. Meanwhile the

Republican Party would seem to continue to represent the best instrument at the moment.

Thus, prolifers should not be the ones to initiate any break with the Republican Party in the short run: let the mis-named Republican "moderates" (although it truly is hard to understand how anything at all about abortion could be considered "moderate"!) be the ones insisting on breaking up the party of Abraham Lincoln, if that is going to be the eventual outcome. Among other things, by leaving now, prolifers would forfeit any chance to help keep the party on the tracks for legislative issues that continue to confront us immediately, such as abortion funding. Prolifers should remember that the vast majority of strong prolife politicians who are currently in office — the Henry Hydes, Christopher Smiths, Robert Dornans, Jesse Helmses, Don Nickleses and many others — are mostly all Republicans and they must continue to receive prolife support unless and until the party itself possibly breaks up over the abortion issue and perhaps over some of the other social and family issues.

Fourthly, just because prolifers must take a principled stand on the right of the unborn to life does not mean that they cannot, as opportunities permit or require, *be flexible in their strategies and tactics*, or accept lesser goals in practice, just as Henry Hyde and his allies were constrained to accept the fake rape and incest indication for abortion in order to win a victory, even a limited one. Prolifers should remember that there are many battles in a war and each battle counts. Merely to set back the proabortion agenda, if only a step, always means at least one battle won, for instance. Winning even partial victories in individual battles also means helping to keep the prolife movement alive and vigorous; it can also mean affecting the enemy's morale, even if real prolife gains remain limited.

In fact, prolifers are *obliged* to be flexible in practice precisely because the abortion situation is so confused and so murky in our country today (it shouldn't be but it is) and its implications so little understood by the public at large. To make progress it is necessary to move a step at a time. Laws requiring informed consent or waiting periods for abortion and the like are hardly ultimate goals; but they are worth working for if they represent the best that can be done at the moment; to persuade a legislator to support such legislation is at least to begin to educate him about abortion. Often the prolife movement has understood this very well in practice, although it has not always been formulated too clearly in principle.

Meanwhile, prolifers should not attempt to read other prolifers out of the movement or start working against them simply because the latter perhaps do not always yet see that the only ultimate political solution to abortion in America has to be a constitutional amendment applying the 5th and 14th Amendment protections to the unborn, exactly as the Republican Party platform language says. But this constitutional amendment is surely a long way off yet. Meanwhile prolifers should be welcoming anyone who claims to be "prolife" — and then leading him on from there! The same principle applies on the other side of the issue: so long as they continue to adhere to non-violence, Operation Rescue and its sister movements should not be boycotted by those prolifers who consider them to be too "activist."

Fifthly, prolifers must *take a more active role in the political process itself*, as it is set up and operates in America today. The best way to have influence within the Republican Party, for example, is to become indispensable to its continued operations and effectiveness, at whatever level. The same thing would be true of the Democratic Party. One of the best ways to influence a legislator's vote is to have been one of those who helped get him elected. One of the best ways to get prolife candidates even to run is to be among those who are selecting them and supporting their efforts.

In the beginning many prolifers thought all they had to do was furnish their — admittedly powerful — arguments, show their slides of aborted fetuses, and so on, and then all the politicians would quickly come around. That idea quickly proved to be a non-starter; most prolifers have since learned that they have to get involved in the political process directly, in particular by working in the campaigns of prolife candidates, if they are really going to have any impact on the political process.

Sixthly, *the prolife movement must continue to be non-violent*. The antilifers have been able to tar the movement with the brush of violence even though it has *not* generally been violent; quite the contrary. But in no case should the antilifers ever be handed a club they can beat the prolife movement with; they are doing well enough at beating up the movement as it is without being handed any additional means to do it. In the present media world of images and sound bites, the very last thing the prolife movement can afford would be to deviate in the slightest from its position of non-violence. Whatever the validity of theoretical moral arguments concerning the licitness of directly rescuing victims from the deadly curettes or suction machines of the abortionists — and the present writer believes that a strong moral case can be made for such direct action — the overall importance of the movement and its future chances for success must still be accorded greater weight. The historical fact of the matter is that non-violence has been the successful principle of those modern "opposition" movements which have *worked*, which have *succeeded*; examples include not only Gandhi and Indian independence and Martin Luther King and the American civil rights movement, but Lech Walesa and Vaclav Havel in Eastern Europe, both of whose anti-Communist movements successfully employed the principle of non-violence in order to *win* and bring down the corrupt and brutal regimes in their respective countries. The prolife movement must not deviate from the principles of non-violence if it expects the same success.

In the seventh place, if there is to be any realistic hope in the foreseeable future for the constitutional amendment insuring the right to life that America so desperately needs, the most important prolife task and priority for the moment is: to continue *to build up the ranks of the prolife movement itself.* This is urgent and essential. Whatever influence the prolife movement has been able to exert on the political process up to this point — and in many ways this influence has been considerable — this influence has always resulted from nothing else but the ability of the prolife movement to make its numbers and its arguments felt in a practical and concrete way. This necessarily means that greater *numbers* of knowledgeable and committed workers are required.

These numbers can be assembled only by continuing to put out the prolife message where people can hear and respond to it. The task of prolife education can therefore never be considered complete; the movement must continually reach out to new individuals and groups. Many people still do *not* know the horrid facts — or won't admit them. Again, continuing to build up its own ranks is something the prolife movement has generally understood quite well in practice and has very successfully done. It is a question of more of the same.

Greater commitment is required too. Once the prolife message has really been heard and grasped, many people do become committed, as a matter of fact. And once there is commitment, then the main obstacle becomes possible discouragement — because the current abortion situation is so bad, because the prolife ranks sometimes seem so thin, because everything prolifers do can so often seem to count for so little — because the harsh world out there seems so little moved by the slaughter of the weakest and most vulnerable of our children.

Prolifers should therefore — finally — never forget that the cause they serve is also the cause of the truth: *veritas magna et praevalebit*; the truth is mighty and shall prevail. A human child is not some object to be disposed of at will like a piece of garbage in accordance with a permissive ethic of naked self assertion; a human child should enjoy the same rights we all enjoy in our democratic system. So it is no real matter if prolifers temporarily happen to find themselves to be orphans within the American political system; the system itself still does provide the means and opportunities for prolifers to recover a commanding position within it; this is something ultimately within the power of the prolife movement itself.

If America's political parties go on being so foolish as to try to deny the truth, then they may one day — sooner than we might think — be gone, while the prolife movement will still remain, and this in spite of present appearances — and also in spite of the self interested calculations of "practical men."

Above all, because prolifers are serving the truth as well as the children, prolifers must learn to be very *patient* and must regularly practice the virtue of patience. For impatience can represent the quickest path to the discouragement, and discouragement can then mean abandonment of the children. Patience is therefore essential to the cause. Prolifers cannot be held responsible for the immediate results they achieve, but only for the efforts they exert; the results, finally, are in "other hands."

Postscript

After the above article — "Is the Prolife Movement a Political Orphan?" — was published, Professor Charles E. Rice of the University of Notre Dame Law School, was among those who responded to the article; he wrote the following letter, raising important points in need of clarification, which appeared in *Fidelity* magazine in April, 1994:

"Kenneth D. Whitehead's long record of prolife advocacy reinforces the credibility of his analysis of the prolife movement in the December issue. However, he dropped the ball. He urged prolifers to 'take a principled stand on the right of the child to life.' But then he urged them to support incremental restrictions on abortion and, worse still, 'to stay with the Republican Party.'

"The prolife movement and the Catholic Church had a brief window of opportunity after *Roe* was decided in 1973. A frontal and uncompromising attack then on *Roe* could have been the catalyst for the needed reconversion of the American people to respect for God and His law. Cardinals Krol, Medeiros, Cody, and Manning, in their 1974 testimony before the Senate, stood on principle and opened the window of opportunity to overturn *Roe* before it became ingrained in our culture. The Cardinals insisted on a constitutional amendment to recognize the personhood of the unborn and they refused to support the Buckley Amendment because it allowed abortion to save the life of the mother.

"Tragically, the pragmatic sophisticates in the National Right to Life Committee and other elements of the establishment prolife movement, including the Catholic bishops' apparatus, sold out the cause by rejecting that no-compromise approach. They insisted on exceptions in Congress and in state legislatures. They opposed the Human Life Bill, they spurned the Paramount Human Life Amendment, and they insisted instead on the states' rights approach of the Hatch Amendment and similar measures. The establishment pragmatists made themselves 'respectable.' And they became a corrupting influence on the public mind. Every time 'prolife' spokesmen propose a law that will allow abortion in some cases, they affirm the basic principle of the abortion and euthanasia movements, that the state can validly tolerate the intentional killing of an innocent human being. In truth, the state may never validly tolerate such killing and is obliged to forbid it. Ideas have consequences. The compromise strategists have increased immeasurably the toll of innocent lives by permeating the public discourse with the message that even the 'prolife' advocates agree that innocent life is negotiable and subject to political compromise.

"The only chance for the restoration of the right to life in our law is for prolife people to insist that the right to life is sacred because it comes from God, not from the State, and that the State can never validly tolerate the intentional killing of innocent human beings. There are numerous principled legislative initiatives, at the federal and state level, that could save lives and shift the right-to-life debate onto ground where we have a chance to begin the educational task that is essential for ultimate victory. It is long past time for us to stop debating refinements of pro-death proposals. Rather, we must shift the debate to our own agenda.

"The prolife movement must insist on protection of life, without exception, from the beginning, i.e., from fertilization. And it must confront the underlying evil of contraception. Unfortunately, the compromise prolifers occupy themselves with advocating marginal restrictions on the surgical abortions which will soon be as relevant as the bronze axe and the spinning wheel. The 'big tent' philosophy of the Republican Party, which accepts advocates of legalized murder as legitimate candidates for public office is worse than useless in this respect."

The author responded to this letter of Professor Rice with the following letter which appeared in *Fidelity* in June, 1994:

I have been rather surprised and generally quite pleased to keep reading the letters which have continued to be printed in *Fidelity* making reference to my article of last December, "Is the Prolife Movement a Political Orphan?" When someone of the stature of Professor Charles Rice of the University of Notre Dame Law School writes in, however, a response is required.

Professor Rice thinks I "dropped the ball." I think he missed the point.

I agree with him that the goal of the prolife movement should be to "insist on the protection of life from the beginning." I believe I made quite clear in my article where I stand on this, although my article was precisely about the varying and in most cases complex and unfortunate circumstances which have been preventing, and are still preventing, the prolife movement from currently being in a position to "insist" upon very much of anything, except within a very limited range of choices. What we are talking about here is not the rightness of the goal but how to get from here to there.

I also agree with Professor Rice that "the prolife movement and the Catholic Church had a brief window of opportunity after *Roe* was decided in 1973." It was a window of opportunity, however, which was very quickly closed, for many of the reasons he correctly enumerates.

Again, however, my article was primarily about where we unfortunately stand now on the prolife issue, not about what could and should have been done in the 1970s; or about where blame should be assigned for the many catastrophes, failures, and even betrayals prolifers have suffered, the consequences of which are still all too tragically with us. Nevertheless, if we grant that we still *have* to go on trying to fight for the rights of the unborn, however unfavorable the present circumstances, then we also have to grant that we have to talk quite concretely about where we are and where it is possible to go given those circumstances.

Professor Rice declares that "every time 'prolife' spokesmen propose a law that will allow abortion in some cases they affirm the basic principle of the abortion and euthanasia movements that the state can validly tolerate the intentional killing of a human being."

No: prolifers working on legislation providing something less than absolute protection of the rights of the unborn are not necessarily "affirming" anything of the sort. The alleged constitutional "right" of a woman to terminate her pregnancy is already as absolute as anything in our legal system; this is what the "law of the land" officially is; what prolifers might "affirm" or fail to "affirm" by whatever bills they initiate or support has no necessary bearing on it at all. It was "legislated" by a Supreme Court decision, *Roe v. Wade*, and nobody has yet found an effective way to get that decision reversed.

In the meantime, any ancillary laws dealing with abortion are not themselves the basis of the legality in accordance with which abortions can be performed; *Roe* is; and so although the decision about whether to support such ancillary laws would have to be based in each case on what the law provides for, support for such ancillary does not in itself necessarily entail support for abortion.

The basic question, of course, remains how the bad "law" stemming from *Roe* can be repealed and a true law based on justice respecting the rights of the unborn put in its place. The constitutional amendment which Professor Rice and I would no doubt both favor to accomplish this has failed for the moment; I doubt if there is a single politician in either house of Congress who would introduce a serious constitutional amendment at this time. Prolifers working in the political arena are therefore necessarily constrained to work for lesser but in some cases currently attainable goals such as prohibiting tax-payer funded abortions, enacting "informed consent" laws or spousal or parental consent laws, waiting periods, and the like.

All these things fall tragically short of what is needed, as I made clear in my article; nor have all the partial measures of this kind proposed or enacted necessarily always been uniformly wise or effective or even, perhaps, always permissible; that is another argument. Nevertheless, I believe it is a grave mistake to hold, as apparently Professor Rice does hold, that "every time" prolifers get involved with abortion legislation which does not afford absolute legal protection to the child's right to life they have somehow "affirmed" the abortionists' principles and have therefore entered into some kind of inadmissible complicity with them. This is a viewpoint which, applied generally, can only lead to the eventual paralysis of any prolife movement whatsoever.

It is a viewpoint which has actually led a number of Catholics that I know to abandon any further efforts to fight abortion in the practical order, on the grounds that they cannot in conscience be involved with any law that "regulates" an absolutely abhorrent practice, one which should simply be outlawed. I agree that it should simply be outlawed — but how are we going to get it outlawed if we can never even be involved with it?

However, looked at another way, in a situation where the existing law already perversely allows the practice of intentional killing of some human beings on the basis of an alleged constitutional right, any abridgment or limitation of the practice in question that can successfully be enacted into law serves to undermine both the absoluteness of this alleged "right" and the legitimacy of the law which affirms it (exactly as the National Rifle Association regularly argues with respect to any abridgment or limitation of the constitutional right to bear arms guaranteed by the Second Amendment!). There may be other objections to some of these laws; that is a matter for prudential judgment in each case; but, in general, laws which limit or abridge the current absolute "right" to abortion do serve the prolife cause.

How important it is in the present circumstances at least to continue to undermine and chip away at the absolute woman's "right" to abortion established by *Roe* can be gauged by the panic, alarm, and fury that inevitably arise on the proabortion side over what we might consider even the most minimal of prolife "victories"; *they* know that to win this battle they cannot ultimately allow or tolerate *anything* except abortion as an absolute "right." Hence to succeed in establishing that the "right" is *not* absolute can be one of the necessary first steps to abolishing it as a "right" entirely.

A further purpose which "partial laws" merely restricting but not outlawing abortion can and do serve is to continue to educate the broad public on the abortion issue — just as election campaigns in which the prolife issue is raised do. It is not clear at the moment, in fact, what *other* more effective ways there are to attempt to educate the public about what abortion really is and what it really does to a society which legalizes it. America does continue to have a bad conscience about abortion, in spite of everything, and this fact must continue to be exploited in every possible way as part of the prolife educational task.

What is amazing at the present moment, in spite of all the defeats and discouragements which the prolife forces have regularly suffered, is that the prolife movement is nevertheless still alive, and, indeed, is actually growing — or, at any rate, more and more prolifers are beginning to take part in the political process and they also appear to understand that they are in it "for the duration." Telling these prolife activists there is nothing they can conscientiously do now except work for a constitutional amendment can only confuse and disorient them. It was to these prolifers increasingly active in the political process that my article was principally addressed; we need them where they are, doing what they are doing. Badly.

For the fact that an impressive prolife movement has sprung into being in order to fight the great evil of legalized abortion also means that the movement *has to have something to do,* awaiting the day when a constitutional amendment to protect the lives of the unborn can again be brought forward with some chance of passing. A movement waiting around for the public to be educated to the point where we can pass a constitutional amendment is unlikely to be a movement that is vital and vibrant — or even viable, for that matter. It is considerably more likely, in fact, that the conditions necessary for enacting a constitutional amendment will only come about *as a result* of the activities of a movement working tirelessly and seizing every opportunity to push the cause forward; in this perspective, the more "partial laws," the better.

From the standpoint of Catholic morality, working contingently in the political order for something less than absolute protection of all human life at all stages can normally be justified, I believe, by the principle of double effect: the *intention* of the measures one enacts or supports has to be to save at least some lives, to uphold recognized rights of parents or spouses, to strengthen public health requirements, to defeat and demoralize the proabortionists (every defeat *does* demoralize them: read their own literature), to educate the public, to advance the prolife cause, etc. None of these things in itself constitutes "doing evil that good may come of it," after all.

So it is time to stop looking down on those prolifers as necessarily minimizers or compromisers who are actually attempting to do something politically in the current horrendous abortion situation. Professor Rice feels able to do this, apparently, even to the point of putting their designation as being "prolife" between quotation marks. Most of them deserve better.

While it is necessary never to lose sight of principles and goals, it is equally necessary to try to find ways of applying them in the situation that actually exists. It is time to start giving more attention to what we can and must be doing *now,* if we are ever going to move this country back to where its own founding principles of "equal justice under law" can again be properly applied to all human life in every condition and at every stage of development.

2

Regarding the Advice Being Given Prolifers by Certain "Friendly" Conservatives

I

In their usual crude, pragmatic way, the politicians seem to be arriving at a rough consensus on how to deal with the abortion issue, namely, this: abortion will continue to be legal, but for the most part the government will not pay for it. This seems to be the meaning of the recent action taken by Congress reaffirming (in only slightly liberalized form) the Hyde Amendment, the perennial measure prohibiting federal funding for nearly all abortions under Medicaid. Even many normally proabortion legislators apparently decided a line had to be drawn at government funding of so controversial a procedure; even if they do not actually read their mail, apparently many of them have at least become aware of the volume of it that comes in against abortion.

With the re-enactment of the Hyde Amendment, the hard-line pro-abortion forces in Congress suddenly had to draw back in disarray and dismay; at this writing they apparently no longer even dare to bring the FOCA (Freedom of Choice Act) bill forward for a vote. They have clearly perceived that a line *has* been drawn by majorities in both houses of Congress. However, this majority is not doctrinaire; some abortion funding has slipped through. Basically, though, the emerging consensus seems to be that the government will not use tax money for a procedure so many taxpayers find objectionable, if not abhorrent; meanwhile the procedure itself will remain legal, and, at the moment, nobody is really pushing to outlaw it. (Never-

Originally published in *New Oxford Review*, January-February 1994.

theless, abortion could prove to be the slingshot pebble that kills the Goliath called national health care reform if the Clinton Administration persists in, what appears at this writing to be, its determination to have abortion covered in the plan.)

This rough legislative compromise pleases neither of the two sides that continue to be passionate on the subject of abortion. But almost all politicians are sick and tired of the subject, and hence are ready to lay it to rest on almost any terms. Some conservative "friends" of the prolife movement also show signs of being as sick and tired of the "insoluble" abortion issue as the politicians; they too are apparently now prepared to see the issue "settled," however minimalist the terms of the settlement.

A case in point of the conservative "rush to settlement" is provided by Irving Kristol. In what he himself described as "friendly but pessimistic advice for prolifers," in a piece in *The Wall Street Journal*, Kristol described abortion as the principal answer of the "culture" to the consequences of today's accepted "sexually active" behavior (what used to be called "promiscuous" behavior). He added:

> It is one thing to deplore abortion, or to believe there is something inherently wrong, even sinful, about it. But it is quite another thing to demand that the secular authorities enforce a theologically defined "right to life" policy. This policy is politically unacceptable to the majority of the electorate, however ambivalent their feelings. It is also unenforceable as new abortifacients come on the market.

Irving Kristol has packed many errors and misconceptions into a single paragraph here. To begin with: prescription drugs must still be licensed by the FDA, and it is not in the least unreasonable to hold that, for many cogent medical and moral reasons, no abortifacient should ever be licensed, regardless of whether such a ban could ever be completely "enforced." The kind of thinking that holds that we must provide people with the means to do "what they are going to do anyway" is the same sort of thinking that has already brought us to the moral nadir of supplying clean needles to drug addicts and condoms to "sexually active" teen-agers.

More importantly, the right to life, an expression which Kristol unaccountably puts between quotation marks, is still assumed — and is supposed to be guaranteed — by the Fifth and Fourteenth Amendments to our Constitution of the United States as well as by our Declaration of Independence. These are the foundational documents of our polity; to place what they assume and guarantee between quotation marks is to signal acceptance of a significant departure from the principles on which this country was founded.

The practical political problem posed by legalized abortion under our system is that unborn children are excluded by simple definition from the equal protection of the laws — as slaves were so excluded until the passage of the Thirteen Amendment. The principle of the right to life is not something inconveniently dreamed up by prolifers in order to gum up the political process; it is a fundamental principle which we cannot give up, certainly not merely by placing it within quotation marks.

Therefore what may or may not be "politically unacceptable" to a given "majority" — if it is a majority — is not the issue. Even though the position a majority takes at any given time may sometimes loom as a virtually insurmountable obstacle for those opposed to it, it is still of lesser moment than the truth about the issue.

If the right to life and the right to the equal protection of the laws are now to be denied to any class of people on account of mere majority opinion at a given time, in spite of what the Constitution and the Declaration of Independence specify, then our system has already been undermined in principle. Hence, whatever "majority opinions" happen to rise up against our foundational principles must be challenged and *changed* — no matter how long it takes.

Actually, the public opinion that currently tolerates abortion seems to be mired in ethical inconsistency. Many polls show that abortion is *needed* even while it is abstractly conceded to be *wrong*. Obviously, public opinion needs to be (further) educated, for we cannot operate a civilized society on the principle that what is seriously wrong should nevertheless be permitted because people want it.

According to *Roe v. Wade*, the unborn are defined as not enjoying the constitutional guarantees available to other Americans. This is the nub of the problem, for the humanity of the unborn is an established scientific fact. Kristol's reference to a "theologically defined 'right to life' policy" is another one of his errors; actually there are two errors in this phrase, since upholding the right to life is in no way a mere policy, but is rather a foundational constitutional principle. Moreover, it is a principle that is not based upon any purely theological finding whatsoever but upon hard scientific fact.

The words "embryo" or "fetus," like the words "baby," "adolescent," or "adult," do not describe some non-human being; rather, all these words describe a human being at a particular stage of development. To deny human personhood to human beings who have not yet been born, as *Roe v. Wade* does, is a purely arbitrary and semantic operation, exactly analogous to denying legal personhood to slaves, as the *Dred Scott* case did.

Nor is affirming the right to life of this as yet unborn human being an instance of "enforcing" a view that is somehow alien to the American system. Before 1966 all 50 states had laws prohibiting abortion except where considered medically necessary to save a mother's life (and in a few states also to preserve her health). Between 1966 and 1972 a number of states liberalized their laws, mostly to allow abortions in accordance with certain so-called "indications" for them, such as the life or health of the mother, rape, incest, fetal deformity, and so on.

Then *Roe* came along in 1973 and simply overturned all these state laws in one stroke, in what dissenting Supreme Court Justice Byron White called at the time "an exercise of raw judicial power." Quite literally, we entered upon a *lawless* period at that time as far as abortion was concerned; we are still living in that lawless period.

People may take legal abortion for granted now. But *Roe* and the other decisions stemming from it are not carved in stone; they really stand on very shaky ground, in fact; and they can be changed. Thus, eliminating legal abortion does not represent some wild, impossible dream; it merely means restoring what was firmly and workably in place everywhere less than a generation ago.

II

At the time our Declaration of Independence and Constitution were adopted, the scientific facts concerning human conception and gestation up to the time of birth were not completely known. Once they became known, it became — and remains — eminently logical to apply existing constitutional and legal rights and guarantees to those human beings who have been conceived but not yet born.

Instead, the opposite occurred. The "culture" was moving in a different direction — one coinciding with the development of new and more reliable technical means for performing abortions. The next thing we knew, we were saddled with the current massive abortion carnage.

What has now occurred, with our society's consciously deciding to reject many of the unborn members of the human family, is a moral revolution in which we have now effectively put ourselves in charge of who is to live and who is to die. Not just the Ten Commandments of the Bible but the "nature and nature's God" of the Declaration of Independence have necessarily been put aside in such a decision. *We* are in charge now, and, considering what we have shown ourselves to be capable of, nobody can be very sanguine about our future.

The unborn baby is a human being. As the journal *California Medicine* stated in a once-famous editorial way back at the dawn of the abortion era, in 1970:

> In defiance of the long-held Western ethic of intrinsic and equal value for every human life regardless of its stage, condition, or status, abortion is becoming accepted by society. . . Since the old ethic has not yet been fully displaced, it has been necessary to separate the idea of abortion from the idea of killing, which continues to be socially abhorrent. The result has been a curious avoidance of the scientific fact, which everyone really knows, that human life begins at conception. . . The very considerable semantic gymnastics which are required to rationalize abortion as anything but taking a human life would be ludicrous if they were not so often put forward under socially impeccable auspices.

The almost universal avoidance in our public discourse of this "scientific fact, which everybody really knows," namely, that a human being is killed by abortion, exemplifies the new and fundamental *dishonesty* which legal abortion has helped bring to our public life. Where abortion as a political issue is concerned, we strive to deny, semantically, that we are taking a life, although that is the reality.

At the same time we understand perfectly well — and act on the logic of it — that if we can take a life by abortion, we can take a life for other reasons as well. And thus the field in which we consider ourselves allowed to take life legally very quickly becomes extended — as it very quickly *has* become extended in our society.

It becomes extended, for example, to the terminally (and to the not so terminally) ill; it becomes extended to the old, the retarded, the defective — in short, to specimens of Friedrich Nietzsche's "botched" and "bungled," or Adolf Hitler's "useless eaters."

Soon, if it has not happened already, the same moral permissiveness in taking life will be extended to AIDs victims, if only in view of the astronomical medical costs associated with their extended care when, all the time, everybody understands that their illness is "terminal" anyway.

None of this represents any hypothetical "slippery slope" argument. We are already on that slope and going rapidly downhill, as witness the nation's current inability to deal with the new phenomenon of "assisted suicide." And it all started with legalized abortion; that was the point where we got on the slippery slope and started downhill towards an open "killer society." Many warned at the time that this was where we were headed, but few paid any attention to such warnings.

Irving Kristol, for his part, finds himself able to accept the current state of affairs and to write:

> In all the Western democracies (including Israel) a public policy has evolved that tolerates abortion while limiting it, regulating it, and discouraging it. It is safe to predict that this is where public policy in the U.S. will end up. And if in Israel the Orthodox — who utterly abhor abortion and do not themselves practice it — can live with such a compromise, there is no reason why our conservative Christians cannot do the same.

Actually there are many reasons. Living with a situation we can do nothing about may be one thing. No doubt the Orthodox are not numerous enough in Israel to affect "public policy" — just as prolifers in the U.S. have not *yet* been able to do too much about the fact of legal abortion. Therefore, for the moment, prolifers do have to live with the current tragic abortion situation in this country — until they can build up their numbers and influence to the point where they can begin to do something effective about it.

But Irving Kristol is evidently arguing for something very different from merely being obliged to live with a situation about which nothing can be done, at least for the moment. He seems to be arguing for the *acceptance* of our current situation, however undesirable even he may think it is.

But this is a counsel of despair. First, much *can* be done about our current abortion situation, as Henry Hyde and his congressional allies have so recently demonstrated in getting the Hyde Amendment re-enacted against all the odds and all the predictions of the pundits.

Other similar concrete prolife measures are also both possible and doable, even in the present unfavorable climate.

But, secondly, abortion *must* be fought against on principle because it is *wrong*: we *cannot* leave our country in the hands of people who have demonstrated that they are perfectly willing to kill the innocent wantonly, meanwhile lying publicly about what it is they are really doing. One of the things that continually motivated the anti-Communists in Eastern Europe and the former Soviet Union and motivated them to try to bring down the rotten regimes that ruled there was the all-pervasive *dishonesty* of these regimes. We simply cannot give America over to the same kind of dishonesty, as practiced by the proabortionists.

With all due respect, then, Irving Kristol is simply wrong about all of this. Legalized abortion is not something that any society can really tolerate or live with without losing its soul. It must be combatted on principle, whatever the odds.

III

Let us not, however, single out Irving Kristol. Over the past several years there has been a veritable spate of articles and speeches by conservatives calling for a more pragmatic, less allegedly "absolutist" position on abortion. There is even a strong trend among conservatives at the present time to assume the existence of some sort of a "consensus" in the practical order in favor of finally accepting legalized abortion under certain conditions.

Prolifers are now being given to understand that their cause can be championed in the political arena only through such measures as those which, in the words of an editorial in *National Review*, "allow states to impose such clearly sensible requirements as parental, spousal, and informed consent. There are solid majorities for such an approach. . .Republican policy should reflect that political reality." So editorialized the conservative journal, which nevertheless continues to represent itself as basically "prolife."

And according to David Horowitz, writing in the same journal, *National Review*, conservative support for recognition of a constitutional right to life would be fatal to the "majoritarian political ambitions" of the conservative movement. No doubt following polls, Horowitz postulated a 30 per cent minority out there determined to be proabortion in all circumstances, a 30 or 40 per cent "center," highly ambivalent about the whole thing, but unwilling to prohibit it by law, and at most a 30 per cent bloc believing in a right to life. Concluded Horowitz: "The arithmetic adds up to an insuperable political barrier." A majority, he thought, "will defeat any political movement that organizes around the code word 'right to life.'" Curiously, he does not even raise the question of principle; one inevitably wonders what other "conservative" tenets he would agree could be decided simply by consulting public opinion polls.

In another article in the same journal, William McGurn exhibits the same pragmatism and frankly advocates doing away with the Republican Party platform plank calling for a constitutional amendment to protect the unborn:

> Taking into account the dramatic shifts in America's political, constitutional, and, yes, moral landscape, Republicans need to shift their position from support for a constitutional amendment outlawing all abortions to support for one asserting the constitutional prerogative of states in restricting abortion.

According to McGurn, holding out for an amendment outlawing all abortions "essentially guarantees there will be no restrictions at all." But this is not true, as proved, *inter alia,* by the recent Hyde Amendment re-enactment. The prolife movement has continued to work, often successfully, for some restrictions on abortion, even while continuing to aim at the principled goal of a constitutional amendment protecting all children. A principal reason the prolife movement has been unable to be more successful in this regard up to now is that we still remain under the thralldom of the courts, especially the Supreme Court, on the abortion issue. The courts keep rejecting what legislatures try to enact.

Traditionally, in both law and morality, no one has the right "to choose" to take the life of another. But since our judges appear unable to understand law or morality where abortion is concerned, a maximalist constitutional amendment remains the best and perhaps the only way they can finally be brought to their senses. Until then, nothing prevents prolifers from working on achieving all the interim measures which *National Review* and William McGurn advocate. Indeed, prolifers are precisely the ones who are out there doing this right now. Who else is working so tirelessly around the country and in the various states for such goals, heart-breakingly limited as they are?

But to disown the *ultimate* goal of prolifers working within the Republican Party by changing or dropping the current platform language would be a catastrophic mistake for the party. Prolifers will not continue to work for or within a party that thinks it has to go to the trouble of expressly repudiating the clear goal of the vast majority of an important constituency — and the reason why many of them are working for the Republican Party in the first place. One recent poll showed that 58 per cent of church-going Republican voters would *leave* the Republican Party if it abandoned its profamily and prolife positions.

All the prolife demonstrators out there — e.g., in the proliferating Life Chains — are hardly holding up signs calling for spousal or parental notification or waiting periods before abortions; they work for such things only because they represent the best that can be achieved at the moment. But the signs they hold up say: "Abortion Kills Children." And what they are really working for is a halt to the killing.

With abortion we are simply not dealing with a normal political issue. If the current arguments for expediency within the Republican Party manage to win out, the party may eventually come to be seen as *doomed* precisely by its inability to deal with the abortion issue on a principled basis, just as the old Whig Party in the last century proved unable to deal with slavery on a principled basis.

And thus the kinds of arguments advanced by the conservative "friends" of the prolife movement such as Irving Kristol and William McGurn are really not too far removed from the arguments of the avowed enemies of the cause; it is the latter who keep on impatiently insisting that the abortion issue must be settled at all costs and that the prolifers are therefore the ones who must compromise.

How can prolifers be expected to take such counsels seriously? With friends like these, we hardly need enemies!

3

Yes, It Is a Holocaust

I

Fifty years ago, in the middle of World War II, in January, 1944, Arthur Koestler wrote an article in *The New York Times Magazine*, "On Disbelieving Atrocities," in which he took public opinion in the democracies to task for shutting out the reality of the evils being perpetrated in Nazi-occupied Europe, evils afterwards abundantly verified and in many ways summed up and symbolized by what we have today come to call "the Holocaust" — the extermination of millions for base and evil ideological reasons.

Today museums are erected so that we will never be able to forget the horror of those now long past events. At the time, however, those who, like Arthur Koestler, attempted to alert public opinion to the atrocities being perpetrated by the Nazis, encountered little but a steady if not grim determination on the part of public opinion broadly speaking never to allow itself to be unduly affected by the gigantic evils being reported by such observers as Koestler.

Himself a refugee in England from Hitler's continental New Order, Koestler described himself as belonging to a group of "escaped victims or eyewitnesses. . .who, haunted by our memories, go on screaming on the wireless, yelling at you in newspapers and in public meetings, theaters and cinemas. Now and then we succeed in reaching your ear for a moment," Koestler noted. "I know it each time it happens by a certain dumb wonder on your faces. . . . But it only lasts a minute. You shake yourselves like puppies who got their fur wet; then the transparent screen descends again, protected by the dream barrier which stifles all sound."

Precisely because the Holocaust perpetrated during World War II represents today everybody's prototypical example of man's inhumanity to man, it is worth quoting further from Arthur Koestler's eloquent testimony in 1944 as to just how things were then. It wasn't easy to get anybody to believe in the horror while it was going on:

Originally published in *The Catholic World Report*, August/September, 1994.

We, the screamers, have been at it now for about ten years. We started on the night when the epileptic van der Lubbe set fire to the German Parliament; we said that if you don't quench those flames at once, they will spread all over the world; you thought we were maniacs. At present we have the mania of trying to tell you about the killing, by hot steam, mass-electrocution, and live burial of the total Jewish population of Europe. So far three million have died. It is the greatest mass-killing in recorded history; and it goes on daily, hourly, as regularly as the ticking of your watch. I have photographs before me on the desk while I am writing this, and that accounts for my emotion and bitterness. People died to smuggle them out of Poland; they thought it was worth while. The facts have been published in pamphlets, White Books, newspapers, magazines, and what not. But the other day I met one of the best-known American journalists over here. He told me that in the course of some recent public opinion survey nine out of ten average American citizens, when asked whether they believed that the Nazis commit atrocities, answered that it was all propaganda lies, and that they don't believe a word of it. As to this country, I have been lecturing now for three years to the troops, and their attitude is the same. They don't believe in concentration camps; they don't believe in the starved children of Greece, in the shot hostages in France, in the mass-graves of Poland; they have never heard of Lidice, Treblinka or Belzec; you can convince them for an hour, then they shake themselves, their mental self-defence begins to work and in a week the shrug of incredulity has returned like a reflex temporarily weakened by a shock.

Clearly all this is becoming a mania with me and my like. Clearly we must suffer from some morbid obsession, whereas the others are healthy and normal. But the characteristic symptom of maniacs is that they lose contact with reality and live in a phantasy world. So, perhaps, it is the other way round; perhaps it is we, the screamers, who react in a sound and healthy way to the reality which surrounds us, whereas you are the neurotics who totter about in a screened phantasy world because you lack the faculty to face the facts. Were it not so, this war would have been avoided, and those murdered within sight of your day-dreaming eyes would still be alive.

At least in 1944 some of the Cassandras such as Arthur Koestler had *access* to the major public media in order to be able to report what was going on — in order to be able to "scream" within the hearing of someone. Maybe they weren't very successful in getting people to believe in the atrocities they were so desperately trying to describe, but at least they disposed of a few substantial public platforms from which to launch their cries. Koestler spoke, after all, of "screaming. . .on the wireless. . .in newspapers. . .public meeting, theaters and cinemas. . ." Koestler's own article "On Disbelieving Atrocities" was published in *The New York Times Magazine*, no less. So it was certainly not the case that the screamers had no access to the media, even if they were not too successful in rousing up people against the evil they were trying to denounce.

II

Today another Holocaust is currently being perpetrated while those who are again desperately trying to rouse the public against it have little or no access to any important media or other public platforms; when this new group of "screamers" are accorded any public notice, it is usually only to be treated as a new class of what Arthur Koestler styled "maniacs." While they are obsessed with the horror of what is going on, the average person goes imperturbably on living in an unreal dream world.

Yet the facts about the new Holocaust are again quite readily available, and are even quite well known to anyone who has taken the trouble to focus on them. Once again, "pamphlets, White Books, newspapers, magazines, and what not" have all been published about this contemporary Holocaust. In spite of this, the indications are that very large numbers of people either do not know about it; or, what is more likely, are determined not to let themselves be affected by the reality of it — they are determined not to admit, in other words, that what is really going on is, in fact, a Holocaust.

For it is not the case that there is never any public reference to today's Holocaust. On the contrary, it is frequently referred to and even rather extensively covered, both in the media and elsewhere; it is the subject of frequent public debate and discussion. Letters to the editor calling attention to it, usually from two opposite points of view, like similar letters to the members of Congress, are common; so are bumper stickers and similar sloganeering about it. What is mostly lacking in all the public attention given to the thing, however, is almost any real, solid, accurate information about just what it really *is* — what it really entails and what its consequences increasingly are for our whole way of life.

It is actually a horror on the level of and even exceeding the appalling atrocities which Arthur Koestler was trying to expose back in 1944. Yet it is most commonly presented to the public in the guise of an absolutely necessary modern "benefit" which helps people live autonomous lives based on their own personal decisions and choices; it is even supposed to stem from the exercise of a woman's "constitutional right."

For the Holocaust of today to which I refer, of course, is the atrocity of legalized abortion. You had probably already guessed by now that this was what I was leading up to. And I can even imagine the rising exasperation level on the part of many the minute anyone attempts to link abortion to the Holocaust. One of the standardized ways in which the reality of abortion is neutralized, obscured, or denied today, as a matter of fact, is to reject, usually indignantly, the notion that legalized abortion is in any way comparable to the Holocaust.

Nevertheless if the World War II Holocaust represented a horrendous institutionalization of man's inhumanity to man, involving the mass extermination of millions, then legalized abortion today — which is nothing else at all but the institutionalized and deliberate killing by medical means, and on a massive scale, of children who have been conceived but not yet born — then this unrestricted killing by abortion surely also qualifies as another Holocaust.

In the United States the lethal procedures used to perform abortions were first institutionalized and have since been maintained by decisions of the United States Supreme Court itself. In its latest major abortion decision, the 1992 Pennsylvania *Casey* decision, the high court ruled that its original legalization of abortion, in its 1973 *Roe v. Wade* decision, must continue to stand because, in the words of the majority decision in *Casey*, "for two decades of economic and social developments, people have organized intimate relationships and made choices that define their views of themselves and their places in society in reliance on the availability of abortion in the event that contraception should fail."

This is indeed what the highest court in the land said: abortion must be available "in the event that contraception should fail"; in such a case we must be able to exterminate at will the children conceived. No thought at all is given to the question of whether these children themselves might not be the subject of rights or have justice coming to them if our constitutional and legal system is still going to be able to claim in any sense that it stands for "equal justice under law." Rather, that proud motto would seem to have already been compromised, and perhaps even fatally undermined, with the *Roe v. Wade* decision of the Supreme Court in 1973.

The New York Times, by the way, which had been willing to print Koestler's jeremiad against the original Holocaust, *welcomed* the current one with the editorial comment that the *Roe v. Wade* decision represented what it called "a noble cry of conscience." (Now we really *do* know what is meant by "the banality of evil"!)

On the purely factual level, there would similarly seem to be no longer even any memory of how contraception was originally promoted in public (against the perceived opposition of, e.g., the Catholic Church) as an indispensable way to *avoid* ever having to resort to abortions. Modern means of contraception had regularly been represented as "alternatives," supposedly preventive of abortion, whereas what has occurred historically is that once contraception came to be considered acceptable and necessary, abortion too came to be considered necessary too, as the indispensable "back-up."

When was it ever debated, at what point was it ever decided that lives could now actually be terminated "in the event that contraception should fail"? Whenever it was, this is what the law of the land now is.

If ever there was a harmful ideology, today's reigning and almost universally unquestioned ideology that a modern autonomous person must be "free" to make his or her own decisions, regardless of their effect on others, who may not have any recourse of their own, surely has to qualify as producing utterly boundless evil. As the current principal argument and justification for legalized abortion, this ideology, now enshrined in law, is producing in the United States every day — "daily, hourly, as regularly as the ticking of your watch," as Koestler said — thousands of abortions every day, and well over 30 million of them since this lethal "medical" procedure was legalized by the Supreme Court over two decades ago.

The latest (1992) statistics do indicate that the incidence of abortion has actually dropped somewhat — to slightly below 1.4 million abortions annually. But this still means that well over a fourth of all the pregnancies in the United States today now terminate in abortions.

But is abortion really killing? I can imagine that exasperation level rising again. The denial that abortion is killing is another one of Arthur Koestler's "dream barriers" designed to enable people to escape from having to face the true reality of the consequences of the Supreme Court's legalization of abortion.

The evidence is overwhelming that abortion is — nothing else but — killing. Moreover it is the killing of a human being. This is in no way a religious or theological judgment. The scientific facts concerning human conception, gestation, and development are all irrefutably established and they all support the conclusion that a distinct human being comes into existence at the time of fertilization; these facts are readily available to anyone honest enough to ascertain them (but once again they are almost never examined or discussed; they are simply denied out of hand and dismissed). The question raised by abortion is not the factual one of whether or not we are killing a human being; we are; the question raised is the moral question of whether we are entitled to do so.

I could dwell upon some of the more bloody and brutal recent techniques by which abortions are currently performed: the so-called D & E procedure where the developing baby is literally cut up into little pieces; or the D & X procedure where the fully formed skull is pierced and the brains sucked out so that the head can be more easily extracted. Yes, these procedures are actually being carried out today by physicians trained in our medical schools.

Or I could dwell upon the process whereby the developing baby swimming in the mother's amniotic fluid sharply recoils in pain from the probing needle which will inject the saline solution which will literally burn him or her to death. I could dwell on this sort of thing at sickening length, in fact, without ever even mentioning the harm that is also regularly done to the *women* undergoing abortions.

But I do not have to dwell on any of these highly unpleasant things to make my point. For the Supreme Court, in effect, has now admitted that abortion does indeed involve the termination of the life of a developing human being before birth; the court has only admitted this, however, in the very act of deciding that this particular kind of homicide is nevertheless permissible anyway and must definitely continue to be legal. A "life" is taken, all right, but, in the words of Mr. Justice Stevens in his concurring opinion in the *Casey* decision, "an abortion is not the termination of a life entitled to 14th Amendment protection."

That's it: it is "defined" as a life which is not "entitled" to the constitutional protections that everybody is supposed to be entitled to.

In a rare moment of judicial candor, a New Jersey judge attempting to rule in a case under the constraints established by *Roe v. Wade* once remarked, quite correctly, that this decision actually "legalized the execution of a human being" but that, as a judge, he was "bound" by the ruling anyway, so long as it remained "the law of the land."

The unborn are thus excluded from the equal protection of the laws supposedly guaranteed by our Constitution by a simple declaration that they are not entitled to it — just as slaves were excluded by definition from the same equal protection of the laws by the *Dred Scott* decision over a century ago.

The comparison of legalized abortion with slavery — like our earlier comparison of America's current abortion plague with the Holocaust — is another one of those things which is again apt to raise the exasperation level the instant the comparison is made. It mightily irritates and annoys all the same reality deniers who are unwilling to face up to the facts of just what abortion is and just what abortion does. But the comparison of legalized abortion with slavery is nevertheless quite exact, just as the comparison of the *Roe v. Wade* decision with the *Dred Scott* decision is quite exact: in each case an entire class of human beings has been deprived by a simple court ruling of the constitutional rights that should have applied to it as a class.

The denial of the reality that legalized abortion is not only sanctioned legalized killing but also stands in direct and stark contradiction to the basic principles of the American constitutional system — which can hardly avoid being undermined generally by such an open contradiction of all that it supposedly stands for — this is a denial which provides abundant confirmation of the fact that millions of Americans today have fallen into Arthur Koestler's category of "neurotics who totter about in a screened phantasy world because [they] lack the faculty to face the facts."

Koestler's contemporary, George Orwell, similarly once wrote that "at any given moment, there is a sort of all-pervasive orthodoxy — a general, tacit agreement not to discuss some large and uncomfortable fact." The reality of abortion in America today would surely seem to be such a "large and uncomfortable fact."

III

Occasionally Arthur Koestler's "dream barrier" protecting treatment of the abortion issue from ever intersecting with reality does get lifted, and some truth is temporarily able to escape. One such occasion was the meeting before the television cameras between President Clinton and Pope John Paul II when the latter arrived in Denver in August, 1993, and again when the president visited the pope in the summer of 1994. The media were obliged to report straight on those occasions the pontiff's pointed remarks about the tragedy of abortion in America; but the events were so unusual that President Clinton knew all the time that he really did not have very much to worry about; and he scarcely even exhibited any discomfort on either occasion.

A similar occasion arose at the annual National Prayer Breakfast in Washington, D.C., in February, 1994, when Mother Teresa of Calcutta told an audience which included both President and Mrs. Clinton and Vice President and Mrs. Gore that:

> . . .the greatest destroyer of peace today is abortion because it is a war against the child, a direct killing of the innocent child, murder by the mother herself. And if we accept that a mother can even kill her own child, how can we tell other people not to kill one another? . . .Any country that accepts abortion is not teaching its people to love, but to use any violence to get what they want.

At that point in her address to the National Prayer Breakfast, Mother Teresa is reported to have received a standing ovation from the audience. President Clinton, however — so journalist Cal Thomas reported — "at that moment. . .quickly reached for his water glass, and Mrs. Clinton and Vice President and Mrs. Gore stared without expression at Mother Teresa. They did not applaud. It was clearly an uncomfortable moment on the dais" — it was the dropping, again, of Koestler's "dream barrier which stifles all sound."

Then Mother Teresa delivered what Cal Thomas called "the knockout punch":

> Many people are very, very concerned with the children of India, with the children of Africa where quite a few die of hunger. Many people are also concerned about all the violence in this great country of the United States. These concerns are very good. But often these same people are not con-

> cerned with the millions who are being killed by the deliberate decision of their own mothers. And this is what is the greatest destroyer of peace today — abortion which brings people to such blindness.

Even though the dream barrier does sometimes get lifted, then, and the truth does sometimes get out, Mother Teresa herself nevertheless most accurately characterized America today when she said that "people are not concerned with the millions who are being killed by the deliberate decision of their own mothers."

Moreover, on those few occasions when the barrier does get lifted, the practical results generally fall tragically short of what is needed. To take yet another example: the terrible truth about abortion has never been more factually or eloquently told, as a matter of fact, than it was by Rep. Henry Hyde of Illinois on the floor of the U.S. House of Representatives at the time of the debate on the Hyde Amendment which for the past eighteen years has generally prohibited federal funding of abortions. Against all expectations, the Hyde Amendment was re-enacted by Congress in 1993 (although the prolife forces led by Rep. Hyde had to agree this time that pregnancies brought about by rape or incest could be terminated at taxpayer expense along with the traditional exception, abortions thought necessary to save the mother's life).

At the time the Hyde Amendment was being re-enacted, there was of course no thought that Congress might ever try to outlaw the horrendous practice of abortion itself. Congress would presumably never have the guts — not until prolife pressures become considerably greater than they have been able to be up to now. The members do heed, though, at least to some extent, the huge volume of prolife mail they regularly receive; and consequently they have so far continued to reject government funding of abortion, even while abortion itself continues to remain legal.

During the debate on the Hyde Amendment, Rep. Hyde himself exhaustively presented, as never before, all the terrible facts about legal abortion; he capably reiterated all the arguments against it (See the *Congressional Record* for June 30, 1993). There is no public record concerning whether the members of the House of Representatives were embarrassed or chagrined or ashamed — as they should have been. What the public record does show, though, is that neither Rep. Hyde's facts nor his arguments ever appeared in any media coverage of the debate.

What appeared in the media coverage were politically correct stories of how the new contingent of female House members — it is virtually taken for granted by the media that any woman in public life today necessarily has to be in favor of keeping abortion legal[1] — the media stories were all about how the inexperienced Congresswomen simply got out-foxed procedurally by an old-boy network in the Congress which included Rep. Hyde. Wait until next year — or at least until "women" finally do come into their own. So the media slant was, and, indeed, this year abortion is again being debated as part of so-called health care reform as just another medical "benefit."

However, the melancholy truth concerning so-called "public policy" on abortion, as any serious inquirer into the real abortion situation will quickly learn, is that our "dominant culture" is quite simply *not interested* in the truth about abortion; it is simply resolved to have abortions. For the moment no facts or arguments will avail. With abortion we are dealing with something totally different from the usual "debate" about "public policy."

It is widely accepted, for example, apparently without argument, that abortion represents an ineluctable and overpowering modern imperative that cannot be opposed. Certainly the so-called "sexual revolution" is inconceivable without it, and the sexual revolution is something that is itself also nearly universally considered to be a simply overwhelming and irreversible modern fact of life. In view of these kinds of assumptions, it is perhaps not even surprising that abortion is typically seen as a juggernaut which we have no recourse but simply to get out of the way of. This is surely one of the strong reasons, though not the only one, for the unreality which pervades nearly every public discussion of abortion. It is also, surely, one of the reasons for the strong disapproval so often expressed against demonstrations by prolifers, the "screamers," the "maniacs," even when they are doing nothing but what demonstrators for other causes are regularly cheered and praised for doing.

Few movements in American history, for example, have been more truly non-violent than the prolife movement. Yet — marking still another casualty for truth — the movement is regularly accused of violence anyway. And the verifiably few violent acts of isolated individuals which do occur are then shrilly and self-righteously laid to the charge of the whole prolife movement — this to the point

[1] Six of the eleven new women House members elected in the 1994 mid-term elections were strong prolifers.

where Congress has now actually enacted a so-called Freedom of Access to Clinic Entrances (FACE) Act, openly abridging the First Amendment rights of prolife demonstrators *only* (and, not incidentally, possibly also encouraging greater violence because now prolife demonstrators can be found guilty of felonies whether they are "violent" or not!). It is almost as if the failed attempt of Count von Stauffenberg and his fellow conspirators to assassinate Adolph Hitler had been taken to be the "problem" in the Nazi-occupied Europe of the 1940s instead of what the Nazis themselves had done!

Whatever your cause, then, it *cannot* be prolife; it is not in fashion. Today's *bien-pensants* irritably repeat like a mantra that the volatile and "controversial" abortion issue must be settled once and for all; prolifers must reconcile themselves and come to terms (since it is plain that the proabortionists are never going to come to terms!). "Practical" people can see no other way out; Americans are tired of the abortion issue — so we are being told so constantly and insistently that perhaps too many of us have come to believe it.

It is, of course, easy to understand why Americans might be uneasy about abortion; it represents, after all, a really monstrous situation in which Americans have nevertheless more or less decided to acquiesce, at least for the moment. Still, there is no way *not* to be uneasy about it, considering what it really is. The idea that legalized abortion just might have to be opposed and fought against on principle, unwaveringly; that it just might happen to be one of those fundamental and unavoidable issues that, if not faced up to and remedied, can undermine our entire legal and constitutional system, and, indeed, is already in the process of doing so; the further idea that America *cannot* be left in the hands of a public opinion apparently prepared to sacrifice a significant percentage of the next generation of Americans to the insatiable demands of a false and sordid ideology — these are all ideas that huge numbers of Americans, including especially too many of our current elected and appointed national leaders, are apparently not yet ready to face up to.

There can be no doubt at all, for example, that the country's present majority Democratic Party political leadership is quite simply firmly and frankly proabortion, no questions asked. The well-heeled abortion lobby has for quite a while been one of the most powerful of all the ideological special interests to which the national Democratic Party is currently enthralled. Democratic candidates generally see abortion, if not always as an automatically winning issue, at least as a clear imperative for their campaigns, often vying with one another in Democratic primaries, for example, as to who is the more militantly "prochoice."

Democratic presidential aspirants have similarly understood for a long time that they stand no chance whatsoever of going anywhere in the Democratic Party nationally unless they espouse a completely wide-open position on abortion; they fear and respect the proabortion forces in a way that none of the Republican aspirants ever seem to fear or respect the prolife forces. Thus, such formerly "prolife" Democrats as Jimmy Carter (he once *said* he was prolife), Ted Kennedy (he did too), Jesse Jackson, Richard Gephardt, and Bill Clinton all found it necessary to renounce whatever real prolife sentiments they may ever have harbored in order even to be able to launch their respective presidential bids. This renunciation of theirs seems not to have caused even the slightest twinge of anguish or afterthought in any of them — itself another symptom of how definitively the abortion issue is already thought by them to have been settled once and for all.

It is hard to know, indeed, what other issue is considered as sacrosanct today. Our Constitution itself, for example, does not seem to be as sacrosanct. Nevertheless, even many who profess to be "prolife" share the same general assumptions about the permanency of the legalization of abortion; and they apparently do believe that this ghastly procedure, unheard of in law for many centuries until V.I. Lenin's Soviet Union first legalized it in 1920, can henceforth only be opposed in the most tepid and minimalistic ways. When William Butler Yeats wrote his oft-quoted line — "The best lack all conviction, while the worst are full of passionate intensity" — he certainly could have been talking about the contemporary abortion issue.

IV

That a modern democratically-elected government could actually be committed to promoting an abortion Holocaust, meanwhile considering the whole thing as respectable, politically correct, and somehow even a plus for freedom and democracy — all this is no doubt bad enough. What is worse is that there is apparently no alternative political leadership in sight prepared to face up to the full horror of the abortion Holocaust or to attempt to do anything significant about it. The situation is exactly the same as the one described by Arthur Koestler in 1944, where neither public opinion nor the political leadership was prepared to admit that the atrocity of the Holocaust was even being perpetrated.

In July, 1993, for example, President Clinton's first proabortion nominee for the Supreme Court, Ruth Bader Ginsbury, was *unanimously* approved by the Senate Judiciary Committee for a seat on the Supreme Court in spite of her assertion before the Committee that "a woman's right to choose abortion is central to a woman's life, to her dignity." The supposedly prolife Senators on the Committee — who have surely solicited and accepted prolife voter support in their election campaigns — nevertheless joined in the unanimous vote for Ginsburg (as did many normally prolife senators on the floor), and this in spite of the disgracefully hostile treatment which the antilife forces in the Senate had meted out to Republican nominees to the Court Robert Bork and Clarence Thomas.

Utah Republican Senator Orrin Hatch, for example, supposedly a "leader" of the prolife forces in the Senate — he once introduced his own constitutional amendment — was actually quoted as saying that a "prochoice" president such as President Clinton was entitled to a "prochoice" justice on the court! William Butler Yeats, where are you now that we need you? Wherever the shadow of the abortion imperative falls, apparently, some Republican politicians no longer seem capable of even being *partisan*, let alone of being principled.

While the Republican Party platform currently does have a prolife plank calling for a constitutional amendment to extend Fifth and Fourteenth Amendment protection to the unborn, the debate that is currently going on is whether the GOP can afford [!] to maintain this position. Strong and influential Republican and even some conservative voices are arguing that a constitutional amendment is simply not in the cards; there is no possible majority of the American people for it, it is claimed; and therefore it is urged that the present prolife plank in the party platform should be eliminated in the name of political realism and of "the art of the possible."

No doubt many Republicans would be enormously relieved to "put the divisive abortion issue behind us" — never mind how; never mind if the party has to sell its soul to do so (since the 1970s the Republican Party has made what were presumably serious commitments to the prolife position in order to attract the large — and still growing — prolife and profamily vote; the party can't have it both ways.)

The truth is, though, that those who think that the Republican Party — or the country — can just "put the divisive abortion issue behind us" are among the charter subscribers to George Orwell's "all-pervading orthodoxy" which has tacitly agreed "not to discuss a large and uncomfortable fact. . ."

What is even more disturbing than the obtuse run-and-hide attitude of those who apparently truly do not see that legalized abortion perforce raises urgent and inescapable fundamental questions concerning the very possibility of the survival of a democratic government, however, is the minimalistic attitude of many of the Republican and conservative leaders and opinion-makers, some of whom even continue to present themselves as "prolife." Most observers who have given any real attention or thought to the matter recognize that no national Republican or conservative victories are even possible in today's climate unless the prolife and profamily constituency remains in Republican ranks.

Yet even in the face of this very hard fact, many Republican and conservative leaders nevertheless go on insisting that a minimalistic position on abortion is the only one that makes any sense. They do not want to lose the prolife votes, of course. However, probably calculating that the prolifers have nowhere else to go anyway, they are determined not to go any farther than they have to in advocating any real prolife "solutions."

Usually the argument is made that the battle to restore the equal protection of the laws to the unborn is already irretrievably lost. Yet such protection was effectively afforded to the unborn by the laws of all fifty of the states up to 1966, less than a generation ago, and scarcely anyone ever protested. But those days are gone forever, it is thought, like the practice of virtue itself perhaps, and those days presumably cannot be recalled.

Little attention is paid, meanwhile, to the question of whether freedom and democracy themselves can survive if "those days" are *not* somehow brought back! No: such ideas are ruled out in advance; and in spite of the fact that they are indisputably in the right on the principle of the thing, prolifers are regularly told that *they* must be the ones who are content to work only for what is attainable today, that is, for half-measures which are merely pinpricks on the skin of the dominant abortion culture: waiting periods, spousal or parental permission for abortions, some limitations on wide-open access to abortions such as time limits, and so on.

National Review magazine, for example, has been regularly advancing these kinds of solutions considered more "practical" or "attainable" than the perceived "absolutist" position of most prolifers (which is still, nevertheless, reflected in the Republican prolife platform language). Over the past several years, *NR* has printed a series of articles advocating a strictly minimalistic approach to the political question of legalized abortion as the only sensible one for Republicans and conservatives (the liberals are not even in the ball game; liberals are certain abortion is here to stay, and should!).

One of the latest of *NR*'s minimalistic advocacy pieces came in an article actually written by three prolife leaders in its issue of December 27, 1993; these writers propose an approach to the abortion issue that would limit access to legal abortion by forbidding the procedure by law once brain-wave activity is verifiably present in the fetus, that is, at around eight weeks of pregnancy. This point in the gestation period was chosen not only because fetal brain-wave activity can be scientifically verified, but also because the legal and medical criteria currently used to define the end of life are similarly tied to verifiable brain-wave activity: once there is no longer any such activity, the plug can be pulled — to use the crude expression which currently is used. It is thought — on the basis of certain dicta of certain Supreme Court justices — that such a test might even enjoy the further advantage of having some chance of being considered constitutional by the high court as constituted today.

Considered an even more compelling reason to adopt this minimalistic approach today, however, is the idea that it would find strong support in current American public opinion, as measured by the polls (*National Review*'s writers on the subject of abortion have regularly appealed to public-opinion polls in support of their "solutions"; one inevitably wonders how they would regard similar polls showing public opposition to the free market!):

Polls consistently show that between 15 and 25 per cent of the public are on each extreme of the abortion issue. That leaves 50 to 70 percent of Americans in the middle. . .According to a recent Gallup survey, 73 percent of Americans support a prohibition on abortion after the first trimester of pregnancy (about ten weeks after conception). This survey shows that 82 percent of those who are strongly prolife, as well as 82 percent of those in the middle would support such a proposal. More surprisingly, even 46 percent of those identified as strongly prochoice agree that abortion should be limited to the first trimester.

Other polls have consistently shown that, while a majority of Americans support a woman's right to choose an abortion in the early weeks of pregnancy, a majority also believe that at some point the government acquires the right to intervene and protect the child. . .

Ergo, what is supposed to make sense today is to work to limit or stop abortions after the onset of fetal brain-wave activity. Other proposals to work for such things as informed, spousal, or parental consent and so on, like proposals to work for time limits on legal abortions, are similarly advanced because these are the things which polls indicate American public opinion might support.

Although such proposals, like the public-opinion justifications advanced for them, are quite obviously based strictly on expediency, they apparently appeal to many people, including many Republican and conservative leaders, some of whom also recognize the prolife and profamily constituency as an essential element of any possible prolife Republican or conservative electoral victories. And hence no little effort is being expended at the present time attempting to convince prolifers that these solutions based on expediency truly do represent the way to go. The "large and uncomfortable fact" that our Constitution presumably cannot consistently permit elective, legalized killing at any stage of life is conveniently left aside.

For the fact is that many of these minimalist approaches to legalized abortion are so framed as to concede in principle that at least some elective killing is permissible. This admission, like the issue of slavery at the beginning of our Republic, fatally serves to divide the house so that it cannot indefinitely stand; and that means that, sooner or later, it will fall.

For those minimizers who protest that nobody will ever convince the average American that a day-old embryo enjoys the same value as a nine-month fetus ready to be delivered, the reply has to be — dictated by the strict *truth* of the matter: "*You* were once a day-old embryo! Did you have a right to life, or not?" We cannot put a comparative price on human life at various stages; that is already to concede the principle. Those who want to prohibit abortion only after viability or the onset of brain-wave activity or whatever are not really against homicide in principle; they are only against the messy blood and gore of later-stage abortions.

V

One of the main troubles with the partial or minimalistic solutions to the abortion question, then, is the illusion that the abortion question is somehow susceptible to a "compromise" or "moderate" solution. In reality no such compromise is possible, and the principal reason for this is that the proabortion people are the ones who from the very beginning have staked out the absolutist position that abortion is a woman's constitutional "right." What constitutional right can anybody ever compromise on?

On the contrary, a very important step towards any solution to the abortion question necessarily has to be to establish and disseminate the truth that there cannot possibly be, under our Constitution, *any* "right" to take the life of another.

In the meantime, precisely because the "absolutist" nature of the problem posed by abortion is perceived, if only dimly, by just about everybody, the habit of speaking of the "extremes" on the question easily arises, even among those who call themselves "prolifers." The proabortionists can be conceded to be "extremists" all right; but then suddenly, unaccountably, those who are strongly prolife can end up being characterized as "extremists" as well.

Yet there surely has to be something radically amiss in an outlook which can categorize those who are *against* legalized killing and aberrant interpretations of our Constitution in exactly the same fashion as those who are *for* these things. One really obvious consequence of setting up such a false dichotomy is that those who are *defined* as the reasonable, moderate people — the ones "in the middle" — are really no such thing. For, all the time, they have actually conceded the argument of principle to the abortionists and have agreed that, yes, we can have some legalized killing — they are simply for less of it. But the truth is, on the abortion issue, that there *is* no middle.

Nevertheless the idea that there ought to be some middle ground on the abortion issue is one of the things that provides a convenient excuse for those who are unwilling to take a principled stand. It is from this standpoint that prolifers are regularly told today, even by many of their self-styled "friends," that their movement can no longer expect satisfactory political solutions, and that they therefore must concentrate on more incremental approaches such as, for example, developing compassionate alternatives to abortion and helping women with problem pregnancies: the prolife movement must seek to change the climate of opinion about abortion by more judicious rational persuasion, it is urged, rather than by rescues, sidewalk anti-abortion counseling, picketing, demonstrations, and other types of agitation. People dislike picketing and demonstrations, prolifers are told, and all the agitation and turmoil they bring; many people even end up opposing the prolife movement as a result of the controversy it inevitably arouses — so it is regularly pointed out.

This sort of advice and counsel to the prolife movement often may even be well meant. However, much of it is also beside the point, and bespeaks on the part of those offering it more than a little ignorance, whether willful or not, of exactly what the current abortion situation in this country is. Compassionate alternatives to abortion and helps for pregnant women, for example, have mostly been long since established, and always with the strong and steady support of the prolife movement. Birthright and similar organizations all came into existence under prolife impetus as quickly as any of the political right-to-life committees and activist organizations — that is, from the moment the abortion explosion was first detonated in our country in the late 1960s and the early 1970s. Churches, which had long been in the same business, have in many cases been redoubling their efforts during the same approximate time frame.

No doubt the total positive effort to help women with problem pregnancies is never sufficient; no doubt there is always greater need. Nevertheless the frequently repeated accusation that prolifers only care about babies before they are born — one inevitably thinks of Clinton's Surgeon General Joycelyn Elders' taunt about the pro-lifers' "love affair with the fetus" in this connection — is nothing but another one of the lies regularly propagated by the media about the prolife movement.

Mother Teresa, for example, in her address to the Annual Prayer Breakfast mentioned above, pleaded with pregnant women not wanting their babies to give them to *her.* "I am willing to accept any child who would be aborted and to give that child to a married couple who will love the child and be loved by the child," she said. "From our children's home in Calcutta alone, we have saved over 3000 children from abortion." Many others similarly stand ready to help women — if "helping women" were really the core problem with legalized abortion.

There is no lack of compassion or of concrete "positive" solutions in the prolife ranks, in fact. But this kind of positive compassionate approach, necessary as it is, does not even begin to compensate for the catastrophic damages and the deep moral corruption which legalized abortion has now spread throughout our entire country and our entire system. The fact is that, by now, *millions* of Americans have actually been involved in providing and undergoing abortions — or have friends, associates, or family members who have been. It is understandable that such people do not wish to be reminded of the evil of abortion. Naturally they are going to view the prolife "screamers" as "maniacs." One recalls the problems Southern slaveholders had with the abolitionists taking aim at their "property." But the possibly offended sensibilities of such people *cannot* be the proper basis on which America has to decide this fundamental moral and political question.

It is not even necessary to look very deeply into the abortion situation today in order to reach the conclusion that the vast — the overwhelming — number of abortions in America today are not done for any of the tear-jerker, "hardship" reasons which figure so prominently in "prochoice" rhetoric — and now even in some recent "prolife" rhetoric. Almost all of today's abortions are done, simply and solely, for *convenience.* They are done because — "the woman does not want the child" — and for no other reason at all. There are always pretexts, of course, many of them of greater or lesser validity; but given the current situation of legalized abortion-on-demand, such pretexts scarcely any longer even have to be cited, in fact; and, increasingly, none are any longer even offered. The women involved simply proceed directly to the brutal exercise of their "constitutional right" by going to the "providers" which our efficient, technologically advanced society has not failed to encourage.

According to a study by the proabortion Alan Guttmacher Institute, 83 percent of all abortions performed in the United States are performed on unmarried women, 26 percent of whom are teenagers. And what reasons do they offer for resorting to abortion? 75 percent of them said that "having a baby would interfere with work, school, or other responsibilities." *Interfere!*

The next most common reasons cited were lack of money and what were called "relationship problems," by which was no doubt meant that the father did not want to marry the mother, or she did not want to marry him. Less than 7 percent of the women undergoing abortions cited any "health" consideration whatsoever (and yet, once again, abortion is supposed to be nothing but a purely "medical" question!). And, finally, a only 1 percent cited rape or incest, one of the contemporary politician's all-purpose excuses for not facing up to the implications of legalized abortion. Well over 90 percent of all the abortions performed in America today, in other words, are performed for reasons or under conditions which polls indicate a large majority of Americans *oppose*.

When we consider the casual, callous, and massive incidence of purely convenience abortions which these statistics point to, then, we may perhaps wonder whether the time has not arrived for fewer patronizing lectures addressed to prolifers pointing to their lack of political "realism" and calling for lowered decibels in the abortion wars, meanwhile summoning *them* to "compromise" solutions and "compassionate" alternatives.

Rather, certain real questions that have been waiting for an answer ever since abortion was first legalized, still need to be addressed before any further put-downs of the prolife movement are offered: where is the compassion for the *babies*, for example? When are those who insist that our Constitution must mandate evil and immorality going to be summoned to accept *any* compromise? How, indeed, can we accept *any* legalized killing and still expect to be able to maintain the integrity of our system?

VI

What, finally, can we think of the twin realities of today's abortion Holocaust, combined with the apparently grim determination of so large a segment of the public and its leaders simply not to face up to the facts and implications of this Holocaust? And what can we think of leaders, themselves often claiming to be "prolife," so breathlessly eager to urge prolifers to be the ones to compromise, while no comparable effort whatsoever is ever addressed to the "prochoice" side?

In what passes for the public "debate" on legalized abortion going on in America today, the proabortion side usually wins the "debate" in question hands down for the simple reason that its positions are tacitly conceded without argument at the same time that the positive arguments for the prolife side never even get presented. How should prolifers proceed in such an unfavorable situation?

First of all, nothing prevents prolifers from working for all those partial goals — waiting periods, limitations on access to abortions, parental, spousal, and informed consent, and, especially, the provision of compassionate alternatives in the case of problem pregnancies. All of these aims and ends can and should be pursued even while maintaining the ultimate goal of a constitutional amendment. Let us, indeed, do whatever we can — and also extract from the political process whatever we can.

All these measures can also be part of the necessary public educational process concerning abortion that has to continue. It is one of the more fatuous aspects of the position of the compromisers, in fact, that they should be busily summoning prolifers to work for measures on which the prolifers are already precisely the ones who are doing the bulk of the work anyway!

Yet no sensible prolifer imagines that these things can serve as ultimate goals; they merely represent what can be extracted from "the system" at the moment. And as things stand, the political efforts that have to be exerted today even to achieve these limited goals are nearly as great as promoting the integral prolife viewpoint anyway, and so it is the latter that has to continue to be the ultimate goal.

Prolifers cannot abandon a principled reaffirmation of what our Constitution already supposedly guarantees, namely, the equal protection of the laws for all. This is in no way some "absolutist," theologically-inspired ideal; it is the actual position set forth in the plain words of the Constitution. Prior to 1966 and the beginning of the leftist ideological push for wide-open abortion, this constitutional position was very largely reflected in the actual statute laws of all fifty states, which made abortion illegal except under the most strictly limited conditions — in almost all cases, the life of the mother. These laws worked quite well once, and they can be made to work quite well again, once the political will to restore them is itself restored.

To abandon a principled position on whatever grounds of expediency, though, is really to abandon not only the unborn but also the Constitution of the United States. If legalized killing in whatever form cannot be abolished under the Constitution, then the Constitution already has, in effect, been abrogated. We are in fact faced today with powerful public movements working for such things as euthanasia and assisted suicide, and soon it will be other forms of legalized killing, which, if current trends continue, can also even become compulsory. None of this is any longer theoretical; in various ways, some of it is already happening; and all of it only became possible and actual *after* abortion was first legalized and the possibility of legalized killing became established in principle.

Even though people do not want to admit that abortion is legalized killing, and many euphemisms are regularly employed to obscure this truth, the fact is that everybody really knows that it is killing, and hence the logic of the thing is irrefutable: if we can elect to kill legally by abortion, we can elect to kill by these other means as well. It's happening. We need think only of the black comedy of the inept efforts of the State of Michigan attempting to bring "assisted suicide" Doctor Jack Kevorkian to justice.

The task of responsible political leadership today is not to acquiesce in the current situation on the grounds that it is no longer easy to fight effectively against it, but rather to find ways to alert the public to our real situation and to the implications of our real situation; and then to find ways to reverse the direction of the past several decades and restore the integrity of our legal and constitutional system.

It is also the task of responsible and serious political leadership to attempt to lead the country on a better basis than merely consulting the latest polls. In 1944 Arthur Koestler discovered that the polls demonstrated that a majority of American public opinion disbelieved in Nazi atrocities. American public opinion was wrong about that; the atrocities were going on. And just as it was the task of political leadership then to convince the people that the evil deeds of Nazism had to be opposed, so today it is the task of responsible political leadership to convince the people that evils of legalized abortion also have to be opposed — on principle.

Public opinion on the abortion issue is notoriously ill-informed as well as mis-informed. It is also volatile. In other words, it can be changed; and it is one of the tasks of political leadership to see that it is changed in order to restore the integrity of our system. Polls, again, have indicated that a majority of Americans still do not understand that what we have in America today is massive abortion almost entirely for convenience. These same polls are even cited by the minimizers as a justification for some of their minimalistic "solutions" — usually fewer and earlier abortions, though still abortions for convenience, with the principle of equal justice under law being conceded in advance.

But once a serious effort has been made to educate the public about the true nature and consequences of our current situation of legalized killing, it is quite possible if not likely, that a new and properly informed public opinion would accede to the necessity of upholding the integrity of our legal and constitutional system as a whole. This, in fact, is the way we *have* to go.

To base a position on the current preferences of Americans as ascertained by highly dubious public opinion polls is to abdicate any claim to principled leadership. This is especially true for Republicans and conservatives who claim to care about the Constitution and its integrity, about the tyranny of the excesses of liberal judicial review, etc.

What *other* Constitutional right is now to be based on public opinion polls, in the opinion of these "conservatives"? Freedom of speech? Freedom of religion? Freedom from unreasonable seizures and searches? How can Americans even continue to *tolerate* the current abuse of legislation by judicial review, which has brought us legalized abortion and so many other evils as well?

In particular, the idea that the Republican Party should abandon its current prolife plank would be a catastrophic mistake. Those who would advocate such a course certainly do not know many prolifers personally; they may sincerely want to see prolife votes remaining in the Republican column; but arguments from expediency or on the basis of supposed "realism" they offer can only alienate most prolifers and bring about massive defections from current Republican ranks.

Even if no constitutional amendment is attainable in the near future, the symbolism of dropping it as a goal for the future would be universally perceived as an abject capitulation before the sorry reality of our current moral corruption, whereas what is precisely necessary for the long term is to keep the fundamental constitutional issue posed by legalized abortion steadily before the public.

The abortion issue is not susceptible of any simple or immediate solution. It is much too serious and fundamental an issue to allow of any solution arising out of the usual compromises and splitting of differences characteristic of politics. The abortion issue really *is* like the issue of slavery, however unpalatable the recognition of this may appear to many. As Arthur Koestler pointed out fifty years ago, the first Holocaust was allowed to take place because the world preferred to live in its own world of illusions and was unwilling to abandon politics as usual when faced with a gigantic evil.

It has often been asked where all the "good Germans" were when the concentration camp gas chambers went into operation and the crematoria chimneys began to smoke. But we Americans today have considerably less excuse than the Germans did under Hitler, since we still do enjoy in this country, at least for the moment, a political system that continues to remain comparatively free and can still be responsive to appropriate political action or pressure determinedly applied or carried out.

It is not clear precisely how much *longer* our freedom will obtain, though, now that we have begun to acquiesce in the legal curtailment of the freedom of, e.g., the unborn to be able to be born — just as the freedom of prolifers too is increasingly being abridged by such laws as FACE; it is no accident that these constitutional outrages have also grown out of the current abortion imperative; it always and inevitably corrupts everything that it touches.

Nevertheless, it still remains true for the moment that most Americans would not be placing themselves in any particular jeopardy today by opposing legalized abortion using normal political means. There are not even any assured penalties today for being a stalwart prolife politician: many of them are in office and continue to do quite well. Many others would find it equally possible to be elected while frankly espousing prolife principles — and this almost in the degree that they forthrightly and unapologetically adopt these prolife principles and then articulate and *explain* them to those who question them. The proabortionists really do not have any answers to the *truths* of the prolife position (but, alas, too many politicians or aspiring politicians "on our side" have to master those same truths themselves first before they can ever articulate or explain them).

It may well be, of course — tragically — that the critical mass of leadership simply does not exist at the moment among the Republicans and conservatives capable of understanding that the abortion question has to be treated on the basis of principle. If that is the case, prolifers must persist anyway; they must persist because they just happen to be in the right about the basic issue: *Does* a woman under our Constitution and laws really have a "right" to take the life of another? The answer is "No": abortion has to be opposed on principle, not only because it entails the killing of a human being; but also because it is a lie.

4

Abortion, the U.S. Government, and the Pope

I

American Catholics can only reflect with deep shame on the role their government played in the preparation for and participation in the recent UN International Conference on Population and Development in Cairo. The Cairo conference itself surely represented some kind of new moral low point in the modern world's relentless slide into official immorality and decadence; and from the outset the U.S. Government played the most active and prominent role in making the Cairo conference what it was.

Would anyone, twenty-five years ago, have thought that there could actually be a UN-sponsored international conference which would attempt to impose through government action a totally materialistic and utilitarian view of human beings upon the whole world?

Or would anyone ever have imagined that those opposed to the ruthless decimation of the next generation by abortion — supposedly required on the pretext that the world is, or soon will be, "overpopulated" — would be the ones automatically assumed to be the "bad guys" at such an international conference? Or that those who do *not* perceive any objection to having large numbers of the next generation killed off by abortion before they have a chance to be born would be the ones automatically assumed to be the "good guys"? The well-worn phrase of Nietzsche, "transvaluation of all values," doesn't succeed in conveying the truth of what has happened to traditional morality in the world of today. And it was Cairo that helped make it all happen. The world surely has traveled very fast and very far in the past quarter of a century.

As the Cairo conference demonstrated, however, the present Administration in Washington proved to be only too willing to enlist all

---

Originally published in shortened form in *The Catalyst*, November, 1994.

the power and prestige of the United States in order to help drive the world yet farther and faster down the wrong road which it has now chosen. The U.S. Government went into the Cairo conference with a firm and well-documented policy frankly aimed at promoting government "population control" by any means, including especially abortion.

And how can anyone even talk about "control" of something by the government without also including the acceptance of actual or potential coercion? To imagine anything else would be like imagining that the IRS will never fail to be benign when reminding people about their delinquent taxes.

More than just trying to promote population control generally, however, the announced U.S. Government aim included specifically the promotion of abortion: the promotion of abortion *everywhere*, both as a method of family planning and as a fundamental right of women, regardless of the legal status of abortion in any given country — for it still just happens to be the case that abortion remains illegal in most countries, at least in some degree. And it seems likely too that, in one sense, the Cairo conference was actually conceived as a way to help change precisely that situation, now seen as inconvenient; conceived, that is, to help get abortion legalized everywhere, just as it has been legalized in the United States.

In promoting a wide-open international abortion policy in this fashion, the United States thus necessarily found itself in a position of disregarding, if not trampling upon, local laws and customs nearly everywhere — but especially in underdeveloped countries.

Furthermore, regardless of what was later stated for public consumption, after the U.S. was constrained to modify its original position somewhat, the U.S. Government was engaged in frankly and openly using its very considerable clout around the world — and not only in such things as foreign aid, technical assistance, and so on — to promote a *Roe v. Wade* regime of abortion on demand throughout the world, even though *Roe v. Wade* and its companion Supreme Court decisions, especially *Planned Parenthood v. Casey,* which have made and kept abortion legal in this country, remain extremely controversial decisions here, decisions which are far from having settled the abortion question in the United States itself.

When publicly challenged, notably by Pope John Paul II, whose unusually pointed criticisms of U.S. population policy were strongly echoed by a letter from six American cardinals addressed to President

Clinton himself, the U.S. Government clumsily tried to deny what its policy was and to deflect the criticisms back upon the pope and the Vatican; and then, when the heat apparently became too great, U.S. Government spokesmen, including both the president and the vice president, openly lied about what the U.S. policy verifiably was and had been all along.

And as if this official, bare-faced lying was not disgraceful enough for the government of a great nation, the proud media of that same nation tamely tended to accept at absolute face value the government's own assertions of what its policy was, rather than inquiring into the real truth of the matter. There were times, indeed, when the Clinton Administration was exonerated in the very same news story which was reporting other, damning facts which should have pointed to a conviction rather than to an exoneration.

Where the U.S. Government's population policy was concerned, however, especially with regard to its position on abortion, the kind of adversarial, "exposé" journalism at the expense of the White House made famous in such affairs as Watergate and Iran-Contra temporarily disappeared from the American media.

What, then, was the U.S. Government's international abortion policy going into the Cairo conference? In March, 1994, the U.S. State Department sent out a cable outlining this policy to all American diplomatic and consular posts abroad; these posts were supposed to inform the governments to which they were accredited about the U.S. policy in question. This State Department cable made it absolutely clear that the U.S. intended to exert its influence with other governments, with the World Bank, and with the International Monetary Fund in order to "advance U.S. population policy interests." The implication was that if underdeveloped countries failed to go along with the policy the U.S. was promoting for Cairo, they might find aid and development money drying up.

And the policy the U.S. intended to push for in Cairo definitely included what was described as "the need to ensure universal access to family planning and related reproductive health services, including access to safe abortion." In the parlance of the modern family planning industry, the phrase "reproductive health services" virtually always includes abortion anyway, as a matter of fact, and precisely as a method of "family planning" — as Americans will discover in connection with health care reform if they are not careful. But in this particular document, the reference to the inclusion of abortion was made explicit, probably in order to be able to stress the safety angle. When carefully perused, though, the text does indeed call for nothing else but "universal. . .access to safe abortions." That was the U.S. Government's international abortion policy going into the Cairo conference.

No matter that at least 95 countries around the world currently have laws that protect the unborn at least in some circumstances. That proved to be a fact of no importance: abortion is considered an idea whose time has come; and so the United States Government was determined to do whatever was in its power to see that the abortion idea's time *would* come.

The State Department cable that was sent out outlining this policy went on to specify that "the United States believes that access to safe, legal, and voluntary abortion is a fundamental right of all women" — that's "a fundamental right of all women."

Earlier, in January, 1994, State Department Counselor Timothy Wirth had made it clear that the whole point of U.S. participation in the Cairo conference in the first place was in order "to provide family planning services, a *comprehensive* family planning package, to every woman in the world who wants them by the year 2000" (emphasis added). Here the word "comprehensive" is the give-away; it is one of the common jargon words used by the family planners and population controllers to indicate, again, that abortion is indeed included in the whole "package."

A number of commentators on the Cairo conference have remarked, by the way, that the strong moral stand taken by the pope against abortion was somehow "compromised" by the pontiff's refusal to yield on the issue of "birth control." Such commentators evidently fail to realize that in modern family planning programs — and this is the case virtually without exception wherever abortion is legal — abortion is always included as an integral part of effective "birth control"; it is considered the indispensable back-up for "failed contraception," as the *Casey* Supreme Court decision, for example, brought out very clearly.

Nor do many of these pro-birth-control commentators realize that many forms of so-called contraception actually are abortifacient in their action anyway, that is, they are really forms of early abortion; they don't prevent conception; they kill an embryo already conceived. Those who continue to imagine today that contraception is some kind of realistic *alternative* to abortion are really ignorant of the real facts about modern family planning: it already includes abortion as a necessary back-up for failed contraception virtually everywhere that this is allowed by the law (and in some perhaps many cases it sneaks it in even where it is *not* allowed by the law).

Over a year ago, in May, 1993, in a formal speech delivered in order to explain the administration's population control policy, the State Department's Timothy Wirth had already flatly declared: "Our position is to support reproductive choice, including access to safe abortion"; and on the same occasion Wirth had actually characterized existing laws against abortion as "violating basic human rights." *This* is the U.S. Government's real abortion policy.

II

The U.S. Government's population policy going into the Cairo conference, then, included abortion; this fact had not been concealed but rather had been made unmistakably clear, over and over again. The policy in question was also well known to the Holy See, since, in the spring of 1994, the whole thing had been abundantly brought out at a preparatory population meeting held in New York at which the Vatican had also been represented. At this preliminary meeting, the U.S. delegation had insisted on the entire package described in the March State Department cable.

At this earlier New York meeting, however, the Vatican delegation had managed to get some of the preliminary conference document's language, especially that related to abortion, "bracketed" for further discussion at the actual Cairo conference. The U.S. delegation, for its part, had hoped to have approval for the whole thing shouted through then and there, at the New York preliminary meeting (where, by the way, the open hostility of the American and other delegations towards the Vatican delegation, and towards the pope personally, was already very intense and was openly expressed, including by the wearing of anti-pope buttons, according to observers who attended the meeting).

Considering what the U.S.Government was by then openly and aggressively aiming at in Cairo, however, it is surely understandable that the Vatican, in accordance with the normal practice of UN-style diplomacy, would immediately be mounting its own diplomatic counter-offensive in order to try to line up support for its own position in Cairo. This was hardly an "aggressive" move in itself; it was precisely what the U.S. itself was trying to do: line up the support of other countries for its position. The U.S. was not only "lobbying" other countries in this way; it is probably no exaggeration to say that it was bullying a fair number of them in a way that the Holy See would never have the clout to do, even if that were its way of operating.

At the same time that it tried to line up support in other countries, however, the Holy See also made public a number of very serious criticisms of the preliminary conference document that had emerged from the New York preliminary meeting. As early as April 5, 1994, John Paul II had sent an open letter to heads of state, including President Clinton, in which he had said that the preliminary document was for him "a disturbing surprise" which "could cause a moral decline resulting in a serious setback for humanity." In particular, the pontiff judged that the preliminary conference document called for "a general international recognition of a completely unrestricted right to abortion," about which he expressed his "deep concern."

Publicly diffusing this kind of severe and pointed criticism, again, was entirely in keeping with the normal rules of diplomacy and UN conference practice. Meanwhile, criticism of the preliminary document was mounting elsewhere; Jewish, Protestant, Muslim, and other groups began to come out against the document and against some of the really extreme anti-life and anti-family plans being projected for approval by the Cairo meeting.

At the end of May, 1994, the six active American Catholic cardinals sent President Clinton an open letter protesting his administration's open and energetic advocacy of abortion, contraception, sterilization, and variant conceptions of "the family" as part of its overall population strategy going into the Cairo conference. "The United States is doing the world no favor by exporting a false ideology," the cardinals told the president.

Two days later, on June 2, President Clinton himself met personally with Pope John Paul II in Rome during a state visit in Italy. In the course of their discussions covering a number of subjects, the pontiff very frankly (but still very diplomatically) urged the president not "to be insensitive to the value of life or appear to be advocating policies that would undermine the strength of the family."

Following this personal meeting with the pope, President Clinton promptly — and rather amazingly, in view of the reality of the situation — declared at a press conference that "the United States does not and will not support abortion as a means of birth control or population control." This statement was simply contrary to the announced policy of his Administration, which was already as well known to the pope, as it had to be to anyone else who had ever bothered to focus upon it.

Moreover, the president's surprising disclaimer came from a politician who, in virtually the first act of his Administration, in January, 1993, had resumed the U.S. payments to the International Planned Parenthood Federation (IPPF) which had been cut off by the Reagan Administration, and he had done so precisely in order to support the IPPF's international birth control and population control efforts. (With yet other strokes of the same presidential pen, the newly inaugurated president on that occasion had similarly decreed a number of other measures by executive order, all of which together had the total effect of extending official U.S. Government support for abortion to its current legal limits.)

In spite of this consistent proabortion record, however, President Clinton went on at his press conference in Italy to inform the world, earnestly, that in his talks with the pope "progress" had been made in narrowing the differences between the U.S. and the Vatican on the issues that would be discussed at the Cairo conference. In the face of such a claim, advanced by the president himself, a Vatican official felt obliged to comment, tactfully, that "if he says there was a narrowing of differences, it is clear that it can only be in one direction," namely, that the U.S. Government had somehow moved closer to the pope's principled, unalterable opposition to abortion. But the president meant no such thing, of course; his comments were entirely semantic and propagandistic; they were merely words strung together, not to communicate his real position but rather to obscure it.

At the same time, back in Washington, White House Press Secretary Dee Dee Myers compounded the semantic confusion further by explaining that the administration's support for the availability of abortion for women in poor countries was "not support for abortion on demand, abortion as a method of family planning, or coerced abortion."

"What in heaven's name *is* it then?" — this would have been the logical question to ask, but no reporter present apparently ever got around to asking it. Myers did concede that the Vatican and the

Clinton Administration basically had "irreconcilable differences" over abortion; and a year earlier, in April, 1993, the same Dee Dee Myers had told reporters that abortion was "part of the overall [U.S.] approach to population control."

Later, at the end of June, the president himself reiterated the same self-contradictory administration position when he told a National Academy of Sciences forum on population that "our goal is to make these [family planning] programs available to every citizen of the world by early in the next century"; in the same breath Clinton again claimed that "we do not support abortion as a method of family planning," again skirting semantically around the fact that all modern family planning programs do include abortion or referrals for abortions.

Once again, this was the very same president who had personally rescinded the so-called "gag rule" which had earlier prohibited abortion referrals in government-funded family planning programs. That had been yet another one of the several initiatives which Clinton took to extend government support for abortion immediately after he took office.

Meanwhile, of course, the exchange in Rome between the pope and the president hardly represented the only or the last word of the Holy Father on the two outstanding subjects of abortion and the Cairo conference. In mid-June, the Holy Father had told a meeting of the cardinals from around the world how much he feared the Cairo population summit would open the door to even more officially promoted and sanctioned abortions, and to an even greater deterioration in the status of the traditional family. Press reports described this address of the pope as "tough language" and "aggressive tactics" — as if there had never been any provocation by the population controllers to begin with — and with all the weight of the U.S. Government behind them. Such is the double standard that typically obtains where reporting on the modern phenomenon of abortion is concerned.

III

As the September 5 date for the opening of the Cairo conference approached, the rhetoric intensified, much of it at the expense of the Vatican, and some of it inspired by the U.S. Government's own efforts in support of population control. This same pattern would be carried on in Cairo itself after the convening of the conference. Papal "attacks" and Vatican "obstructionism" were regularly deplored in press accounts. National Public Radio — which employed the virulently anti-papal Frances Kissling of the oxymoronic "non-organization" Catholics for a Free Choice as its expert on the Cairo conference — characterized the papal position as "strident."

The Vatican was out of step and out of date, it was reported — or else out of touch, isolated, with perhaps only a couple of Latin American countries going along with its views, a Liechtenstein, or a Malta, for example. How could the pope even continue to hang on? Surely he was already on the ropes.

No: suddenly the Vatican was responsible for stirring up Muslim opposition, for encouraging Islamic fundamentalism: it was reported that the Holy See was actually seeking support for its positions even from such radical regimes as those in Libya and Iran. *Washington Post* columnist Jim Hoagland described this as a "moral nadir" for the Vatican.

One of the favorite approaches of the pro-population-control, anti-Vatican media was to feature prominently the vaporous emissions of Catholic malcontents and turncoats prepared to take a public stand with the neo-pagan modern world against the Church they still claimed to belong to (although they were apparently not equally prepared to fulfill some of the traditional requirements of true Church membership).

Or else the media resorted to citing polls indicating how many Catholics today supposedly disagreed with the teachings of the Church on such topics as abortion, birth control, sexual morality, and the like — as if such disagreement by individual Catholics somehow invalidated the Church's position or nullified her ancient claim to be the authoritative interpreter of a divine revelation which she has guarded and handed down from the time of the apostles — her ancient claim, that is, to be literally the authoritative voice of Jesus Christ in the world speaking to each generation.

For, as everybody really knows, the Catholic Church bases her "policies" neither on the results of public opinion polls nor upon any democratic majority vote, but rather upon what she firmly believes to be the special guidance of the Holy Spirit promised to her by Christ concerning what we must believe and do in order to achieve our sanctification and salvation.

And one thing the Cairo conference abundantly demonstrated, of course, is how desperately Christ's voice is needed in the world today! It would be difficult to argue against the proposition that the way the world is going today is not the way the world should be going. The idea that government power and modern technology should be employed to "control" population — an expression that cannot possibly mean anything else but controlling — coercing — human beings — has already been proven to be one of the most tyrannical ideas ever to arise in the history of mankind; this has been proven, notably, in Communist China, where unprecedented government repression and coercion have already been in effect over the past decade and more in order to implement the Chinese government's infamous one-child-per-family population control policy. In China, if a woman becomes pregnant with a second child, she is forced to have an abortion.

This is not something that is theoretical or fanciful; it's happening in China right now. Highly symbolical of the way the world is going, therefore, was the announcement in Cairo of the next big international conference to be held by the new totalitarians; the Fourth International Conference on Women is to be held nowhere else but in Beijing, China, in September, 1995. Same script, same cast, as well as same producer and director, apparently.

Nor does Communist China represent the only regime where the totalitarian idea of population control has been taking hold. It took hold, after all, among most of the official delegations represented at the Cairo conference. Regardless of the semantic disclaimer in the final conference document that "coercion" was to be eschewed (a point the Vatican delegation singled out for praise at the end), the entire logic of the Cairo conference was that government power and technology must be employed henceforth to dictate externally and from above what in God's plan should be the most intimate and sacred decision of a married couple, namely, the decision to bring new life into the world.

Nor can the population controllers tolerate, apparently, any opposition to their highly immoral and inevitably tyrannical plans. The zeal of ideological true believers visibly fueled the attacks on the pope and the Vatican for opposing the new international "consensus" on the need for population control, by whatever means, which was supposed to be arrived at and confirmed in Cairo.

Once unleashed, however, the campaign against the pope and the Vatican eventually got out of hand, at least from the point of view of the Clinton Administration. In late August, just before the conference convened, and even while asserting that the U.S. Government did not want the conference to become a "U.S.-Vatican showdown," the State Department's population coordinator, Faith Mitchell, nevertheless said that the Vatican's disagreement with the U.S. had to do, in her view, "with the fact that the conference [was] really calling for a new role for women, calling for girls' education and improving the status of women." (On the evidence of such a statement as this, it surely could not have been a surprise to anyone to learn that this same Faith Mitchell had been a population-control activist in San Francisco before joining the Clinton Administration.)

Among other reactions to this false and bigoted statement, the Catholic League for Religious and Civil Rights was obliged to publish in *The New York Times* an open letter to President Clinton signed by Harvard law professor Mary Ann Glendon and endorsed by a number of other distinguished Catholic women and women's organizations. The open letter pointed out the irrefutable fact that the Catholic Church had long led the world in providing for the education of girls and it called on the president to direct Faith Mitchell to retract her statement.

At a certain point this kind of mounting heat on the Clinton Administration was perceived as being too great. After all, Catholics still do vote in the United States. And certain Catholics close to the White House who also possessed a modicum of political savvy, including current White House chief of staff Leon Panetta, and former California Congressman Tony Coelho, who was working with the Democratic National Committee, were suddenly to be found conceding candidly to reporters that yes, indeed, some members of the Clinton Administration *had* been guilty of anti-papal and "anti-Catholic sentiments requiring White House discipline," according to one press report in *The Washington Times*.

No doubt privately the same or like-minded officials apparently succeeded in convincing their own Administration that continuing the on-going open warfare in the media with the pope and the Catholic Church was hardly likely to be conducive to electoral success with many traditionally Democratic Catholic voters. However that may be, the Clinton Administration's principal "solution" to the public embarrassment it now realized it faced turned out to be even more insulting and mendacious and demeaning than its creation of the original "problem."

The solution in question was this: on August 25 Vice President Al Gore himself stepped before the cameras and microphones at the National Press Club and, without batting an eye, declared that "the United States has not sought, does not seek, and will not seek an international right to abortion." Anyone who pointed to the obvious fact that the preparatory document for the Cairo conference which had been largely engineered by the United States did attempt to call for precisely that — or that U.S. policy on numerous previous occasions had, again, called for precisely that — was guilty of an "outrageous allegation," the vice president unblushingly declared. In other words, the pope himself, who knew and had said what the real U.S. policy was, could only be the one who was wrong and, indeed, at the head of the line of the guilty ones making outrageous allegations.

The Clinton Administration just couldn't seem to get it right. The official Vatican spokesman, Joaquin Navarro-Valls, was surely exhibiting both restraint and considerable diplomatic tact, therefore, when he found himself obliged to set the record straight by remarking, rather awkwardly, but nevertheless quite accurately, that "the draft document, which has the U.S. administration as its principal sponsor, contradicts, in reality, Mr. Gore's statement."

However, instead of fastening gleefully on the patent fact that yet another American politician had been caught out in a blatant contradiction — something American reporters generally love to uncover — the American media, almost uniformly, reported the Gore statement as simple fact. Gore's speech was widely described as a "conciliatory speech" or even as an "olive branch" extended to the pope — as if the vice president's mere words could cancel out and compensate for all the U.S. Government's previous hard-nosed words and actions promoting abortion worldwide. Moralizing *Washington Post* columnist Jim Hoagland weighed in once more describing the Gore obfuscation as "a high-road search for conciliation," while his colleague on the same influential newspaper, political commentator David Broder, maintained that the administration had shown "convincingly" that it was not trying to promote abortion; Broder further averred that the U.S. Government had all along been acting "with due deference to religious principles, moral scruples, and nationalist pride." Lewis Carroll did not realize the half of it about words meaning only what somebody wants them to mean.

New York Times pundit William Safire even declared that the careful Navarro-Valls *mise au point* of the false claim of the vice president of the United States "impugned the sincerity of Gore's conciliatory assertion that the U.S. did not seek an international right to abortion." "Conciliatory?" one might ask. Was it *true*, or not? Safire did not ask. For him it was "a personal insult issued in the pope's name." "Unless corrected," Safire wrote further, "it will stand as an unprecedented papal meddling in U.S. politics."

In the face of this kind of reporting and commentary on the Gore speech, it does not seem to have occurred to anybody to comment on what appeared to be a looming threat to the whole genre of hard-hitting investigative journalism itself — to the idea that hard-boiled reporters are supposed to dig out the truth, regardless of where the chips might fall. It fell to Bishop James T. McHugh of Camden, New Jersey, a member of the Vatican delegation to the Cairo conference, to point out the obvious, namely, that what the Gore statement really signified — if, that is, Gore was speaking the truth *this time* — was "a shift in U.S. policy."

The U.S. policy certainly *had been* to promote abortion internationally, the vice president's statement notwithstanding to the contrary. That much was clear enough. Bishop McHugh recalled the preparatory New York meeting, which he himself had attended, where the American delegation had been "determined and intransigent" in continuing to insist on including abortion as a method of family planning because, according to the American delegation, it was a basic woman's right.

Now, however, Vice President Gore was *apparently* signaling that henceforth this was no longer going to be U.S. policy. When he himself limped up to the rostrum in Cairo on crutches as a result of a sports accident — although the crutches surely constituted a very apt symbol of how the Clinton Administration had been handling the whole thing generally — the vice president, in what turned out to be an unusually mild speech, repeated his claim that the United States did not seek to impose the legalization of abortion on other countries. Correspondent Morton Blackwell, reporting from Cairo in *Human Events*, wrote that "this was contrary to the frequently expressed position of President Clinton's U.S. delegates and that of the conference managers, but leftists here quietly accepted Gore's sop to Roman Catholic opinion in the United States."

IV

In the event, because of what turned out to be the opposition of more than 30 countries out of the 152 which sent delegations to the Cairo conference, the conference itself was forced to back off from the initially proposed universal-access-to-abortion language in its final document, even though the speakers there who advocated this position were the ones who were cheered on the floor of the conference itself, while those who agreed with the Vatican's position were as often as not unceremoniously booed. The headline of one *Washington Post* story datelined Cairo gave the flavor of the reporting: "Vatican's Abortion Stance Riles Many at Forum." (It appears that Catholic Christians today will simply have to get used to the fact that the tenets of their faith no longer enjoy much acceptance or respect in certain rather prominent sectors of today's world!)

In the end, the Cairo conference was evidently forced to retreat from the extreme position most of the delegates there favored; this came about largely because the U.S. Government had been forced to retreat from its extreme position. As one story in *The Washington Times* reported: ". . .the informal coalition between the Vatican and Islamic fundamentalists appears to have caught the U.S. Administration by surprise. U.S. officials were certain a month ago that the issue of contraception and abortion could be pushed through, if necessary, by a formal vote, since the Vatican at that time was supported by only four other small countries. Now even moderate Arabic nations are backing away from any suggestion that they should permit abortion. . ." (Concerning all this, American Catholics can only muse how God truly *does* work in mysterious ways. . .)

Thus, the much ballyhooed 1994 UN International Conference on Population and Development in Cairo finally ended up deciding, contrary to what the American delegation among many others had originally pushed for, that "in no case should abortion be promoted as a method of family planning." Similarly, the Holy See and its allies successfully insisted on language to the effect that family reproductive health matters should conform to local laws, cultures, ethics, and religion, and that the conference proposals were not intended to overturn national laws or social customs.

These points represented notable victories for the Vatican and for what by common consent was conceded to be its very competent delegation in Cairo. Correspondent Morton Blackwell reported in

Human Events that "the best speech given here was by the head of the Vatican delegation, Monsignor Renato Martino. In 20 minutes of sensible and eloquent remarks, first he advised the conference to focus more on achievable economic development. Then the assembly quieted noticeably as he urged delegates not to dismiss the moral dimension of irresponsible or immature behavior."

In his Cairo speech, Archbishop Martino took note of the fact that there had "been efforts by some to foster the concept of a 'right to abortion' and to establish abortion as an essential component of population policy." This concept, the archbishop went on to say, correctly, "would be entirely innovative in the international community and would be contrary to the constitutional and legislative positions of many states, as well as being alien to the sensitivities of vast numbers of persons, believers and unbelievers alike."

At least on a few such points, then, the Vatican prevailed against all the odds, proving itself to be the true defender of the underdeveloped countries against the arrogance and excesses of the rich, developed countries, including, unfortunately, the United States. And behind all the work of the Vatican delegation at the conference there were the words and example of Pope John Paul II himself — an adversary President Clinton and Vice President Gore, like Joseph Stalin when he inquired how many divisions the pope had, had probably never taken very seriously in the beginning.

Of course the degree to which the Vatican "victory" in Cairo is going to alter very many things in practice in today's world should not be exaggerated. The population controllers, after all, did end up getting their official reference to making abortion "safe." They got some of the other things they wanted as well, so that the Holy See could only endorse the final document in an "incomplete" and "partial" manner.

Over 150 countries, for example, approved a plan of action in Cairo that now sanctions universal government birth control programs. If the Catholic Church's firm teaching about *that* is correct (and, to say no more on that subject here, the Church's track record to date demonstrates that she has been mysteriously, amazingly *prophetic* concerning all of these "human life" issues!), then this kind of massive government intervention in what should be private and intimate family affairs can only serve to lower further the already low state of sexual morality, marriage, and the family around the world.

Not even John Paul II, apparently, could fight and win the whole battle, though. The victories stigmatizing legalized abortion and favoring local autonomy were probably the most that could be won in the present climate which is so highly favorable to "population control." For American Catholics, however, even these small "victories" cannot be anything but very bittersweet ones, considering how vigorously their own government pushed for universal legalized abortion for as long as it perceived it was able to do so; and then, when it was forced to retreat, it resorted to a disgraceful series of official lies and obfuscations.

More than that, if "anti-Catholicism" were against the law, and the present U.S. Government were ever put on trial for it under such a law, it is hard to see, on the evidence, how it could ever expect to be acquitted.

5

Will the New Republican Congress Save Us from Our Culture of Death?

I

Will the new Republican Congress save us from what Pope John Paul II has aptly styled our contemporary "culture of death"? The short answer is "no," but it is nevertheless highly instructive to inquire in more detail into how the dramatic changes wrought by the 1994 mid-term elections are going to affect what are commonly called our on-going "culture wars," especially current prolife and profamily issues.

Conservatives in general and prolifers in particular have been busily congratulating themselves on the results of these elections, as well they might: the new Congress of the United States is surely the most conservative in a generation, the House of Representatives in particular having become, overnight, between November 8 and 9, 1994, what in French history was once dubbed the *chambre introuvable*. And the president of the liberal — and mis-named — People for the American Way organization seems to have observed quite correctly that "the ideological shifts in Congress are much deeper than the leadership changes and much broader than the party tallies."

On the prolife front, not a single prolife incumbent of either party was defeated in either the Senate or the House. Meanwhile, in the House, a total of twenty-nine prolife challengers succeeded in defeating as many proabortion incumbents, while prolifers won a majority of the open seats as well. In the Senate, of the eleven new senators elected, only Olympia Snowe, Republican of Maine, seems to be militantly proabortion. Most observers of the congressional scene agree that the 1994 elections brought about a net gain of

---

Originally published in *Culture Wars*, May, 1995.

around forty plus new prolife votes in the House, and probably as many as six new prolife votes in the Senate.

In normal times such drastic changes in a legislative body would betoken significant changes in the legislation it produces, and this is surely likely to be true of the new Congress on a whole broad range of issues. Nevertheless the times are distinctly not normal as far as prolife issues and some other moral issues related to our current "culture wars" are concerned, and it is not at all clear at the moment that there will in fact be legislative changes on these issues in the 104th Congress proportionate to what the new numbers would seem at first sight to call for.

Certainly the new session will be nothing like the last one, when Congress was thought to be on the verge of passing a Freedom of Choice Act (FOCA), which would have had the effect of simply removing the grisly practice of abortion from the province of our legal system. The last Congress was also thought to be poised to pass a comprehensive health-care reform bill which would almost inevitably have included abortion as a "benefit" as well. In the event, these things did not happen, although the Congress did pass a Freedom of Access to Clinic Entrances (FACE) law, abridging the First Amendment rights only of prolife demonstrators, not of other kinds of demonstrators, so it is in no way an exaggeration to label the 103rd Congress as a "proabortion" Congress in a way that should not be at all true of the current one.

Thus the 1994 election results have had the effect of putting the proabortionists on the defensive. Neither FOCA nor health-care reform are likely to be raising their heads again soon. On the other hand, prolife initiatives are rather conspicuous by their absence from the lists of all the great new Republican initiatives currently being touted and talked about, including, in particular, the Republican "Contract with America" in which, before the election, several hundred Republican incumbents and candidates, most of whom were elected or re-elected, laid out the urgent priority items they were going to enact in the first 100 days of the new Congress. No prolife items, as such, were included, however.

This absence of specific, announced prolife initiatives does not mean there will be no prolife initiatives, but it does mean, unfortunately, that they evidently do not figure very high up on most Republican priority lists.

Almost certainly the Hyde Amendment forbidding the use of federal funds for abortions under Medicaid will be handily re-enacted — and this time, hopefully, minus the fake "exceptions" for rape and incest which got written into the law during the last, "pro-abortion," session. With so many new prolife legislators — and so many prolife legislators now chairing committees and subcommittees — we may also see a number of initiatives designed to overturn Clinton Administration measures such as allowing abortions in military hospitals and abortion referrals in federally-funded family planning programs, or encouraging the importation of the French RU 486 abortifacient pill.

President Clinton's own apparent rejection in November of the proposal of a blue-ribbon panel at the National Institutes of Health to allow federally funded research involving the creation of human embryos *in vitro* for the express purpose of performing experiments on them was surely dictated by the White House's own belated, reluctant reading of the election results. The new Congress may go farther and flatly prohibit such embryo experimentation or fetal tissue experiments.

Moreover, with the elevation of prolife stalwart Republican Representative Henry J. Hyde of Illinois to the chairmanship of the House Judiciary Committee, there may even be a serious effort to repeal the FACE law on what would appear to be very sound First Amendment grounds; the votes for the repeal of FACE should be there if the new prolife numbers in Congress mean anything.

All these things are to the good as far as they go. And from the point of view of prolife and profamily strategy and tactics, we should also not forget — or neglect the significance of — the fact that the proabortion forces are now demoralized and in serious disarray — indeed in a veritable panic — over the results of these elections. The National Abortion Federation's Donna Singletary, for example, described herself as "shell-shocked" and predicted a "scorched earth" policy on the part of the victorious Republicans (if only!). Kate Michelman of the National Abortion and Reproductive Rights Action League called election day 1994 nothing less than "a devastating and disastrous day."

In spite of all the undeniable good news for prolife and profamily Americans coming out of the 1994 mid-term elections, however, the most optimistic and realistic estimate nevertheless has to be that the 104th Congress will probably do little beyond, if it goes that far, moving the country back to the status quo *ante* Clinton as far as, for instance, the abortion issue itself is concerned. No serious challenge to the continued legality of abortion itself appears to be contemplated anywhere by anybody. *Roe v. Wade* and its companion Supreme Court decisions which keep abortion legal are apparently not threatened in any way on the legislative front at the present time.

And if legalized abortion as such is apparently considered beyond challenging by this great new "conservative" and "prolife" Congress, there is probably even less chance that this same Congress will ever dare to take on some of the other government-sponsored and government-funded programs which continue to corrupt the morals of large segments of the American people — such as the government-subsidized so-called family planning programs which have done so much to bring condoms into the schools and onto the airwaves, as well as providing abortion referrals without parental knowledge or consent to teen-aged girls or placing Norplant implants under their arms. These kinds of "services," unfortunately, are only too likely to go on without serious challenge as long as the present climate remains what it is.

II

Although nobody can predict how the actual presence of increased numbers of prolife legislators might change the whole climate in the new Congress, the hard fact at present is that hardly anybody at all in Congress is really talking about any substantial prolife or profamily initiatives. Certainly the Republican leadership is not saying much about these issues. On the contrary, whenever the subject of the prolife cause is raised, the tendency on the part of the major Republican leaders and spokesmen is to downgrade its importance, intimating how the "divisiveness" of some of the prolife issues could compromise the success of all the economic and tax issues and the like which the Republicans plan to enact.

The current indications are that the Republican leadership will stay as far away as it feels able to do from social and moral issues — which they nevertheless surely must know were on the minds of many, many voters.

As things now stand, however, incoming Speaker Newt Gingrich has announced that the Republicans are indeed ready to go for a constitutional amendment — but it is a School Prayer Amendment, not a Human Life Amendment. New Senate Majority Whip Trent Lott, when questioned about any possible prolife initiatives, candidly admitted that "I don't think you will see a lot of action there." Similarly, an aide to Senate Majority Leader Robert Dole has been quoted as saying that abortion would definitely be considered to be "on the back burner."

All these esteemed conservative leaders, of course, have long been considered solidly "prolife," as that term is understood in the Congress. And so the question immediately arises: "If they do this when the wood is green, what will happen when it is dry?" (Lk 23:31). If it is really the case that with its solid new phalanx of prolife votes the Republican leadership is not even going to consider any basic measures to halt the horror and carnage of legalized abortion in America — if, in other words, the new Republican leadership truly does not understand that legalized abortion is simply *intolerable* and *impermissible* if the integrity of our legal and constitutional system is to be maintained, not to speak of the divine retribution which is certain to overtake this country if we do not soon repent — then it is doubly unlikely that they are going to exhibit much moral leadership where a number of other current moral and social issues are concerned. Rather, what is likely is that they will exhibit enormous reluctance at the very idea of even seeing raised any questions about whether the government should be funding some of the immoral programs which it in fact continues to fund.

New House Republican Majority Leader Richard Armey, for example, is an aggressive, imaginative, tireless, and persistent leader in promoting his favorite tax and economic programs. He too also regularly votes prolife, of course. Yet he has positively thrown cold water on the idea that, for example, the Republicans might ever want to do anything about Title X of the Public Health Service Act under which millions of tax-payer dollars flow annually into providing so-called "family-planning services," that is, contraceptives, abortion referrals, and the like.

At one time — and not so very long ago, either — this kind of thing would have been almost universally understood as simply undermining and corrupting people's morals; today it is simply considered to be one more imperative and indispensable social "service" that even our conservative and prolife leaders apparently do not dare question — even though, we should imagine, there is also an excellent and purely "conservative" argument against government funding of such programs.

For if in the broadest terms conservatives stand for less government — and certainly conservatives do generally stand for keeping the government out of providing tax monies for dubious social programs of questionable benefit — then government-subsidized family planning programs ought surely to be almost automatically to be high up on the list of government programs that should simply be zeroed out in the next budget, regardless even of what might be thought of the morality of such programs.

But no: nothing of the kind. Nowhere in the Contract with America, in fact, is there anything on this subject at all. Meanwhile Congressman Armey is quite specific and explicit that such programs are *not* to be targeted by the incoming Republicans. Nor does it seem likely that he would get any serious arguments on this score from Senators Dole or Lott, Congressmen Gingrich, or other Republican leaders such as the current crop of budding 1996 presidential candidates, judging from *their* typical words and actions. In his book *Standing Firm*, for example, Dan Quayle seems to be doing the opposite of standing firm; he seems to be carefully distancing himself both from his Murphy Brown speech as well as from his earlier steady prolife stand, even though it would seem that his early championship of "family values" has in fact been strongly vindicated by events.

Why is this? Why are the Republicans suddenly so nervous and even negative about social and moral issues which they themselves, when seeking support, have intimated to the American people that they were the party to champion such moral and family values? Specifically, why could the Republicans not simply declare that they are going to get the U.S. Government out of the family planning and contraceptive business, among all the other good conservative things they are planning to do? Why not indeed?

III

There is one major obstacle which prevents the new Republican Congress from even attempting to get the U.S. Government out of the family planning and contraceptive business — which more or less insures, in fact, that the Republicans are going to stay as far away from such an issue as they possibly can. This obstacle is: the sexual revolution.

Yes, the sexual revolution. Between the time when people generally understood that providing people the wherewithal to commit fornication and adultery was morally corrupting, and the present time when doing this is now considered to be a necessary social service, there has supervened — nothing else but — the sexual revolution of the 1960s. Before that time society generally understood and accepted the truth that the powerful and insidious human sexual drive present in everybody perforce has to be tightly reined in by effective moral and social constraints. That is why society once more or less endorsed "traditional morality," the morality of the Ten Commandments, the Judeo-Christian ethic, or whatever you want to call it, even though a cynical blind eye was often enough turned to breaches of this code. Still the code itself was not assailed.

All that has now been changed, indeed reversed. Today *nothing* is assailed and mocked more frequently and regularly than traditional sexual morality. Today it is simply taken for granted and affirmed that people can do what they like in the sexual area. Initially, there was one stipulation included in this, namely, that people could do what they wanted in the sexual area provided that "nobody was harmed." Sex between "consenting adults" was the phrase often employed, as it is still often employed.

But this stipulation that nobody should be harmed very quickly got dropped. For example, it very, very quickly became almost universally accepted that it did not really matter if the unborn child who happened to get conceived while people were exercising their freedom to sexual expression got harmed.

Similarly, it very soon no longer seemed to matter much if the innocent party in a no-fault divorce got harmed when one spouse decided it was time to move on to a more tempting and fulfilling liaison. And so it went. The important thing was that freedom to elective sexual expression was henceforth the primary thing that had to be maintained, and by whatever means was found to be necessary.

That is about where we stand at present. And few very strong voices beyond the voice of Pope John Paul II are ever publicly heard really opposing this state of affairs. Even the champions of traditional morality resort to nothing stronger than euphemisms such as "family values," as, notably and probably understandably, the Republican Party resorts to these euphemisms — or, at any rate, that portion of the Republican Party does which perceives that the state of galloping moral decadence to which America has currently been reduced really does constitute an urgent national problem in spite of what all the Republican "moderates" continue to pretend.

In this situation, nobody should imagine that any mere Republican political leaders in Congress will go up against the near universal contemporary mentality which is more or less accepting of the sexual revolution and its consequences, even if sometimes quite reluctantly; and which is also accepting, therefore, of the notion that the government too must accept and act on the consequences of the sexual revolution.

In any case, the media would instantly and probably effectively mock and crown with thorns and crucify any politician who seriously dared to question the "gains" that have been achieved for American society by the sexual revolution. Look what has happened, again, to Dan Quayle in spite of the careful and circumspect way he made reference in his Murphy Brown speech to what are in reality mounting national tragedies, namely, growing illegitimate births and welfare-dependent female-headed single parent homes, especially among blacks.

Senators Dole and Lott, Congressmen Gingrich and Armey may well all vote "prolife," as, indeed, they do. Abortion itself, after all, really is generally recognized to be a nasty business even by those who also believe it is a necessary evil. Anyway, a politician *can* be at least broadly "prolife" and survive, as the recent elections have abundantly proved.

But few or no contemporary politicians imagine that they could ever take the sexual revolution itself on head-on and still expect to survive. Whether or not this is really true, there do not at any rate seem to be many or any politicians around willing to test it out. Politicians today are manifestly not going to go beyond merely being "prolife" in general unless they are compelled to by more powerful pressures than are likely to be brought to bear in the present climate.

Nor are they merely cynics, accepting prolife and profamily support, but never allowing it to affect their judgments or their actions — just as Francis Bacon said he was willing to accept bribes. No: they can generally be counted upon to deliver the prolife votes on the issues that come before them.

They are probably even quite pleased with themselves when they vote to restrict federal funding of abortions or deny government aid to international family planning programs that utilize abortion as a method of family planning. These are the kinds of things they generally are called upon to vote on, after all, and they appear to have no trouble positioning themselves on the "prolife" side of such issues. They will deliver, in other words, the necessary prolife votes on the issues as the issues are currently framed today.

Anyway — they might well go on to argue — is it their fault the way the issues are framed? The fact is that hardly anybody is talking any longer about banning, say, family planning, if only for the simple reason that hardly anybody is even talking about banning abortion either, making the whole ghastly practice illegal. Prior to the mid-1960s, few had ever even imagined that there could be legalized abortion in America. Today it is hard for most people to imagine ever making it illegal again. This is, precisely, the legacy of the sexual revolution.

Neither the current Republican leadership nor, probably, even most of the Republican rank and file, even want to go into such things. They are certainly not about to go on any moral crusades about them. Few or none of them would ever want to be caught bucking what is considered, at least for the moment, to be the accomplished and irreversible fact of the modern sexual revolution.

And this sexual revolution is clearly understood by nearly everybody today, whether reluctantly or not, to be based squarely on the current universal availability of contraception — with legal abortion as the necessary back-up for failed contraception.

Thus, the Republicans, however prolife and profamily they profess to be, are about as likely to speak out against the sexual revolution in the present climate as they would be to advocate nuclear war or concentration camps for the "underclass." If you speak to them of the tragedy and horror of today's massive legalized abortion, they will respond with lectures about politics being the art of the possible. If you argue that at the very least the government should get out of the business of subsidizing whatever pills or condoms or implants people today think they have to resort to, they will tell you that "times have changed" and that we can never "go back to the 1950s" (as if that were the issue). So this really is about where we are. . .

IV

It is increasingly repeated today that political parties in a democracy are not really in a position to bring about very much in the way of what is euphemistically called "cultural change" (what is meant is today's galloping moral decadence). And this is no doubt true in the sense that ultimately our salvation does not reside in politics. It is also true in the sense intended by Dr. Samuel Johnson when he wrote about "how small of all that human hearts endure" ever turns out to be "that part which laws or kings can cause or cure."

In another sense, however, pointing out how little politics can really do about our current "culture wars" represents a very convenient excuse, if not a cop-out, for those politicians who are unwilling to face the full implications and consequences, including the undeniably political consequences, of the current low state of morality, especially sexual morality, in America today; and about how government has steadily helped promote and subsidize this current immorality.

Take abortion. Through legalized abortion we are currently sacrificing a substantial portion of the next generation to the pagan gods of untrammeled sexual expression; this is the case because everyone understands in practice that there has to be an ultimate, fail-safe "remedy" for the unintended consequences of recreational sexual activity. Legalized abortion constitutes that fail-safe remedy. Nothing in the nature of things obliges us as a nation to resort to such horrendous mass crime in this fashion and for such a purpose; on the contrary, reason and morality cry out to bring the carnage to a halt, and this independently of any purely religious imperative.

So why do we do go on, in such a way and on such a scale? How did we arrive at what John Paul II calls our contemporary "culture of death"? Here in the United States we arrived at it when we made abortion legal. Although this came about by a decision of the United States Supreme Court, as everybody knows, it was nonetheless a quintessentially "political" decision in the sense that it was intentionally brought about by "government"; it was a measure deemed necessary by "government"; and "government" has not failed to ratify the original Supreme Court decision on a number of levels.

Those who argue that sexual morality is irrelevant to politics on the grounds that it concerns only the "private" behavior of people could not be more tragically wrong; our entire political and legal system has now been skewed and distorted and corrupted in order to accommodate the ghastly "remedy" of mass abortion for the unintended consequences of people's "private" sexual behavior; these unintended consequences are "unwanted children," whom millions of

Americans have now been easily persuaded should not be born if indeed they are "unwanted."

How could abortion, which always involves the killing of a living human being before the onset of natural birth, ever have become legal under a Constitution which says that no person can be deprived of life, liberty, or property without due process of law, or be denied the equal protection of the laws? Clearly, abortion deprives unborn babies of life, and, as a class, they are quite patently now denied the equal protection of the laws as well. How could this ever have become legal under our Constitution?

The 1973 decision which legalized it, *Roe v. Wade*, simply bypassed the question of the full humanity of the unborn, asserting, erroneously, that this could not be known; and then it went on to assert further that the unborn had never been considered legal persons "in the full sense." From these very precarious and highly questionable assumptions, the *Roe v. Wade* decision then simply went on to make a spectacular leap to the assertion that there existed a woman's "right. . .to terminate her pregnancy," which was grounded in something the Court held was a prior constitutional "right to privacy."

Although no such right is mentioned anywhere in the Constitution, of course, *Roe v. Wade*'s mere assertion of such a woman's right nevertheless effectively cancelled out whatever protection the unborn might have been thought to enjoy in accordance with the rights the Constitution does mention.

Around twenty years and some thirty million abortions later, in 1992, the Supreme Court's *Planned Parenthood v. Casey* decision finally threw over this jerry-built "right to privacy" subterfuge and openly grounded the American woman's supposed right to abortion upon the simple empirical fact that "for two decades of economic and social developments people have organized intimate relationships and made choices that define themselves and their places in society in reliance on the availability of abortion in the event that contraception should fail."

Yes, you read this sentence right, in case you were wondering: we now maintain the legality of abortion in the United States solely in order to make it available to women "in the event that contraception should fail." People are now able to make choices and organize intimate relationships on this basis; any children that might be conceived do not count.

The highest court in the land has thus now ruled that we may and indeed must be able to kill unborn children in order to provide — a back-up for failed contraception. No other reason or justification is adduced or required. And this is "the law of the land," as all the commentators, like the Court itself, keep reminding us.

When abortion was first legalized, many people urged the promotion of more and better contraception on the grounds that contraception was merely preventive of conception, while abortion killed the child after he had been conceived. At first glance this position seems plausible, and many continue to advocate it. However, quite apart from the fact that some of the methods of so-called contraception are actually abortifacient, pills, IUDs, and what-not — the French RU 486 abortion pill which the Clinton Administration wants to make available in the United States is regularly described in the press as being a "contraceptive" — perceptive observers nevertheless soon began to notice something else about this idea of promoting birth control before the fact in order to preclude abortion after the fact.

What these observers discovered was considerable hard evidence that the promotion of birth control does not normally *decrease* the incidence of abortion but rather tends to *increase* it!

There is a reason for this: for it is the acceptance of contraception by modern society which, historically, also led to the acceptance of legalized abortion. The acceptance of contraception established the firm principle that we human beings are in complete control of who is to be born and who is not to be born — indeed it established that we are in control of whether sexual activity is even to be allowed to *have* any consequences or not beyond its perceived value as interpersonal pleasure — and this quite apart from any considerations such as God's law or the teachings of a Church in any case thought to be dominated by celibate males; such things very quickly came to be considered entirely extraneous, irrelevant.

But then it turned out that in spite of our supposedly foolproof modern contraceptive technology, our human control of conception actually proved to be less than one hundred per cent effective. When this was discovered, then abortion logically had to be brought in as the necessary back-up to make effective the need for "birth control" already inalterably established as an irrevocable modern imperative — something we simply must have, and could never get along without.

Historically, this is exactly how our society arrived at the acceptance of legalized abortion. As late as the early 1960s, even Planned Parenthood was still arguing for birth control in the publicity it issued in order to preclude the need to have abortions, which Planned Parenthood itself frankly recognized and stated at the time meant killing the baby. As the abortion juggernaut got underway late in the 1960s, however, Planned Parenthood led our whole society in climbing aboard; and thus as a society we made the choice, in effect, that effective control of births was the basic imperative; and it therefore had to take precedence over the question of whether or not we were actually resorting to killing in order to achieve our already settled goal.

Legally, abortion came about strictly in accordance with precedents which followed this same logic. The legal precedents for *Roe v. Wade* were concerned with, precisely, contraception. In 1965, in its decision *Griswold v. Connecticut,* the Supreme Court established that contraceptive information and means could not be legally denied to married people; later a follow-up decision, *Baird v. Eisenstadt,* established that such contraceptive information and means could not be denied to *single* people either — single people have a legal "right" to engage in sexual intercourse under our current law!

And then, finally, *Roe v. Wade* itself came along; it was squarely based on both these earlier Supreme Court decisions, from which it consciously lifted its famous "right to privacy." And the latest Supreme Court *Planned Parenthood v. Casey* decision affirming the legality of abortion simply follows in strict logic from these earlier decisions.

If the initial acceptance of contraception by our society is what led to its later acceptance of abortion — which was then ratified by "government" when the latter practice became legalized by the Supreme Court — then what becomes almost equally clear is that, in a very important and even fundamental sense, we now have government-sponsored abortion today precisely because we had earlier agreed as a society to go along with government-sponsored birth control. Again, then, it is *not* true that governmental action can do little to affect the "culture"; government action in our time in the area of human life has manifestly helped decimate what was once the more-or-less Christian "culture" of America.

Back in 1959, when a commission appointed to deal with U.S. foreign aid ended up recommending that the U.S. should help requesting countries deal with what was already then being called "the problem of rapid population growth" by sponsoring birth control research and the like, the Catholic bishops of the day roundly denounced this commission recommendation as a "morally, humanly, psychologically, and politically disastrous approach to the population problem." The heat generated at the time was so intense that President Dwight D. Eisenhower quickly repudiated the recommendation of the commission and declared that he could not "imagine anything more emphatically a subject that is not a proper political or governmental activity or function or responsibility. . ." Such was the climate in 1959. The "sixties," obviously, were still to come.

Within five brief years, however, President Lyndon B. Johnson was declaring in his 1965 State of the Union Address that he would "seek new ways to use our knowledge to help deal with the explosion in world population. . ." Already the problem of world population was thus believed to be an *explosion*, by the way, and it was considered a kind of problem, moreover, which almost without thought or analysis was held to justify resorting to means formerly thought unwise if not immoral.

In the meantime, contraception, believed by all Christians to be immoral up until around 1929, when the Church of England's Lambeth Conference caved in and allowed the practice in "hard cases" — in the meantime contraception had rather quickly come to be viewed in an entirely different light, including by Christian denominations pretty much across the board; it came to be viewed as a positive, indeed an indispensable, personal and social good; this "idea whose time had come" *came*.

By 1966, tax supported family planning programs were already to be found in over forty states — up from only about 13 in 1963. Publicly financed birth control clinics around the country nearly doubled in numbers in the same three-year period — although not always without opposition. For example, when in March, 1964, the District of Columbia announced itself to be a recipient of a federal appropriation of $25,000 to distribute birth control information and devices at health department clinics, Archbishop (later Cardinal) Patrick A. O'Boyle of Washington vigorously protested the action and promptly set up his own clinic to provide instruction in the rhythm method.

However, the birth control juggernaut was already effectively launched and was encountering opposition almost nowhere. Contraception *had* by this time come to be almost universally considered a boon to humanity. The Catholic bishops nevertheless did go to the wall one more time over the issue. In November, 1966, they called upon "all — and especially Catholics — to oppose vigorously and by every democratic means, those campaigns already underway in some states and at the national level towards the active promotion by tax supported agencies, of birth prevention as a public policy, above all in connection with welfare-benefit programs."

This effort by the bishops was seriously meant, but it did not succeed in rallying any significant opposition to the government birth control juggernaut. In any case, the Catholic bishops were destined to be effectively neutralized in the whole battle anyway when Pope Paul VI's anti-birth-control encyclical *Humanae Vitae* came out two years later, in July, 1968, and immediately became the target of vociferous dissenters from both inside and outside the Church. In the eyes of the world, the encyclical seemed to be repudiated even by most Catholics, following the lead of probably a majority of North American Catholic theologians, who issued a famous statement of "dissent" from the encyclical which made headlines even before the text of the encyclical itself became available.

The same Cardinal Patrick O'Boyle of Washington who had almost alone consistently tried to counter the whole new pro-birth-control mentality was also practically the only Catholic prelate who seriously tried to defend the encyclical *Humanae Vitae* in public, and for his pains he very quickly became discredited in the media because of his attempts to discipline priests and theologians who dissented from it.

The results of the widespread and continuing Catholic dissent from *Humanae Vitae* — which continues to this day — have been nothing less than catastrophic: the Catholic bishops have virtually never again spoken out on birth control since they were routed in the media and in the public eye by the initial theological dissent against the pope's encyclical; and this in turn has created a near universal impression, both inside and outside the Church, that the Catholic Church no longer seriously believes or upholds her teaching that contraception is immoral.

In this hazy situation, even the strong statements against abortion that the Catholic bishops have regularly continued to make have been vitiated by the current received public wisdom that "even Catholics no longer agree with the pope and bishops on birth control and abortion." This is the standard line that has been repeated as recently as *Time* magazine's 1994 "Man of the Year" story on Pope John Paul II.

Moreover, the fact that the Catholic bishops have for the moment virtually ceased to teach or speak out on birth control has had consequences even more far-reaching than merely the fact that many individual Catholics have thereby found it possible to approve of or even resort to birth control (and even abortion) with untroubled consciences. What the effective neutralization of the Church on the issue has meant is that Catholics in public office have also been able to represent themselves as Catholics in perfectly good standing, even while acting to promote birth control and abortion by government action. The "I'm-personally-opposed-to-abortion-but" Catholic politician may have become a contemptible stereotype today; but nearly all Catholic politicians in office today apparently share the current near universal public perception that the Catholic Church is simply wrong about birth control; and that the world, Catholics included, must simply move on, whether or not the Church wants to go. (Yes, and look where the world has moved on *to*!)

The era of universal contraception which we are still living through in America was, in fact, if not actually inaugurated, at least solidified for the foreseeable future when a Catholic politician, Senate Majority Leader Mike Mansfield of Montana, in December, 1970, pushed through, with virtually no opposition, the Family Planning Services and Research Act authorizing grants to non-profit organizations to establish and expand family planning clinics offering medical advice and contraceptives on request, especially to low-income women. The federal government was thus launched into birth control in the major way that continues on an even more massive scale today.

At the time, abortion was officially excluded (as theoretically it has been excluded throughout the life of government-subsidized family planning); but all that exclusion has meant in practice is that clinics have had to arrange their budgets so that none of their "federal" money shows up as financing abortions. And, in the meantime, the fact that some of the birth control devices, pills, IUDs, etc., that the clinics have purveyed *are*, in fact, abortifacient, has simply been "fuzzed," creating yet one more of the many and on-going official dishonesties involved in our contemporary culture of death.

VI

Once we realize how our contemporary culture of death came about — that it is based upon a sexual revolution unthinkable without both universal birth control and abortion as a necessary back-up, and therefore has enjoyed an enormous, indispensable boost from the government itself promoting these very things — then it becomes absolutely clear that there inescapably *is* a political and "government" front on which our current "cultural war" also has to be fought. (Yes, it is a matter of "changing hearts" too, as is so often repeated; but it is not only a matter of changing hearts.)

Abortion was legalized by government action and can only be finally countered by rescinding this legalization. The government has similarly gotten itself into totally illegitimate areas such as so-called family planning — not to speak of what it has been doing more recently promoting "alternate lifestyles" and the like, all based on the premises of the sexual revolution.

Many of the other direct consequences of the sexual revolution besides the ones we have been concerned with here could also be cited: divorce, teen-age pregnancy, illegitimacy, epidemics of sexually transmitted diseases, and so on. As is increasingly being realized, these things too, like abortion and birth control, are unfortunately often encouraged, if not always by direct positive government support, at least by the failure of the government to act appropriately considering the nature of the problems themselves.

Given the magnitude and variety of all these problems, then, what is our new conservative and prolife Congress really likely to do about them? Anything effective? In order to realize how far we still are from any even minimally effective political solutions to the real problems which beset us, we need only look at what the new Republican majority's Contract with America *says* it proposes to do about America's current problems.

What is included in this Contract with America is: budgetary reform, anti-crime measures, welfare reforms, support for families, tax relief, small business incentives, increased defense spending, tort reform, and term limits for officeholders. The announced Republican plan is to introduce bills addressing each one of these problem areas in the first 100 days of the Congress.

Most of these measures, of course, have little or nothing to do with the current social and moral problems we have been reviewing here. Probably as a gesture recognizing earlier Republican pledges concerning "family values," there will be included, for example, bills to provide tax credits for families with children and to remove the current tax penalty by which married couples are forced to pay more taxes than if each spouse filed separately.

Another Contract with America bill actually entitled the Family Reinforcement Act would do such things as: beef up child support enforcement by requiring states to honor child support orders from other states, while developing uniform court-order language that would help agencies collect child support; increase penalties in cases of child pornography, sexual abuse, or prostitution; provide tax credits for those families caring for aged or disabled parents or incurring expenses adopting children; and, finally, require parental consent before minors could participate in federally funded surveys on religious beliefs, sexual behavior, or psychological problems.

While it would be hard to argue with any of these things, and while all of these areas are no doubt important — certainly they are immensely preferable to some of the kinds of things the Clinton Administration has been trying to promote, such as homosexual "rights" or health care reform with mandatory abortion as a "benefit" — not a single one of these initiatives really addresses the real current moral and family crisis in America today. Indeed, some of the proposed bills may only make things worse.

For example, there is a welfare reform bill also included in the Contract entitled the Personal Responsibility Act; this is the initiative in connection with which Newt Gingrich has been talking about reviving orphanages and recommending that people go pick up the video of Spencer Tracy playing Father Flanagan of the original Boys Town. Again, this is all very well. Nevertheless the actual effect of such a bill as this in the present environment might actually be to encourage more abortions by cutting off welfare benefits to mothers who are minors and denying increased aid for any additional children they might bear.

While "personal responsibility," especially in the sexual area, is perhaps the greatest single need of our society today, trying to use the legal system to force on welfare recipients alone a standard of behavior currently required nowhere else in our society — where the sexual revolution still holds sway — hardly seems the most intelligent or even the fairest way to proceed. (In his Murphy Brown speech, for example, Dan Quayle was very careful to question the morality of the whole yuppy middle class, not just to fault the "welfare queens" or "princesses.")

What seems evident even from this very brief look at the highly touted Republican Contract with America, then, is that nothing like this Contract is really going to save us — certainly not from our current culture of death. After all, it is the pope, and not the Congress of the United States, who understands that it *is* a culture of death. The seriousness of the moral and social crisis which we really do face in America today is scarcely even recognized by the Congress; and the inadequacy of the public measures that are currently being brought forward are totally — even ludicrously? — incommensurate with this crisis. On the evidence, our new "conservative" and "prolife" Congress scarcely understands what the questions are, let alone having any clue about what the answers might be.

Nevertheless the current Congress, by itself, should not be blamed unduly. In fact, the current Congress very largely reflects the current state of the country. If there are no crusades by the Republican leadership for a Human Life Amendment, for example, we also have to ask who is effectively crusading for it outside of the Congress, or lobbying the Congress for it. Many of the prolife organizations, including those supported by the Catholic bishops, have apparently long since been content to focus on such things as fighting FOCA and possible health-care abortions or working for such things as parental notification and waiting period bills and the like. This is perhaps understandable in the current situation, but what our ultimate goal has to be cannot be lost sight of either.

Yet at this very moment, influential Republican and conservative theorists are now expressly recommending, in fact, that the Human Life Amendment plank should be dropped from the 1996 Republican platform and that the prolife focus should henceforth be placed upon helping women with "problem pregnancies." What this counsel amounts to in practice is that any real political solution to the legalization of abortion should now be abandoned. . .

As for birth control, who is opposing that *anywhere* — except, again, Pope John Paul II? Is anyone at all even lobbying Congress against Title X of the Public Health Service Act, for example? Does anyone dare? A Dick Armey can surely be pardoned, at least in some sense, if not even the Catholic bishops any longer actively oppose our current government-subsidized birth control, as they actively opposed it up to as late as 1966. It is hard to imagine the current bishops' conference making the kind of statement the bishops were capable of making back then. Meanwhile, our current social wounds are surely going to continue to fester until someone does finally summon up the courage to recognize in public what it is that really afflicts us.

For the moment, however, we live in a world in which birth control is seen as both an urgent social necessity and an unalloyed personal good. The recent UN Conference on Population and Development in Cairo illustrates the whole problem. Prolifers are jubilant, as they should be, at the unexpected and wholly praiseworthy victory of the Vatican delegation and its unlikely allies in getting abortion as such excised from the conference recommendations, while decisively besting the massed proabortion legions of the modern world led by the United States of America. What is less often recalled, though, is that the Cairo conference, while excluding abortion, nevertheless approved an international plan of action that now sanctions universal government-promoted birth control programs everywhere — exactly what we have in the United States which has helped bring us to our present pass.

In other words, the forceful and imaginative leadership of Pope John Paul II, which has now brought him the grudging honor of being named *Time*'s current "Man of the Year," has indeed succeeded in excluding "abortion as a method of family planning," just as the prolifers in the U.S. Congress have long since achieved the same goal there. Abortion itself may formally be excluded, but the radical superstition of "family planning" remains; and it is nothing else but the world's current addiction to contraception which continues to support the whole sexual revolution. So it is the sexual revolution itself which has to be overturned and reversed. And nobody has even *begun* to work effectively on this (except, again, Pope John Paul II).

Yet it has to come: "God is not mocked" (Gal 6:7). Our society is barely keeping its nose above water in a raging sea of promiscuity, pornography, illegitimacy, sexually transmitted diseases, no-fault divorces, and no-fault abortions, all going back to the tragically mistaken beliefs that we can do what we want in the sexual area, and that modern contraceptive technology is the guarantee of this.

Before a situation can come about where the Congress of the United States could seriously begin to address some of the real moral problems we face, another whole moral reformation in society has to come about — one not unlike the moral reformation which came about as a result of the original establishment of Christianity in the world. Today the Catholic Church is the only substantial body in the world that both understands and teaches that man is *not* in charge of life, and that, specifically, birth control is *wrong* and gravely harmful to society, as it is to individuals.

No matter how many people, even among Catholics, continue to disbelieve this at the moment, it nevertheless remains strictly and starkly true, as the current and growing pathological evidence from our own gravely disordered society more and more dramatically shows. It is upon the Catholic Church, therefore, that naturally devolves the task of working for the moral reformation in our society that inevitably has to come about if our society is indeed going to survive. No other imaginable entity exists in the world that could possibly bring about the moral reformation that is needed.

Those of us who have believed all along that the Catholic Church is the extension of Christ in the world and in history should not be surprised to see her now cast in this obviously providential role. We should not be surprised, in other words, to see her still "standing erect amid the moral ruin that surrounds her," as Pope Pius XI prophetically said in his encyclical *Casti Connubii* in 1930, directly responding to the cave-in of the year before by the Church of England's Lambeth Conference — and on what else but birth control?

6

The Prolife Movement Is a Non-Violent Movement — and Why It Has to Remain That Way

I

The year 1994 proved to be a year of definite electoral gains for the prolife cause, but at year's end a sensational incident of individual violence directed against abortion clinics, following upon similar incidents earlier in the year, could, tragically, serve to place some of these prolife electoral gains in jeopardy: in Brookline, Massachusetts, a gunman dressed in black opened fire with a rifle inside two separate abortion clinics about a mile apart, killing a woman at each clinic and wounding at least five other persons..

The gunman, identified as John C. Salvi of Hampton, New Hampshire, was later apprehended some 600 miles south of Massachusetts, in Norfolk,Virginia, where he had driven the covered black Toyota pick-up which had been spotted at the scene of the Massachusetts shootings; and where he then futilely peppered with rifle fire the outside glass doors and windows of a building housing Norfolk's Hillcrest Clinic on the same building's second floor. He was quickly captured by the police, thus bringing to an end what had already and immediately become a massive nationwide manhunt.

We have seen it all before: the intense, troubled loner, representing no prolife organization or constituency, who is, in fact, at odds with the non-violent philosophy of the movement, and who decides to take the law into his own hands — but only succeeds, in the nature of the case, in arousing all too justified outrage at his own mur-

---

Published in an earlier version in *Fidelity*,January, 1995.

derous act, outrage which then gets directed at the prolife movement as a whole, meanwhile diverting public attention from the similar deadly acts which regularly go on *inside* the abortion clinics that are targeted.

At the same time, the proabortionists are the ones who are handed the golden opportunity to cry "murder," which they are hardly loath to do: "This reign of terror must end!" cried Pamela J. Maraldo, president of the Planned Parenthood of America, speaking about the shootings in Brookline; she was certainly not referring to the particular "reign of terror" which the PPFA has itself undeniably been conducting over the past two decades and more in America against unborn children (it is curious that prolifers are instantly stigmatized for crying "murder," while proabortionists can use the word all they want with no apparent ill effects).

Given the peculiar circumstances of this latest instance of anti-clinic violence, the proabortion Governor of Massachusetts, William F. Weld, was also enabled to jump in quickly on PPFA's side, which *he* was hardly loath to do, either: "The man is nothing but a terrorist," Governor Weld declared. "Nobody's cause was advanced today," he added — and prolifers, sadly, have to agree.

Prolife organizations quickly themselves jumped in to denounce and disavow Salvi's actions. The National Right to Life Committee condemned the shootings "in the strongest possible terms." A spokeswoman for Massachusetts Citizens for Life described their members as "heartsick" and "grieving" for the victims of the shootings, while the organization's executive director called the whole affair an "atrocity," and added that "this person is either deranged or evil. We are outraged by this violence." Cardinal Bernard Law of Boston even felt obliged to call for a temporary halt to prolife demonstrations of any kind.

Unfortunately, the damage was already done, and the whole panoply of law and order *cum* media chorus was enabled once again to come out massively against the prolife cause itself because of the actions of one loner. Governor Weld immediately made the state police available to help guard the clinics. The Attorney General of the United States, Janet Reno, instantly announced that she would use recently expanded federal powers to pursue the assailant and prevent a recurrence. U.S. marshals have in fact been guarding some abortion clinics since last summer's clinic shootings in Florida, although, ironically, the Brookline clinics were not among those receiving such federal protection.

Even the Chief Executive of the United States was enabled to weigh in on the issue: "I am strongly committed to ending this form of domestic terrorism," President Clinton said. "I have called for a thorough investigation into this attack, and Attorney General Reno and FBI Director Freeh have already begun that task." Impossible to buck the issue up any higher in importance than that. . .

Even more ominous for prolife prospects than these statements representing an avowedly proabortion administration, however, was the reaction of new Senate Majority Leader Robert J. Dole, a legislator who up to now has pretty reliably voted prolife on the legislative issues that have come before him. Senator Dole declared on the CBS program *Face the Nation* after the shootings that the federal government might actually have to beef up the Freedom of Access to Clinic Entrances (FACE) Act passed by Congress and signed by President Clinton earlier in the year precisely in order to clamp down on anti-abortion demonstrations. Dole characterized the latest incidents as acts of terrorism that could require even tougher federal action. "I think we may be reaching that point," he said.

One of the real questions posed by the whole tragic affair, though, was whether the FACE Act, and recent Supreme Court decisions in the same vein, also directed exclusively against clinic protests, but not other kinds of protests, were not themselves an important factor in this most recent outburst of violence and killing. Perhaps. When legal and peaceful means of protest are cut off, those inclined to protest can get ever more desperate.

For one thing which our system fails to take into account generally is the continuing and enormous disproportion between the massive, inexorable government machinery that swings into action, accompanied by a chorus of media and public approval, in order to pursue, apprehend, and bring to trial the isolated individual abortion clinic assassin — while the regular killing that goes on all the time uninterruptedly within the clinics themselves proceeds not merely with the passive acquiescence of our society and government, but under their active — and belligerent — protection.

It cannot really be any wonder that, in the face of the largely silent abortion holocaust that grimly goes on, while the media and public attention are directed elsewhere, there are occasionally a tiny few among the millions of Americans who bitterly object to legalized abortion, and to the national shame of the abortion holocaust that it has brought about in this country, who can suddenly "snap" and turn to violence — in spite of all the vigorous and continuing efforts on the prolife side to keep the movement itself non-violent. No: in the present atmosphere, it cannot be any surprise if these sincere prolife efforts do not always succeed. The present situation is simply too awful to resign oneself to.

There can surely not be any question, however, that the efforts by the government and the courts to discourage, if not eliminate, anti-abortion protests as such, have also hampered the efforts of the prolife movement to keep those who march in its ranks on a non-violent course. Some prolifers have been warning for a long time, in fact, that to the extent peaceful protests are rendered more difficult, violent protests become more likely. This may very well be true as a bare fact.

In a larger sense, however, the prolife movement cannot concede this. Violence consciously directed against clinics, their personnel, or their "patients," can never be considered anything but a willed act of a kind which prolifers must *never* engage in or approve of. What this latest tragic affair proves, again, is how catastrophic for the cause as a whole can be the mindless, irresponsible acts, such as those in Brookline and Norfolk, even though carried out by only one individual on his own. Far from "saving babies," violent actions of this kind serve to turn both the public authorities and public opinion against the prolife movement; they surely set back the day when we will ever be able to see justice done to the unborn in America.

We are nevertheless far from seeing the end of the difficulties and disadvantages which this and similar incidents have unfortunately been fastening upon the prolife movement as a whole. Thus it is both necessary and instructive to review the whole burning issue of abortion clinic violence, in which these latest instances in Brookline, Massachusetts, and Norfolk, Virginia, now have to be included.

II

The July, 1994, killings of an abortion doctor and his escort outside a clinic in Pensacola, Florida, by an ex-Presbyterian minister named Paul Hill, constituted another much publicized abortion clinic violence case. Paul Hill's capture and trial were extensively covered in the media; he was speedily tried both for a federal crime under the new FACE law (which was enacted and signed only two months before he unleashed his deadly assault) and then for murder under Florida law; he was convicted in both trials.

Then, on December 6, 1994, Paul Hill was condemned to death for murder; the jury itself recommended capital punishment in his case. Quite possibly the anti-capital-punishment sentiment which is normally so common in America today is not nearly so pronounced when the murder is carried out in front of an abortion clinic; but this still remains to be seen. (John Salvi faces a maximum sentence of life in prison without parole under current Massachusetts law; whether this incident will motivate any return to the death penalty in Massachusetts also remains to be seen.)

Throughout the entire period of Paul Hill's trial and conviction, virtually no approval of his action was voiced anywhere within prolife ranks. Some isolated individuals, again, saw his action as justified in order to save babies — and, as usual, the press was avid to report such voices — but they represented no one within the movement. Rather, Hill's action was immediately condemned — roundly and unequivocally condemned, as it should have been — by all of the major prolife organizations. Cardinal Roger Mahoney of Los Angeles, chairman of the Catholic bishops' Committee for Pro-Life Activities, surely spoke for the overwhelming majority of prolifers when he said that this shotgun killing "makes a mockery of everything we stand for."

Speaking for its numerous affiliate organizations throughout the country, the National Right to Life Committee said in a statement that it was the media itself that had "created the illusion that [Hill] represents a constituency within the prolife movement." The NRLC pointed out that "unfortunately, over the past year, many in the media — including *USA Today*, the *New York Times*, and the NBC *Nightly News* — have given Mr. Hill a national spotlight, providing him undeserved attention and likely increasing delusions of self-importance."

The media were willing to give this kind of attention to Mr. Hill after he had emerged, following the killing of another abortion doctor, also in Pensacola (though outside another clinic), in March, 1993, as one of a tiny handful of people in prolife ranks who were publicly trying to justify attacks on abortionists in order to save babies; and also following the wounding of yet another abortion doctor in Wichita, Kansas, in August, 1993.

Following these episodes, Paul Hill appeared at his own suggestion on, among other programs, Phil Donahue's television show. No doubt Phil Donahue likes to host extremists claiming to represent causes he opposes; their extremist views will then serve to discredit their announced causes in the eyes of his audiences. It is a common and obvious media strategy, all the more conspicuous because the media tend to report so little — and so unsympathetically — on the manifold positive activities of one of today's major national movements, the prolife movement.

Instead, on ABC-TV's *Nightline*, in December, 1993, Paul Hill was featured declaring that "it would be just as justified to shoot and kill a doctor who's about to kill an unborn as it would be to shoot a doctor who's about to kill a born child."

The principal effect of a statement such as this, of course — and the principal reason why the mass media are always so ready to give wide coverage to such statements — is to damage the prolife movement in the eyes of public opinion. The aim is to brand the prolife movement as violent, when in reality its largely consistent and near unanimous espousal and practice of non-violence as a mass movement is surely one of the most remarkable phenomena in recent American history. There can be little doubt that the records of, say, pro-labor, anti-war, or even pro-civil rights demonstrations do not come close to the record of the prolife movement on the score of non-violence.

In fact, prolifers tend to be more keenly conscious than anyone of how much damage can be done, and has been done, to the movement by isolated instances of violence such as the recent assaults perpetrated by loners in Florida, Kansas, and now Massachusetts and Virginia. The typical prolife viewpoint on this was never better expressed than it was at one point directly expressed in person to Paul Hill himself — by a Florida prolife activist quoted in the press, Vicki Conroy, when Hill showed up to join the regular on-going — and peaceful — picketing against the Pensacola abortion clinic.

"When he showed up on the scene and started espousing his views," Conroy said, "We would tell him: 'Paul, your theology's wrong. You do not have the right to take the life of another human being.'" The same dictum applies exactly to John Salvi.

This, in fact, is what the prolife movement is really all about. Nor is it just a matter of preventing damage to the prolife movement by employing the wrong tactics (although it is that too). More importantly, it is a question of the fundamental integrity of the prolife movement itself: *we* of all movements can never resort to taking life even to achieve a good and important end or goal.

If a principal goal of the prolife movement is to persuade the American public that no one can resort to killing an unborn child, no matter how good the aims and intentions involved in wishing to terminate a particular pregnancy might be, then the movement cannot itself sanction the taking of life, even if immediate defense of the unborn is sincerely offered in justification for this.

If another principal goal of the prolife movement is to convince the American public that the unborn child is entitled to the equal protection of the laws under the Constitution, then the movement itself cannot resort to illegal acts which undermine the rule of law: the prolife movement must remain non-violent.

So widely and deeply is this understood and accepted by prolifers today that, just as occurred immediately in the Massachusetts case, all of the major prolife organizations similarly denounced Paul Hill's act without any hesitation or consultation, as soon as it was reported in the news. The proabortion *Washington Post* had said condescendingly in an editorial: "The large majority of abortion opponents who abhor violence must speak out, not only after an atrocity but continually." They did, and they will.

The militant American Life League, for example, called the assassination of the Florida abortion doctor "a horrible, tragic, heinous, serious crime." A leader of the even more activist Operation Rescue declared that "the prolife movement has no room for violence or vigilantism. There are no qualifiers." The national director of Rescue America emphasized that his group "does not condone violence either inside or outside of abortion mills." Even the militant American Coalition of Life Activists, which tries to expose doctors who perform abortions, requires a non-violence pledge from its activists.

In an editorial in his journal *First Things*, Father Richard John Neuhaus expressed something of a movement consensus when he wrote: "Bizarre. Beyond the pale. Outrageous. Mad. These are some of the terms applied to the suggestion that killing abortionists in order to defend unborn children may be morally justified." Similar statements from many other prolife leaders could be cited.

But it was a Church of Christ pastor in Pensacola who probably said it best following the whole sorry, tragic Florida incident: "Abortion is abhorrent to God, but that does not justify killing people. . .We are here to do the will of God, but we need to use his methods. . ."

III

Even though the prolife movement's typical strategies and tactics have been consistently non-violent, then — even though the movement has exhibited near unanimity in eschewing and condemning violence — those on the other side have rarely been willing to grant or concede this; the movement as a whole is almost always instantly blamed. This has proved to be the case in the Florida, Kansas, and Massachusetts *cum* Virginia cases.

And the prolife movement is blamed not only by those on the other side: no, what should be the "neutral" government and the courts, not to speak of the media, themselves regularly tax the prolife movement with promoting or condoning violence. The movement is taxed with this charge by the very fact of continuing to speak out concerning the evil of abortion. "Opponents of choice must take responsibility for creating a climate in which this terrorism thrives," declared NARAL's Kate Michelman after the Brookline incident.

Earlier, following the double Florida assassination, a spokesman for the same NARAL organization had asserted as follows: "We believe a significant portion of the blame for this murderous act rests with the leadership of the antichoice movement, which has been unwilling or unable to control the violent extremists within their midst" — as if prolifers had no right to espouse their cause unless they could also guarantee that there would never be any violence; or as if prolifers were strictly obliged to accomplish what the police and the U.S. marshals have been unable to accomplish, namely, "to control the violent extremists."

Such standards have surely never been demanded of any other social protest movement in America. The movement for black civil rights in the 1960s, for example, which everybody now concedes to have served justice, occasioned no little violence, and there were even some killings. None of this was itself justified, of course. Nevertheless the civil rights movement as a whole was not blamed for it.

But the prolife movement today is being held to very different standards. In May, 1994, as already mentioned, Congress enacted and President Clinton signed, the Freedom of Access to Clinic Entrances (FACE) Act, making it a federal felony offense to block access to abortion clinics, to damage clinic property, or to injure or intimidate clinic patients or staff. The "criminal behavior" thus established by this law does not apply to protesters in general but only to prolifers protesting what goes on in abortion clinics. Abortion is thus now not only legal on demand in the United States; it now enjoys special protection from the law as well.

And that a normally prolife legislator such as Senate Majority Leader Bob Dole now thinks FACE even needs to be beefed up simply underlines the damage violence does to the prolife cause.

The very next month after FACE was enacted, in June, 1994, the United States Supreme Court, which quite evidently remains in thrall to its own misbegotten 1973 *Roe v. Wade* decision legalizing abortion, in yet another decision entitled *Madsen v. Women's Health Center*, further curtailed the freedom of, again, abortion-clinic protesters only, upholding protective buffer zones around clinics because of the confrontational tactics of clinic picketers — as if any kind of strike or protest, no matter how peaceful, were not in some sense "confrontational." That is the whole point of any strike or protest, even a peaceful, non-violent protest of the kind the prolife movement typically advocates and carries out.

Anyway, when did mere "confrontation" as such become a crime? What happened to the approval and even praise which protests for "social justice" normally garner in our society? We have already asked whether the placing of such severe restrictions on avowed peaceful protests against abortion actually encourage more violence by individuals, since there is now less incentive to eschew violence if one is going to be charged with a felony anyway. And just as the fringe element prone to violence is fed and egged on by avid media attention, so those denied legal, peaceful channels of protest can unfortunately sometimes be tempted into illegal, violent channels.

Earlier, in January, 1994, the same Supreme Court had ruled that the famous Racketeer Influenced and Corrupt Organizations (RICO) Act — a law originally directed against organized crime — could also be used against abortion-clinic protesters, thus not only expressly equating prolife demonstrators with *criminals* but also making them liable, if convicted in civil lawsuits, for triple money damages. (It should be duly noted, however, that both the 1994 Pensacola and the later Brookline shootings took place *after* all these stringent measures had come into effect.)

Surely both the FACE law and the Supreme Court's *Madsen* and RICO decisions represent serious assaults upon the First Amendment rights of all Americans. Nevertheless it would surely be naïve to count on any support from civil libertarians; such support has been conspicuously lacking whenever the so-called "woman's right" to abortion ever comes into play. Normal rules are typically suspended where abortion is concerned.

Unless and until a new climate can be created in the Congress and on the Supreme Court, these recent enactments only underline how utterly serious and important it is for the prolife movement to remain non-violent: for if Congress and the Court are so ready to move against a movement that truly is non-violent for the most part, we do not need much imagination to figure out how the prolife movement and those in it would be treated if the movement ever did turn to violence in any degree. And this is why the Massachusetts killings, coming as they did after the prolife movement was already being pushed to the wall by FACE, *Madsen*, and RICO, represent an especially tragic development.

IV

One of the things that has been most dramatically brought out in the aftermath of both the Massachusetts and Florida assassinations is how insecure and even frantic the proabortionists themselves remain even as, by all objective standards, they would seem to be winning almost everywhere. An officer of the national Organization for Women (NOW) reacted to the Pensacola shootings by asserting that "we believe there is a conspiracy across the country to terrorize abortion providers and women. . .We want the FBI and federal marshals to protect clinics and enforce the law."

Make no mistake: the proabortionists *believe* in this conspiracy theory. After the Brookline shootings, a vice president of the National Organization for Women (NOW) told the press that the fact that a "domestic terrorist" like Salvi wound up way down at the Hillcrest Clinic in Norfolk, after having carried out shootings up near Boston, simply reinforces NOW's settled conviction that there currently exists a "national conspiracy" of violence and terrorism directed against abortion clinics.

This theory was already operative at the time of the Florida shootings. A lawyer with the Washington-based Feminist Majority

Foundation spoke of a "wave of domestic terrorism" against clinics and called for a "a multi-jurisdictional task force" to investigate violence against abortion clinics and propose measures to strengthen security. Eleanor Smeal, president of this same Feminist Majority Foundation, claimed at same time, in reference to the Pensacola shootings: "This is not an isolated event. We have repeatedly called for a national investigation. . .The extremists have embarked on a murder strategy."

This kind of talk is taken with the utmost seriousness when it comes from the proabortion side, and Smeal herself has long been one of the most prominent voices calling for further drastic government action against prolifers. "We passed [FACE]," she was quoted as saying — note the "we"! — "so that federal investigation of anti-abortion violence would be undertaken, and we want it now."

The federal government has evidently been only too happy to comply. President Clinton's own statement on the Pensacola incident, like his later one on the Brookline shootings already quoted above, echoed the near hysteria of the proabortion forces themselves; the president spoke with a straight face of clinic violence as being a "form of domestic terrorism that threatens the fabric of our country."

Perhaps a little perspective is needed here. Besides the Florida and Massachusetts shootings, there were only *two* other reported attempted burnings of abortion clinics in the United States in the course of the entire year 1994. There have been a total of 146 such incidents in all in the dozen years since 1982. This is very serious, of course, but as serious as, for example, drug-related crime, with its gang wars and drive-by shoot-outs? Tragic as the clinic killings have indubitably been, gangs snuff out as many lives in a single night in some of our large cities. Yet in spite of this disparity, the president himself believes that it is the clinic violence, not the drug violence, or the gang-war violence, which "threatens the fabric of our country."

Meanwhile, the president has evidently long since communicated this viewpoint of his quite effectively to his Department of Justice. Attorney General Janet Reno actually met with officers of NOW immediately following the Florida shootings and then issued a statement which affirmed what she called "the importance of law enforcement's continuing efforts to determine whether there is any organized criminal effort directing these horrible acts of violence. . . We will. . .use every federal tool at our disposal," Attorney General Reno promised.

By the first of the next week following the Florida shootings, which occurred on a Friday, the Attorney General of the United States had made good her promise, dispatching with wide publicity U.S. marshals to guard around the clock abortion clinics in a dozen different localities around the country. Nobody cared to speculate how long these federal marshals would continue to be deployed twenty-four hours a day around these abortuaries. In some cases, these same U.S. marshals are now providing door-to-door protection for abortionists coming and going to work.

As it happened, the clinics in Brookline were not among those receiving around-the-clock and door-to-door federal protection when the shootings took place there; but what was already in place for the later incident was a massive federal apparatus always held in readiness to be directed against clinic protests.

For the Reno Department of Justice had also set up a task force which included the FBI and the Bureau of Alcohol, Tobacco, and Firearms (BATF), along with lawyers in the Department's criminal and civil rights divisions, in order to pursue the whole business. Actually, according to press reports, Janet Reno had already promised to launch a federal initiative against the prolife movement following the earlier 1993 shooting of the abortion doctor in Florida, and so things were no doubt already in readiness for the 1994 Pensacola events; they were certainly in place for those in Brookline.

As the Justice Department officials were meeting to consider all these elaborate measures, including possible next steps against prolifers, proabortionists were noisily demonstrating outside the Justice Department building — confrontational? — with its famous motto carved in stone over the door: "Equal Justice Under Law." Not all protests in this country, however, are considered equally serious threats to the fabric of the nation, it would seem.

In fact, as the *New York Times* revealed in a special report on the subject, bringing the FBI into the picture after the Florida shootings constituted a wholly new dimension of federal action, a "first" for the Clinton-Reno Justice Department, since the FBI has not previously been involved in abortion-clinic-related cases. "Setting aside a long-standing reluctance to involve itself in cases of abortion-related violence," the *Times* story related, "the Federal Bureau of Investigation has begun a broad inquiry into accusations that the use of force against women's clinics and their doctors is the work of a conspiracy by antiabortion militants." A confidential teletype message to this effect was sent out to all 56 FBI field offices only one day after the Pensacola shootings: things indeed *were* in readiness! Now that the FBI is fully in the picture, it would be naïve to expect any further "reluctance" on its part.

V

Once such a vast and wide array of federal power has been set in motion, we can be pretty sure its effects will hardly be confined only to violent activists on the fringe of the prolife movement; the movement itself is evidently going to be in for considerable harassment, the ultimate consequences of which are surely not yet even in sight.

Thus, what we see today with regard to what is so often and so blandly called "the emotional, controversial abortion issue" is: irrefutable evidence that the federal government itself has now decisively taken one side in this supposed "controversy"; for the federal government it evidently is no longer a controversy; the issue has been decided, and not in favor of the prolife movement. The power of all three branches of the federal government is now being methodically brought to bear on the proabortion side. Not only do the rights of the unborn not count; the rights of peaceful protesters do not count. Indeed the rights of all who object to abortion do not count, since their tax money is now being used not only to pay for abortions (although we have regularly been told that it is all nothing but a matter of "choice"); their tax money is also being used to pay for around-the-clock special police protection of abortion purveyors.

All this can only be considered a rather remarkable and dismaying set of results, considering how predominantly non-violent the prolife movement truly has been from the beginning. Nevertheless, it remains true that, precisely because the proabortionists have been able to get the government itself to serve their cause so diligently, they now have the *means* to administer to the prolife movement some telling blows from which it would be very difficult for the movement to recover — and which could only further delay the day when a serious effort to outlaw legalized abortion by legal means can be attempted.

As has been most aptly remarked, for the prolife movement to be attempting to use force against the massed power of — nothing else but the federal government itself — would be to attack the other side's strongest point with the prolife movement's weakest possible weapon. All the federal government needs now in order to do grave, perhaps even fatal, harm to the prolife movement is some actual *proof* somewhere that the movement is indeed a "violent conspiracy." No one professing to be "prolife" should ever want to be guilty of providing any such "proof."

The real results of the violent actions of Paul Hill and John Salvi, then, may turn out to have been of greater harm to the prolife movement as a whole, and to the innocent unborn as well whom these men declared they were trying to save, than can yet be seen. In fact, it is not at all clear how many more of these disasters the prolife movement can afford.

The prolife movement's major weapons must, therefore, remain truth and right and the ability to appeal the justice of its cause to the conscience of the American people. While continuing to proclaim the truth about the evil of abortion from the housetops, the prolife movement must itself remain consistent in its own defense of life, never forgetting how it was a similar principled, non-violent strategy which finally brought even the Communist empire crashing down — after all the attempted armed uprisings against it had failed.

The prolife movement must remain non-violent. This is imperative; it is the only strategy that, in God's providence, *can* work, considering all the relentless worldly forces currently arrayed against the prolife cause. This is still God's world, after all, although especially in the climate of today it sometimes seems mysteriously given over, as it was in biblical times, to "the world rulers of this present darkness" (Eph 6:12). If we truly do want to do God's work, though, we do have to try to follow God's way.

Postscript

John C. Salvi was sentenced to two consecutive life terms without the possibility of parole for his role in the Brookline shootings. His court appointed lawyer attempted to have him found insane, but the prosecution opposed that defense on the grounds that he had planned his clinic assaults so methodically and had carefully taken steps to escape. In the event, he was found guilty and sentenced and committed to prison accordingly. However, on November 29, 1996, Salvi was found dead in his prison cell, an apparent suicide.

7

Will the Republicans Alienate Prolife Voters?

I

No doubt the Republican Party wants to keep the prolife vote in 1996, but does it understand what it has to do to keep it?

Although most of the declared or probable Republican presidential candidates describe themselves as prolife (except, of course, maverick Pennsylvania Republican Senator Arlen Specter, frankly running on what he calls a "moderate, prochoice" platform), none of them wants to emphasize the prolife issue.

Although a majority of Republican members, as well as all the Republican leaders, in both houses of Congress, are similarly "prolife," few of them really want to emphasize the issue, either. It is notorious that the Contract with America contains no specific prolife initiatives, and, meanwhile, leaders such as Majority Whip Senator Trent Lott candidly admit that "I don't think you'll see a lot of action" on the prolife front.

Then there is Republican National Chairman Haley Barbour, also self-described as prolife, who has nevertheless been declaiming for the past couple of years that anyone who thinks legalized abortion should be a defining issue for Republicans "ought to have his head examined."

In spite of this obvious lack of enthusiasm on the part of the Republican leadership — almost as if the prolife vote did not supply the margin of victory in the 1994 mid-term elections! — the Republican Platform nevertheless still does call for a Human Life Amendment that would make operative for the unborn the right to life and to the equal protection of the laws which the Constitution is already supposed to guarantee to everyone anyway.

A shorter version of this article appeared in *Crisis* in May, 1995.

However, a number of Republicans appear to have become quite nervous, and then some, about this; they want to drop the HLA goal as unobtainable, meanwhile simply affirming that the Republican Party, unlike the Democratic Party, opposes "abortion on demand" and is therefore "the prolife party."

This desire to drop the HLA plank from the platform persists in spite of the prolife gains in the 1994 elections. The abortion issue is regularly seen as too emotional and divisive. Polls indicate that while Americans do not favor abortion on demand, they do not want to see abortion banned outright, either. Appearing to be too "harsh" or "extreme" on the issue will meanwhile alienate voters in the middle; so it is thought.

"We shouldn't continue to fight on ground we cannot win," former U.S. Education Secretary and Drug Czar William J. Bennett was recently quoted in the *Washington Post* as saying — a position he has held for some time, along with other prominent Republicans and conservatives. The same *Post* article revealed, in fact, that "active. . .negotiations to moderate substantially the Republican positions on abortion and school prayer" have been going on for some time among important Republicans and conservatives.

But it seems that something of a monkey wrench was thrown into these "negotiations" when Ralph Reed, executive director of the surging Christian Coalition, recently told the Conservative Political Action Conference (CPAC) that prolife voters will not tolerate any watered down Republican platform in 1996. Reed said that "prolife and profamily voters, a third of the electorate, will not support a party that retreats from its noble and historic defense of traditional values, and which has a national ticket or a platform that does not share Ronald Reagan's belief in the sanctity of human life."

Media reports tended to interpret Reed's statement as indicating that the Christian Coalition would not support any candidate on the ticket who was prochoice on abortion; but Reed plainly said "platform" as well as "ticket," and thus he would also seem to have been warning restive Republicans that backing away from the HLA platform language could alienate large numbers of prolife voters and trigger a major "walk" by them in 1996.

If so, Ralph Reed is right: prolifers have not been moving increasingly into GOP ranks for no reason. They have been voting Republican because they believe that, as their Life Chain signs proclaim,

"Abortion Kills Children"; and so they have supported the party that has officially declared at least a theoretical commitment to stopping the wanton slaughter of children by abortion. Republican leaders will trifle with this deep-seated prolife conviction at their peril.

William Bennett thus has it all wrong: you do not ground a point of principle as basic as the right to life on what you can easily "win," much less on what opinion polls say Americans want. America *must* enact a Human Life Amendment if our Constitution is to go on meaning what it says. We will have willfully abandoned the whole basis of our democratic and constitutional system if we ever admit that there is a class of people — such as the unborn — to whom the guarantees of the Constitution do not apply.

II

The lack of enthusiasm for a Human Life Amendment on the part of Republican leaders and influential conservatives does not date from yesterday, just as actual efforts to "moderate" the Republican Party platform position on abortion have a history. For a long time there have been more than a few rumbles and complaints from various quarters about the party's position; they go back to the 1980s and before; the Republican "big tent" philosophy of the late Lee Atwater was formulated and announced precisely in order to try keep happy those same Republicans who never wanted a prolife plank in the Republican platform in the first place. Most of them have been from the centrist or even liberal wings of the party; often they have been "country club" or Planned Parenthood-type Republicans. But they are not the only ones who want the platform changed.

Many party conservatives have apparently also long since decided that the party's principled prolife stand is a liability. *National Review* magazine, for example, has been printing articles and editorials in this vein for several years, meanwhile rejecting articles arguing the contrary position, namely, that the party has to continue to take a principled stand on an issue as fundamental as the right to life.

In June, 1994, a major initiative was launched with no little fanfare in an effort to persuade party conservatives in particular that the time had come to remove the perceived abortion albatross from the neck of the party. This initiative was put forward by William Kristol of the Project for the Republican Future and George Weigel of the Ethics and Public Policy Center.

In the same breath, Messrs. Kristol and Weigel declared themselves to be prolife; but they were nevertheless quite firm that they wanted to get beyond what they evidently consider the traditional prolife fixation on the right of the child to life and on the consequent need for a constitutional amendment in order to guarantee that right (since the *Roe v. Wade* Supreme Court decision had so effectively voided it).

In their proposal, Kristol and Weigel favor what they style a more positive and incremental approach to the abortion issue, one aimed at helping women with problem pregnancies and at reducing the total number of abortions being performed; they also want to concentrate on efforts in the states to "curb the incidence of abortion by seeking maximum feasible legal protection for the unborn."

"Maximum feasible" evidently means, in the context of their discussion, not very much, if any, real "legal protection for the unborn" at all, since, even if their strategy succeeds in reducing the number of abortions, the unborn will still admittedly lack any basic legal and constitutional protection for their right to life.

Their proposal thus does not touch the basic issue, even though they claim to believe that "the unborn child has an inalienable right to life." As a practical matter, however, they go no farther than arguing that since the Supreme Court's 1973 *Roe v. Wade* decision legalizing abortion was wrongly decided, the American people should at least be able to debate the issue in a democratic forum; they further argue that what they call "the $500-million-a-year abortion industry" should be regulated by instituting such things as informed consent and parental consent for the abortions of minors. They also reject government funding of abortions or the promotion of abortions through international organizations or aid programs.

Although the Kristol-Weigel proposal met with some immediate and probably predictable vocal opposition in Republican ranks, notably from the Phyllis Schlafly and Pat Buchanan camps, a number of other prominent Republican prolife leaders seemed only too ready to endorse the new initiative. Reagan Administration stalwart Gary Bauer of the strongly prolife Family Research Council, for example, called the Kristol-Weigel proposal "needed." Conservative columnist Mona Charen, also prolife, was actually laudatory, describing the Kristol-Weigel proposal as "a service" to the prolife cause, "not a surrender. . . [This] is not the language of capitulation. The Human Life Amendment idea is dated. . ."

Following these endorsements from conservatives and even prolifers, the Kristol-Weigel presentation ended up appearing in print in August, 1994, almost inevitably, in the pages of that steady siren-singer, *National Review* — siren-singer, that is, of the song that Republicans and conservatives can still be "prolife" while not really attempting to do very much of anything, in practice, about legalized abortion.

In September, 1994, at a meeting of the Christian Coalition in Washington, the proposed new approach to legalized abortion evidently made further progress, even in the face of an eloquent contrary appeal made by Pennsylvania's Democratic Governor Robert P. Casey never to say die on the abortion issue. Even the redoubtable Phyllis Schlafly was reported to be coming around in favor of "simplifying the Republican Platform. . .[in order to] just uphold the principle that the unborn child has a fundamental, individual right to life." Ralph Reed of the Christian Coalition, however, was already reported by then as saying that his group was not ready to take such a position; and that "any changes in the plank must not appear to alter the party's prolife position, lest many religious conservatives defect from the GOP."

But there is no denying that the Kristol-Weigel proposal had considerable immediate impact. At the moment it was first launched, pundit Fred Barnes, who has himself also apparently voiced personal prolife sentiments, even hazarded what he called an educated "guess" in *The New Republic* that "the new Republican position on abortion has *arrived*. . ." (emphasis added).

Later on, pundit Ben Wattenberg waxed positively enthusiastic, "offering to eat the pages, one by one. . .if there is a tough anti-abortion plank in the 1996 Republican platform" (Wattenberg is proabortion). Typical Washington "insiders" that they are, such "experts" as these are seemingly oblivious to the effect any such watered-down platform plank would have on rank-and-file Republican voters; such considerations do not enter into their analysis.

The new position surely does represent a no doubt tempting "solution" for professional Republican politicians and their handlers as a class, however, anxious as all these people surely are to get out from under the perceived abortion-incubus, no matter how.

Nevertheless, if the guesses by Fred Barnes and Ben Wattenberg prove to be correct, and if the Kristol-Weigel proposal really does represent the Republican wave of the future on the abortion issue; if the Republican Party, that is, does attempt to go on presenting itself as "the prolife party," while dropping its call for the constitutional amendment which the prolife forces in Republican ranks have insisted upon in past platforms — then what the real result will be is a serious erosion in the Republican party's current voter strength — a major "walk" by prolifers in 1996.

III

Prolifers are not opposed to, indeed they strongly favor, the positive strategy outlined by William Kristol and George Weigel which "recognizes the need for an extensive and on-going process of public persuasion, and one that provides care, assistance, and alternatives to women caught in the dilemma of unwanted pregnancy." Former National Right to Life President John Wilke has similarly spoken most persuasively of the need to concentrate more strongly on the needs of women with problem pregnancies.

Prolifers generally are not only favorable to this positive approach; they are the ones who are principally carrying it out; they also pioneered it. Prolifers had already established such pregnancy assistance organizations as Birthright even before *Roe v. Wade* legalized abortion nationwide. One of the best kept secrets about the prolife movement, courtesy at least in part of near total media non-attention to the activities of the movement, is the extent to which substantial pregnancy crisis and counseling work has been for a long time and continues to be carried out by prolifers.

Several years ago Cardinal John O'Connor of New York publicly pledged to take care of *any* woman anywhere with an "unwanted pregnancy" who was nevertheless willing to carry her child to term. That's "any woman." A few years later the cardinal sadly had to report at a mass rally on the Mall in Washington that he had been unable to get any of the major media even to *report* this remarkable offer. Nor did the media report it *then*, either, even though the cardinal revealed the whole story in front of a mass audience of several hundred thousand people.

Mother Teresa of Calcutta recently made the *same* offer at a national prayer breakfast that has been widely reported and commented on, then and since, probably because both President and Mrs. Clinton, and Vice President and Mrs. Gore, were all present in person to hear this particular pledge made by Mother Teresa. These pledges to any women truly facing problem pregnancies still stand; women facing problem pregnancies enjoy unprecedented opportunities for assistance and sympathy today, as they should. Nor are religious leaders the only ones dedicated to helping such women.

It is therefore time to lay to rest the falsehood that prolifers do not care about women and only care about babies before they are born; this is yet another one of the many lies fabricated by the proabortionists and diffused by the generally proabortion media; and it represents mis-information that anyone claiming to be prolife in any way — or even claiming to be objective — ought not to want to perpetuate, even indirectly.

Meanwhile, however, for Kristol and Weigel, and all the Republicans who have already been climbing on their bandwagon with great sighs of relief, to imagine that the *political* problem of abortion can in any way even be adequately formulated solely or even largely in terms of women unable to deal with problem pregnancies is naïve in the extreme; it makes one wonder where these people have been for the last twenty or thirty years, and whether they have ever really reflected very seriously at all on the real problem of legalized abortion in America today.

Women with "problem pregnancies" in America today are in fact dealing with them quite decisively and efficiently; they are getting abortions. Massively: the statistics on abortion are well known, amounting to around 1.5 million per year (thus, well over 30 million since *Roe v. Wade* legalized the practice). Each year more American lives are lost by abortion than in all the wars of American history (the latter figure amounting to a grand total of 1.2 million dead in all, according to the *World Almanac*).

And for every dead child, as the bumper sticker expresses it, there is a wounded woman.

Such statistics indicate an unprecedented, previously unimagined lethal assault by this generation upon the next generation:

They even offered their own sons
And their daughters in sacrifice to demons
They shed the blood of the innocent
The blood of their sons and daughters. . .(Psalm 106)

This is an intolerable situation for any nation calling itself democratic, or, indeed, civilized. The prolife movement holds that the fundamental political question of abortion today remains whether this society, or any society, can go on indefinitely permitting this kind of elective taking of human life, not just on this scale, but in this way.

A Human Life Amendment protecting innocent human life at all stages and in all conditions, far from being any "lost cause," is a strict imperative for the future of our democratic and constitutional system.

Given the huge dimensions of the problem in our current legal and cultural climate, it is quite true, of course, that the prolife movement has not yet been too successful in advancing its viewpoint very far in American society at large. Weigel and Kristol are perceptive observers of the current scene and they naturally see this. And at least something of what they say about the prolife movement and some of its leadership — rather too condescendingly, however, one senses — may even be correct. They do propose that the Republican Party should forthrightly "salute right-to-lifers" and "those dedicated women and men who have already made alternatives to abortion widely available," and no doubt they are sincere in all this.

But Kristol and Weigel are not merely perceptive observers; they also apparently aim to be smart operators. And it seems pretty clear that at least one of their principal aims is not perhaps so much to deal effectively with the abortion question itself in any really fundamental way, as it is to defuse the whole controversial and volatile issue generally for the perceived good of the Republican Party — without, meanwhile, alienating the prolifers in the party's ranks and possibly precipitating the dreaded "walk" by them in 1996.

IV

While the Kristol-Weigel proposal to downgrade the abortion issue is perhaps understandable for those whose primary motive is to unite the Republican Party, theirs is an initiative that is nevertheless bound to fail in the nature of the case. The prolife movement hardly arose merely in order to provide workers and votes for Republican candidates or merely in order to serve as a component of a winning Republican coalition (as it was basically treated by both the Reagan and Bush administrations). Rather, the prolife movement arose in order to stop legalized abortion, a callous, violent, bloody, and immoral practice, and an impermissible blot on our entire constitutional and democratic system.

Moreover, the prolife movement is here to stay, regardless of how uneasy Republican mainstreamers may feel about it (while continuing to covet its votes). The prolife movement has long since become nationwide in scope; it is solidly motivated and organized, especially at the grass-roots level; and it continues to grow all the time. By any standards, it has become a force which can no longer be ignored, either by those who oppose it or by those who are trying to court its favor. It certainly cannot be manipulated by mere smart operators who perhaps imagine they can direct it from the outside in the interests of Republican electoral victories.

Indeed, the prolife movement would seem to be an especially formidable force to reckon with, considering that it has been able to attain the position it now occupies in the face of the strong and active disapproval, if not the outright hostility, not only of "the 500-million-a-year abortion industry," but for the most part of the media, the courts, the organized political classes, government bureaucracies at all levels, as well as of the legal, medical, teaching, and social work professions, the universities and foundations, and powerful economic forces such as the pharmaceutical industry.

Nor has the movement even had the churches always effectively and consistently on its side. While it genuinely is "antiabortion," the Christian right is often prone to accept the most minimalistic of measures, abortion clinic regulation and what-not, as resounding prolife "victories," even though the basic questions of the legality of abortion, and the alleged justifications for it, are never seriously challenged.

As for the Catholic Church, the Catholic bishops of the United States, even while never deviating from a strong principled stand against abortion, have nevertheless often seemed to be more interested in practice in such things as their pastoral letters on peace and the American economy than in supporting any really effective political action against legalized abortion; certainly many of their experts in the United States Catholic Conference find it difficult to summon up the same degree of enthusiasm for the fight against abortion as they exhibit for some other issues. Even while maintaining their strong stand on principle against direct inclusion of any abortion in proposed health care reform, the Catholic bishops have similarly been quite strangely muted in opposition to some of the other morally objectionable features in most of the current health care plans proposed in the last session of Congress, features which would almost certainly have provided support for abortion and other immoral practices in some fashion (whatever happened to the principle of subsidiarity?).

Meanwhile, "respectable people" almost everywhere continue almost instinctively to turn up their noses at the prolife movement whenever they encounter it, and "enlightened opinion" generally appears to be quite certain that legalized abortion is here to stay, and ought to be here to stay.

The wonder is, in the face of all of this, that there is any prolife movement at all. To underestimate it or dismiss it because it has not yet been able to achieve all of its announced goals, however, would appear to be short-sighted in the extreme. At least some of those in the Republican Party do realize, of course, that the prolife movement cannot be ignored, and we may now even hope that this includes many of the newly elected prolife legislators. There are indeed some signs that this may be so. Evidently, though, not all the important Republican leaders and opinion makers do realize this. They fail to do so at their peril.

Far more than just not being ignored, the prolife movement's own views on matters of interest to its cause are going to have to be taken into account by those courting its votes; the movement cannot be manipulated or dictated to by those Republicans whose motive would appear to be — all too sadly understandable in one sense — to "settle" a contentious issue without alienating the party's many prolife voters too much.

Whatever its own deficiencies and even failures, however, the prolife movement has already moved far beyond the point where mere smart political operators, even though they may be sincerely trying to do the right thing — but who have not, themselves, hitherto been active in the prolife movement, nor have they contributed anything to it — can really be the ones to pretend to develop its "strategies" for it. The prolife movement generally has a very clear idea of why it exists and what it is supposed to be doing, regardless of how successful it may have been to date. Like it or not, Republicans are not only going to have to take this into account; there are some things *they* are going to have to accept as the price of continued prolife support.

From this perspective, the Kristol-Weigel approach does not in any way represent an adequate position for the Republican Party to adopt in 1996 if it expects to retain the prolife vote. It is not that prolifers are against whatever practical possibilities may exist out there to reduce abortions in the present circumstances still basically governed by the irrational *Roe* decision; prolifers are principally the very ones who continue to work on these kinds of measures out there in the state legislatures and the courts and elsewhere, after all.

Nor is it the case that prolifers are against trying to educate the public on the issue. On the contrary, it is again the prolifers themselves who have been out there doing most of the education on the issue that has been done.

But prolifers also understand that there is a basic principle involved. To guarantee to the unborn the constitutional protections which the Constitution is in any case supposed to extend to everybody is not merely some obstinate prolife "demand." It is a question of whether the U.S. Constitution is really going to continue to mean what it says and to be taken seriously or not. Maintaining the principled *goal* of constitutional and legal protection for all is, meanwhile, in no way whatsoever incompatible with promoting the more positive and incremental *approach* which Kristol-Weigel and many others want. All the things they think need to be pursued can and should be pursued right now, but without giving up the ultimate goal.

Messrs. Kristol and Weigel think the whole debate on abortion has been debased by too much "rights talk," which they say has proved to be an "electoral winner for the other side" (this was before the 1994 elections); but that has been the case at least in part because too many of those on the prolife side politically have been unable or unwilling to engage in a little more "truth talk," namely, that it just happens to be *true* that a child has a right to life — while it is *not* true that a woman has a "right" to take her child's life. When the merits of the case are considered, the prolife side wins hands down; but too few ever argue the merits if they can possibly avoid it.

Nevertheless, if the Republican Party, impelled by a basically media-created perception of the real issues involved, while ignoring the lesson of the 1994 elections, does decide to go ahead and modify or downgrade the current plank in the Republican platform calling for a constitutional amendment, then the prolifers who have done so much to support and even revitalize the Republican Party in recent years — and, especially, in the recent elections — will get the clear message that, while the party may want their votes, it does not really care enough about their cause to maintain a principled stand on it.

It does not matter that a Human Life Amendment is probably not yet possible in the present state of public opinion. Prolifers are as aware of that as anybody — although they are also keenly aware of how volatile public opinion is on the abortion issue, and, especially, of how much *ignorance* there is out there concerning the real facts about legalized abortion in our society — and about the real consequences which have followed in its wake.

However, this ignorance concerning abortion will certainly never be dispelled if prolifers themselves are ever persuaded to give up the consistent public advocacy of their cause. It is foolish to talk about "educating" the public about the evils of abortion if it has already been, in effect, conceded that abortion is henceforth to be both tolerable and legal.

While the necessary "extensive and on-going process of public persuasion" that the Kristol-Weigel proposal calls for goes on, therefore, prolifers must continue to maintain the principle on the fundamental issue at stake. Most of them will in any case not accept the minimalist position that the people merely have "a constitutional right to deliberate on the question [of abortion] in their legislatures." Although the people surely do have that right, prolifers will also have to insist that the child's right to life itself has to be maintained if the Constitution is to mean what it says.

Re-iterating that very point on all possible occasions, in fact, is a necessary *part* of the public educational process on the issue. The Kristol-Weigel proposal, however, as pundit Fred Barnes accurately noted in *The New Republic* when it was first advanced, has in reality "accepted that abortion may never be banned, just curbed." It is accommodationist by definition.

The majority of prolifers will never accept that position. And if by chance any among prolife leaders do say that they will accept such a position — perhaps flattered by the attention of political powers-that-be who usually pay so little attention of any kind to the prolife movement — those leaders will not be followed by most grassroots prolifers. The latter *know* why they are out there active in the movement, after all, and it is not merely to implement the programs political operators or policy wonks may have decided on their behalf are all that is doable or desirable at the present time.

Killing its children is something no civilized society can continue to sanction as just one more consensual public policy option.

Whether or not the Republicans agree with prolifers on this point, they would do well to get it into their heads that the prolifers themselves believe it; and they are not going to stop believing it to gain some supposed tactical or temporary political or electoral advantage.

Nor will arguments of supposed political realism or prudence persuade people who are thus motivated. Rather, political realism and prudence would seem to require that the Republican Party should take into account the real sentiments and convictions of one of the most important of its political constituencies.

8.1

The President's Choices for Surgeon General One: Jocelyn Elders

I

What by normal standards should have been the relatively non-controversial position of Surgeon General of the United States has instead become one of the most hotly contested battlegrounds in our current "culture wars." In a governmental sense, the position had long since become almost superfluous, once there was in place an Assistant Secretary for Health in the Department of Health and Human Services. Former Health, Education, and Welfare Secretary Joseph Califano has described it as "a health post that carries with it little staff, no programmatic budgets, and no clout in the federal bureaucracy." In short, there is serious question whether the position of Surgeon General should not long since have been abolished.

It was not abolished, however, either because of the Surgeon General's remembered important role in the national crusade against smoking, or because of sheer bureaucratic inertia, or, more troubling, perhaps because the liberal side in the culture wars had learned how effectively the position could be used to advance their cause.

Meanwhile, especially in recent years, the position has become mostly a "bully pulpit" — a platform for launching national crusades such as the one against smoking launched over thirty years ago by then Surgeon General Luther Terry. As things have turned out, of course, some considerably more dubious crusades have been launched since then.

The recent battle over the confirmation of Dr. Henry W. Foster, Jr., to be Surgeon General of the United States provided ample

---

The first part of this chapter, on Dr. Joycelyn Elders, appeared in *Culture Wars*, July/August, 1995; the second part, on Dr. Henry W. Foster, Jr., appeared in *Fidelity*, December, 1995.

proof, if added proof were needed, of how politicized the position had become; and this, in turn, indicated how hot our present culture wars have now become. But the fight did not begin with Dr. Foster. It did not even begin with the unlamented former Clinton Administration Surgeon General, Dr. Joycelyn Elders. It goes back at least to Ronald Reagan's unfortunate (as it turned out) pick for the job, Dr. C. Everett Koop.

As much as Dr. Elders ever did, Dr. Koop too apparently let the bully pulpit, all the attention, the ridiculous surgeon general's uniform with its gold braid, or something, go to his head. Koop turned out to be one of the most spectacular defectors in all of the culture wars, in fact, he turned out to be a kind of Kim Philby of American social conservatives.

Dr. Koop had been recruited by the Reagan Administration precisely because, at the same time that he possessed eminent medical credentials as an outstanding pediatric surgeon, he was also a practicing evangelical Christian and outspoken prolife physician — this at a time when the rest of the medical establishment had more or less gone over to the other side.

Few now remember that, as soon as Dr. Koop was nominated, the liberal-leftist ranks instantly closed ranks against him; the controversies over either the later Joycelyn Elders or the Henry Foster nominations were mild compared to the original furor over Koop's nomination, perhaps because liberal Democrats really do fight bare-knuckled for their causes, while conservative Republicans are almost always looking for ways to avoid fighting for theirs. This always present tendency is strongly re-enforced, of course, by the fact that the media tend to cheer liberal-leftist causes on, while belittling conservatives almost in the degree that they ever dare to take a stand on the morality of anything.

At any rate, Dr. Koop's nomination was bitterly contested and held up for over nine months, at a time when the early Reagan Administration was otherwise still racking up what turned out to be its most impressive achievements. Dr. Koop was contemptuously labeled "Dr. Kook" and other names even less complimentary.

At first Dr. Koop seemed to be what he had been supposed by the Reagan people to be. Then, whether because he had seen some kind of light on account of the very bitterness of the liberal opposition to him — it is amazing how liberal opposition manages to concentrate the attention of anyone who ends up on the receiving end of it — or because of a sincere conversion to the other side, Koop began taking, to the astonishment and chagrin of his original supporters, positions which were "objectively," as the Marxists used to like to say, those of the other side.

Before long, Dr. Koop was espousing causes such as sex education in kindergarten and condom ads on television. Eventually, this erstwhile prolife doctor was even saying that a pregnant woman with AIDS ought to have the "option" of an abortion. This is what the media like to call "growing in office."

In the end, Dr. Koop's principal "legacies" turned out to be his 1986 AIDS report calling for a massive, aggressive federal response to the disease, and his famous letter declaring that there was no conclusive scientific data about the possible harmful effects of abortion on women. Dr. Koop thus succeeded in divorcing medicine from morality, even more effectively than he otherwise might have done, precisely because of his Christian and conservative credentials — much as the "conservatives" Nixon and Kissinger could do what no liberal would ever have dared to do when they opened up diplomatic relations with Communist China; or much as the "conservative" Charles De Gaulle could alone bring the Algerian War to an end for France because he had come to power with the support of the very right-wing ultras who insisted on Algeria remaining "French."

When reproached by those who had been instrumental in putting him in office in the first place, Dr. Koop replied with the typical jargon of those who believe that medicine and public policy can be divorced from morality: "I am the Surgeon General of the heterosexuals and the homosexuals, of the young and the old, of the moral or the immoral, the married and the unmarried." To his fellow Christians, Dr. Koop announced (in his view, no doubt coruscatingly): "I am the surgeon general, not the chaplain of the Public Health Service."

This was the *conservative* surgeon general, then! We may well deplore, but we can hardly be surprised about, what the position he held has become since. But Dr. Koop had demonstrated, as Dr. Luther Terry had shown much earlier on the smoking issue, that the office was ideal for putting the federal government behind advocacy of a cause.

How and why did it become such a battleground, though? Why did this third-tier position in the government, even if it did have its uses for advocacy, become such a hotly contested strategic objective for both sides in the culture wars? Why, in particular, did the Clinton Administration expend so much of its energy and credit trying to get or keep such obviously unsuitable Surgeons General as Dr. Elders and Dr. Foster? It would be hard to defend either of these two on the basis of any normal political calculations whatsoever. Their pretensions to be able to fill the job, indeed, would have been ludicrous, if the whole situation surrounding them had not been so tragic. What was at stake?

What was at stake was the validation and legitimation of legalized abortion in our society, and, behind legalized abortion, the validation and legitimation of the sexual revolution, which strictly requires legalized abortion in order to exist and perpetuate itself. Without modern contraceptives, and legalized abortion to back them up, the contemporary sexual revolution is not even thinkable, let alone doable. Given this hard fact, the liberal side in the culture wars therefore understands that legalized abortion must be maintained at all costs.

In order to maintain legalized abortion, the nation's chief medical officer must be a convinced proabortion physician; and this chief medical officer must also have for the country at large a message which includes the validation and legitimation of our current regime of legalized abortion. This was the all-important cause which made this otherwise dispensable federal position a critical one.

It is especially important that it be a "medical" officer who validates abortion. The Supreme Court shamelessly reduced the whole issue of abortion to a "medical" question between a woman and her doctor, prescinding from any morality in the matter. And now, once in place, the principle that a woman has a constitutional "right" to elect an abortion, courtesy of the Supreme Court, cannot in any way be conceded by those who are proabortion. Such a concession of principle could well mark the beginning of a rollback, both of legalized abortion, and of the sexual revolution that lies behind it — and that would be simply unthinkable.

Hence the nomination of a Dr. Henry Foster had to be defended at all costs; if at all possible it had to prevail, regardless of both the political cost, and the manifest harm, that defending such an unsuitable and, indeed, quite hopelessly unqualified, candidate turned out to involve. Generally speaking, politicians are the first to try to avoid defending the indefensible; but that principle has certainly not been true in the case of both of President Clinton's choices for Surgeon General. Why? Why should the Surgeon General position be any different from any other high-level federal political appointment?

The problem for the liberal-leftist side in the current phase of our culture wars did not begin with Foster. The earlier saga of Dr. Joycelyn Elders is at least as significant, and bears retelling in the light of the Foster fiasco. Both of these bungled Clinton Administration choices of black professionals throw considerable light, in fact, upon how the culture wars are going in at least one crucial sector of the battlefront.

II

Dr. Joycelyn Elders was one of the original Clinton Administration people the new president brought with him to Washington. Although her name was not yet the national household word it was going to become, there was never a time when she was not an embarrassment to the President, if only Bill Clinton had been capable of realizing it; but it already explains a great deal about this President and his administration, to note that the young President never did seem to realize what an embarrassment she was. By the time he decided to appoint her to a high and visible public position in Washington, she should have already been an entirely known quantity for him; nothing she ever said as Surgeon General could possibly have come as much of a surprise to him, for she had said it all before, and then some.

While governor of Arkansas, Bill Clinton had appointed Dr. Elders, a pediatric endocrinologist, to be director of the Arkansas Health Department. This was in 1987. On paper she probably seemed to be a good choice, quite apart from the fact that she was a black professional woman, and thus she fit doubly into what was no doubt already by then Bill Clinton's consistent affirmative action approach to government appointments. But in addition to practicing medicine as a black woman, she had also been on the faculty at the University of Arkansas for 26 years and even had some 150 scholarly research papers to her credit.

She was also already known even back then (although to a relatively limited circle) for the kinds of distinctly non-scholarly, and, indeed, quite outrageous, statements, usually having to do with sex, with which the whole country would be regaled after she was named Surgeon General. Her pre-Surgeon-General-era remarks included, for example, her glib talk-show recommendation that the birth control implant Norplant should be provided to prostitutes addicted to drugs "so that they could still use sex if they must to buy drugs" and not become pregnant.

Then there was her early characterization, in the American Medical Association's *American Medical News,* of teen-aged unmarried mothers as "America's newest slave class." She even once called those opposed to abortion "very religious non-Christians," and said that "they love little babies, as long as they're in somebody's else's uterus."

These were neither lapses nor isolated statements; they were strictly vintage Elders, as Governor Clinton already knew very well. Right after her appointment as Arkansas health director, a Little Rock reporter asked Dr. Elders how she proposed to combat teen pregnancy. She replied with the standard contemporary dogma that school-based clinics offering a wide range of "services" to teen-agers would be one way.

"Would these clinics hand out condoms to the kids?" the reporter wondered.

"Well, I'm not going to put them on their lunch trays, but yes," she replied.

Later, recalling the moment, Joycelyn Elders was to laugh heartily while recounting the reaction of young Governor William Jefferson Clinton: "I'd say his face turned about the color of this dress I'm wearing," she remembered. She was wearing a dress somewhere between purple and red at the time. "I realized I had just dropped my governor in an ocean of jello," she remarked, going on with her story. And then, according to her own account, Bill Clinton "sort of cleared his throat. He said, slowly, 'I support Dr. Elders.'"

When we consider this president's choices for Surgeon General, we should never think in terms of his possible ignorance, of inadvertence, or of his being blindsided by his people. No: Bill Clinton has consciously chosen the kind of candidate he *wants* to be Surgeon General. There can be no mistake about this. When they were both still back in Arkansas, Dr. Elders would go to him and ask, "Governor, should I back off? 'No, no, Joycelyn. I love it. Keep it up,'" he would say. And when he selected her for the post of surgeon general, Bill Clinton actually said to her: "Joycelyn, I want you to do for the whole country what you've done for Arkansas."

This strong Clinton support for a woman who was destined to give the term "loose cannon" new meaning was nothing if not consistent. After she had been Surgeon General for nearly a year — and, by then, her name *had* become a national household word! — syndicated columnist Robert Novak reported that "President Clinton has rejected requests from the Catholic Archbishop of Washington to disavow Joycelyn Elders comments about sexuality, signaling that she must be treated with kid gloves, no matter how embarrassing her statements." (It bears recalling that when the Cardinal Archbishop of Washington persisted in his complaint against her, the Clinton White House simply persisted in its defense of her.)

"When she recently said the reason more federal funds should be spent on AIDS than on cancer was that its victims are younger," Novak went on in his column, "her superiors rolled their eyes but could not reprimand her. 'The president feels very strongly about Joycelyn Elders.'" So Novak was informed by a high-ranking Clinton Administration official.

This seemed obvious. In another interview, widely disseminated to a mass audience by the *USA Weekend* Sunday supplement magazine, Dr. Elders herself claimed that both the president and the first lady "think I'm enough of a visionary to know what I need to do. I've known them both for many years, and the president has never asked me to speak out or take certain positions, and he has never asked me not to speak out on anything."

Considering some of the things she did speak out on in the course of her tenure as Surgeon General, it is scarcely any credit to the president that he allowed such license to someone as irresponsible as Dr. Elders proved to be. The U.S. Senate deserves no credit here, either. Even before she was finally confirmed by the Senate to her position as the U.S. Government's top-ranking medical officer, she had surely already delivered herself of enough of her trademark outrageous statements to have killed the nomination of anybody else.

But these outrageous statements did not kill the nomination of Joycelyn Elders; she was always a special case, inexplicable on the basis of any normal political calculations.

III

More than a few groups and individuals attempted to prevent the confirmation of Dr. Joycelyn Elders as Surgeon General of the

United States. In one unusual display of across-the-spectrum ecumenism, for example, the Catholic League for Religious and Civil Rights joined the Christian Life Commission of the Southern Baptist Convention to co-sponsor a joint statement strongly opposing the Elders nomination. Among the typical Elders utterances which this joint statement objected to were: the perennial Elders "brag" that "I tell every girl that when she goes out on a date, put a condom in her purse"; and the even more famous Elders statement that "we've had driver's ed for our kids" — as she opined on April 2, 1993 — "We've taught them what to do in the front seat of the car, but not what to do in the back seat."

In yet another sally on this latter subject, later on, when she was Surgeon General, she strongly countered opponents of modern "value-free" sex education, who believe this kind of instruction actually contributes to sexual permissiveness, rather than providing any remedy for it. She remarked about sex education, characteristically, that "nobody has to teach us how to have sex. God taught us how to have sex."

This typical Elders public "frankness" about sex and condom use — which until very recently would have violated what were still strong moral and social taboos — is supposed to be justified today by the need to curtail teen pregnancies and the spread of sexually transmitted diseases, especially AIDS. In reality, all that has been achieved by bringing the discussion of condoms and condom use out into the open is that — the discussion of condoms and condom use is now out in the open. The taboo on discussing these things in public has now been broken down; it is now just one more taboo that has gone the way of so many others taboos.

But this is all that has been accomplished: it has had scarcely any effect at all in curtailing either teen pregnancies or AIDS, if, indeed, it has not had a net negative effect because some people may have been wrongly persuaded that condoms are efficacious when they really are not. Meanwhile, the message that any kind of sex that the individual chooses to engage in is now acceptable in our society *has* been strongly re-enforced. At the same time, the things said by people such as Elders, who have abandoned traditional morality, are further legitimated; they are allowed to get away with saying things that would once have resulted in the instant social demonization of practically anybody else on any other subject.

But since our society has now at least tacitly agreed in advance that everything having to do with sex must now be allowed, and that no restrictive-type morality can any longer be applied by society to any freely chosen sexual activity, it is supposed to follow that all of today's advocates of sexual freedom must now be allowed to trumpet their "solutions" featuring condoms and such on prime time television as well as in the classrooms of mere children.

In reality, the catastrophic social consequences which have resulted from our society's practical abandonment of any prescriptive sexual morality remain very much with us. Nevertheless the thinking seems to be that, if the morality is gone, the "taboos" obviously have to go too; it's logical, after all. Thus, in the case of an Elders, her "frankness" simply gets chalked up to "candor" or "feistiness," and nobody thinks anything more about it.

As Arkansas state health director, Dr. Joycelyn Elders kept on her desk a "condom tree" — an artificial plant constructed out of wrapped, curled condoms mounted in a clay pot. She labeled it the "Ozark Rubber Plant" (it had yet another suggestive label on it which could not be printed here!). That Dr. Elders earned her sobriquet "the condom queen," no one can dispute. What speaks even more eloquently about the moral standards of our times, however, is that she became something of a modern cultural heroine in the process; in some of the backwoods fever swamps of liberalism-leftism, apparently, there are still people who believe that Puritanism and the Victorian Age are not yet dead, and still need to be fought against; but there surely cannot be included very many people who either read the daily newspapers or watch the evening news.

In opposing the nomination of Dr. Elders to be Surgeon General, the Catholic League-Southern Baptist joint statement was able to point out that "under her tenure as director of the Arkansas Health Department, the teen pregnancy rate rose by 12 per cent. . .What is most striking about this figure, however, is that it is a complete turnaround in the period just prior to Dr. Elders' tenure, when the teen-pregnancy rates had actually declined."

This joint statement further pointed out that Dr. Elders had knowingly ordered the continued distribution of a specific lot of condoms understood to be defective, thus playing "rubber roulette" with the recipients of these condoms, as one press account characterized it. It had been established that the condom lot in question had a defective rate more than ten times higher than the limit which had been set by the agency itself. Dr. Elders, however, decided not to inform the public about these leaky condoms; she justified the continued distribution of the whole lot of them on the grounds that "public confidence" in condoms might have been undermined if the health department had ever acknowledged that some of these free "health products" being given out were in fact defective.

Maintaining "public confidence" — more commonly called "stone-walling" in other famous cases such as Watergate — was evidently more important to Dr. Elders than responsibility, honesty, or truth; and since the subject, again, was sex, Dr. Elders was naturally not held to any of these other standards.

When questioned about this particular decision at the Senate hearing on her nomination, Dr. Elders airily dismissed the whole business by claiming that "as a public health decision, you try to do the greatest good for the greatest number of people." Jeremy Bentham himself could not have articulated better the totally utilitarian morality which our modern sexual freedom fighters espouse and promote — and which our government now promotes and subsidizes.

The Catholic League-Southern Baptist joint statement, which vainly attempted to head off the confirmation of Joycelyn Elders, added its voice to a veritable chorus of complaints against the nominee when, among the many statements of hers which it deplored, it included the one on abortion which the Arkansas public health director had made at a so-called prochoice rally in January, 1992. On that occasion, Dr. Elders had said that "we would like for the right-to-life, antichoice groups to really get over their love affair with the fetus, and start supporting the children."

On this occasion, she accused the Catholic Church in particular of being "silent" and "doing nothing" about everything from slavery to the holocaust, and added: "Look at who is fighting the prochoice movement: a celibate, male-dominated Church!"

When Cardinal John O'Connor of New York protested, and declared Dr. Elders to be "unfit for high public office"; and when Baltimore Archbishop (now Cardinal) William H. Keeler, the sitting president of the National Conference of Catholic Bishops, then followed up on his colleague's protest by writing directly to President Clinton about her "contemptuous" characterization of the Catholic

Church, Dr. Elders was evidently finally prevailed upon by somebody in the Clinton White House to do something in response; and so she did then finally issue an apology of sorts.

At that particular point, of course, a vote on her confirmation was imminent in the U.S. Senate, after all. So she wrote an extremely self-serving reply to Archbishop Keeler saying that "*if* my statements have caused any offense, I sincerely apologize." She did not admit that her statements *had* caused any offense, though there can be no doubt that they were grossly offensive.

In the event, though, none of these things prevented her from being confirmed by the Senate as Surgeon General of the United States. Such are the public moral standards to which the perceived inevitability and permanence of the sexual revolution have now caused us to sink in the United States — and which few public figures, including most churchmen, generally dare to question publicly in any fundamental way. And even when they do, as was proved in the case of Dr. Elders, it turns out not to matter very much anyway.

IV

In retrospect, it seems pretty clear that no champion of "sexual freedom" such as Dr. Joycelyn Elders had proved herself to be could possibly have *failed* in the climate that has prevailed in recent years in all our public life. Certainly none of the other objections raised about the fitness and qualifications for high public office of Dr. Elders seem to have counted any more than "rust on the scales," as the Prophet Isaiah poetically puts it. Nothing would do but that this person should be Surgeon General of the United States.

Yet there were plenty of other facts on the record against her, any one of which, again, might well have sunk the nomination of any other candidate for any other office.

For example, Dr. Elders had been among a group of former members of the Board of the National Bank of Arkansas who had been taken into court in a lawsuit on the grounds of "negligent management" and "bad lending and investment practices." The bank in question was evidently found by the U.S. Comptroller of the Currency to have in fact been badly mismanaged during the tenure of the Board on which Dr. Elders had served. This is the kind of "moral issue," of course, into which the members of the U.S. Senate normally do love to sink their teeth, usually egged on by the media, which also find in this sort of thing their idea of a grave moral issue. In the case of Dr. Elders, though, the issue was passed over in almost complete silence.

It transpired too that Dr. Elders had a financial interest in a Little Rock Nursing Home that was not reflected on her financial disclosure forms for 1991, 1992, and 1993. Imagine: financial disclosure forms filled out improperly! — another ready-made, cut-and-dried contemporary "moral issue" for the U.S. Senate to probe! This is exactly the sort of thing that, today, is typically represented as deserving the same moral stigma that used to be aroused only by crimes involving moral turpitude perpetrated against innocent and defenseless victims. On this occasion, however, no hard questions from senators were allowed to embarrass the nominee unduly; nor did any baying journalistic hounds set off in pursuit of her.

There was more. Yet another earlier misstep of hers of the type which, in Washington, can be fatal, was the fact that Dr. Elders, after being named by President Clinton, was apparently involved in some "double-dipping" before completing her old duties and taking up her new ones. Before her confirmation and actual entry on duty as Surgeon General, that is, she served as a paid "consultant" to the U.S. Department of Health and Human Services, meanwhile continuing to draw her full salary as Arkansas health director. At her Senate hearings, she explained that she came to Washington only on "paid vacation days," and that there was nothing illegal about the arrangement anyway (thus implicitly admitting, it would seem, that she *had* been double-dipping). But this too was overlooked in her case.

Finally, it seems that Dr. Elders' husband, a high school athletic coach, had failed to pay social security taxes for the nurse hired to take care of his ninety-plus-year-old mother — exactly the misdeed and infraction which had caused the withdrawal of President Clinton's first two nominees for attorney general, Zoe Baird and Kimba Wood! Again, with the decline of what was once universally understood to be morality, this is the kind of "moral issue" that is most frequently emphasized in public life, especially, no doubt, because Social Security remains one of the few things in our society that is "sacred" any longer.

So, at her confirmation hearings, Dr. Elders was let off on this hook too; she explained that she "was not involved in these day-to-day affairs. Maybe I should have been, but I wasn't."

Attempts by Senators who opposed her nomination to discredit her on any of these grounds proved unavailing. At her hearings, Republican Senator Dan Coats of Indiana kept trying anyway. For example, he asked her to explain why she had decided not to go public concerning the high failure rate that had been discovered in at least one lot of the condoms that were distributed by the Arkansas health department. He might as well have been asking her if, as Surgeon General, she planned to have the famous Surgeon General's Warning Label placed on packages of condoms as they are placed on packages of cigarettes (and as the president of the Catholic League for Religious and Civil Rights, William A. Donohue, has seriously and aptly proposed!).

Dr. Elders lamely explained that it was difficult to get young men to use condoms in the first place, and that she did not want "to make anybody afraid of condoms." She maintained stoutly that, under the same circumstances, she would make the same choice again. In her case, this attitude was instantly chalked up to courage and forthrightness rather than to any shocking malfeasance and misfeasance in office.

We can only imagine what a Senate panel would think, say, of a candidate to head the FAA who failed to reveal to the public that one in five flights of a particular aircraft were destined to crash. It is doubtful whether the desire not "to make anyone afraid of flying" would be considered an adequate excuse in such a case.

But the reality is that *condoms are lethal* in about this same proportion as a so-called protection against AIDS. But where elective sex is concerned, making this point does not count: it has already, in effect, been *decided* by society that elective sexual activity is to remain entirely free of any restrictions, especially moral restrictions. The rules that would apply anywhere else are not to apply here.

Reflecting the same widespread current social attitude (and presumed universal consensus) in favor of permissive sex, the Senate Labor and Human Resources Committee proved to be adamantly determined to see Dr. Elders' nomination approved, regardless of how she may have acted in the defective condom affair, or in other similar affairs; the Committee was as determined to confirm Dr. Elders as the White House was determined to appoint her — no matter what the opposition might be or what the evidence brought against her was. This would turn out to be a pattern.

At a certain point, the chairman of the Senate Labor and Human Resources Committee curtly cut off a no doubt still incredulous Senator Coats, who continued to imagine that the nominee's record should have something to do with whether or not she should be confirmed, and that the whole Senate hearing process should bear some causal relation to the outcome. Senator Coats therefore went on questioning the nominee, but the committee chairman interrupted him: "You've listened to the answer three times," the chairman said at one point.

But the Indiana senator could apparently not get it straight that it did not *matter* what Dr. Elders' answers were. Shortly after that, the committee chairman in question adjourned the hearings. No surprise: the chairman was none other than Democratic Senator Edward M. Kennedy of Massachusetts, who had taken a personal and protective interest all along in shepherding Dr. Elders through her confirmation hearings, personally intervening to help her evade or blunt the force of as many obstacles as possible.

Nothing would do in the mind of a "new-morality" man such as Senator Kennedy but that Dr. Joycelyn Elders should be the Surgeon General of the United States. The committee chairman championed that viewpoint entirely, consistent with other positions he has taken (and exemplified).

The Elders hearings were held in July, 1993. In September, when the full Senate voted on the nomination, Dr. Elders was confirmed by a vote of 65 to 34. It was a foregone conclusion: she represented, in rather pure form, the philosophy to which, with the advent of the sexual revolution, the country had more or less decided to go over — for how long a period still remains to be seen.

Certainly, at the moment, we not seeing very many effective protests about it, any more than we are seeing very many effective protests against legalized abortion in establishment institutions such as the U.S. Senate.

V

It was not until the Clinton Administration came into office that the government finally got around to admitting that, yes, the country now had definitely bought into the sexual revolution; and legalized abortion, in particular, was definitely now here to stay. The facts and statistics already strongly showed this, of course, but up to this point there had been a strong reluctance to concede, openly and officially, what the facts and statistics bore out.

President Clinton had certainly not run for office calling for any new morality; he ran on "the economy, stupid," as was notorious. The whole "values" question during the 1992 elections, in fact, was used only to show how "shrill" and "strident" some members of the Republican right were in somehow imagining that a return to traditional morality might involve a few benefits for society. For many others, and at least for the time being, traditional morality appeared to represent an entirely lost cause, its champions having come to be almost automatically labeled as "extremists."

It is true that, prior to the election of President Clinton, there had been more than a few rumbles to the effect that the government now did recognize that traditional morality was indeed a lost cause. The office of the Surgeon General had even provided the locus for some of these same rumbles. The White House wanted a permissive sex educator and proabortionist in the position precisely because it provided such a ideal forum to preach the new morality (as a "medical" benefit, of course. What else?).

Dr. C. Everett Koop, as we have noted, had already provided more than a small indication of how valuable the position could be for promoting the new morality and the new permissive society; he also provided, not incidentally, an example of the damage that can be done to society when the nation's chief medical officer prescinds from the nation's long moral tradition and pretends to be able to validate a sexual revolution on purely "medical" or "scientific" grounds.

Well before the arrival on the scene of Dr. Elders, Dr. Koop had already put the prestige and influence of the office of Surgeon General of the United States behind some of the dubious causes stemming from our contemporary sexual revolution. So Joycelyn Elders was not the first Surgeon General to provide official government sanction for today's typical divorce of sexual behavior from morality. Dr. Elders did enthusiastically follow up, however, proclaiming both the ideal and the fact of the new morality. She colorfully articulated for the masses the new reality that the Sixth and Ninth Commandments had now finally been abrogated in America, at least as far as "official" America was concerned. Henceforth anybody *could* covet his neighbor's wife — or anybody else for that matter. As for adultery, could it any longer even be classified as a crime anywhere, regardless of what the law books might continue to say in certain backward jurisdictions?

Modern thinkers and philosophers have expatiated for us at length on the modern "autonomous person," the man (and, today, especially, the woman) who is the measure of all things and who fashions his or her own new morality, especially in matters related to sex. Friedrich Nietzsche scarcely dreamed of all the things out there beyond good and evil that we have seen since his time!

Comes now a Joycelyn Elders and announces the entry of the modern autonomous person into prosaic everyday American life, as representing, indeed, the new moral norm of society — and all this with the sanction and encouragement of the federal government! Perhaps even Nietzsche would have rubbed his eyes in disbelief! Joycelyn Elders represents what happens when Nietzsche's "transvaluation of all values" is brought down to the level of Karl Marx's formerly oppressed masses subsisting on various kinds of opium.

In her June, 1993, *USA Weekend* Sunday supplement interview, Dr. Elders articulated the new modern moral understanding of things, bluntly and without beating around the bush. *Inter alia*, she affirmed the following propositions:

— "Sexuality is up to the individual; it's not for the rest of us to decide."

— "Sex [is] pleasurable, and it's not just for procreation."

— "None of us is good enough, or knows enough, to make decisions about other people's sexual preferences." (This last proposition was formulated in connection with Dr. Elder's view that the Boy Scouts should admit declared homosexuals and the Girl Scouts avowed lesbians.)

What are we dealing with here? What we have here is a plain and unvarnished statement, for mass consumption, by the Surgeon General of the United States, that henceforth the U.S. Government approves and endorses the view that no moral restrictions are henceforth to be placed by American society upon any type of human sexual activity that individuals may elect to engage in.

The surgeon general not only does not exclude, but specifically includes, children in her casual, sweeping dismissal of millennia of sexual rules, restrictions, and mores such have been enjoined by every known society prior to our own. A necessary corollary to her wide-open permissive position, of course, is that the very idea or concept of "moral corruption" through the use of sex is no longer even intelligible on her terms.

This has apparently long been the view of some our self-selected elites. The same general outlook is often simply taken for granted in contemporary Hollywood movies or on broadcast network programs: if two people are attracted to each other, they go to bed; that's all and that's it; no complications or consequences, such as those which in fact occur in real life, are typically portrayed. "Doing What Comes Naturally" would be the new national anthem except that, where sex is concerned, what is *un*natural is now sanctioned as well!

There is no way, of course, that any society or civilization can ever operate on this basis. But there can be a time lag, even a considerable one, before people find this out or admit it. America today seems to be taking her own sweet time about it, for example. Meanwhile, all the horrendous statistics that follow from acting on this philosophy of life are out there: the infidelity, the divorces, the disturbed children, the illegitimacy, the abortions, the sexually transmitted diseases, AIDS, etc., etc. And these statistics are even readily cited and insisted upon when it is a question of raising money, getting a government appropriation, starting some remedial program to be run by social workers, putting condom ads on TV, or whatever.

But the same statistics are generally kept quite separate from the culture's generally positive presentation of all the advantages of the already taken-for-granted new sexual freedom. In this context, Madonna-type songs warning "daddy" not to "preach" rule the airwaves (as if anyone *were* preaching any longer. . .).

The maintenance of a status quo of sexual freedom such as the present one logically requires the availability of all modern technological contraceptive and abortifacient means — with legal surgical abortion as a necessary back-up. The new sexual freedom now considered to be a fundamental human and constitutional right would be unthinkable without these means. For there *are,* in reality, serious consequences stemming from this kind of untrammeled sexual "expression," or to any utilization of the sexual faculties, and so there has to be some way of eliminating these consequences. That is why the votaries of the new sexual freedom become so frantic whenever the so-called constitutional right to abortion is ever questioned. Without legalized abortion, the whole modern sexually permissive view of the world would fairly soon be seen to be untenable.

That is why the issue of legalized abortion, no matter how much almost everybody may try to evade or avoid it, is really at the heart of the whole contemporary debate about "values" in modern America. It is also why this debate about "values" itself cannot go on indefinitely yielding to issues of economics, taxes, and the like. At the moment our society is coughing and choking and retching uncontrollably on the basically economic and political medicine our leaders, including especially our conservative leaders, keep on trying to offer us for what really ails our society.

What principally assails and threatens our society today, what threatens to make any civilized society impossible, in fact, and perhaps sooner than anyone imagines, is — let us say it plainly — massive and publicly-sanctioned immorality. It is the idea that people can just do what they think they have decided they want to do, without society attempting to place any moral restrictions on them. *This* idea is only going to continue to make things worse — until such time as the leaders of our society finally do realize that the problem has to be faced and remedied; it is certainly not going to go away by itself.

Meanwhile, giving a bully pulpit to such as Joycelyn Elders to allow her to go on promoting the very way of life from which America is currently strangling only underlines the degree of decadence into which we have sunk. Her flamboyance, along with her highly touted "frankness," similarly underlines the degree to which she has consistently been part of the problem rather than part of the solution.

In the end, she turns out to be nothing but a rather gaudy front for the prototypical degenerate institution of our age: Planned Parenthood. Once the various layers of pungent onionskin have been peeled off her often colorful rhetoric, her basic message turns out to the same message Planned Parenthood purveys: "All I want is every child in America to be a planned and wanted child," she has said (as if even God could ever guarantee this to anyone).

In the more than two decades that have passed since the Supreme Court legalized abortion, Americans should have learned that the necessary corollary to the Planned Parenthood message that every child should be planned and wanted is that any child who has *not* been thus "planned" and is therefore not "wanted," by that fact alone, no longer enjoys any right to life at all. So far, America has been obstinately and, indeed, willfully, obtuse in refusing to learn this lesson.

But Dr. Joycelyn Elders understands it perfectly. Her defense of legalized abortion has been an integral part of her total position. "We've got to fight to get our post-coital contraceptives available in government-funded family-planning clinics," she has said. But there is no such thing as a "post-coital contraceptive." What she and the Planned Parenthood legions call post-coital contraceptives, acting as they do after conception, would necessarily have to be abortifacients, as Dr. Elders, a physician, must know. This does not bother her. Speaking of Norplant, Depo-Provera, RU-486, female condoms, and the like, she has declared: "We've got to have all of them, if we are going to be able to take care of all the problems that we face with low-income women. . ."

This totally utilitarian, indeed "mechanical," approach to low-income women, or to any other women, will never result in anything but making our current problems worse; for this kind of approach represents a radical denial, on the most fundamental level, of the human dignity of women in particular. . .

VI

When the end finally came for Dr. Joycelyn Elders as surgeon general, as it did in December, 1994, it was really an anti-climax. The particular "outrageous statement" which caused her to be fired, while bad enough, in absolute terms, was no worse than other, similar statements which she had been regularly making.

What she said on this occasion was said in answer to a question by an AIDS activist, who had been commenting on how "the campaign against AIDS [had] already destroyed many taboos about discussion of sex in public." Given the new climate of openness created by the abandonment of the old taboos, this AIDS activist wondered whether masturbation should not now be something to be taught in the schools. Dr. Elders replied: "I think that [masturbation] is something that is part of human sexuality and it's part of something that perhaps should be taught. . ."

Far from this being a novel idea in contemporary society, the kind of classroom sex education which Planned Parenthood and Joycelyn Elders alike favor and promote has *always* included telling children as young as five about masturbation; educators in the field are perfectly well aware of this and are apparently not generally alarmed by it. Alarmed parents, however, have been steadily branded as kooks for years now for attempting to get across to responsible officials, if there still are any such, that such things as masturbation *are* being taught in this way, precisely, to children in so-called value-free sex education classes. Anybody who imagines that modern sex education — or, euphemistically, "family life education" — is still about the birds and the bees is back in a 1950s time warp. Sex education has long since moved far, far beyond that.

Nevertheless, Dr. Elders' overt statement in favor of teaching masturbation in the schools was used as a pretext to get rid of her, once the White House had finally decided it wanted to get rid of her. In making the request for her resignation, President Clinton stated that "his own convictions" were at variance with what Dr. Elders was now saying about masturbation. What seemed likely, however, was that Republican gains in the November, 1994, were what finally caused the White House to focus on what nearly everybody else realized was the continuing embarrassment of Dr. Elders. Up to that point she had been able to say pretty much whatever she liked — she had even called for the legalization of drugs! — but there had never been any consequences.

Prior to the 1994 elections, in September, 1994, there had even been introduced into Congress a resolution with 44 co-sponsors calling for her resignation. Later, Republican Congressman Cliff Stearns of Florida persuaded 87 Republican members of Congress to co-sign with him a letter to President Clinton calling for the same thing. None of this availed. The position of Dr. Joycelyn Elders remained "safe" prior to the 1994 elections.

After the elections, however, the atmosphere became very different. By then also the White House chief of staff was Leon Panetta, a former California Democratic Congressman thought to be wise to the ways of Washington and shrewd in his understanding of what President Clinton needed. From a political point of view, the president no doubt *did* need — among other things — to be divested of the particular albatross named Joycelyn Elders; but then he had surely "needed" this for a long time without ever apparently understanding that he needed it. But if his new and shrewd chief of staff now thought that the departure of Dr. Elders was important to the viability of his presidency, then who was Bill Clinton to question this?

In no way did this appear to mean, however, that there now existed in the Clinton White House any new or increased understanding of the reasons why someone like Dr. Elders could never be anything but bad for America — could never accomplish anything, indeed, except help fuel the on-going culture wars. It did not appear that anything whatsoever had been changed in President Clinton's understanding of the moral issues currently facing America. All that had happened was that a perceived embarrassment to his presidency, which he had resolutely refused to admit up to that point, had finally, belatedly, been recognized and dealt with, mostly at the insistence of the people around him — but it did not appear that the young President himself even then understood *what* an embarrassment and a liability she had been.

One question that hung over the whole Elders saga, as it would over the whole Henry Foster saga later, was this: how much did the fact that both these physicians were *black* have to do with the travesties that their respective nominations became? This was surely an important factor in the calculations of the Clinton Administration, and it was true in both cases, because it generally meant that no opponent of either nomination could ever pull out all the stops in opposing either one of them. These particular nominees had to be treated with kid gloves. No matter how valid and principled the objections to them may have been, or how truly deficient and compromised their own records, bringing these things out would still always and inescapably be viewed as an "attack" on a black person, and one only too likely to be viewed as "racist."

These are simply the facts of life in the United States today, as the disgraceful O.J. Simpson murder trial has dramatically brought out. The Clinton Administration could therefore always be confident of promoting the kind of proabortion candidate desired for Surgeon General at considerably less political cost if a black were named. It had become a distinct advantage to name a black, in fact.

This is just one more of the numerous ways in which the sexual revolution has continued to be promoted in our society as a supposed legitimate child of the civil rights revolution. Unfortunately, the child in question is *il*legitimate — and the blacks are all the while the ones who are suffering disproportionately from the deleterious, indeed disastrous, effects of it all.

So the Clinton Administration may have understood some things well enough; but these things unfortunately did not include the moral state of the nation or its real need for moral reform. When the

President got around to naming a successor to Dr. Elders, in February, 1995, it would once again become clear, that not only did the President not "get it" about all this, the people around him did not really get it either. Apparently nothing essential was really going to change.

8.2

The President's Choices for Surgeon General Two: Henry W. Foster, Jr.

I

Early in 1995, the Clinton Administration's attempt to name a new Surgeon General of the United States as quickly as possible demonstrated that neither the President nor those around him, like the royalist *émigrés* of French Revolution fame, had ever really learned anything — in this case, from the disgrace of having a Dr. Joycelyn Elders as the nation's chief medical officer during the first half of the Clinton Administration. Nor had they forgotten anything either, apparently, about what their real agenda for America was, regardless of what they might put out for public consumption.

Only belatedly and reluctantly had the irrepressible, but also spectacularly irresponsible, Dr. Elders finally been asked to leave, the pretext being one of her trademark "outrageous statements" about sex with which the whole country had become familiar by then. But the statement which caused her to be fired was scarcely any more outrageous than many of the other things she had been regularly and consistently saying while serving as Surgeon General, thus regularly identifying the Clinton Administration thereby with the most extreme manifestations of today's sexual revolution.

The particular statement that happened to bring her down just happened to come at a politically difficult time for the President. It came after the 1994 elections, in which Republicans had won control of both houses of Congress. So Dr. Elders was finally allowed just to go quietly — uncharacteristic as doing anything quietly was for her.

The White House waited until after the new Republican Congress had been installed and the State of the Union address was over, however, before trying to replace her. Then, February being Black

History Month, the White House made history of its own of a sort, as the whole country would shortly come to realize, by announcing the nomination of another Arkansas-born black physician to be Surgeon General; he was Henry W. Foster, Jr., of the Washington-based Association of Academic Health Centers but, formerly, of the Meharry Medical College in Nashville, Tennessee.

Apparently the quota-conscious Clinton Administration had come to see the Surgeon General position as now "reserved" for minorities, and Dr. Foster was therefore eminently qualified on this score, although, as things turned out, it was hard for an outsider to see what *other* reasons the president could possibly have had for naming Dr. Foster. With almost dizzying speed, the Foster nomination turned into perhaps the most deplorable and embarrassing nomination to date of an administration that already had succeeded in getting an Attorney General confirmed only on the third try, and had spectacularly failed, with maximum negative publicity, in getting nominees confirmed for the positions of Secretary of Defense and Assistant Attorney General for Civil Rights, respectively. Similarly, a candidate to head the CIA would soon have to withdraw in the face of public criticism.

The nomination of Dr. Henry W. Foster, Jr., though, proved to be even more ludicrously unsuitable and inappropriate than any of these other failed nominations. Of all the possible medical specialties that might have been considered after the Elders-era controversies over condoms, sex in the back seat of the car, and alleged "love affairs with the fetus," obstetrics and gynecology was surely the medical specialty most likely to breed further controversy of the same type.

So, naturally, obstetrics and gynecology turned out to be the specialty the White House selected. What else? The Clinton Administration had already long since proved itself to be almost totally oblivious to any of the problems or sensitivities in this particular area, no doubt because the Clinton Administration actually *believes* — the evidence for this is overwhelming — in the permissive kind of world represented by the two nominees for the post of Surgeon General which this president has made.

However, the chairman of the Senate committee that would be examining Dr. Foster's qualifications, Republican Senator Nancy Landon Kassebaum of Kansas, was acutely sensitive to the problems posed by this particular nomination. While Senator Kassebaum has herself consistently voted the proabortion line in the Senate, she was at any rate sensitive to the problem; and so, according to press reports, at a meeting on welfare reform, she informally asked Clinton's Secretary of Health and Human Services (HHS), Donna Shalala, whether Dr. Foster had ever performed abortions.

In yet one more instance of the apparently inexpugnable moral obtuseness of most Clinton Administration people, Secretary Shalala reportedly asked: "Why? Should that matter?" Well, whether it mattered or not, Senator Kassebaum wanted to know.

Dr. Foster himself later explained to Ted Koppel on ABC's TV program *Nightline* what happened next: "The day before the president announced his intention to nominate, I was asked by someone in the administration if I had done abortions. And I said, 'Yes.' And the one I remembered most was a woman who had AIDS. And that was essentially the end of the conversation."

From the fact that Dr. Foster remembered doing one abortion in particular, Donna Shalala and her people in HHS apparently concluded that he had only done "one" abortion in his entire medical career, a career spanning several decades. And so that was the word passed back to Senator Kassebaum: yes, Dr. Foster had done "one" abortion. However, this particular answer turned out to be an especially momentous error on the part of the Clinton Administration, since, although many United States senators can be found to tolerate and even to promote abortion, few or none can be found to tolerate being lied to, including the antilife Senator Nancy Landon Kassebaum.

For it quickly came out, of course, that Dr. Foster had performed considerably more than one abortion in the course of his medical career. In fact, it quickly became one of the *justifications* advanced in his favor by his supporters to point out that any ob-gyn doctor of his generation would have *had* to perform many abortions as medicine is practiced today. A medical colleague of his from New York was shortly quoted on the front page of the *New York Times* as speaking of "the need to conduct an abortion in cases where a woman is in danger of dying or when she is having a miscarriage is sometimes part of the job."

But this was simply another one of the typical mendacities behind which too many members of the medical profession today, and others too, continue to hide their unwillingness to oppose legalized abortion on principle; the kinds of cases the New York doctor was talking about constituted exactly what was already legal everywhere in the pre-legalized-abortion era when abortion, *except* for the kinds of cases the doctor was talking about, i.e., if a woman's life was in danger, was otherwise illegal. It was hardly necessary to legalize it in order to deal with such cases.

Medical practitioners of all people should know better anyway. Even before *Roe v. Wade*, there were no longer any truly medical indications for abortion, just as there is virtually no *medical* justification for abortion today. The idea that abortion is even considered a "medical" issue at all is mostly a gigantic hypocrisy. Abortions today are done almost entirely for convenience — and *because* they are legal, of course. The statistics bear this out: in well over 90 per cent of all the 4000-plus abortions performed every day in the United States, no "medical" reason is even any longer advanced or alleged.

The U.S. Supreme Court may have placed the abortion decision in the hands of "a woman and her doctor"; but in no sense does abortion today constitute "medical care." More and more, abortions are done in special clinics today, and abortionists are simple technicians, whether or not they have an M.D. degree; the procedure is hardly "care giving" in any way. The idea that abortion even has anything to do with "medical treatment" is just one more of the dishonesties and hypocrisies that surround the whole issue of legalized abortion in our society.

Nevertheless, Dr. Henry W. Foster, Jr., turned out to be very definitely one of those contemporary physicians willing to include abortion as part of his medical practice — and then some, as the world soon learned.

II

The question of how many abortions Dr. Foster had performed very quickly became the focus of his credibility as a nominee. The figure of one abortion given to Senator Nancy Kassebaum had to be corrected almost immediately. At that point, Dr. Foster was directly quoted in a statement issued by HHS as saying that he thought he had "performed fewer than a dozen pregnancy terminations. None were in outpatient settings; all were in hospitals and were primarily to save the lives of the women or because the women had been victims of rape or incest."

It soon turned out that this new figure of "fewer than a dozen abortions" had to be corrected too. It seems to have been arrived at when somebody on the Clinton team was again questioning the good doctor about the abortions he had done — and doing so in what seemed to be the team's usual slipshod fashion. "I was asked how many I had done," Dr. Foster related during his later interview on Nightline. "'I really don't know,' I said. 'Was it a hundred?' 'No, I don't think so.' They said, 'A dozen?' I said, 'Yes, perhaps a dozen. Maybe less than a dozen.'"

In providing this explanation, Dr. Foster also tried to deflect criticism of his record by stressing that he had "personally delivered more than 10,000 babies." Here again, though, he seems not to have kept count any more accurately than he had kept count of the abortions he had done. Speaking from the Roosevelt Room of the White House itself during his hastily arranged *Nightline* appearance, after a new controversy had exploded over his nomination, Dr. Foster went on to ascribe the false "fewer than a dozen" figure to a "faulty memory." Records at the Meharry Medical College dating back to 1973, he indicated, revealed that he had actually been physician of record in 39 abortions.

This figure of 39 also proved to be as accurate as it was when Radio comedian Jack Benny, as one of his gags, used to give it out as his age. For prolifers had meanwhile turned up an article in the May, 1985, issue of *Obstetrics and Gynecology* describing a program of experimentation with abortifacient drugs at Meharry. The experiments described in the article were financed by the Upjohn pharmaceutical company and conducted by a medical team headed by none other than Dr. Henry W. Foster, Jr. These experiments involved the use of prostaglandin drugs inserted into pregnant women by means of vaginal suppositories; the medical journal article reported that the experiments were successful in the cases of 55 of the 60 pregnant women participating in the program (surgical abortions were carried out on four of the remaining five women). Abortions procured by prostaglandins, by the way, are almost always late abortions, sometimes very late; often the baby would be viable outside the womb or close to it.

Although Dr. Foster headed the team that performed these 55 chemical plus 4 surgical abortions in the course of this experimental program, Dr. Foster disclaimed performing any beyond the 39 his medical logs showed he performed. Medical residents did the "work," he explained; none of the "patients" was "his." "Those were not patients I knew; they weren't my private patients," he said — as if this in any way exculpated him for responsibility for the deaths for which he was ready enough to take *credit* in the medical journal article reporting them. In a later 1981 newspaper article, he said the medication used in this program had resulted in 75 abortions.

In any case, none of these abortions, quite evidently, was done to save anybody's life or to help any victim of rape or incest, as he had initially claimed. This was pure experimentation on human subjects. Moreover, an HHS spokesman later belatedly conceded that Dr. Foster "may have administered some of the medications." That, of course, is how prostaglandin abortions are performed: by administering the "medications."

In spite of the contradictions clearly on the record, Dr. Foster nevertheless maintained in the course of his *Nightline* interview that: "I abhor abortion. I abhor war. To me abortion is failure. I don't like failure." (If only "failure" were *all* that abortion is!)

Asked how he could carry out and supervise actions that he professed to "abhor," the Tennessee physician explained, as far as the experimental program was concerned: "To keep my veracity. We are in a medical setting. We had a research grant. We have to do that to train our residents. We were in a multi-center study with the Upjohn company, and we tested a product, a suppository, not a mechanical procedure, to train residents. . . That's part of keeping our program accredited. . .20- per cent of all universities survive on grant funds. That was a grant."

It is *not,* of course, necessary to take pharmaceutical company money to do prostaglandin abortions in order to maintain the accreditation of a medical residency program. Ironically, Dr. Foster's ob-gyn residency program had *lost* its medical accreditation in 1991 — clearly raising the question of his medical competence to be Surgeon General — but this inconvenient fact did not stop him from making a big thing out of it on his *Nightline* interview.

In any case, the chilling attitude exhibited by this supposedly benevolent practitioner really resembles nothing so much as the attitude of, say, an Adolf Eichmann: *"Ich sass am Schreibtisch und machte meine Sachen*; I sat at my desk and got on with my work. . ." Eichmann's "work" happened to be arranging the transport of human beings to the place of their mass execution, Foster's arranging the termination of the lives of human beings in a "medical setting," using a "research grant" to test a "product. . ."

It soon became clear, however, that the involvement of Dr. Henry W. Foster, Jr., with abortion was not yet exhausted by referring to the Meharry Medical College logs or to the 1985 article in *Obstetrics and Gynecology*. A few days after his *Nightline* appearance, the Associated Press circulated a story that quoted a relative of Dr. Foster's back in Alabama, as well as a medical colleague of his there, both of whom indicated that he had also performed an unspecified number of abortions in Tuskegee, Alabama, where he had lived and practiced medicine between 1965 and 1973. In those years, of course, abortion was *illegal* in Alabama, except to save the life of the mother; back then, the Supreme Court's 1973 decision *Roe v. Wade* which legalized abortion nationwide was still just a glint in Supreme Court Justice Harry Blackmun's eye.

There was more on Dr. Foster, and worse — and in the attempted cover-up of which the White House, HHS, and Dr. Foster all shared complicity in roughly equal measure. For all the time that the "numbers game" of Dr. Foster's abortions was being publicly played out, with the numbers being given, variously, as one, less than a dozen, 39 plus 55 (or 59), an authentic "smoking gun" was being uncovered in the form of actual documentary evidence that the 1985 medical journal article did not represent the only instance when Dr. Henry Foster had been prepared to take credit before his medical colleagues for the abortions he had performed.

A veteran prolife worker, Randy Engel of the Michael Fund and the U.S. Coalition for Life in the Pittsburgh area, had had a funny feeling about Dr. Henry Foster all along. So she consulted some of her files and rather quickly came upon a transcript of a meeting of the then Department of Health, Education, and Welfare's Ethics Advisory Board, a meeting which had taken place back in November, 1978. In the course of this meeting, a Dr. Henry W. Foster, Jr., had told the HEW ethics panel that he had, in his own words in the transcript, "done a lot of amniocentesis and therapeutic abortions, probably near 700."

Amniocentesis is a procedure by which a needle is inserted in the mother and a sample is taken of the amniotic fluid in which the child floats in the womb; from this sample it is possible to ascertain certain fetal genetic characteristics such as the child's sex or possible genetic defects. In our present legalized abortion culture, it goes without saying that the use of amniocentesis has often led to eugenic abortions; prolifer Randy Engel has specialized, among other things, in monitoring and working to counter today's abuse of the amniocentesis procedure.

In the transcript found by Randy Engel in her files, Dr. Foster is directly quoted as having said at the 1978 HEW Ethics Advisory Board meeting: "We do amniocentesis *in order to decide* whether or not the pregnancy should continue and *to provide a therapeutic abortion. . .*"(emphasis added). It is not clear from the transcript whether the figure 700 mentioned by Dr. Foster refers to amniocentesis procedures, to actual abortions, or to both. It is possible that not all the 700 amniocentesis procedures carried out terminated in abortions; but in view of what Dr. Foster's own description of the purpose for doing the amniocentesis procedures, i.e., solely to determine whether an abortion was called for and for no other therapeutic purpose, he can scarcely be accorded any moral credit in the cases where it may have been decided in the end that abortion was not indicated. At no time, apparently, would he have failed to proceed to the lethal abortion procedure, if he had thought it indicated, according to his own testimony.

Incidentally, among the other damning statements made by Dr. Foster in the 1978 transcript, there is language suggesting that, already back then, Dr. Foster approved of fetal tissue research as well as of the *in vitro* creation of human embryos for the purpose of experimenting upon them. In short, the man is a veritable modern ghoul; the evidence for it is indisputable (but don't imagine that, in the present climate, any of this evidence can really be effectively brought out in order to establish anything against Dr. Foster!).

As things turned out, the White House was determined to hang tough. It was new presidential press secretary Michael McCurry himself who first suggested that the 1978 transcript was a fabrication, an outright fraud, he thought; and he intimated that Dr. Foster had never even been present at the HEW Ethics Advisory Board meeting. At that point, a *Federal Register* notice for June 18, 1978, was quickly produced, recording that a Dr. Foster had indeed been scheduled to testify at that very meeting. Moreover, Randy Engel, soon joined by others, had very quickly sent or faxed the incriminating transcript to so many places that it no longer seemed possible to ignore either the document itself or the implications of it.

Nevertheless, press secretary McCurry seems never to have backed off from his false accusation that the document was a fraud; nor does it seem that the famed White House press corps, ever vigilant to ferret out the truth (provided the case was Watergate or Iran-Contra), ever got around to holding McCurry accountable for his mendacious attempt to "stonewall." The zeal which usually accompanies contemporary investigative journalism inexplicably fades when the subject is abortion.

HHS spokeswoman Avis LaVelle, however, did eventually concede that the transcript was real. But Dr. Foster himself meanwhile continued to deny flat out that he had ever said what the transcript plainly recorded him as saying: "The transcript says what it says," Avis LaVelle granted. Dr. Foster "can't account for what's is the transcript. It could be an error. . .The transcript is absolutely wrong," she maintained — and simply left the issue hanging. Nor was she apparently pressed, then or since, to resolve it. Nor was Dr. Foster pressed. After a day or two of interest, the media tended to move away from the whole issue, and the figure 700 soon stopped being mentioned at all in news stories about the Foster nomination.

It was at this point, according to the *Washington Post*, that "the Planned Parenthood Federation of America brought 100 representatives from around the country to Capitol Hill to form what it called a 'Foster Truth Squad' to counter allegations by abortion groups. . ." There was only one problem with this PPF "Foster Truth Squad," of course — one that any objective observer would have noticed right away — and that was that it had, as yet, scarcely any "truth" at all to work with. . .

III

One of the principal keys to the understanding of the whole Foster phenomenon — as of the whole Elders phenomenon earlier — resides in what we may call the Planned Parenthood connection: both of these M.D.'s are typical Planned Parenthood physicians, Dr. Foster persistently and aggressively so. He served on the national Board of Directors of Planned Parenthood between 1978 and 1981, and on the Board of Nashville's local Planned Parenthood in 1988-89. In recent years he has been on the Board of PPF's slate of "Key Public Policy Advocates." He was a member of the PPF-sponsored Physicians for Choice in the early 1980s and was also on the National Leadership Committee of Planned Parenthood's Campaign to Keep Abortion Safe and Legal in the late 1980s — this latter organization is one that was organized in the wake of the Supreme Court's *Webster* decision; this decision had allowed the states to enact certain rather minimal restrictions on abortions, such as parental consent or notification laws, bans on third-trimester abortions, and the like; and therefore it was imperative that these erosions of the absolute abortion "right" be opposed, and Dr. Foster was among those ready to oppose it.

Anyone who has looked very closely at what Planned Parenthood is (the nation's leading provider of abortions and abortion referrals, among other things), and at what Planned Parenthood does (last year utilizing around $160 million of the taxpayer's money), cannot be too surprised at anything that has surfaced in the course of either the Foster or the Elders spectacles. Doing abortions and providing justifications for doing them, while working to insure that they will not fail to be available — these things are Planned Parenthood's principal business. That an organization engaged in such a business could ever have become "respectable," attracting large corporate donations as well as country clubbers and affluent society women — including, unhappily, the wives of several prominent United States Senators, who adopt and promote it as their "charity" — is just another one of the many indications of the low moral state to which our society has now sunk.

Where Planned Parenthood is concerned, however, it is not just abortion that is at issue; for the very term "planned parenthood" (which that stout-hearted prolife fighter, Fr. Paul Marx, O.S.B., has rightly dubbed "planned *barren*hood"!), as well as the organization which bears the name, both include a whole complex of beliefs and attitudes, some of which, outlined immediately below, will instantly be seen as incompatible with the Judeo-Christian ethic, to put it mildly:

— That human beings are completely in charge of human life and human sexuality, without regard to the morality which was formerly believed to apply to these things.

— That the use of the human sexual faculty need not be limited to a man and a woman married to each other, but may be employed for pleasure or self-expression with any other partner, or with no partner, at the unfettered option of the individual.

— That the self-interest and self-expression of the autonomous individual takes absolute precedence over any responsibility human beings may once have been thought to have towards one another.

— That the scientific and technical means now exist either to prevent the "unwanted" natural consequences of sexual intercourse in the form of pregnancy, or to provide the "remedy" for any such unwanted pregnancy after the fact; and that the use of these scientific and technical means is always entirely licit and indeed desirable.

— That these same scientific and technical means may licitly be further employed both to "improve" the race in the case of those pregnancies that are "wanted," and also to prevent "undesirable" people from reproducing themselves (as Supreme Court Justice Oliver Wendell Holmes once infamously expostulated in a famous sterilization case: "Three generations of imbeciles are enough!").

— That the laudable goal of reducing perceived "overpopulation" similarly justifies the use of any and all scientific and technical means to prevent unwanted pregnancies, especially, again, among "undesirable" races and classes of people.

— That all of these new attitudes and beliefs regarding human life and human sexuality should now be instilled in the up-coming generation, especially by means of school courses in "sex education" or "family life education," regardless of the wishes of the parents of children thus being indoctrinated in a new morality.

These are some of the principal attitudes and beliefs by which Planned Parenthood lives. They are, as we have remarked in the slightly different connection of the similar moral beliefs of Dr. Joycelyn Elders, incompatible with the successful operation of any society or civilization. The goal of reducing world population is a relatively new one, while the "eugenic" goal of improving the race through modern scientific and medical means of birth control has only in recent years imperceptibly come back into vogue, after having been for many years in relative eclipse because of the bad name eugenics acquired during the Nazi period in Germany.

Planned Parenthood has not hesitated to embrace the modern movement for population control, however; and the organization's connection with the eugenics movement goes all the way back to the PPF foundress, Margaret Sanger. Sanger's worldview always included both a sexually permissive lifestyle *and* plans to "improve the race".

Among those programs with which the Nazis helped discredit the eugenics movement for a time, there was included the sterilization of the "unfit." As a result of the bad odor into which sterilizations of this type were brought by the Nazis, they became almost non-existent in the immediate post-World-War-II period, after having been quite common in this country in the 1920s. In the 1960s, however, sterilization started coming back into fashion in our society along with the increased use of contraceptives.

One of the particularly depressing aspects of the whole Foster affair is that, along with all of the other immoral practices this black physician has adopted in the course of his medical practice, he has also given himself, apparently whole-heartedly, to the eugenics movement. It is heart-breaking even to think about this, considering that blacks have always been prime targets of the eugenics movement, the "unfit" by definition in the minds of some. How a Dr. Foster could *join* the declared enemies of his race is hard to understand, but the facts are what they are. Among his published medical journal articles, there is at least one discounting fears of some blacks concerning black genocide and calling for more "family planning" in the black community.

Nor have his efforts in the field of eugenics been confined to mere advocacy. In 1976 he published an article in the *Southern Medical Journal* in which he wrote, candidly: "Recently I have begun to use hysterectomy in patients with severe mental retardation. . ."

In other words, Dr. Foster has publicly admitted here to having engaged in the sterilization of the unfit, without their consent, and for the sole reason that they are considered unfit. This constitutes yet another area of immoral experimentation in which Dr. Foster was actively engaged well before he ever got into doing prostaglandin chemical abortions for the Upjohn company. And it is worth noting in passing that such procedures scarcely accord with the current jargon-dogma that what is involved in all these things is "choice for women in reproductive health matters."

In order to perform this kind of sterilization today, a physician must secure the consent of a retarded woman's court-appointed legal guardian and then get an actual court order allowing the procedure to take place. It is unclear what legal steps Dr. Foster took, if any, when he was sterilizing the retarded back in the 1970s by surgically removing healthy uteruses without any therapeutic purpose. When asked, an HHS spokesman said that Dr. Foster — once again! — could not recall the details; the HHS spokesman said the issue was "under review," according to syndicated columnist Charles Krauthammer (himself a trained M.D.).

Krauthammer further pointed out in his newspaper column on this subject that, two full years before Dr. Foster published his paper on the sterilization program in which he was involved, the U.S. Department of Health, Education, and Welfare had already published regulations banning the use of federal funds in the involuntary sterilization of the mentally incompetent unless: 1) an independent review committee approved; and 2) "a court of competent jurisdiction determined that the proposed sterilization [was] in the best interest of the patient."

As soon as the issue of Dr. Foster's ethics in this matter was raised, however, the White House immediately defended the nominee on the grounds that his actions were in accord with the accepted medical practice at the time, and, indeed, were "in the mainstream of medicine." Charles Krauthammer's information by itself, however, shows this pretty clearly not to be the case. In any case, could any federal nominee today ever get away with saying that he was in favor of segregated schools *before* the Supreme Court's *Brown v. Board of Education* decision, but saw the light after the Court ruled? Segregation was surely "in the mainstream" of education in the South in the pre-*Brown* days. How could this kind of excuse or subterfuge ever be accepted in Dr. Foster's case today?

Nor did Dr. Foster's sterilizations of the retarded without their consent represent his only apparent lapse from accepted medical ethics. No sooner had the flap over these sterilizations died down than another one arose over Dr. Foster's knowledge, or lack of it, of the notorious Tuskegee Experiment in Alabama. This was a medical experimentation program that began back in the 1930s as an apparently legitimate medical effort to study the epidemiology of syphilis: poor black men afflicted with the disease were placed under medical observation in an effort to chart the progress of the disease. In those days there was no effective treatment for syphilis.

After the discovery in the 1940s of penicillin, which could be used to treat syphilis, however, the Tuskegee Experiment took a sinister turn; the researchers decided not to treat 400 of the men in their cohort, but simply to monitor the effects of the progress of their disease, comparing the results with those for others who were being treated with penicillin. The men themselves were never told anything about this.

At one point, Public Health Service doctors involved with the study decided to brief the local Macon County Medical Society on the still on-going experiment, and, reportedly, they received "approval and support" for the continuation of the experiment from the local doctors. This was in 1969. Dr. Henry W. Foster, Jr., was vice president of the Macon County Medical Society in that year.

In 1972, when the facts about the Tuskegee Experiment finally came out, considerable public outrage was expressed. The continuing fall-out from the experiment even contributed to the passage of the National Research Act the next year, which codified stricter rules concerning informed consent. By this time, Dr. Henry Foster was president of the Macon County Medical Society, and he apparently added his voice at that point to the general outrage over the experiment; we need not doubt nor question his sincerity on this score.

But he also claimed that he had neither attended the 1969 medical society briefing on the Tuskegee Experiment, nor had he ever even heard about it — or about the experiment itself — until all the facts became public later on.

Meanwhile, however, another former Alabama physician, a Dr. Luther McRae, now living in Georgia, came forward to give a different account. Dr. McRae said that he would testify under oath that Dr. Foster had indeed been present at the 1969 briefing, knew about the study, and, at the very least, had made no protest about it at the time. Dr. Foster, naturally, denied this, and the White House declared that Dr. McRae's remarks were "inconsistent with the facts."

In addition to Dr. McRae's statement, the Senate Labor and Human Resources Committee later turned up a sworn deposition made in 1974 by the then head of the Alabama State Health Department in connection with the Tuskegee experiment in which the latter recalled a conversation with Dr. Foster. This deposition rather clearly indicated that Dr. Foster did know about the experiment before knowledge of it became public; but again the actual dates were not entirely clear.

Whatever the truth of the matter, the Tuskegee episode on its face nevertheless provided yet one more instance where significant negatives concerning Dr. Foster were not refuted, nor any counter evidence offered; the allegations were simply denied and then dismissed out of hand and then set aside and forgotten.

Yet in releasing copies of Foster articles and speeches to the press (after having been forced by the overwhelming publicity to do so), John Podesta, a White House official in charge of managing the Foster nomination, was actually heard to grumble that "antichoice opponents may try to comb through his writings and distort his record." This charge might have been more believable, if there had ever been any *reason* to "distort" his record; all that seemed to be necessary, it seemed, was to *cite* it!

For it certainly did not seem to be the case that the good doctor's practices had ever been "in the mainstream of medicine." Rather, he seems to have positioned himself rather consistently in the mainstream of — Planned Parenthood? Ethics-wise and otherwise, he seems to be nothing else but a Planned Parenthood doctor, through and through. And so the question becomes whether, even as low as America has already fallen morally, a Planned Parenthood doctor really is what is needed as Surgeon General of the United States. . .

IV

That Dr. Henry W. Foster, Jr., is a Planned Parenthood physician first, last, and always, would seem to apply especially to his work as a so-called "abstinence educator." The White House touted this aspect of his work from the beginning, intimating that "fighting teen pregnancy" was what the debate should be all about, not abortion. Anything but abortion. The White House even strongly suggested that his work against teen pregnancy was the real reason for Dr. Foster's selection.

Even some of the legislators and commentators otherwise critical of his appointment were generally prepared to concede that, well, yes, his work against teen pregnancy was no doubt meritorious. This idea very quickly began to be treated as established fact in various press stories, columns, and the like: Dr. Foster came to be credited as being an educator of proven effectiveness in the kind of education required today for the disadvantaged.

The principal educational program with which Dr. Foster has been associated is the Tennessee "I Have a Future Program," which he founded at Meharry in the 1980s. This program targets disadvantaged adolescents aged 14 to 17, and it has been praised as highly effective. Few actual figures demonstrating its effectiveness seem to have been given out anywhere, however; a laudatory article about it which appeared in the *New York Times* was not able to cite any actual figures, but merely quoted the program's current director to the effect that "there have been only a few pregnancies among the 800 to 1000 young women who took an active part in the program."

The wish was no doubt father to the thought, and almost immediately this program started being described as an "abstinence program" for teens. Dr. Foster himself declared in his famous *Nightline* appearance: "I favor abstinence. That is what I favor."

According to the documents which describe the program, however, it appears that one of the main objectives of the program is, rather, to "increase contraceptive availability" for teens. At the same time, in these same documents, there is no mention of abstinence or of the delaying of sexual activity; the youngsters are taught that they can be "intimate" without actually having sex; a "non-judgmental approach" is stressed throughout the program; and condoms are actually distributed to the kids along with instructions about how to use them.

Even the laudatory *New York Times* article on the program confirmed all these features of Dr. Foster's type of "abstinence education" when it noted that "doctors who have worked with Dr. Foster through the years credit the program using common sense and incentives, *not just speeches about abstinence*, to keep teen-agers from being held back by the weight of newborn children" (emphasis added).

In another, in-depth analysis of this "I Have a Future Program," the *Washington Times* confirmed the above and mentioned an actual *refusal* of the program's current director to give out any hard evidence on the program's actual effectiveness — on the grounds that "we're writing a journal article." This attitude dismayed even some pro-sex-education observers disposed to be favorable to the program. Later, the same *Washington Times* secured a staff training manual for the program which confirmed all of this and more. This manual for the "I Have a Future Program" included the following, quoted verbatim:

— "Each individual family member must decide what his/her personal values are towards sexuality. As adolescents, it is important to understand one's personal values even if these values may be in conflict with one's parents."

— "Each family member has the unique decision of when and what age to engage in sexual activity. Family members values do not have to mold the values of the developing adolescent."

— "The African-American family in all of its diversity should be respected, acknowledged for its strengths and not compared negatively to Eurocentric family standards."

— "Condom Exercise: Group members will divide into pairs. In pairs, each participant is to open the condom and place two fingers within the condom. They are to explore the condom and feel its texture. The group leader will

> discuss how to select condoms, check the expiration date, and application of condoms. Group leaders need to emphasize the importance for both males and females to become comfortable with handling."

Regardless of what anyone might think of the morality of all this, could anyone seriously argue that this kind of approach could ever have any effect whatever in *preventing* teen-age pregnancies? Could Dr. Foster possibly have been *serious* when he told Ted Koppel that he favored *abstinence*? In point of fact, when the Senate Labor and Human Resources Committee finally succeeded in prying loose a report on the effectiveness of the "I Have a Future Program" which had eluded all other investigators up to that point, it transpired that this report, prepared in 1991 for the Carnegie Corporation in order to get a grant for the program, actually showed that *not only did it fail to reduce the number of pregnancies among teen-age participants, but those in the program were more likely to engage in frequent sex than those in a control group!*

In spite of all this, during the confirmation hearings for Dr. Foster held in early May, 1995, pamphlets on the IHAF program were nevertheless circulated claiming that the program promoted abstinence. Senate staffers, however, discovered that the purchase order for these particular pamphlets from the Meharry Medical College were dated March, 1995, as was the shipping invoice on them — that is, *after* Dr. Foster's nomination to be Surgeon General!

In short, as far as anyone can tell, Dr. Henry Foster's highly touted model IHAF program for combatting America's current epidemic of teen pregnancies out of wedlock turns out to be both a patent fraud and a spectacular failure — another one of those programs which the Southern Baptist Convention, in opposing Dr. Foster's nomination, called "the failed, 'safe-sex' model of sex education" — the kind of "value-free" sex education that, in fact, at long last, has been taking a few hits lately, after virtually a generation during which the claims of the educators who have devised these programs have been uncritically accepted in the face of all the contrary evidence.

In a widely quoted article in the *Atlantic Monthly* in October, 1994, however, social scientist Barbara Dafoe Whitehead, author of the earlier "Dan Quayle Was Right" article in the same journal (and no relation to the present writer), concluded: "There is no evidence that [this kind of sex education] works. Teen-age pregnancy is up, and so is the incidence of sexually transmitted disease. It is a gumbo of ideas based on no known field of knowledge."

Specialists in real abstinence education have long noted that, even where abstinence is explicitly encouraged and promoted — which is clearly *not* the case with Dr. Foster's program — the abstinence message can nevertheless get lost if condoms and other contraceptives are promoted as well. For the kids do not fail to get the "double message" inherent in talking about abstinence but handing out the contraceptives anyway; the double message, even when it is not explicitly stated, is: "We know you're really going to do it anyway, in spite of what we tell you is best for you, so you better take some of these. . ."

Dr. Foster's approach to teen pregnancy, then, proved to be of a piece with the rest of his practice: it was, once again, nothing else but the Planned Parenthood model. Planned Parenthood has long endorsed and promoted the guidelines of the Sex Information and Education Council of the United States; this means promoting not only the "safe sex" model of "value free" sex education, relying primarily on far from uniformly safe contraceptives; it also means telling children quite explicitly, and giving emphasis to, such things as that homosexual and heterosexual "lifestyles" are equally valid; finally, it also means that teachers are encouraged to discuss things like masturbation in a morally neutral fashion with children aged 5 to 8 — exactly what Dr. Joycelyn Elders got fired for advocating!

What were the differences, then, between President Clinton's first choice, and his second choice, for Surgeon General? Were there any? The president's choice of a successor to Dr. Elders appeared to believe exactly the same things that she did, particularly with regard to how children are to be educated.

If there were any differences between them, in fact, they would mostly seem to tell in Dr. Elders' favor! For at least she had apparently not herself performed abortions and sterilizations of the "unfit," and experimented on human subjects, etc. Who would ever have imagined that the President of the United States could have found a successor to Dr. Joycelyn Elders who could actually make her (in suitably relative terms, of course!) look good?

V

How did President Clinton manage it? How did he manage to pick a candidate worse than the one he had just had to fire? The conventional wisdom in Washington quickly came to the conclusion that the main problem which had caused such embarrassment was White House bungling and stupidity, failure to "vet" the nominee properly before publicly announcing his name. President Clinton himself said the problem was that legislators just do not want to have to vote on anybody who is in the least bit "controversial." In one of his radio talks he complained that "every time anybody is appointed who is controversial, some [senators] will call and say, 'Please pull it down so I won't have to vote on it.'"

So why did he keep on selecting "controversial" candidates then? Offering this lame kind of excuse was surely merely another pretext for not engaging the most important substantive issue involved, namely, whether Dr. Foster would make a suitable Surgeon General or not.

The Republicans, for their part, seemed as little ready as the Democrats to discuss the substantive issue of his suitability for the office or even to get into what the real issues were. The fact that he was also a black whom nobody wanted to be seen opposing was surely a factor, but it was not the only or perhaps even the most important one. Generally Republicans wanted to stay as far away from the abortion issue as they could. Speaker Newt Gingrich, for example, opined that: "I would focus in on the incompetence of the White House and the potential dishonesty. I would never touch the abortion issue. There's no point in picking fights inside your own majority if you can help it."

As for Senate Majority Leader Senator Robert Dole, he was certainly the one leading the pack of those initially calling for President Clinton simply to withdraw the nomination: anything but a debate on abortion! Later, of course, Dole forthrightly came out and said that he opposed the Foster nomination; he added that he might not even bring it out on the floor of the Senate for a vote if it ever got through committee, which he doubted. Later still, though, after the Foster nomination had been favorably voted out of the Senate Committee, Senator Dole said that, well, maybe he would bring the nomination to the floor for a vote after all; but he wanted to talk personally to Dr. Foster first.

Certainly, none of this came out as very principled opposition to abortion as such, however. While Senator Dole is no doubt sincere in his generally prolife voting record, if the political process was nevertheless about to produce the Senate votes for confirming an abortionist and unethical medical experimenter as Surgeon General, who was he to object? Politics has been his whole life; how could he possibly stand against a decision of the "political process"?

Senator Dole is scarcely aware, apparently, that there is even a culture war going on, in spite of his rather strained efforts to garner conservative Christian votes by such tactics as bashing Hollywood. Dole's rival presidential aspirant, Pat Buchanan, was to charge, with considerable justification, that the Senate Majority Leader always had the "one vote" to deny Henry Foster's confirmation, i.e., by declining to bring the nomination to the floor. Dole himself had several times noted that the Democratically controlled Senate had failed to bring to a confirmation vote no less than 192 Reagan and Bush nominees in all (once again, a feature of the "political process"!).

But, of course, it was not really as simple as that, either: because the Democrats were threatening to hold up other Senate business if the Foster nomination was not acted upon, and this could make Senator Dole look very, very bad in the middle of his presidential bid. Minority Leader Thomas Daschle of South Dakota plainly put him on notice that "we may start objecting to moving to other legislation. We may need to make it clear that cooperation is a two-way street." Daschle turned out to be a formidable tactician in managing these developments.

Dole's original threat not even to bring the nomination to a vote had, of course, been issued back when Dr. Foster had still looked like a goner. Pat Buchanan's later challenge to Senator Dole was in any case described by some observers as an attempt to prevent his and Senator Dole's rival presidential aspirant, Senator Phil Gramm of Texas, from scoring points with prolife voters by carrying through with the latter's threat to filibuster Dr. Foster's nomination if it ever reached the Senate floor.

Yes: both Senator Dole's and Pat Buchanan's rival, Senator Phil Gramm, did come out strongly against Dr. Foster, and from the beginning. Early in the game Gramm had threatened to mount a filibuster against any substantive vote if his nomination were ever brought to the floor (maybe this was even why rival Dole, later, declared that *he* would *not* bring it to the floor! — Ah, politics!). Gramm no doubt early saw an opportunity to gather prolife support by opposing a nominee as obviously bad as Foster — even though he too continued to avoid taking a stand on the fundamental issues posed by legalized abortion, murmuring along with all the others that there was no "consensus" (even Pat Robertson felt obliged to make *that* point!). Nevertheless, it should be recorded that Gramm did not back off from his position, even after the Senate Committee voted in favor of confirming Dr. Foster.

But the idea that *creating* a consensus on a matter that represented a crucial moral issue for the whole nation might just be one of the functions of responsible leadership did not seem to occur to very many politicians of any stripe. The whole thrust of most of the efforts to oppose Dr. Foster seemed mainly to be not to alienate the prolife vote by allowing him to get through — but meanwhile not to allow the abortion issue to be the deciding factor in his defeat. At first, Dr. Foster seemed to be a bad enough candidate to lend to this basically dishonest approach some plausibility.

In such a climate, even a prolife Republican senator such as Dan Coats of Indiana, a legislator who all along was perhaps most consistent and persistent in fighting both the Elders and Foster nominations, nevertheless also proved himself to be quite reluctant to admit that abortion was the core issue. "There is a litmus test here, but it is not abortion," Senator Coats explicitly said. "The litmus test is truth telling, and on this point the president's and Dr. Foster's version of the truth differ from day to day."

In fact, many Republicans quickly decided, somewhat to their relief, that Dr. Foster *was* a pretty easy man to oppose; there were so *many* grounds! It was apparently not going to be necessary to take a principled stand after all. And so, not surprisingly, many legislators did not do so.

Republicans generally, including many prolife Republicans, visibly dreaded the emergence of the abortion issue, or most other social or cultural issues, for that matter. Many of them still recalled how, in 1992, the Democrats and the media had used these issues, only too successfully, it was thought, to convict the Republicans of meanness and exclusivity as a result of certain 1992 Republican Convention speeches, and also to depict Republicans as "anti-woman." This Republican fear of even getting into the social or cultural issues tended to persist in spite of the major prolife gains in the 1994 midterm elections (which some studies have since ascribed *to* profamily and prolife voters turning out massively — in other words, the media interpretations of the 1992 Republican Convention speeches as showing how "mean-spirited" the Republicans were were simply *mistaken!*).

Both the Democrats and the Clinton Administration, however, once the furor and confusion of the first days after Dr. Foster's name was launched, and the negatives on him had surfaced, had dissipated somewhat, decided to take their stand squarely *on* the abortion issue. They continued to perceive it as a winning issue; they wanted to present the nomination as indeed, in some sense, a "referendum," one from which they expected to profit, regardless of whether or not Foster was confirmed.

"Ultimately the fight is not about all the extraneous issues that are being cited," declared White House Press Secretary Michael McCurry. "Nobody should be under the illusion that these groups that are working with the Republican majority. . .are fighting this nomination for any reason but to make abortion criminal."

McCurry himself evidenced a unusual zest for the combat and became quite aggressive in pursuing a frank proabortion line (surely not without at least the tacit approval of his boss). "The truth is," he said, "that there are extremists within the right to life who have now hooked Republicans and Congress by the nose and they're dragging them around."

Various pundits credited the White House with great political sagacity in frankly adopting a proabortion stand in defense of Dr. Foster; they saw this as splitting the Republican ranks at the most likely fissure point of the latter. That these pundits may well have had something could be seen by the consistent Republican reluctance to face the core issue which became quite obvious.

However, the White House really had little choice in deciding to take a frank proabortion stand; the liberal-leftist interest groups so influential in the Democratic Party had, from the start, been fuming that there could ever have been any suggestion of abortion being anything anyone might have to apologize for. Abortion was legal, wasn't it? It was the law of the land. It should accordingly be forthrightly — indeed, aggressively — defended. Thus many of the liberal-leftists typically thought and said, especially the radical feminists among them.

At bottom the White House seemed to agree with this point of view, and, once the decision was made to stay with the Foster nomination, come what might, the "usual suspects" in the way of liberal-leftist interest groups were called to a special meeting at the White House, where Chief of Staff Leon Panetta earnestly re-assured them that President Clinton was never going to abandon Henry Foster.

Included at this meeting were such obvious groups as PPF, NOW, NARAL, and the homosexual-rights Human Rights Campaign Fund.

But one more indication of how seriously the new morality and the sexual revolution have now co-opted formerly legitimate, if not mainstream, groups, could be seen in the fact that, at this same special pro-Foster White House meeting, there were also representatives from such organizations as the National Education Association, the American Association of University Women, and no less than eight different professional medical associations — the American Medical Association (AMA) having almost immediately come out in favor of Dr. Foster, as a matter of fact.

Strong White House support continued even after Dr. Foster committed yet another pre-confirmation hearing blunder, stating in a speech that "*white* right-wing extremists" were the ones trying to thwart his nomination, thus injecting into the controversy the very race issue which everybody on all sides up to then, including the Clinton Administration, had been at great pains to keep away from. In the event, Dr. Foster himself was the one who introduced it into the debate. "He misspoke," the White House's Michael McCurry quickly said. "It was a slip of the tongue." (It was not the first one for Dr. Foster, whose tongue at another point had apparently "slipped" when he said: "I have done *illegal* abortions. . .")

Anyway, to speak of a slip of the tongue was hardly to excuse Dr. Foster, certainly not in the political climate that prevailed. House Majority Leader Richard Armey, just days before, had been excoriated up and down the land for a similar slip of the tongue, when he inadvertently said "Barney Fag" for "Barney Frank," the avowed homosexual Congressman from Massachusetts. Rep. Armey had been obliged to apologize abjectly for his slip of the tongue; nor were his apologies even accepted with very good grace by Mr. Frank and the latter's friends and allies.

Dr. Henry W. Foster, Jr., however, named to be Surgeon General of the United States, emerged from this latest episode as relatively unscathed as he had apparently emerged from all his earlier gaffes. The Associated Press story that went out about his accusations against "the right-wing extremists" that he claimed were after him even failed to include the word "white." Most people only learned about after Dr. Foster's use of the word after the White House had issued a *correction* of his original statement.

A month later, Dr. Foster raised the race issue again, at least indirectly, when he told a National Newspaper Publishers Association luncheon that there was something definitely "fishy" in the way "minorities" continued to be attacked, him among them. Still the White House showed no signs of wavering in its support of him. "I know there is an agenda by a significant minority who want to turn the clock back, who want to see criminalized the right of a woman to choose," Dr. Foster said, noting that, after all, abortion *is* legal. "That's what this is all about," he said. He had spoken no truer words than these, in fact, in the course of his entire saga, in which all of the words he had spoken, apparently, not always *were* necessarily true. . .

VI

The confirmation hearings on the nomination of Dr. Henry W. Foster, Jr., to be Surgeon General of the United States took place on May 2-3, 1995, and they surely represent some kind of low point in political unreality, evasion, and dishonesty. Although he had just told the National Newspaper Publishing Association a month before that "the right of a woman to choose" was the core issue behind all the controversy over his nomination, Dr. Foster's prepared statement presented to the Senate Labor and Human Resources Committee chaired by Republican Senator Nancy Landon Kassebaum of Kansas turned around and *began* by asserting: ". . .Some. . .say this nomination is about abortion. It is not."

Another "contradiction"? It was not the only one. Dr. Foster's prepared statement similarly claimed that his "I Have a Future" program "was working," although by then the Committee already had in its hands the report originally submitted to the Carnegie Corporation which showed that it was not working. Even so, Dr. Foster was able truthfully to inform the Committee that the IHAF program had received an award from the American Medical Association, as well as a designation from the Bush Administration as one of America's Thousand Points of Light.

In answer to questions by Senators, he similarly delivered himself of such dicta as that "race has no part in this" (although he was the one who first injected the issue of race into the controversy too). His "*white* right wing" phrase was again explained as "a slip of the tongue." "We had a prepared text," Dr. Foster explained. "It wasn't even there." With regard to one of his other slips of the tongue, he told proabortion Maryland Republican Senator Barbara Mikulski, in answer to a direct question about whether he had ever performed an illegal abortion: "Never," he said.

He also told Senator Mikulski that he did not believe that parental consent or involvement should be required of a teen-aged girl seeking an abortion. This position is contrary to the belief of around 75 per cent of all Americans, who believe there should be parental consent for abortions performed on minors, according to a 1992 Gallup Poll. In normal times, this position alone should have been disqualifying for a Surgeon General nominee.

But the times are evidently not normal; nobody on the Senate Committee batted an eye about his answer concerning teen-aged abortions, any more than most of them expressed any concern about the eight or ten other objections to the Foster nomination, any one of which, again, would probably have sufficed to sink the nomination of any other candidate. But not Henry Foster.

Dr. Foster explained the discrepancies in his earlier accounts of how many abortions he had performed by explaining: "In my desire to provide instant answers to the barrage of questions coming at me, I spoke without having all the facts at my disposal." "It was a mistake," he said. The Committee members proved only too ready to excuse any avowed "mistake": too bad Dr. Foster did not see fit to admit a few other mistakes. As it happened, he had plenty of mistakes to work with; but he probably would have gotten away with most of those too.

Concerning the number of abortions he had performed, he went on to refer to the famous "log" at Meharry Medical College listing his 39 abortions of record; but this in no way explained the additional figures of one, less than a dozen, 55, 59, 75, or 700. Nevertheless, he was not pressed about any of these. Incredibly, the 1978 transcript of his testimony before the HEW Ethics Advisory Board was in no way even adverted to — as if the 1974 Watergate Committee had decided not to raise the question of the tapes President Nixon had made of his conversations in the Oval Office!

All in all, then, the Committee was exceedingly gentle with Dr. Foster, even when the questions being raised were of such a nature that they could not have been anything but embarrassing. Committee Chairman Kassebaum asked him about the IHAF program, for example: "Were you not concerned that the program was not only failing to discourage sexual activity, but possibly increasing it?" Dr.

Foster replied that epidemiological studies were difficult, and anyway, of those "most active" in the program, only one got pregnant; the program participants with higher rates of pregnancy were thus *defined* as "less active" in it!

In response to this evasion, Senator Kassebaum simply admonished him not to oversell the program. Dr. Foster got away with a number of other instances of this sort as well. He was not even questioned, for example, about how his ob-gyn residency program lost its accreditation, although this surely had a bearing on his competence to be Surgeon General.

Dr. Foster's most persistent critic at the hearings was Republican Senator Dan Coats of Indiana, who honestly did try to raise the issues of abortion, involuntary sterilization, and the Tuskegee syphilis experiments. "In at least three areas, Dr. Foster and the public record are disturbingly at odds," Senator Coats pointed out. "A Surgeon General is to lead so that others will want to follow. He must do more than avoid violating the law."

The Indiana Senator hammered away at various inconsistencies (he too had plenty to work with). Unfortunately, he expended a considerable amount of his own questioning time reading from various documents and depositions which supported his points; they were no doubt damning enough, if only anybody had been disposed to pay any attention to such documentation. Senator Coats thought that they posed "a great problem" for him, one which he just could not "overlook." Time would soon tell, however, that not all members of the Committee were of the same disposition as he was.

Generally, all Dr. Foster had to do was deny with words the plain meaning and import of the various inconsistencies and the various documents. Neither evidence nor rebuttal was usually offered. "Nothing is more offensive to me than the litany you put forth," he told Senator Coats, who was trying to establish his prior knowledge of the Tuskegee business; how indeed could anyone have the "audacity" to accuse a black person of complicity in such a "dastardly experiment"?

Dr. Foster scared off proabortion Vermont Republican Senator James Jeffords from pursuing a similar line of questioning by the same technique of injured righteous indignation. Senator Jeffords had wondered how Dr. Foster could not have known about the Tuskegee experiments in a medical society as small as the one in Macon County. "Nothing has offended me more than this," Dr. Foster thundered. "I was outraged!"

At the conclusion of it all, the former chairman and now ranking minority member of the Committee, Senator Edward M. Kennedy of Massachusetts, actually declared that "it is Dr. Foster's opponents who have a credibility problem, not Dr. Foster." Senator Coats was not satisfied, of course; he later circulated a letter to his colleagues pointing again to some of Dr. Foster's inconsistencies. "It appears that as a result of media reporting of the hearings," Senator Coats wrote in this letter, "there is a fairly widespread perception that Dr. Foster satisfactorily answered the many disturbing questions surrounding this nomination. In several respects, I don't believe this is true." It was one of the understatements of the year.

But again, it was all to no avail. If ever there was a case of merely going through the motions in order to arrive at a pre-selected outcome, the Foster confirmation hearings before the Senate Labor and Human Resources Committee was surely it. Anyone who still held to the view of the United States Senate as the world's greatest deliberative body surely had to revise his view as a result of these hearings. Personable and baby-faced, cracking jokes, Foster was able to win over them all. Even Senator Dan Coats said after the hearings that "Dr. Foster has many good qualities. . ."

As was to be expected, the media generally reported the Foster hearings quite favorably. "In hours of questioning," wrote the *Washington Post*'s very liberal Mary McGrory about Dr. Foster's testimony, "he displayed no spite, no pettiness, not a shred of self-righteousness." This became the issue: Dr. Foster's benign personality, which "disarmed the inquisitors, at least most of them," wrote McGrory. Senator Kassebaum was lauded for having conducted the hearings in such great style (she *excluded* any outside witnesses, for or against Dr. Foster, from the start!). The Washington elite was congratulating itself, in fact, on having once again gotten over yet another once seemingly insurmountable hurdle.

A couple of weeks later, though, Dr. Foster had to "correct" the record again: he had testified under oath, in answer to a question by Missouri Republican Senator John Ashcroft, that there was no more recent data on the IHAF program than what had been provided in the 1991 report to the Carnegie Corporation. In his letter to Senator Ashcroft, however, he said that this particular report had merely been an interim report and that he was now enclosing the final one; whereas the interim report had indicated a negative effect of the IHAF program, the final one "correcting" the record merely indicated that the IHAF had had *no* effect on preventing teen-age pregnancy. . .

Out of such unlikely materials are favorable Senate committee votes sometimes fashioned: on May 26, 1995, the Senate Labor and Human Resource Committee voted 9 to 7 to send the nomination of Dr. Henry W. Foster, Jr., to the full Senate with a favorable recommendation. That a committee of the United States Senate could thus favorably report out a candidate against whom the questions had been raised that had been raised against Dr. Foster — and no answers provided, or, in most cases, even attempted — was a virtual admission of intellectual and moral bankruptcy on the part of a key American institution. The fact that Dr. Foster belonged to a "minority" which the senators — perhaps even understandably — did not want to offend can in no way extenuate or excuse the failure of this Senate Committee to look at the real facts of the case and arrive at a responsible judgment about them.

The key person in this remarkable outcome was new Tennessee Republican Senator Bill Frist. Elected to the Senate with considerable profamily and prolife support, Senator Frist, himself a physician, nevertheless assisted Dr. Foster considerably at his hearings. "On more than one occasion," as one press account in the *Washington Post* reported, "Frist seemed to rescue Foster from fiery questioning — either by explaining standard medical practice, or by introducing contrary information."

Senator Frist did not reveal his position on the Foster nomination at the time of the hearings. It was known all along that proabortion Republican Senator Jeffords would vote with the eight Democratic members of the Committee for Dr. Foster; this would have meant an 8-8 tie, and the nomination would then have had to go to the Senate floor with no recommendation.

However, after hearing at least a good part of the same record we have been reviewing in this essay, Senator Frist said, in announcing his vote:

> It should not be our purpose to search for every possible mistake or imperfection in Hank Foster's life. The question before us is a much more narrow one: does this man have the commitment, the intelligence, the training, the honesty, and the integrity to be the chief spokesman for Americans on is-

sues concerning public health? These are the issues I've considered, and I'm satisfied with what I've seen and heard. . .

While most of us could perhaps agree with Senator Frist's definition of the issue in the abstract, it is pretty hard to see how anyone acquainted with what we have seen of Dr. Foster's public record could ever answer Senator Frist's question in the affirmative, as this "prolife" Senator apparently found himself able to do. His conclusions were as tragically evasive and mistaken as the Committee's.

We live in an era when people are literally in thrall to today's abortion imperative: those who voted for Dr. Foster evidently believe unalterably that the "right" to abortion simply must be affirmed; and they were and are prepared to "go to the mat" to defend this position. Those who opposed Dr. Foster, by contrast, were unable to oppose him on the basis that abortion is tragically wrong and can never be countenanced, whatever the practical difficulties in the way of abolishing it today may be; they could only oppose him on the basis that the man lacked credibility, was dishonest, or unforthcoming, or whatever — but none of these things sufficed to kill the nomination. It is not surprising which side won in this particular contest.

No part of this remarkable outcome is easy, or perhaps even possible, to understand, except in the light of the continuing, even desperate need of our society today to legitimate legalized abortion, along with the sexual revolution that stands behind it. These are things that the Clinton Administration, and the cultural forces that stand behind *it*, necessarily favor. Long after normal political calculation would have pronounced this nomination doomed, the president himself, at a news conference, was still saying that *he* would "go to the mat" for Dr. Foster. This phrase described the president's policy and predilections to a "T."

The Foster nomination, like the Elders nomination before it, consistently broke all the usual rules: nobody, on the basis of pure political calculation, would ever have named, or have attempted to hold on to, either of these totally unsuitable, indeed absurd, candidates. On normal political calculation, indeed, one would even have imagined that perhaps a partisan Republican mole somewhere deep within the bowels of the Clinton Administration had all the while been the one to come up with such inconceivably bad candidates. . .

But this sort of imagining would have failed to take into account the one all-important element here, the element of legalized abortion, which always corrupts everything it touches, as it has now apparently corrupted our society and our normal political processes as well. The Clinton Administration is hardly alone in believing that America simply "must have" legalized abortion; the whole system often seems to be conspiring, openly or furtively, to ensure the same thing.

VII

The denouement of the Foster affair was an anti-climax which altered none of the essential elements in the case. Senate Majority Leader Robert Dole had his personal meeting with Dr. Foster, in which the latter's answers to the senator's questions were evidently as unsatisfactory as his answers before the Senate committee. Even so, Senator Dole appears still not to have tumbled to some of the graver implications of the whole affair: he expressed amazement that his phones started "ringing off the hook" merely because he had agreed to *meet* with the nominee.

Following this meeting, Senator Dole brought the Foster nomination to the Senate floor — but only after ensuring that he had enough votes to prevent a successful motion for cloture, or the cutting off of any further debate, especially that interminable type of continuing debate known as a "filibuster."

The majority leader's move was a shrewd one. By bringing the nomination to the floor, he de-fanged Democratic threats to obstruct other legislation over the Foster affair. He also pre-empted the initiative of his rival presidential aspirant, Senator Phil Gramm, to lead a filibuster against the nomination and thus be able to take credit for opposing Foster with prolife voters. Under current Senate rules, a bill being filibustered, or threatened with a filibuster, can be temporarily set aside and a cloture vote scheduled. This is how Dole proceeded. A three-fifths vote (60 senators) is required to impose cloture, after which the substantive issue before the Senate would then have to be voted on, in this case whether Dr. Henry W. Foster, Jr., would be the next Surgeon General of the United States.

That question was never voted on. Senator Dole had lined up beforehand 43 solid Republican votes against cloture. The word on Capitol Hill was that the majority leader called in all his IOUs to insure the outcome of this particular vote. Even so, eleven Republican senators voted to impose cloture, in effect, voting *for* Foster; they were: Campbell (CO), Chafee (RI), Cohen (ME), Frist (TN),

Gorton (WA), Jeffords (VT), Kassebaum (KS), Packwood (OR), Simpson (WY), Snowe (ME), and Specter (PA).

In two cloture votes on two successive days, June 21-22, 1995, an identical vote of 57 to 43 was recorded. Thus the motion failed. The nomination was effectively killed. Senator Dole had demonstrated that he could "deliver the goods" by a more effective method than by exercising his "one vote" not to bring the nomination to the floor at all; this latter approach would have left the whole thing hanging in a limbo perceived as "undemocratic." As it was, the Kansas senator again proved to be a master of the political process.

However, there was more at stake in the whole Foster affair than is apparently even dreamt of in the philosophy of a Robert Dole. In spite of the fact that we have now been spared the indignity of having a Henry Foster as Surgeon General, the fact remains that *a majority of the United States Senate* was nevertheless fully prepared to confirm this man notwithstanding the record we have examined here. This cannot but be disquieting to anyone who cares about the moral health of this country. Although the sinking of the Foster nomination, if only by a procedural vote, may represent a tactical victory of sorts in the culture wars, the overall strategic situation remains little changed.

Following the vote, Senate Republicans were talking about dealing with the whole embarrassing and unpleasant situation by abolishing the position of Surgeon General entirely. In theory this could be accomplished by the simple expedient of declining to provide any funds for it in the upcoming HHS appropriations bill. However, this tactic would require the cooperation of the House of Representatives, and the chairman of the appropriations subcommittee for HHS there happened to be none other than doctrinaire pro-Planned Parenthood, proabortion Illinois Republican Representative John Edward Porter.

Thus, nobody should be holding his breath waiting for any "relief" in this particular fashion. Once again the ghastly abortion specter is seen to raise its ugly head, blocking the way; it rarely fails. The proabortionist legislators will almost always fight for their cause, it seems. Too many of the prolife legislators, though, would apparently rather avoid seeing theirs come up at all. It is true that the office of Surgeon General could be abolished by a particular bill, such as the one already introduced by prolife California Republican Representative Robert K. Dornan. Even so, it is not clear how likely this could ever be, or how great a "victory" it would represent anyway.

The liberal-left establishment, though temporarily in partial political eclipse, remains as committed as ever to the evil imperative of legalized abortion which supposedly enables people to solve otherwise intractable problems and to "control" their lives. Pennsylvania Senator and would-be presidential candidate on a frankly proabortion ticket Arlen Specter actually called Henry Foster a "hero-martyr" to this cause. *Washington Post* columnist Mary McGrory, always a Foster cheer leader, described him after the cloture votes a "a decent and honorable man who was treated like a dog by the Republicans. For pettiness, spitefulness and sheer meanness, it had few parallels," she added.

The *Washington Post*'s own editorial, though more moderate in expression, was equally divorced from anything resembling reality when it concluded that Foster was "a thoughtful and dedicated physician [who]. . .seemed genuinely to care about. . .bringing down the teenage pregnancy rate and uplifting poor children. . ." This is surely nothing but highly pernicious delusion. . .

President Clinton himself surely best articulated what was fundamentally at stake in the whole absurd and melancholy Foster affair — once again contradicting Dr. Foster's own assertion at his hearings that abortion was *not* the issue! — when he declared apropos of the Senate vote that:

> Today 43 Republicans in the Senate failed the fundamental test of fairness. *By choosing to side with extremists who would do anything to block a woman's right to choose*, these senators have done a disservice to the nominating process, and sent a chilling message to the rest of the country (emphasis added).

9

The On-Going Saga of Title X

I

One of the big surprises of the 1995 legislative session was the action in July of the House Appropriations Committee eliminating the U.S. Government's flagship program providing massive financial support for so-called "family planning." This program is authorized by Title X of the Public Health Services Act of 1970, as amended. The action excising the program was accomplished by the simple expedient of transferring all $193 million of the funds originally budgeted for Title X to another child health program. Without money the program could no longer go on.

For a brief but gratifying time, all the *bien-pensant* liberals in the House, on both sides of the aisle, were in a veritable panic; the world had in effect been turned upside down overnight. How could family planning, of all things, not be supported by the U.S. government? But the action of one House committee was not destined to last. Very quickly, in early August, 57 House Republicans were found to join 167 of the 202 Democrats there to restore funds to the Title X program, thereby keeping it alive. The world returned to normal.

For the temporary, bi-partisan working majority of the House of Representatives that was patched together to restore Title X funding, it was simply unthinkable for the U.S. Government *not* to be supporting family planning on the massive scale that it does in fact support it, and has supported it for years. It was especially unthinkable considering how essential so-called family planning has come to be considered in our culture at large. At the moment, not funding family planning with tax moneys might even be considered equally unthinkable in the minds of a majority of Americans — who may or

---

Originally published in *Culture Wars*, October, 1995.

may not realize that government-supported "family planning" has little or nothing to do with "planning" families at all.

Title X is concerned, rather, with *preventing* families if at all possible, meanwhile helping to fuel the sexual revolution by the indiscriminate and wholesale distribution, especially to the welfare class, of pills, condoms, diaphragms, and such — as well as providing counseling and referrals for abortions. Abortions come into the picture not just when the contraceptive methods fail, as they often do; under current Clinton Administration regulations, family planning clinics are *required* to give pregnant women and girls counseling in abortion as a "pregnancy management option."

The applicable law is "Title Ten," by the way, and not "x," as in "x-rated." Originally enacted a quarter of century ago with strong bi-partisan support, supposedly in order to "assist" the poor and the welfare class, the program has long since expanded its services into the general public arena, financing such things as school-based contraceptive clinics near affluent suburban schools. Much of the money under the program goes to affiliates of Planned Parenthood, in fact: the organizations which is the world's largest provider of abortions and abortion referrals.

From the beginning of Title X, abortion was always supposed to have been excluded as a method of family planning. In practice, however, all the clinics and the other beneficiaries of the law have had to do is, on the one hand, to keep their book-keeping separate for the abortions they might be performing (which are supposed to be funded from other sources); and, on the other hand, to use their Title X money for their other "family planning services."

The whole thing has never been anything but a gigantic public fraud and hypocrisy, however. For one thing it is not clear that Title X grantees have ever been seriously monitored or audited to verify that their abortion activity *was* being kept separate from their other family planning services. For another thing, abortion referrals by Title X clinics have pretty much been standard all along. In practice it is virtually impossible to exclude abortion as a method of family planning anyway, since it is all inextricably part of the same grisly modern life-prevention "industry."

Many people may even remember what an enormous controversy was generated in the 1980s when the Reagan Administration finally issued regulations, nearly two decades after the original law had been passed, prohibiting family-planning counselors in Title-X-funded programs from making referrals for abortions. Dubbed a "gag-rule," this was one of the proabortion measures which President Clinton rescinded by executive order immediately after taking office, henceforth *requiring* such counseling. Also in the 1980s, a conscientious Title X administrator, Jo Ann Gasper, was fired by the supposedly prolife Reagan Administration for attempting to require some Title X grantees to adhere to the no-abortion policy nominally part of the law from the beginning.

Actually, Title X is not the only vehicle by which the U.S. Government funds family planning, including abortions. Medicaid, or medical assistance to the poor, has regularly been providing around a half billion dollars annually for these purposes. This is larger in money terms than Title X, and it is surely an inevitable outcome of defining abortion and contraception as "medical" procedures. In addition, family planning services have been included in other government programs such as Community Health Centers and Child Health. It was to this latter program that the House Appropriations Committee attempted to transfer all of the Title X funds; even then, some of the money could still have been spent for family planning services, but, under this program, this would no longer have been the *required* use of the funds appropriated.

Had the opponents of Title X in Congress succeeded in killing the program in this fashion, an enormous moral victory would have been won: even though the U.S. Government would not have ceased to be in the family planning business in a big way, at least the significant government *commitment* in principle to so-called "family planning services" would have been enormously compromised and weakened. Conversely, the principle that the government does not necessarily *have* to support this dubious kind of activity would have been firmly established at long last. The significance of all this was only too well understood by the proponents of government-supported family planning in Congress, and hence they immediately determined to launch a strong counter-offensive to see that Title X was restored.

II

The overall bill in which the transferred Title X money was included was the huge $260-plus billion appropriations bill for Education, Labor, and Health and Human Services. Substantive provisions or requirements are not supposed to be included in appropriations bills, according to regular House rules. In recent years, however, these rules have been increasingly by-passed by both parties on certain controversial issues such as abortion. For one thing, from the prolife point of view, a substantive bill aimed at curbing abortions would not only have less chance of passing; it would also be a certain target for a presidential veto under the present Administration. This may, in fact, be the fate that awaits the Partial-Birth Abortion ban bill recently passed by the House Judiciary Committee.

Most successful prolife legislation has so far come in the form of amendments to appropriations bills, as a matter of fact. The famous Hyde Amendment restricting Medicaid abortions is a classic example.

In the case of this particular Education-Labor-HHS appropriations bill, not only did the House Appropriations Committee initially succeed in eliminating Title X by transferring out all of its funds, prolife members had also succeeded in attaching several other important prolife amendments, such as measures 1) forbidding the use of federal funds for research or experimentation on human embryos (introduced by Republicans Jay Dickey of Arkansas and Roger Wicker of Mississippi); 2) stipulating that federal funds could not be denied to medical schools refusing to teach abortion techniques, as the Accreditation Council of Graduate Medical Education had been attempting to require nationwide (introduced by Republican Tom DeLay of Texas); and 3) allowing states to deny payment for Medicaid abortions on grounds of rape or incest, as the Clinton Administration had been requiring states to do even when this was against their own state laws on the matter (introduced by Republican Ernest Istook of Oklahoma).

The amendment to "x" out Title X was offered, and all of the other prolife amendments were consented to, by Appropriations Committee Chairman Bob Livingston of Louisiana, who commented that it was "pay-back time" for the Prolife Caucus for the strong support it had given to so much of the Republican agenda up to that point. It had been fairly widely noted, in fact, that the famous Contract with America, which the new House Republican majority had substantially passed in the first 100 days of the new Congress, was admittedly very short on prolife and profamily elements. More than that, the House Republican leadership had been regularly putting prolife members off, and scotching some of their initiatives, fearful of splitting the Republican majority on the always volatile abortion issue.

As Rep. Livingston recognized, however, it was time for the prolife members to start moving some of the items on their own agenda. Nor was this the only appropriations bill to which important prolife amendments were being attached; provisions denying the use of foreign aid funds for abortions and abolishing abortion coverage in federal health insurance had already been enacted in connection with other bills, for example, as had amendments forbidding the performance of abortions in military hospitals or payment for abortions by the Bureau of Prisons.

In the case of this particular Education-Labor-HHS bill, however, it turned out that the so-called "moderate" Republicans were not going to stand still; they were simply not prepared to let all the prolife measures in the bill pass unchallenged. (How the term "moderate," by the way, ever came to be applied to members who are, precisely, promoting the use of taxpayer dollars to corrupt the morals of the recipients of family-planning services, and to fund the killing of the innocent by abortion, is another one of those anomalies of our very confused times.)

Proabortion Republican House members prepared two amendments of their own to the Education-Labor-HHS appropriations bill. One of these amendments, introduced by Congressman Jim Greenwood of Pennsylvania, restored to Title X the nearly $200 million which had been taken away from the program by the committee action. Another amendment, by Congressman Jim Kolbe of Arizona, would have again forced states to pay for rape and incest abortions under Medicaid. The "moderates" behind these measures, over two dozen of them, then let the Republican leadership know that they would oppose the entire appropriations bill if their amendments were not allowed — and this could have effectively prevented the bill's passage.

Meanwhile, the House Republican leadership was already on notice from the prolife side, which had already prevailed in committee on its own measures, that prolife members too would take a walk on the issue unless their amendments were included. What was involved for the leadership was deciding which amendments would be protected by rule from challenges on the floor; all such substantive amendments were vulnerable on the floor precisely because of the regular House rule against substantive law-making in appropriations bills.

Now the Republican leadership, consisting of Speaker Newt Gingrich of Georgia, Majority Leader Dick Armey of Texas, and Whip

Tom DeLay of Texas is supposed to be officially "prolife"; all of them ran for office and thus they presumably solicited the support of the voters on that basis. In fact, the prolife amendment concerning medical schools was Tom DeLay's own personal amendment. But the leadership was not prepared to take an integral prolife stand on this bill.

It is not at all clear whether a firm prolife stand by the leadership — sending a strong signal that it *was* indeed "payback time" for the prolifers in the Republican coalition — would not have proved to be sufficiently persuasive for most of the proabortion Republican members, who all have plenty of other reasons for wanting to go along with the leadership, after all. If it had been almost any other issue except abortion, it seems pretty clear that the leadership would have insisted much more strongly that the bill embodying language demanded by such an important component of the Republican coalition had to be passed intact.

Based on the records of Gingrich and Armey to date on prolife issues, however, such a firm, uncompromising stand by them in this instance would probably have been an even more surprising development than the elimination of Title X funds by the Appropriations Committee.

In the event, Speaker Newt Gingrich made the decision that the leadership would not insist on party discipline on the bill which the Appropriations Committee had crafted; the speaker told both sides that he would take the bill to the floor without any rule protecting any of the amendments, any of which could then have been stricken from the bill on the floor. The speaker pointedly passed out a list of all the measures in the bill that would be jeopardized in that event. In this situation, it was the prolife side, with all of the important prolife measures already written into the bill, which had the most to lose. The head of the Prolife Caucus, Representative Chris Smith of New Jersey, understandably complained that Gingrich's decision really favored the proabortion side.

What the Gingrich decision led to was, in fact, a legislative compromise. After lengthy and, press reports said, tempestuous negotiations, it was agreed that the proabortion side would drop the attempt to continue to force the states on the matter of Medicaid abortions. However, the Greenwood Amendment restoring Title X funds would be accorded an up or down vote on the floor (that is, the Livingston amendment excising of the Title X money would *not* be protected by rule). On the floor, of course, 57 Republicans were thus found to join the Democrats in restoring the $193 million to the program by voting for the Greenwood Amendment.

Meanwhile, however, the three prolife amendments on embryo experimentation, medical schools, and Medicaid abortions remained in the final bill, which then passed with a total of 219 affirmative votes.

Up to the last minute, however, some members on both sides continued to balk at support for the entire bill. One group of 23 prolife members actually resorted to a public prayer service in order to seek divine guidance on the matter, before they finally decided that the positive and definite prolife advances which the bill did contain justified their support for it. This is a relatively new thing in Congress: a group of knowledgeable and cohesive prolife members determined not to be put off, even while they are realistic about working the system effectively; it bodes well for the future of the prolife cause.

In the meantime, though, the other side was equally obstinate. Even though it can be argued that the prolife gains were not all that great, considering the enormity of the evil of legalized abortion, the fact is that almost *any* prolife gain at all tends to unhinge the proabortionists, who once thought this issue had been settled for good in their favor. Speaker Gingrich reportedly had to resort to his notable powers of persuasion in order to convince some of the "hardline moderates" (a contradiction in terms?) to go along with the entire bill at the end: having won on Title X, they finally decided they had to bend a little too.

Given the typical mind-set of this "moderate" group, however, we should not be too surprised if its adherents do not attempt some kind of really aggressive and determined action against the prolife cause. Although the prolife gains made are relatively modest, these people already see them as forerunners of an unstoppable juggernaut. If only. . .

According to press accounts, though, Speaker Gingrich was reported to be absolutely furious at what he considered to be prolife obduracy on this particular bill. This could well be because he now realizes that prolife members really are going to insist on measures which the speaker himself does not see as essential to the Republican program for America — but which he clearly does see unhinge the proabortion members of his shaky coalition and jeopardize his control of the whole legislative process.

Although the issue is not entirely clear cut in this particular case, it still does seem that the speaker leaned farther than he had to towards the proabortion side; if so, he may be underestimating the importance of the Prolife Caucus to his larger Republican Coalition. It would hardly be the first time that the Republican leadership has been short-sighted in this regard. Nevertheless, the passage of the whole Education-Labor-HHS appropriations bill was generally seen and reported in the media as yet another triumph for the astute politician from Georgia.

III

In many ways, the passage of the 1995 Education-Labor-HHS appropriations bill by the U.S. House of Representatives represented just another day orchestrating "the dance of legislation." The initial and surprising elimination of Title X of the Public Health Service Act, followed by its rather prompt restoration, was just one more example of how coalitions shift and deals are typically made in Congress. What does it mean for the prolife movement?

First, it is sadly evident that prolife and profamily forces in Congress, in spite of the impressive gains registered in the 1994 elections, still do not possess the overall strength simply to get rid of a program even as bad as Title X is. What is surprising for veteran observers of the congressional scene is that the initiative even got as far as it did, namely, that it succeeded in garnering a winning vote in the House Appropriations Committee. This was an especially impressive achievement, considering that the House Republican leadership probably never wanted the issue brought up at all; the fact that it got as far as it did means that many House members now do understand how bad it is and want to see it eliminated.

This represents yet one more indication that the prolife gains registered in the last election were not negligible. Not only are more prolife measures being pushed, even contrary to the wishes of the leadership; some of them are even getting enacted. This is all to the good. Nevertheless the defeat in 1996 of more proabortion members, and the election of more prolife members, surely remains an imperative necessity.

Regarding so-called "family planning," though, there is not likely to be a major breakthrough on it any time soon. Title X should have been a prime target for an aggressive conservative majority looking for wasteful and harmful government programs to cut. But this would have been to reckon without the almost sacrosanct status that family planning programs, in spite of their documented failure and indeed the positive evidence of all the harm they have done, have come to occupy in our contemporary mind-set and in our culture. A verifiable majority of the House of Representatives evidently continues to believe these programs are doing good; and, in this, these law-makers very likely reflect the majority view of their constituents. People today not only see "nothing wrong" with birth control; birth control has long since come to be accepted as an essential feature of modern life; it is not seen as in any way an evil but rather as a positive and necessary moral and social good. Why shouldn't the government be promoting it?

There is little sense, either in the Congress or among the public at large, that in indiscriminately providing both contraceptive counseling and the wherewithal to practice it, the government is really contributing to the further moral breakdown of our society. The message that these family planning programs actually deliver to their clientele is: we do not believe that you possess inherent human dignity or are capable of ordering your life and behavior in accordance with reason and the moral law; on the contrary, we believe you are no better than a rutting animal out of control, and that you are going to engage in permissive sexual activity exactly as you please, regardless of age, condition, or marital status; the government's only concern, therefore, must be to limit to the extent possible the *consequences* in the form of unwanted pregnancies of the untrammeled sexual activity that is expected of you.

That this sort of argument applies as readily to abortion as it does to family planning — and this is what the actual experience of our society has shown — is obstinately never noted or admitted either by the proponents of family planning or by their media parrots. A number of members of Congress argued strongly against the elimination of Title X because this would allegedly increase abortions; eliminating support for family planning was "a bad, bad agenda" for decreasing abortions, in the words of Illinois Republican Representative John Edward Porter, the subcommittee chairman who had put the $193 million in Title X to begin with (which the full Appropriations Committee under Livingston then attempted to excise).

Republican Representative Connie Morella of Maryland similarly declared that "to eliminate this program when we're trying to reduce the number of abortions. . .flies in the face of common sense. . ."

Actually, "common sense," if that is what it is, is wrong about this: there is no evidence that contraceptive use reduces the number of abortions; the evidence all points the other way. Once the really fundamental decision has been made that it is the unwanted pregnancies that have to be eliminated, rather than the sexual promiscuity, then nobody any longer distinguishes very carefully between the various "methods" to accomplish this, whether they come before or after the fact of the conception of a child.

This is exactly the way in which legalized abortion came to our society, as a matter of fact: whatever else it might be, abortion surely was a foolproof method for the elimination of unwanted pregnancies; and it was the elimination of these unwanted pregnancies which had already been decided to be the primary objective. No matter that our society was now actually resorting to legalized killing in order to realize this objective; the objective itself was what was deemed fundamental. Congressman Porter and Congresswoman Morella precisely illustrate the point, as do all of the others of their way of thinking, by the undeniable fact that they consistently vote for *both* family planning *and* abortion; they cannot consistently pretend to be the champions of the former as against the latter, or claim that the former reduces the latter; their whole approach is just more piece of sham and dishonesty.

Thus, "family planning" continues to remain relatively invulnerable in today's atmosphere. Even the House members who opposed Title X, apparently, opposed it not so much because it provided family planning services, but rather because it provided massive funds for Planned Parenthood and also thereby promoted abortion. One of the strongest Title X opponents was Republican Representative John N. Hostettler of Indiana, who authored and published an article forcefully opposing the restoration of Title X. At the same time, though, the good Congressman felt obliged to include the question: "But don't poor people need family planning assistance?" "Yes," he answered, "which they can get through. . .other programs. . ."

The notion that perhaps neither poor people, nor anyone else, in fact *do not need government family planning assistance at all*, is an idea that seems never to have crossed his mind.

We are not yet very far along towards restoration of the moral order in the United States when even prolife members of Congress do not yet understand that not just legalized abortion, but government family planning assistance itself, as such, is gravely harmful and morally corrupting — and inevitably dehumanizes those who are involved in it.

We should, of course, be very happy that some members of Congress have been motivated by their opposition to abortion to try to eliminate Title X as well. But we should not be under any illusions about how far we probably still have to go before we will ever succeed in convincing our fellow citizens, along with our representatives in Congress, that modern family planning itself — the attempt to implement the modern error that sex can be separated from both procreation and from the moral law — must itself cease to be considered respectable in any society or polity that is truly seeking the authentic moral health of its people.

10

The Significance of the Pope's New Encyclical

I

Pope John Paul II's new encyclical *Evangelium Vitae*, "the Gospel of Life," has received high praise as a remarkable and perhaps unique modern explanation of the meaning of the commandment, "You shall not kill." Certainly there is very little about the meaning and implications of this commandment in today's world that the pope has not covered, at least in some fashion.

In the encyclical, though, the pope concentrates on the peculiarly modern evils of abortion and euthanasia; and he condemns these twin evils, along with the killing of the innocent generally, in a particularly solemn way, expressly invoking "the authority which Christ conferred upon Peter and his successors," and explicitly declaring that he is teaching "in communion with the bishops of the Catholic Church " (EV #57. #62. and #65). Thus, the pope clearly intends his teachings on these points to be both definitive and binding upon the faithful.

Moreover, as Vatican II's Dogmatic Constitution on the Church *Lumen Gentium* (#25) informs us, when the pope and the bishops are "in agreement that a particular teaching is to be held definitively and absolutely," such a teaching must be considered as taught "infallibly" by the Church. Although the encyclical does not say in so many words that the pope's solemn condemnations of abortion and euthanasia and the killing of innocent are infallible teachings, nevertheless, because the pope does invoke his full authority and also declares that he is teaching in agreement with the Catholic bishops of the world, it would now seem to be exceedingly difficult, if not impossible, to consider these teachings as anything but infallibly taught.

Certainly the pope expressly intends to make clear, once and for all, the Church's unchanged and unchangeable position on these cry-

---

First printed in *Fidelity,* July/August, 1995.

ing contemporary evils. The pope's condemnation of abortion, euthanasia, and the killing of the innocent may well even constitute the strongest official pronouncements the Catholic Church has ever made on any moral question in her entire history.

On the other hand, nobody ever imagined that the pope and the Church were ever anything but strongly opposed to these particular evils all along. So, in another sense, there is little that is really new in the encyclical. Indeed, the perceived "absolutism" of the pope and the Church on questions of this type is the very thing they are most often reproached for in the cultural climate of today, when former moral absolutes — such as the Ten Commandments — are now widely considered to have "evolved" to meet today's alleged new situations.

In America today, after all, we already do have legalized abortion, along with a "contraceptive mentality" that sees human beings as in complete charge of human life. The maxim of the Greek sophists reigns: Man is the measure of all things. Not surprisingly, this mentality of total control over life, and the transmission of life, has brought with it a number of actually ghoulish, Frankenstein's monster-type related evils, which the pope does not fail also to condemn, such as in-vitro fertilization and experimentation on human embryos and fetuses.

Soon, the way things are going, we will no doubt have legalized euthanasia and doctor-assisted suicide as well. These things were recently approved in a popular referendum in the state of Oregon. Once society has decided, as with legalized abortion, that "You shall not kill" no longer applies across the board, it seems inevitable that this commandment will indeed turn out not to apply in more and more instances. The logic of it is inexorable after all.

Meanwhile, in the minds of many, it is the Catholic Church that is seen as out of line on these things. The Church, in the view of many people today, some of them members of the Church, is supposed to be moving with the times. Or, at any rate, the Church is not supposed to be raising too much of a fuss about all the unheard of new things that are happening: that would be undemocratic. "Society" has decided on these things, after all. Besides, who else is protesting? The Church has no right to interfere and set herself up as society's judge in such matters; separation of church and state is still supposed to apply in this country — so it is typically argued.

But Pope John Paul II has now definitively judged for the Church anyway; and he has ruled that, from the standpoint of God's unchanging laws, which by the will of Christ the Church authentically interprets with the help of the Holy Spirit, our society has in fact been moving in the wrong direction for quite some time now. At this point in time, in the pope's view, it is clear that society has decided to go where Christians cannot follow and still remain faithful to God. The Catholic Church, therefore, is going to have to keep raising a fuss about it. The Church cannot help this; she could not remain true to Christ if she did not continue to raise her voice, separation of church and state notwithstanding.

This, in fact, is precisely where the principal significance of this encyclical lies: its issuance, at this time and in this manner, means that the Church is in fact not going to stand still while the modern world goes on perpetrating and promoting the evils it has tragically decided to embrace. The Church has no choice but to resist, and she also has to teach her faithful that they have to resist too.

The answer to the cynical question Cain asked after he killed his brother Abel, "Am I my brother's keeper?" (Gen 4:9) — the answer to this question, according to Pope John Paul II in this encyclical, is: "Yes, every man is his 'brother's keeper' because God entrusts us to one another" (EV #19). We are responsible for the weakest and most defenseless among us. The Church cannot remain silent in the face of today's assaults and outright crimes against human life. Neither can anyone who professes to follow Christ. This, then, is one of the principal things this encyclical has to teach us.

The theology and arguments used by Pope John Paul II in *Evangelium Vitae* are, for the most part, not new. Most of them have long since been set forth in other Church documents such as the Congregation for the Doctrine of the Faith's Declarations on Procured Abortion (1974) and on Euthanasia (1980). Similarly, the pope's reiterations in this encyclical of the Church's condemnations of contraception, sexual activity outside of marriage, artificial insemination, in-vitro fertilization, and related evils have also long since been set forth, if not in papal encyclicals such as Pope Paul VI's *Humanae Vitae* (1968), or in Pope John Paul II's own apostolic exhortation *Familiaris Consortio* (1981), then in Instructions from the Congregation for the Doctrine of the Faith such as the one on Respect for Human Life in Its Origin and on the Dignity of Procreation, *Donum Vitae* (1988), or the earlier one on Certain Questions concerning Sexual Ethics, *Persona Humana* (1975).

The Church had thus already spelled out in some detail her position on all of these issues well before this encyclical was ever thought of.

The same thing is true of the pope's *obiter dicta*, or mention in passing, of most of the other issues he touches upon in the encyclical such as war, the arms trade, economic exploitation, and environmental degradation: the position of the pope, and of the Church's contemporary magisterium, are all very much on the record concerning these issues; they are available to anybody who wants to know what they are. Indeed, virtually everything in the new encyclical is covered, or at least mentioned, in the new *Catechism of the Catholic Church*.

This is even basically true of the pope's remarks on capital punishment found in this encyclical. Much has been made about what the pope says on this subject, and many press articles on the encyclical have singled out the capital punishment issue for special comment. Cardinal Joseph Ratzinger, prefect of the Congregation for the Doctrine of the Faith in Rome, said in his statement introducing the pope's encyclical to the press, that John Paul II's "reservations with regard to the death penalty are still stronger than those already presented in the *Catechism*." According to Cardinal Ratzinger, this represents a distinct "development of doctrine" which will be incorporated into the *Catechism* when the latter is revised.

It is true that the pope's reservations about the use of capital punishment today are even "stronger" than those in the *Catechism*, as Cardinal Ratzinger correctly noted; but they are not different in kind. Both the pope and the *Catechism* continue to recognize and affirm the Church's traditional teaching regarding the moral licitness of legitimate state authority resorting to execution provided by law for proportionate reasons of those who are guilty of grave crimes — capital punishment is, precisely, not the killing of the innocent, which is what this encyclical basically condemns. Capital punishment involves a somewhat different moral question, as the Church has traditionally recognized, and as this encyclical continues to recognize.

Neither the pope nor the *Catechism*, however, thinks very highly of capital punishment as it has been practiced in the past. This "development" in the encyclical is based on the pope's judgment that, since "penal justice" must be "ever more in line with human dignity," offenders should not be executed "except in cases of absolute necessity" — and in today's world the pope judges these cases to be "very rare if not practically non-existent" (EV #56).

In an encyclical in which he takes excruciatingly great pains to defend human life and human dignity against all the callous, wanton, and even gruesome evils that regularly assail them today, it is perhaps not surprising that the pope has also come to view capital punishment too as contributing today to the further cheapening of the value of human life and of human dignity generally. Our era is an era that no longer places anything but utilitarian value upon human life and human dignity. So in a document which intends among other things to recall today's utilitarians back to a sounder respect for the dignity and sanctity of human life, placing too great an emphasis on the distinction between the death penalty and today's other peculiarly modern ways of taking life may have struck the pope as not particularly helpful.

In today's climate, the disrespect if not contempt for the sanctity of life that manifests itself in so many ways mark this era as one in which it is counterproductive to insist too strongly on the state's traditional prerogative under certain narrowly defined conditions of taking the life of those who have forfeited their innocence — better to affirm human life and human dignity across the board, even where the sinner or the hardened criminal is concerned: so John Paul II concludes.

Nevertheless, the pope still does carefully distinguish between the legal execution of the guilty, duly convicted under law, and the wholly immoral, always unjustifiable killing of the innocent; and it is the latter which he singles out for solemn condemnation "with the authority which Christ conferred upon Peter and his successors" (EV #57).

II

Evangelium Vitae confirms that the Church has been nothing if not consistent on all of the burning life and death issues covered in this encyclical; nor has the Church in any way neglected to set forth her carefully considered teachings on all of these issues. This encyclical, however, coming as it does in the midst of what Pope John Paul II has often styled our modern "culture of death" — and the pope does not fail to repeat this characterization in this encyclical (e.g., EV #21) — and embodying, as it also does in the highest degree, the supreme teaching authority of the vicar of Christ — in view of these things, the appearance of this encyclical at this juncture cannot be considered anything but an event of the very greatest importance. It may even turn out to be something of a watershed event, a turning point in enlisting the Church and Catholics more actively against the galloping antilife developments increasingly being manifested in our contemporary society.

The importance of the document lies not merely in what it says, but even more in the fact that the pope has chosen to cover all of these human life issues again, carefully and definitively, this time in his own name and in a special teaching document devoted especially to them, meanwhile invoking the full teaching authority he has from Christ in the cases of abortion, euthanasia, and the killing of the innocent.

And he has chosen to do this at a moment when the premises and presuppositions of our contemporary culture of death are increasingly being accepted and taken for granted as "necessary" and "inevitable" modern developments. Who, indeed, is effectively speaking out against these things in our society at large except the pope? As the head of a worldwide Church, he is at least able to get the attention of world leaders and world public opinion; and even when his views do not command general agreement, it is recognized that his voice carries considerable weight and represents a significant challenge to the way the modern world has been going.

The issuance of *Evangelium Vitae* thus means that the Catholic Church does not, and cannot, accept the way the whole modern world has been going. The Church is not going to back down or back away from the principled defense of life in the midst of today's culture of death. One of the things about solemn declarations made by the supreme magisterium of the Catholic Church is that they *cannot* be taken back. Certainly there is no way anything in this encyclical could ever be taken back, even supposing some future pope would ever want to do so. Nor does the solemn way in which the pope has elected to teach in this instance suggest that these human life issues might simply be neglected or quietly forgotten, either.

So the issuance of this encyclical means that the Church cannot accept, and is not going to accept, that today's utilitarian control of life by abortion, euthanasia, fetal experimentation, and similar practices represent irreversible modern developments which are now simply here to stay. The corruption of society that they represent is too fundamental. These evils must be opposed and combatted. This is the message of the pope.

It does not matter what the practical difficulties might be in the way of effectively opposing and combatting them; they have to be opposed and combatted anyway.

The Church cannot accept, and is not going to accept, that making evil "the law of the land," even democratically, can ever settle anything so alien to the law of God as abortion, euthanasia, or the killing of the innocent. *Evangelium Vitae* represents, in effect, an ultimatum to the modern world and to its culture of death. A gauntlet has been thrown down, and further confrontation and struggle are inevitable.

Nevertheless, Pope John Paul II has issued this ultimatum to the modern world at a time when, if polls are to be believed, he apparently cannot even count on the support of all Catholics to back him up on the positions he has taken, let alone find mass support among the public at large. Nor is the pope unaware of the formidable opposition to what he is saying that exists out there.

But this, of course, is surely one of the very reasons the pope has raised the banner in the way that he has at this particular time. The Catholic Church has always been, and is widely known to be, against abortion, euthanasia, and the other evils that the pope condemns in the encyclical; indeed the Church is notorious for precisely this stance of hers today. Vatican Council II did not fail to call abortion an "abominable crime" (*Gaudium et Spes*, #51), and the U.S. Catholic bishops have regularly issued statements against legalizing it going back at least to 1967. The prolife office sponsored by the bishops' conference has continued to do invaluable work on the prolife front.

On the other hand, the "seamless garment" approach which has also been promoted among Catholics, in effect placing concern for poverty, economic exploitation, and the like on the same moral leveal as the legalized killing of the innocent, gets the priorities all wrong. While this approach reflects Catholic social teaching in certain respects, and in a sense is even reflected in the various concerns listed in this encyclical — for the Catholic Church still *is* concerned about poverty, economic exploitation, and the like — what the seamless garment approach has nevertheless too often provided in practice has been an excuse for those Catholics who have continued to support proabortion politicians and their type of legislation, provided only that the latter were *for*, let us say, welfare, Medicaid or other benefits for the poor and disadvantaged.

Moreover, Catholics, along with other Americans, have been living for so long in a society where legalized abortion and other antilife manifestations are not only tolerated, but are actually encouraged by the powers that be — in this situation, Catholics have often come to accept these things as a matter of course, and, indeed, to take them for granted. They are thought to be irreversible developments; there is nothing much anybody can do about them; it is futile to go on protesting them; and so on. Society, after all, accepts them, regardless of how immoral they may be regarded by the magisterium of the Church. And we have to live in this society.

Anyway, what can the Church, or Catholics, effectively do about what society has decided — even if it is manifestly against the law of God? The prevailing rules in the secular society we live in effectively prevent any religion or denomination from opposing what "society" has thus decided (even if a majority of Americans still nevertheless profess to believe in the God whose laws are being transgressed by society).

In this situation, no majority or even critical mass of Americans, including Catholics, has yet been formed in the body politic so as to make the de-legalization of abortion either thinkable or doable at the present moment. In this same climate, the pro-euthanasia forces continue to make considerable — and chilling — progress. The prolife movement may have accomplished many things in the more than two decades it has been around; but we do not even seem to be close to being able to make abortion illegal again. Moreover, "practical people" immediately see this, and so this becomes yet one more reason why the culture of death is not seen as something that has to be fought against.

But now Pope John Paul II has solemnly issued *Evangelium Vitae*, saying, in effect, that this common passive attitude in the face of so many of today's gigantic evils is itself illegitimate; it is inadmissible. Abortion and the other evils the pope catalogues must be fought against; nobody has the right to sit on the fence while these evils triumph; they are literally capable of destroying our society, and they are in the process of doing so.

There is no longer any room, then, for being "personally opposed to abortion" — as too many Catholic politicians have professed to be, and have been tolerated in this by too many Catholic voters.

Now, however, the Vicar of Christ has made all this a matter of "the authority which Christ conferred upon Peter and his successors." The realization may still be slow in coming, but the fact is that all of these

Catholic politicians and voters are going to have to decide somewhere in the secret recesses of their consciences whether they really are, or want to go on being, Catholics. Many may decide, of course — many may have already decided, in effect — that no, their Catholic profession of faith is not important enough to trump their desire to go along with what the world wants. "They have their reward" (Mt 6:2).

Others, however, may decide very differently. The growing horrors of the culture of death, along with the now undeniable realization that the only real Catholic position on the various human life issues with which we are confronted in our society is the one which the Holy Father has now unmistakably set forth in his encyclical — the realization of these things may eventually influence more people than we can currently imagine. It will not happen overnight; too many Catholics have become accustomed in recent years to thinking that certain positions are optional for Catholics, positions which Pope John Paul II has now made clear are not optional.

Then there are all those sincere Christians who are not Catholics, who may even have been brought up with prejudice against Catholics and the Church, but who now look out upon the dismaying spectacle of our culture of death and find no leaders in their own ranks effectively opposing the truths of Christ to what they see out there — the only visible leader on the world scene who is both articulating the truths of Christ and opposing the culture of death turns out to be the Catholic bishop of Rome, the Roman Pontiff! How long has it been since a pope has been *seen* to be the world leader of all who believe in Christ the way John Paul II has now currently come to be seen as such in the face of the culture of death?

When such Catholics and other Christians "have turned again" (Lk 22:31) in greater numbers, therefore, their numbers may then perhaps be added up in order to make up that critical mass of convinced prolife voters that we must have in order oppose the culture of death on the social and political planes. These changes of mind and heart will not come about instantly, but there is real hope that they can and will come about. Pope John Paul II, among others, is counting on it.

III

In conclusion, it is worth briefly summarizing what several of the practical implications of John Paul II's encyclical *Evangelium Vitae* would appear to be for the prolife movement in the United States.

(1) The prolife movement must work to restore to the unborn the full legal right to life and to the equal protection of the laws which the Constitution is already supposed to guarantee to all. Since it is a faulty interpretation of the Constitution by the Supreme Court which has permitted legalized abortion in the United States since 1973, a constitutional amendment making clear that we cannot have elective killing of any kind under our Constitution is undoubtedly going to be required in order to achieve this. If properly framed, such an amendment can and should deal with other issues such as assisted suicide, euthanasia, the illicit creation of human embryos *in vitro* and experimentation upon them, and so on. The sanctity of human life must be inviolable at all stages. Incidentally, it is likely that John Paul II was thinking of the U.S. Constitution when he remarked in his encyclical that some countries have legalized abortion while "perhaps even departing from basic principles of their constitution" (EV #4).

(2) While working towards the necessary ultimate goal of a Human Life Amendment, the prolife movement in the United States can also, appropriately and legitimately, work to limit or restrict legalized abortion — which is currently unlimited by virtue of the *Roe v. Wade* decision — by favoring legislation or other measures short of the absolute protection of the unborn which a constitutional amendment would provide. The pope explicitly states in *Evangelium Vitae* that "when it is not possible to overturn or completely abrogate a proabortion law, an elected official whose absolute personal opposition to procured abortion was well known could licitly support proposals aimed at limiting the harm done by such a law and at lessening its negative consequences at the level of general opinion and public morality" (EV #73). It is to be hoped that this papal statement will put an end once and for all to the long-standing and harmful controversy within the prolife movement to the effect that any support for antiabortion measures short of absolute protection of the right to life of the fetus means complicity with the abortionists, since to agree to "regulate" a practice in itself abhorrent means, it is argued, to "accept" it. It does not necessarily mean any such thing; rather, it can be seen as one step on the way to outlawing the abhorrent practice in question — and this is the way the prolife movement should now view legalized abortion with the express endorsement of Pope John Paul II.

(3) Neither Catholic politicians nor Catholic voters should any longer be able to take refuge in the statement that they are "person-

ally opposed" to abortion but that they have to abide by what the law is in the United States. No: Pope John Paul II endorses and ratifies the view of St. Thomas Aquinas that a law contrary to right reason "ceases to be a law and becomes instead an act of violence" (EV #72). This dictum has never been truer than when applied to *Roe v. Wade*, a decision that is truly nothing else but "an act of violence."

(4) The "seamless garment" approach which tends to place all social evils on the same level can no longer be used as an excuse for continuing to tolerate — and even support — politicians who vote the proabortion line but who hold other views on, say, welfare, which presumably accord with Catholic social teaching. But the Holy Father has now singled out the evils of abortion, euthanasia, and the killing of the innocent in a solemn way which now makes it impossible to place other things on the same moral level. If there remains some kind of a stigma in being a "one-issue voter," the Holy Father himself proudly displays his own stigmata on these particular issues. It is time for Catholics to begin looking at the comparative moral seriousness of these human life issues, and not go on imagining that it is enough just to be liberal, in favor of the poor, etc.

(5) In view of the seriousness which, in the light of the encyclical, we now know abortion, euthanasia, and the killing of the innocent to be, the prolife movement cannot be content with partial solutions to the abortion issue which allow "some killing" to go on provided that, say, the total numbers of abortions are reduced. Above all we can no longer settle the issue on the basis of what Americans currently believe about abortion, namely, that they want some abortions to remain legal even while they admit that abortion is wrong. No: the goal of the prolife movement must be to stop the killing. No system claiming to be based on a Constitution which protects natural rights can maintain its own integrity if it allows legal abrogation of some of those rights. We must stop looking at public opinion polls and begin thinking about what needs to be done to educate American public opinion in the harm that legalized killing does to our entire system.

The fact is that, if the battle for human life in which we are currently engaged is lost, then American freedom and the American system are going to be lost as well. Nobody could say this better than Pope John Paul II has already said it in *Evangelium Vitae*:

> To claim the right to abortion, infanticide, and euthanasia, and to recognize that right in law, means to attribute to human freedom a perverse and evil significance: that of an absolute power over others and against others. This is the death of true freedom. . .In this way, democracy, contradicting its own principles, effectively moves toward a form of totalitarianism (EV #20).

11

Still Not "Getting It"

I

In staging the Republican National Convention which nominated Bob Dole and Jack Kemp in San Diego in August, the leadership of the Republican Party — including both of the candidates, most of the speakers, and, especially, the party and convention managers — made consistent, sustained, and perhaps even partially successful efforts to present what was surely one of the most conservative and prolife gatherings in American history as instead everything the major media and the supposed American mainstream imagine a political party is supposed to be, that is, "politically correct."

In particular, the issue of legalized abortion, which for hundreds of the delegates was probably the most important political issue at stake, almost disappeared from sight — at least as far as the official proceedings were concerned — once what was admittedly a very strong prolife platform calling for a constitutional amendment to protect the right to life of the unborn had been decided upon.

In the planning and execution of the San Diego convention, almost all traces of the Republican Party's (nevertheless well-known!) "extremism," "intolerance," and "mean-spiritedness" were carefully scripted out; in no way, if the Republican leadership had any say in the matter, was this going to be a reprise of the notorious Houston Republican Convention of 1992, when speakers such as Pat Buchanan were supposed to have declared a culture war on mainstream America, a culture war which, in the mythology of the major media, was then responsible for the subsequent ill fortune of the Republicans — except that the Republicans did not suffer any notable ill fortune after 1992, winning both houses of Congress overwhelmingly in 1994, in elections in which, in particular, no prolife incumbent, anywhere, was defeated, and in which considerable prolife and conservative gains were otherwise registered.

Published in *Culture Wars*, October, 1996.

No culture war was "declared" in 1992, then. The only question, then and now, was whether and to what extent the political conventions would take cognizance of the fierce culture war already going on in America today. The Republican convention in Houston had at least addressed the issue.

By 1996, however, mythology had triumphed over reality in the minds of Republican planners, and scarcely a hint about any culture war going on was allowed at the San Diego convention; all the talk was programmed to be about such things as freedom and opportunity, individual initiative and working moms, cutting taxes and getting the government off the back of the average American.

However pertinent and valid such topics as far as they went, they scarcely got to the heart of the increasing social decay and even disintegration and galloping moral decadence in our society which troubles an increasing number of Americans who have been looking to the Republicans for political leadership in these troubled times; but the requisite leadership was little in evidence at this convention.

Instead, smiles and optimism were decreed by the convention managers as expressive of the obligatory mood, even if they sometimes had to be expressed through gritted teeth. The principal watchwords decreed were "tolerance" and "inclusiveness," especially the latter: nobody here but us "moderates," boss.

In our current political vocabulary, of course, "moderate" is a favorite code word signifying tolerance, or even approval, of the current constitutional situation in America which allows for the legalized killing of babies by abortion. To be "moderate" means to agree that, while the U.S. Supreme Court may have wrongly decided its *Roe v. Wade* decision in 1973 legalizing abortion, or may even have exceeded its competence entirely in attempting to decide any such question at all, nevertheless nothing can or should now be done about this absolutely extraordinary and unprecedented situation; it should not even be discussed, in fact, because it always turns out to be so "divisive" — and so anybody who disagrees with *that* must automatically be marked as an "extremist" too!

But since people holding such "moderate" views need to be included in Republican ranks if the party is ever to make up a majority, continuing to include them becomes imperative, and "inclusiveness" inevitably becomes another code word, as it did at this convention.

And what "inclusiveness" means is that the Republican Party, in spite of its official prolife stance as set forth in its platform, nevertheless does not require its candidates, members, or supporters to be prolife if they are inclined to some other view. Indeed the hope is that many voters will support the Republican Party for its other positions even if they disagree with its prolife position. Considering that rallying a majority of Americans around a constitutional amendment prohibiting abortion is not a likely prospect at this time, it no doubt makes good political sense to try to project the idea that, even while the Republican Party does remain the nation's prolife party, it nevertheless wants and welcomes others who do not share this particular position. Hence the convention's emphasis on "inclusiveness."

Unfortunately, however, this particular emphasis was carried to such lengths in San Diego as to constitute a distinct put-down, if not an actual insult, to the Republican Party's huge prolife constituency, including what was surely a large majority of the delegates present in the hall. From the tone and substance of the official proceedings it sometimes seemed that everybody was being included *except* the prolifers, who have worked so hard for the party over the past few years.

For "inclusiveness" meant: pointedly choosing prominent "prochoice" Republicans such as General Colin Powell and keynoter Rep. Susan Molinari of New York precisely in order to send the message that the prolife issue is not really all that important in spite of what the party platform says. Inclusiveness meant: making prochoice New Jersey Governor Christine Todd Whitman the convention co-chairman in order to reinforce the same message.

And as if it were not enough to load the official program with prochoicers, even when actual prolifers were up there on the podium, they almost never spoke on the subject of abortion itself or affirmed their own or the party's position on the matter. Former Vice President Dan Quayle was perhaps the only speaker who even mentioned the subject of abortion within the hearing of the entire convention, and he confined himself to the relatively "safe" topic of the Partial Birth Abortion Act which Bill Clinton had vetoed.

Erstwhile presidential aspirant Alan Keyes, who conducted an impressive and honorable if losing prolife primary campaign, and who is an eloquent and exciting speaker, was accorded a heavily edited 30-second videotape appearance before the convention. "They don't want people like me here," he remarked ruefully. And added: "Why would you have a convention where you retreat from a positive prolife position? The prolife stance is not a political liability. It has never hurt a Republican when it is presented right."

But the party leadership and the convention managers were not interested in trying to present it at all. Rather, they went far out of their way in order to downplay the whole issue. Not only did the party's presidential nominee and hence current head, Robert J. Dole, go equally far out of his way in order to tell an interviewer that he had not even bothered to read the platform containing the famous prolife plank; Republican National Chairman Haley Barbour and Speaker of the House Newt Gingrich both said exactly the same thing, emphasizing that *they* had not read it either. Even former President George Bush felt obliged to echo this "consensus" when he told yet another interviewer that he had not read either of the platforms on which he ran in 1988 and 1992.

No doubt the principal motive of all these Republican leaders, all of them officially "prolife," by the way, was to underline the message that the Republican Party does not set up any one issue as a "litmus test" and it sincerely does want to attract the support of the maximum number of voters whatever their views. This policy may even be understandable, though it surely depends upon how it is presented.

But is it legitimate — is it even honest — for a political party to seek the support of a portion of the electorate by announcing a particular stand and by adopting, say, a prolife amendment, and then, in effect, deliberately downplaying or even nullifying that stand in order to appeal to another portion of the electorate?

Did it not occur at any point to any of these distinguished Republican leaders what the effect might be of expressly and publicly stating that the party's professed principles, as expressed in its platform, were really not of any real importance to them? Surely none of these leaders would have been willing to give the impression that lowering taxes, say, or balancing the budget, were not really important to the party and to its presidential candidate. Why is it different on the question of restoring the right to life to the unborn?

Did these Republican leaders in some strange way wish to project themselves as cynical politicians without principles? *Are* they really cynical politicians without principles willing to say in words whatever their prolife constituents want — but then go on to hint at what their antilife constituents want as well? Whatever the explanation, it is hard to mistake the message that the abortion issue does not really count as far as the top Republican leadership is concerned.

Similarly, a panel of some of the presidential hopefuls bested by Bob Dole in the primaries, including Texas Senator Phil Gramm, Indiana Senator Richard Lugar, and former Tennessee Governor Lamar Alexander — again, all of them supposedly "prolife," though the case of Alexander is more than doubtful — went on the record before a national television audience expressing the view that a political party's platform — its publicly announced operating principles and convictions — were really of no practical importance in the real world at all. The party's nominee would properly and necessarily decide such questions on his own, they opined in chorus before the cameras.

The context of this remarkable bit of political doctrine was a discussion of why their fellow failed primary candidate Pat Buchanan had not yet endorsed victorious candidate Bob Dole. Evidently it had not occurred to any of these estimable leaders who had sought the presidency that in issuing a platform perhaps a party might seriously intend to announce that it stood for something. For them, apparently, no party has to stand for anything; what was important for them was winning elections.

All of these prominent Republicans seemed oblivious to what the possible effect might be of declaring before a national audience that their party really had no principles that anyone had to pay any attention to. The fact that they were all so totally oblivious to such a fundamental matter should perhaps provide us with a clue as to what was really happening here: all of these veteran politicians were reflexively engaged in what they perceived as essential damage control; the importance of the Republican platform obviously had to be downplayed, in their view, because it was the platform that contained the party's unequivocal, principled affirmation of the right to life and to the equal protection of the laws of the unborn; and *that*, as everybody knows, was "controversial" and hence to be avoided to the extent possible.

Most of the reporters, commentators, interviewers, and pundits at the convention, of course, were only too well aware of what the party's platform contained, and hence they tirelessly kept bringing up the subject of abortion at every turn. This threatened the carefully crafted positive image of moderation and inclusiveness which the party leaders had been at such pains to project. On the one hand, though, they could hardly single out and repudiate the abortion plank itself, which they knew had to stay in to consolidate their prolife base; on the other hand, they could hardly just stand still while the party was again accused of "intolerance" and "extremism," as at Houston in 1992. The whole platform, therefore, had to be downplayed and dismissed as of little importance. Very probably, the Republican leadership did not even confer about this; it was just obvious to all of them.

As the Republican leaders saw it, they had already made their maximum concessions to their prolife constituency; they had done this by agreeing to a prolife plank calling for a constitutional amendment; prolifers could not reasonably expect anything more; if anything, they had already been given too much, given the present climate. Now it was incumbent upon the party leaders to reach out to others, to Republican prochoicers and, especially, to what they still thought to be the majority of American voters at large; a party has to be practical and realistic if it expects to win elections, after all.

Faced with the inevitable media question on abortion posed by an interviewer, Reagan-era spin-doctor Michael Deaver, called back into service to help organize this convention as a media event, replied without a trace of irony or embarrassment: "Oh, that question was *settled* in the platform. . ." Nothing else to say or do.

So that is how the Republican leadership consistently saw the matter. Bob Dole in particular, as we shall see, made repeated efforts — at times almost to the point of jeopardizing his quest for the presidency — to see to it that "tolerance," and not the fundamental right to life of all, was the basic operating principle of America's prolife party.

It still remains to be seen at this writing, of course, whether Dole and the rest of the Republican leadership have not already undermined their prolife and profamily support base to the point where the 85 to 90 percent of Republican voters always needed to insure a Republican victory will not be there for them on election day. The prolife and profamily delegates attending the convention seem not to have reacted very strongly to the regular downplaying of their cause; the prolife and profamily organizations which represent them similarly seemed to be basically satisfied with the platform victory and with the choice of a prolife vice-president. Even Pat Buchanan professed to be basically satisfied when he finally endorsed the Dole-Kemp ticket.

Nevertheless, by constantly trying to obscure and downplay the party's official commitment to the prolife cause, and keep the whole issue out of the media, Bob Dole and the Republican leadership may have alienated more prolifers, both at the convention and among television viewers, than is now apparent. Only time will tell. (Denying speaking time to such doctrinaire proabortionists as Governors Weld of Massachusetts and Wilson of California, by the way, evidenced no great commitment to the prolife cause on the part of convention organizers; the media kept suggesting that this was the case; but the convention organizers just did not want the issue stirred up in any way; their decision in this regard was entirely in keeping with all their other efforts to keep the abortion issue from even being raised at all.)

Meanwhile, the real story of election year 1996 remains the fact of the growing, almost commanding, influence that the prolife movement now has within the ranks of the Republican Party: the professional politicians, against all of their normal political instincts and typical wishes, have been forced by the grassroots to acknowledge the central importance of legalized abortion anyway. Not all of the old line politicians, such as Bob Dole himself, either recognize or accept this as yet; but it has increasingly become the case.

If present trends continue, and if prolifers continue to bring more voters into Republican ranks in comparable numbers to those they have been bringing in, the time may already have passed when a prochoice Republican presidential or vice-presidential candidate is even any longer thinkable. Or: if the party somehow, against its own interest, decides instead to try to go back on its prolife commitment, the resulting hemorrhage from Republican ranks will be so huge and unprecedented that there will virtually not be any national party left any longer. The "moderates" and country clubbers *cannot* carry the party by themselves. When will they finally realize this?

Confirming a national trend evidenced in such state party conventions as those of Texas and Virginia, today's grassroots Republican prolifers in effect *dictated* the strong prolife plank in the party platform this year; they dictated it not only in the face of a flurry of efforts over the past couple of years to water down or remove the prolife plank; they did it in the face of the express and repeated wishes of the current party's standard bearer.

Prior to the final showdown on the platform the week before the convention, Bob Dole had publicly declared more than once that a "tolerance" plank specifically linked to abortion had to be included in the platform; on at least one occasion he said that this was "non-negotiable." And his own stubborn efforts to insure this result continued even after the platform committee had acted in a vein contrary to his express wishes.

But Bob Dole had to yield in the end; the prolife forces on the platform committee succeeded in overruling the party's nominee. Pat Buchanan, among others, was surely justified in "declaring victory" on this particular point. The almost frantic efforts at perceived damage control on the part of the candidate and the rest of the Republican leadership could almost surely be traced back to the fact that the platform committee's rejection of what the leadership wanted had rather embarrassingly taken place in full view of the major media. The media were henceforth avid to keep bringing up the subject of abortion whenever possible.

Thus, Bob Dole and the Republican leadership still do not "get it" where abortion is concerned. Their futile and failed efforts to downplay and neutralize the issue may turn out to be *the* enduring story of the 1996 elections. Some may question this, asking of what importance a platform is which the leaders of the party have already in effect declared they do not care about and do not intend to be guided by.

Those inclined to ask this question should think back to 1948 and the introduction of the first civil rights plank into the platform of the Democratic Party in that year. Within a little more than a decade, the issue of civil rights was on the way to becoming the dominant American domestic political issue of our lifetime, and it has remained so pretty much up to our own day. Given the absolutely fundamental legal and constitutional issues raised by legalized abortion, we should not hastily imagine that this issue does not have enormous potential for the future; those who imagine that it is somehow going to go away are surely deluded.

Certainly it is not going to go away just because most practicing politicians quite evidently *wish* it would go away. On the contrary, there is no possibility of any unilateral truce at all in a real culture war, and this *is* a real culture war. The saga of the abortion plank in the 1996 platform of the Republican Party may one day turn out to have sent an abiding message not only to the still uncomprehending Republican leadership but to the country at large.

II

Why *don't* the politicians ever quite manage to "get it" where the abortion issue is concerned? Nothing illustrates the problem more clearly than the long-running dispute over the prolife plank in the Republican Party platform which unfolded over the summer, and culminated in a platform fight the week before the convention.

Actually the platform problem goes back a long way. When abortion was first legalized in 1973, many politicians were willing to take a prolife stand in order to gain prolife votes; there was little chance under *Roe v. Wade* that anything very substantive could be decided about abortion by means of legislation anyway; so being "prolife" largely meant voting against government *funding* of abortions, and many politicians were willing to sign on as prolife without much understanding of or much conviction about the issue.

The famous Hyde Amendment denying Medicaid funding of abortions was the prototype of prolife legislation early on. Otherwise prolife legislation was generally confined to such things as defeating the proposed — and infamous — Freedom of Choice Act (FOCA) of a couple of years back which would have codified *Roe v. Wade,* and more.

Supreme Court decisions subsequent to *Roe* had opened up a few fairly narrow legislative possibilities: parental and spousal notification, waiting periods, and the like. What really opened up the abortion issue as a national issue, though, were the great Republican and prolife victories of 1994. With new majorities, especially in the House, a number of initiatives besides prohibiting abortion funding were mounted — against such things as fetal tissue research, abortions in military hospitals, "family planning" assistance to organizations that performed abortions, abortion coverage in federal employees' health insurance, and so on. The Congress even held hearings and passed the now well-known Partial-Birth Abortion Ban Act, which President Clinton then shamelessly vetoed.

At the same time that new prolife legislative muscles were being flexed within the new majority party, however, ominous signs were already appearing indicating how ambivalent the Republican leadership really was where abortion was concerned. The new Speaker Newt Gingrich, for example, explicitly rejected the idea of including any prolife initiatives in his famous Contract with America; and he further both discouraged and sometimes actively even scotched certain prolife initiatives that had been brought forward.

With the 1996 presidential elections on the horizon, the question of the abortion stance the party would be taking in its platform soon became an issue that rapidly heated up. Especially in connection with the possible candidacy of the prochoice General Colin Powell, influential figures in Republican circles favoring a Powell candidacy begin working for a watering down of the party platform calling for a constitutional amendment; such figures included former Education Secretary and Drug Czar, William Bennett, and Bennett's former chief of staff and editor of a new neoconservative journal named *The Weekly Standard,* William Kristol.

Bennett's basic argument was that a plank calling for a constitutional amendment currently impossible to enact did nothing to reduce the number of abortions which, utilitarian-fashion, this trained philosopher, lawyer, and self-appointed teacher of virtue to the nation considered to be the principal issue posed by legalized abortion in a democratic polity. Kristol's magazine, claiming to be prolife but aiming in particular at the Buchanan forces, immediately became the apologist both for a Powell candidacy and for a watered-down abortion plank (the articles in favor of these things did nothing to enhance the new magazine's intellectual stature).

As for Bob Dole, who at that point was also courting Colin Powell as a possible running mate, a remark on NBC's Meet the Press in December, 1995, got him in very hot water with the prolife and profamily base which it was still thought he understood he needed to have in his corner to win. Dole seemed to say on the program, at least as understood by some of his hearers, that he no longer supported the constitutional amendment that the Republican platform had called for since 1980; he remarked that he had supported such an amendment in the past but could no longer support one.

A sharp public outcry by various prolife and profamily organizations, including grassroots right-to-lifers in Kansas and Iowa (where the Iowa caucuses were looming), quickly brought a clarification from Senator Dole's office (after consultation with various prolife and profamily organizations) that the Kansas Senator still favored an amendment, but one with exceptions for the life of the mother and rape and incest.

This whole unedifying sequence scarcely points to a prolife legislator with unshakable convictions on the abortion issue. This melancholy fact should be kept in mind as we review the Republican nominee's flipflops on abortion culminating with the final 1996 platform fiasco on the issue. For it turned out that supposedly prolife Republican presidential candidate Robert J. Dole not only felt able to disregard the right-to-life movement, which had remained unusually loyal to him, and thus risk alienating this large and growing prolife segment of his own political base; apparently he felt in some sense *obliged* to do so when, beginning in mid-June, 1996, he inexplicably moved to upset a compromise on the abortion issue which he himself had successfully fashioned only a few days earlier. He did this by insisting that what he called a "declaration of tolerance" had to be attached to the Republican Party platform plank calling for a Human Life Amendment.

Of course the issue of this platform plank was not the only issue which candidate Dole bungled in the course of the summer. The media enjoyed more than a few field days at Dole's expense keeping before the public the Republican standard-bearer's successive ineptitudes concerning the possible addictive properties of tobacco, concerning his reversal of position on the banning of assault weapons, and concerning his apparent unwillingness to address the convention of the National Association for the Advancement of Colored People — in several of which instances the candidate also testily declared that he had been "set up."

But his bungling of the abortion issue was of a wholly different order of magnitude than his other missteps; for in bungling this issue he risked alienating a core constituency which would loyally stay with him regardless of all his other ineptitudes, provided only that he stick to prolife principles. But this was precisely what the former Kansas senator and Senate Majority Leader proved unable to do.

Earlier, candidate Dole had actually agreed that he would neither seek nor accept any modification in the current platform language calling for a constitutional amendment. To this Dole added only that the platform should include a declaration of tolerance recognizing that some Republicans do have divergent views on this issue, as, indeed, many Republicans do on a number of other issues on which the party takes a position in the platform, issues such as term limits, gun control, and tax cuts, for example.

It was initially understood that the declaration of tolerance which Dole wanted in the platform would apply generally and would not single out the abortion plank specifically, thus implying that this plank, in particular, was the only one that was optional for Republicans. Apparently the Dole campaign even made firm representations to this effect to various party constituencies. Bob Dole himself had even said at one point that he did not care where the declaration of tolerance was attached to the platform. "What's the difference?" he asked in a TV interview.

Most prolife leaders almost immediately agreed to this initial compromise, as did not a few of those on the other side of the issue. Indeed there was a rather widespread collective sigh of relief that apparently an ugly abortion battle at the Republican Convention in San Diego was going to be avoided. Bob Dole seemed to have almost miraculously solved the party's abortion dilemma at one stroke. It was hard to see how the so-called "moderates" could even raise the issue any longer without themselves being stigmatized as "dividing the party" (a charge previously leveled mostly at prolifers).

But no: Bob Dole himself came out on his own a few days later and specified that the declaration of tolerance he wanted had to be linked specifically to the prolife plank; and he also said that this point was "non-negotiable." As anyone knowledgeable about the prolife movement could have predicted, prolife leaders reacted quite negatively and with more than a little dismay to this sudden new development, which, of course, served to reopen the whole abortion controversy once again.

Bob Dole, in turn, reacted waspishly to the prolife reaction, and even went so far as to launch a personal attack on one of the Republican prolife leaders who had objected to his sudden switch, former Reagan Administration official Gary Bauer, president of the Family Research Council.

The prolife reaction to this personal attack, as well as to the whole spectacle of Dole incomprehensibly back-tracking towards the Republican "moderates" for no reason that anybody could grasp, was equally predictable. James Dobson of Focus on the Family, whose influential television program reaches millions, declared that while Dole obviously could not afford to alienate his prolife and profamily base, in Dobson's words, "he has just done that."

The nearly two-million-strong Christian Coalition issued a statement saying that it had "no choice but to go to the convention in San Diego to lead the fight to preserve the existing plank and to oppose the naming of a prochoice running mate." "The Christian Coalition may have to sit the election out," a spokesman said. Later, the head of the Christian Coalition, Ralph Reed, declared that the forces allied to his camp included enough delegates to *win* any battle on the convention floor, even against the party's presidential candidate.

Clearly Bob Dole had gotten himself into some very serious trouble. Why did he stir up the whole abortion issue again after having just "settled" it? How could the veteran legislator, who has himself voted prolife for just about as long as abortion has been around as a political and legislative issue, have so little sense of what was bound to alienate if not outrage his indispensable prolife constituency?

Some saw his move as simply the obligatory "move to the center" which any presidential candidate usually makes under our system after he has secured his party's nomination. But surely any candidate savvy enough to win his party's nomination would also understand that this "move to the center" would have to be carefully made without obviously alienating any significant part of his political base; it was hardly something that a candidate would attempt to manage by off-handedly throwing out a "non-negotiable" demand about.

But then perhaps Dole acted because he sincerely believed — and as some have no doubt kept telling him — that he would have greater appeal to "women" if he insisted on a declaration of tolerance specifically on abortion. The language of his sharp put-down of Gary Bauer in June similarly suggested this motivation; Dole accused Bauer of somehow objecting to "women" supporting him if they wanted to. Of course the Republican Party, along with Dole himself, is supposed to suffer from a "gender gap" anyway; people who believe the media on this point almost always believe they have to run scared. In some ways, the Republican convention, for example, seemed to have been planned with nothing else but this famous Dole "gender gap" in mind.

But again, other polls show that, apart from ideological feminists, a majority of women do *not* favor wide-open abortion; polls over the last decade have on the contrary rather consistently shown women generally to be more prolife than men. Thus, the advantages of trying to appeal to "women," that is, to feminists, on this score, particularly if one is already marked down as a conservative and prolife anyway, have certainly not been shown; feminist women who do believe in abortion as a woman's "right" are surely mostly already signed up with the other party anyway.

Or perhaps Bob Dole was honestly groping for a formula that would preclude the Republican Party from being attacked by the media as "intolerant" the way it was attacked after the Houston convention in 1992; this did prove to be a major factor in the planning and execution of the convention after all. Abortion is a "moral issue," Dole explained, as if that did not make it all the more important for him to take a principled stand rather than dithering and waffling about it; he would surely not advocate tolerance where "racism" is concerned just because it was a "moral issue," for example.

Anyway the particular formula for tolerance that he in fact hit upon would practically seem to insure the very kind of "controversy" at the convention which Bob Dole was supposedly seeking to avoid.

Yet another possible explanation for Bob Dole's otherwise almost inexplicable sudden switch on the placement of the declaration of tolerance issue related to his coming selection of a running mate. The prolife elements in the party had been making it very clear that a "moderate," proabortion vice-presidential candidate would be absolutely unacceptable to them; for them *this* point was non-negotiable. Bob Dole himself, however, has never conceded this point; and, indeed, he continued to grouse and make noises and give other intimations that a prochoice candidate such as General Colin Powell would still be just fine with him.

Dole has certainly been encouraged in this view by all the reporters and pundits who mindlessly continued to talk up this same "dream ticket" — without realizing that the choice of Powell would precisely have *insured* the loss of such a significant part of the Republican prolife base that this by itself might have insured Dole's defeat (forget about the favorable polls for a Dole-Powell ticket; the right-to-life question was never factored into these surveys, nor indeed brought up at all in connection with them).

Bob Dole appears not to have ever had any sense of all of this; to the extent that he realized there was even a problem, perhaps he had come to resent the idea that *any* party constituency could presume to "dictate" what kind of vice-presidential candidate he, the head of the ticket, might wish to choose. Do not successful presidential candidates always get to choose their running mates? Has this not become a firmly established custom of our political life? How could the prolife movement now presume to "dictate" to a candidate about this?

The truth is, of course, that where the abortion issue and the prolife movement are concerned, the Republican Party, if it seriously wants to continue to be the prolife party, no longer does have the option of nominating a proabortion candidate. If it did nominate one, it would instantly lose a vital part of its own base which it could never afford to lose; prolife and profamily voters constituted around forty percent, or perhaps even more, of the victorious Republican electorate in the 1994 elections.

Thus, a new political reality has been brought about in the wake of the legalization of abortion and the subsequent rise of the prolife movement. This new political reality is still not very widely understood, and this is precisely what is meant when it is stated that the politicians still do not really "get it" where the abortion issue is concerned.

Be that as it may, as late as July 1, 1996, Bob Dole was still saying on NBC's "Today" show that he would definitely consider a proabortion running mate. "That may distress some people," he said. "But I am the nominee. I need to make the choice and I need to find someone who can be president."

In the event, of course, Bob Dole did choose in Jack Kemp a running mate with a solid prolife voting record; but there is no evidence that the prolife question was one of the factors in his choice. Syndicated columnist Charles Krauthammer wrote that he knew "for a fact" that Dole offered the position to William Bennett before he offered it to Kemp, and Bennett, as we have noted, has been one of the leaders in trying to water down the principled Republican stand on abortion. Probably on this as on just about everything, trying to respond to his prolife constituency is the farthest thing from the candidate's mind.

For on the evidence, Bob Dole surely really doesn't "get it." The erstwhile Majority Leader, with all his proven skills, nevertheless appears to inhabit and take seriously the artificial world created by the media where, contrary to the results of actual polls, "women" supposedly need to be appeased by telling them that it really is all right if they want to have the children they have conceived killed.

In the face of the immense social and moral crisis posed by legalized abortion, Dole has gone on blissfully playing by the usual political rules, making the typical deals and compromises, courting the various factions and playing one of them off against the other as if they were all on exactly the same level, meanwhile never taking his eyes off the latest poll results; he seems to have no idea at all that the legalization of abortion by the U.S. Supreme Court has necessarily introduced a radically new dimension into our national life, one which will not disappear until legalized killing itself disappears. And in all of this he is, unhappily, only too typical of politicians generally, including some "prolife" politicians.

Newt Gingrich, for example, doesn't "get it" either. The Speaker of the House displayed none of the astuteness for which he is famed when he reacted to the whole June platform flap by criticizing prolife leaders for "nit-picking" Bob Dole. The Georgia Republican averred that the prolife movement was surely applying an unreasonable standard to Dole by reacting so strongly to the candidate's reversal of position when he unilaterally decided that the prolife plank was going to be optional in the Republican Party platform after all.

Gingrich declared: "I hope every person involved who believes in right to life is going to take a deep breath, take a step back, look at the big picture, and decide that the commitment is to defeat Bill Clinton, that the cause of the unborn children in this country is best served by defeating Bill Clinton." Of course few or no prolifers would dispute the desirability of this outcome; however, it was Dole himself who jeopardized his own and his party's prospects by his abrupt turnabout, overturning the compromise that prolifers had effectively agreed to; the great deal-maker apparently didn't even realize when he had a deal.

Gingrich added: "To the degree that we get sucked into some internal fight, I think this is frankly self-destruction." So why did candidate Dole not just leave well enough alone? Newt Gingrich's notion that it is for him as a party leader to be lecturing prolifers about what they should think surely fails the test of political realism. Rather, it is for the party leaders such as Gingrich to be ascertaining what the party needs to do as the price of the prolife support it has enjoyed up to now.

A week before the Republican convention, Newt Gingrich published an "Open Letter to Republican National Convention Delegates" in which he did demonstrate that he realizes that our society is truly in a crisis situation. "No civilization can survive," he wrote, "with 12-year-olds having babies, 14-year-olds doing drugs, 15-year-olds killing each other, 17-year-olds dying of AIDS, and 18-year-olds receiving diplomas they can't even read. All of these things are happening in America today." Gingrich could and should have added — except that he doesn't "get it" — that no civilization can survive when 4400 of its children are legally being killed every day, while the country's leaders, including him, refuse even to discuss the implications of this as a serious political and social problem.

House Majority Leader Dick Armey, for his part, doesn't quite "get it," although he seems to come a little closer than either Dole or Gingrich. He also, like the other two, has a personal prolife voting record, and he even stated it as a preference that any declaration of tolerance should be in the preamble to the platform, not directly linked to any particular plank. "I would prefer to have it in the preamble," he said on CNN. "But I'm not going to get myself exercised if it's in the plank, because the plank states clearly our position on abortion as it has been."

But how would it continue to state it with any chance of being taken seriously if it forthwith went on to declare it optional and of less importance than the other planks not thus singled out to include declarations of tolerance?

However that may be, Dick Armey professed not to understand "why everyone is so upset" over the issue. For him too, apparently, abortion is just one more issue, not nearly as important as, say, tax reform or welfare reform. "I really don't understand what the flap is all about," he further said on CNN. "First of all, Bob Dole is prolife and has been, and nobody can question that."

However, Armey did distance himself ever so slightly from the Dole-Gingrich common front when he noted that a platform issue had never been one for the party's presidential candidate to decide. Rather, the convention as a whole should decide and vote on the platform, according to Armey. "That is the way the process should go," he said.

In making this particular point, the Majority Leader could well have been ever so gently pointing the way for candidate Dole to get out of his self-made impasse: let the platform committee decide, the platform committee chairman being Mr. Prolife himself in the U.S. House of Representatives, Rep. Henry J. Hyde of Illinois. When Hyde was named platform chairman, some speculated whether he was not being placed there so that he could do a Nixon-to-Red-China turnabout on the abortion issue for the Republicans; but the Illinois Congressman immediately moved to scotch these rumors by quoting Winston Churchill's famous statement that he did not become his Britannic Majesty's first minister in order to preside over the liquidation of the British Empire (some pessimists, however, remember what eventually happened to the British Empire anyway!).

When Bob Dole decided that the declaration of tolerance had to be linked specifically to the prolife plank, some press reports described Henry Hyde as so "angry" that he was ready to resign as platform committee chairman. Certainly Henry Hyde is one of the few politicians who generally does "get it" where the abortion issue is concerned.

Meanwhile, though, Bob Dole, himself always the conventional political deal maker, was reported as saying that the whole controversy would be handily resolved once he had personally talked to Henry Hyde. "We're going to confound the press," Dole stated on an Illinois TV station. "We're going to have it all resolved before the convention." "Piece of cake," he added.

In the event, the issue did get resolved before the convention was gaveled to order; but it was not resolved in the way Bob Dole had envisaged — certainly it was not resolved without the necessity of an explicit repudiation of the nominee's own views and wishes by the party's platform committee.

III

The politicians are not alone among those who don't "get it" as far as the abortion issue is concerned. For the most part the media and the pundits have the same problem. Scarcely any of the media reports concerning the Dole turnaround on the placement of the declaration of tolerance in the Republican Party platform got very far beyond making the simple point that the whole episode was an embarrassment for Dole. But then any public reversal on almost any issue always constitutes at least a temporary embarrassment for any politician running for office.

It is true that the media do understand that anything related to the abortion issue also represents a special kind of embarrassment in today's climate. Abortion is nothing if not a hot button issue today, even while it is an issue that most people on all sides of the question try to avoid bringing up entirely if at all possible; but the media do pounce on it gleefully whenever it comes up as a potential embarrassment factor, as certainly proved to be the case in the course of the Republican Convention itself.

Most of the media reports in the course of the controversy over the platform also understood the further point, which was in any case obvious, that alienating your base is always a very risky business for a politician. Few of these reports, however, understood exactly *why* Bob Dole was alienating his prolife base simply by insisting on a particular placement of the declaration of tolerance in the platform.

Much of the reporting on the incident, especially the comments of various experts or pundits, singularly failed to grasp or report on what was really at stake in the whole business. Some commentators actually saw Dole's move as in some sense a net gain for him and the Republicans. For example, a story in the *New York Times* quoted an academic, supposedly an "authority on the politics of abortion," who declared, fatuously, that "these prolife people will probably vote for Dole anyway, and to have them scream at him makes it look like he's not a captive."

The *Washington Post* ran an even more absurd story comparing Dole's move to one made four years earlier by candidate Bill Clinton, when the latter, in the words of the *Post*'s story, "challenged the most ideological wing of the party and one of its most prominent leaders, Jesse L. Jackson, for giving a public platform to Sister Souljah, the controversial rap singer."

Sister Souljah, for those with short memories, was the black woman who had said in a widely reported interview: "If black people kill black people every day, why not have a week and kill white people"? In promptly repudiating this point of view, of course, Bill Clinton risked nothing and probably alienated few or no voters, even among blacks. Not even "the most ideological wing" of the Democratic Party favors the views of a Sister Souljah; and except for the fact that she is black, she represents no visible constituency of any kind. Thus, to compare, in effect, the "extremism" of Sister Souljah to the "extremism" of the prolife movement, as the *Post* article does, simply represents one more of the ways in which the mainstream media regularly attempt to put down and discredit the prolife movement.

In fact, though, as we have already seen, the prolife and profamily movements supplied more than forty percent of all the Republican voters in the victorious 1994 elections. To pay Bob Dole compliments for having distanced himself from *them* is surely not to evince any real interest in or solicitude for Bob Dole's electoral prospects — or for the Republican Party's electoral prospects. Yet more than one supposedly Republican or conservative expert was also quoted in the same *Post* article precisely as complimenting or congratulating Dole on this: "Bob Dole has established that he is his own man," said one Alex Castellanos, described as "a conservative Republican media consultant." "This does very much what the Sister Souljah incident did for Clinton; this makes Bob Dole a little taller, a little stronger, and more his own man."

Similarly, another political pollster, Linda DiVall (whose clients, significantly, include the Republican Coalition for Choice), is quoted as saying that "Senator Dole instinctively knows that the party's position on abortion signals intolerance to many women, moderates, and suburbanites." Of course it signals something quite different to another large, growing, and convinced segment of the American electorate. It is true that only the actual election in November will reveal which of these blocs of voters proves to be more important to Bob Dole's election — or to his failure to be elected. Even then it is likely that other factors will obscure the meaning of the final result anyway.

Meanwhile, however, trying to appeal more to "women, moderates, and suburbanites" at the expense of the solid prolife and profamily base the Republicans already have would seem to be a very iffy proposition for Bob Dole; the whole idea does not seem to be either very well grounded or very carefully thought through. Would very many of those who believe abortion to be a woman's "right" vote for the Republicans anyway, even with a declaration of tolerance in the platform?

By contrast, where prolifers stand is very well known; and the party's prolife base of support can and will be seriously eroded if it ever agrees to sacrifice its present clear and unambiguous affirmation of the right to life of the unborn to the nebulous and half-baked notions of "tolerance" of its current presidential candidate.

Among those pundits who, on the record, could scarcely be thought to favor a Republican victory, but who have not for all of that refrained from offering their expert advice to the Dole campaign anyway, is syndicated columnist Ben Wattenberg. In a column on the topic of the platform, Wattenberg made the important points that 1) the notion of an "intolerant" 1992 Republican convention in Houston was a myth created by the media; and 2) that it was actually the Democratic convention in New York which exhibited intolerance when it refused even to let then Pennsylvania Governor Robert P. Casey speak on the abortion issue. Prochoice Republicans, by contrast, had ample opportunity to state their views in Houston; and, according to Wattenberg, even such "extremists" as Pat Buchanan and Pat Robertson who spoke in Houston gave speeches that were really quite tame when coldly examined; they were simply blown all out of proportion by the way the media reported them and then kept going back to them, according to Wattenberg (too bad the planners and managers of the San Diego convention apparently never read the man!).

For those who live in, or even spend any time in, the world created by the media, though, the myth of the intolerant Houston convention has been a very powerful one; it is enough for them that the Republicans were *perceived* to be "intolerant" and "extremist" in 1992. And as Ben Wattenberg correctly noted, one of the main things about the convention that continued to be branded as extremist was the Human Life Amendment in the platform; the negative view adopted by the media about this was, according to Wattenberg, "spun and respun, doubled and redoubled in spades by the Clinton campaign of 1992. Why not? It was good politics. It traumatized the Republicans then, and it traumatizes them now."

Evidently it never ceased traumatizing Robert J. Dole. For it is hard to imagine *what else* could have moved him, so abruptly and clumsily, to place in jeopardy the solidest basis of his electoral support in order to try to appeal to committed prochoicers unlikely to vote for any Republican. Columnist Wattenberg stated so well how the issue was perceived, and indeed still plays in the media, that his summary is worth quoting in full; it throws light on what otherwise has to be considered irrational and, indeed, almost incomprehensible actions by Dole and his convention managers:

> Traumatized, many Republicans are now seeking a way to show that they are not kooks. The press plays the abortion is-

> sue as No. 1, early and often. So Republicans try to deal with it. But the prolifers say: Do not change a single word in the Human Life Amendment plank. Prochoicers say: Take the whole thing out of the platform. Candidate Bob Dole favors a "tolerance" plank, which doesn't quite do it for me, prochoice and anti-condescension. Then they argue about whether the tolerance should be promulgated in the preamble, or linked to the abortion plank.

This states the general case quite accurately, although it also reduces the whole question to something that seems trivial and inconsequential, if not absurd. But this is assuredly not true about the question of whether or not all human beings, from conception through natural death, really do enjoy a right to life and to the equal protection of the laws under the legal and constitutional system of the United States. This question, precisely, is what the abortion issue really is all about.

Shrewd as he is, then, pundit Wattenberg turns out to be yet another one of the many who still do not "get it" where the abortion issue is concerned. This failing of his comes out quite clearly in his recommendations concerning what the Republicans should do about the situation he so succinctly described; these recommendations too are worth quoting in full; they are only too typical of how the pundits and experts do tend to see the abortion issue; according to Wattenberg, the Republicans should:

> Write a brand new plank. Stress that Supreme Court rulings (*Webster*, 1989, and *Casey*, 1992) have changed the playing field. There are now things that can be done to make abortion more rare, here and now and legally. These include: 24-hour waiting periods, parental consent, adoption counseling. Such a plank will allow both prochoicers and prolifers to declare victory. Continue to oppose federal funding. Dare the Democrats to challenge their feminists and endorse these popular measures, while denouncing Mr. Clinton's endorsement of so-called "partial-birth" abortions. (Do Republicans want a plank or a president?)

Of all the possible solutions to the Republican platform dilemma, these recommendations, if the Republicans had ever tried to act on them, would most surely have insured a "walk" by prolifers from the Republican convention and have caused a serious, perhaps fatal, erosion of the party's prolife base. Ben Wattenberg too clearly doesn't "get it" if he imagines that the prolife movement could seriously "declare victory" merely as a result of getting such things as 24-hour waiting periods and parental consent for the continued legalized killing of children. Making abortion "more rare" is *not* the goal of the prolife movement; this is, rather, nothing else but the stated goal of, of all people — Bill Clinton! The prolife movement has quite another goal.

IV

What is the "it" concerning the abortion issue which so many politicians and pundits still fail to "get"? Most of them still see legalized abortion as just another conventional political issue about which typical political compromises and give-and-take apply. To some extent this is true, of course, at least on a certain level. However, by the nature of what abortion is, it is impossible to compromise on the basic political issue posed by the legalization of it without in fact conceding defeat and handing victory then and there to the other side. The basic political issue posed by legalized abortion is this: is the right to life spoken of in the Declaration of Independence really "unalienable" or not?

Does the Constitution of the United States really guarantee that no one "shall be deprived of life, liberty, or property without due process of law. . .or be deprived of the equal protection of the laws," or not? So long as an entire class of human beings — currently children who are alive and developing but not yet born — can be legally killed at the option of third parties, then the Constitution of the United States is clearly being violated, and the constitutional guarantees upon which our whole legal system is supposedly based are in a state of practical suspension.

This is the exact situation in which we presently find ourselves as a result of the United States Supreme Court's irrational 1973 decision to allow legal abortion of unwanted children contrary to the Constitution's guarantees. Not only are the lives of numberless children being brutally and wantonly sacrificed as a result of this decision; the very integrity of our legal and constitutional system is also at stake.

Moreover, if this current suspension of our constitutional guarantees is allowed to go on, then there is no longer any *other* constitutional right of anyone that is not at least potentially at risk, since the principle will have been established and ratified that our supposed constitutional guarantees *can* be abrogated — at the option of any five out of nine Supreme Court justices, for example.

The logic of all this is perfectly clear, although it is rarely explicitly stated. Recognizing, however, that the right to life is no longer operative and absolute under our Constitution, the courts are already proceeding to extend the new, court-manufactured "right" to take the life of others to other situations, as we can clearly see in the recent Second and Ninth Circuit Court decisions on assisted suicides.

In the confused and very fluid situation that now exists as a result of our increasing legal acceptance of optional killing in more and more situations, the right to life is being rapidly shredded in more ways than one. The State of Michigan, for example, is now no longer able to prosecute successfully and put behind bars a serial killer such as Dr. Jack Kevorkian. The man actually shows up at police stations and turns in the dead bodies of people whose deaths he has "assisted"; the bodies are accepted and no further attempt is made to prosecute him. Rather, after three acquittals, he is lionized. The man could bring *anybody* in, no questions asked, at this point. This is what our legal system has descended to under the sway of the legalized killing introduced by the legalization of abortion.

And public opinion, of course, quickly reacts to the steady erosion of the idea of the sanctity of life, just as the Supreme Court was once said to react to the election returns: juries acquit Dr. Kevorkian and his ilk as readily as judges find arguments to justify and extend the legalized killing that was in fact accepted into our system only with the legalization of abortion.

The logic of all this is inexorable even as its forward movement steadily gathers momentum. None of it can be legally controlled or stopped until legalized killing itself is stopped at its source. In practice this means that the Constitution of the United States must be amended to exclude interpretations of it which allow elective killing at various stages of human life or as a result of various conditions of human life.

This is what the Human Life Amendment plank in the Republican platform is all about. Prolifers *cannot* compromise on a constitutional amendment as their ultimate goal because they cannot concede that elective killing can ever be acceptable under our legal and constitutional system; elective killing must be opposed on principle and absolutely; in thus opposing it, prolifers are, among other things, functioning as the guardians of the integrity of our system.

And as a practical matter, and in the present climate, any retreat by the Republican Party from its current principled affirmation of a constitutional right to life would amount to conceding this principle and admitting, in effect, that legalized killing is and can be legitimate under our system. This is why all the politicians and pundits simply miss the point when, pointing to public opinion polls, they declare a Human Life Amendment to be impossible, now or in the foreseeable future, and say it should therefore be abandoned as the goal of the prolife movement.

Prolifers, they say — condescendingly — should concentrate on lowering the total number of abortions performed, on getting enacted measures such as those waiting periods and parental consent laws which polls indicate current public opinion does support, and on outlawing such horrors as partial-birth abortions, where the skulls of nearly delivered children are pierced and their brains sucked out before their collapsed heads are then removed from the birth canal. It is necessary to ask: what *other* constitutional guarantee do these people think should be operative only insofar as current public opinion approves of it according to current polls?

It must be strongly emphasized that prolifers are precisely the ones who are out there working on and sometimes achieving some of these other partial or lesser "solutions" so regularly being recommended to them as goals. None of these things would be happening if prolifers had not been out there steadily pushing the politicians on the abortion issue all along. But prolifers who have come to understand the total dimensions of the abortion horror also understand that all these partial solutions together do not add up to nearly enough: elective killing has to be prohibited in principle; we cannot have a society where it is practiced and sanctioned; certainly we cannot call ourselves a civilized society until it is outlawed.

This is why there can be no compromise on the ultimate goal of a Human Life Amendment to the Constitution. No matter how impossible it seems. No matter how long it takes. It has to remain the ultimate goal, and there cannot be any compromise of principle on it. Perhaps it will come to seem less impossible once a few of our aspiring national leaders finally do begin to "get it" where the abortion issue is concerned; it is little wonder that public opinion polls are so ambivalent and confused on the abortion issue when most of our national leaders are so ambivalent and confused on it as well, and even most of our leaders who are prolife spend most of their time running away from the issue. It should, however, be seen as a very clear and basic constitutional human rights issue; and it is the historic task of the prolife movement to keep at it until it does finally come to be seen this way.

Bob Dole was therefore initially correct to state that he would neither seek nor accept a change in Republican Party platform language calling for a Human Life Amendment. Unfortunately, however, he then did seek to change it; his declaration of tolerance, if attached to the prolife plank, would have had the effect of calling into question the goal of a Human Life Amendment as a real goal — precisely, compromising on the principle of it. While affirming it in words, the plank would then have immediately blunted and even nullified it by adding, in effect: "No, this isn't *really* one of the goals of the Republican Party; we make a specific exception precisely here."

So as a practical matter there could be no compromise on the placement of the declaration of tolerance, either. It had to be kept separate from the prolife plank and it had to apply generally. There remains a sense, of course, in which such a declaration really is nothing more than a statement of fact: many Republicans do not in fact agree with the party's goal of enacting a Human Life Amendment.

Nobody disputes this as a statement of fact. But the real point is that, whether or not all Republicans agree with this particular goal, they do have to agree that it can and must remain in the platform as the party's official goal. A near majority want it in the platform as a condition of their continuing to be Republicans. This is thus the price the party has to pay in order to get the prolife support which the party has enjoyed up to now. In one sense, it is a matter of simple political realism.

It is also the "it" the politicians and the pundits must begin to "get" if they really ever expect to understand the abortion issue.

V

So how did Bob Dole try to get out of the trap he himself dug and then fell in as a result of his failure to "get it" where the abortion issue was concerned? He had confidently predicted, of course, that the solving of the problem would be a "piece of cake" once he sat down with platform committee chairman Henry Hyde.

The two men met privately on June 21, and the Dole campaign then issued a statement in which both men "reiterated. . .that they share the same strongly held views on the abortion issues." Both men also recognized, according to the statement, "that there is a diversity of views among Republicans on this and other issues. Both agree there should be language in the platform reflecting this diversity. They also agree that the real tragedy on the abortion issue is President Clinton's support for the indefensible partial-birth abortion procedure."

This last, of course, is *not* "the real tragedy on the abortion issue." Legalized abortion itself is. *All* abortions — deliberately and legally killing children by whatever means — are "horrors"; the children are just as dead as if their brains had been sucked out. Most abortions are just less visible than the partial-birth kind which, finally, have at least enabled a few more people to grasp what abortion really is — although in today's climate, as we saw above, even a Ben Wattenberg still believes he has to qualify this ghastly procedure as a "*so-called* partial-birth abortions."

In the wake of the Dole-Hyde meeting, press reports quoted unnamed Republican sources as indicating that the "careful wording" of the statement put out by the Dole campaign meant that a compromise had been reached which Rep. Hyde could live with. The fact that this compromise was not immediately made public, however, suggested otherwise; it suggested that Bob Dole was *not* immediately willing to unlink his declaration of tolerance from the prolife plank, thus laying upon loyal Republican but prolife stalwart Henry Hyde the very difficult task of either trying to convince the candidate to change or to sell Dole's position to prolifers in order to avoid an open party split.

But not even a Henry Hyde would be able to convince many prolifers that Dole's capricious embrace of "tolerance" at the expense of prolife principle was anything but a sellout of the prolife cause. He could only hope that Dole himself would finally come around and agree that his declaration of tolerance could be placed elsewhere in the platform. Prior to his meeting with Dole, Henry Hyde himself, in a special briefing of members of the Catholic press, had suggested that, instead of placing the declaration of tolerance anywhere in the platform, the Republicans should instead approve a separate Statement of Republican Principles that would outline "the principle of the open door, if not the big tent," according to Hyde.

But no mention was made of this proposal following the Dole-Hyde meeting itself. After the meeting Bob Dole himself went on to New York to campaign, where his answers to a question by a woman lawyer in a delicatessen concerning his views on abortion indicated that the meeting with Hyde had had no apparent effect on him at all. He clearly still didn't "get it"; he was still much more concerned about getting "tolerance" into the platform than he was with meeting the known minimum requirements of his large prolife constituency. When the woman, a declared Democrat and prochoicer, asked Dole a question about abortion (she surely already knew where the Republican Party stood), Dole shot back ("in his inimitable sarcastic style," a reporter wrote): "What are you, with the press now? I know they put you up to it!"

Doesn't Dole understand that "they" are tirelessly going to be "putting people up to it" on the abortion and similar issues throughout the entire presidential campaign? This particular incident preceded the similar one where the candidate complained to Katie Couric on national TV of having been "set up." Why doesn't Bob Dole just learn how to *defend* his party's position in public? He will never see the end of this kind of questioning until he does. And it may well be the thing that brings him down.

However that may be, he certainly did not answer this New York delicatessen woman's question; she wasn't asking him about tolerance; she was asking him about abortion. He went on anyway to expatiate on how *he* really sees the whole problem: "We hope to have a very strong statement of tolerance in the platform. We're an inclusive party. We're going to work it out. We would like to know where the Democrats are on abortion. They have different views but they are never presented. . ."

Thus, for Bob Dole, being prolife is strictly *pro forma*; what really engages him is whether the party is going to be "tolerant" or not. Only in November will it be seen whether the bloc of voters for tolerance in the Republican Party will end up offsetting the prolifers who may either now sit on their hands or begin to look elsewhere for a champion for their cause as a result of Dole's continuing performance on this issue.

In the event, not even tolerance turned out to be a firm principle for this candidate. On July 12, nearly three weeks after the meeting with Henry Hyde, the Dole campaign issued language intended to resolve the whole problem by : 1) retaining the Human Life Amendment language stated in the strongest possible terms; but then adding *another plank*, separately from the prolife plank, affirming *inter alia* that:

> While the Party remains steadfast in its commitment to advancing its historic principles and ideals, we also recognize that members of our Party have deeply-held and sometimes differing views on issues of personal conscience like abortion and capital punishment.

It is not at all clear how the question of capital punishment ever got into this mix (perhaps Henry Hyde had been reading Pope John Paul II's encyclical *Evangelium Vitae* and discussed it with Dole?); nor is this statement at all satisfactory since neither abortion nor capital punishment are questions of "personal conscience," any more than the fact that abortion is a "moral issue" is the reason why there has to be "tolerance" concerning it, in Bob Dole's confused formulation.

Nevertheless, the fact that the tolerance statement was separated from the prolife plank meant that prolife forces had certainly obliged a no doubt reluctant Bob Dole to back off from his insistence on linking tolerance specifically with abortion. At any rate Henry Hyde professed himself satisfied with the solution. Ralph Reed of the Christian Coalition similarly declared the new solution to be a prolife victory. Not all prolife leaders were equally pleased, however, and there were rumbles of further possible agitation over the issue at the convention in San Diego.

Meanwhile, it was the *pro*abortion elements in the Republican Party who seemed most dissatisfied with the supposed compromise solution. Massachusetts Governor William Weld called the two-plank solution "transparently begrudging towards those who hold the prochoice point of view" and said that he planned "to continue the fight for a more inclusive party platform." The director of the Republicans for Choice Political Action Committee, Ann Stone, called the new language a "disaster" and claimed that the religious right "got everything they wanted." In other words, at what was supposed to be the end of his adventure, candidate Bob Dole singularly failed to please the very people he was seeking to reassure with his "declaration of tolerance."

Nor was it the end of the adventure. The leaders of interested prolife organizations, reflecting further upon the compromise, increasingly began to question whether even a separate tolerance plank could be considered acceptable; the same thing was true of the reference to abortion as a matter of "personal conscience." It is *not* just a matter of personal conscience; there is a baby involved, a human being entitled to the protection of the law; to concede on this point would be to eviscerate the prolife plank itself.

The leaders of the principal prolife organizations involved, who became known as the "fearsome four" when the actual platform hearings began in early August, included Phyllis Schlafly of the Eagle Forum and the Republican Coalition for Life; Angela "Bay" Buchanan, chairman of her brother Patrick's presidential campaign; Gary Bauer of the Family Research Council; and Ralph Reed of the Christian Coalition. These prolife stalwarts had not been entirely free of disputes among themselves as to whether any among them might have gone "soft" or too easily gone over to the "Dole camp." On the day the platform hearings began, however, they all appeared conspicuously together as a united group.

In the meantime, the Dole campaign managers, in an attempt to insure that the candidate's views prevailed, had already overruled the choice of Henry Hyde to chair the abortion subcommittee of the platform committee and had placed their own chairman in that position. This proved to be a serious miscalculation. The courtly and always loyal Henry Hyde made no protest himself about who the chairman of the subcommittee was (although Phyllis Schlafly later told the press that it was an "outrage" the way the Dole people had treated Hyde); but the Illinois legislator did exercise his prerogatives as chairman of the platform committee to insure that sufficient prolife *members* of the abortion subcommittee were named to insure that a prolife plank would be voted out of the subcommittee which the full platform committee could only have overruled by an embarrassingly public left turn — which the conservative platform committee was unlikely to make.

In the event, the abortion subcommittee crafted a plank, aimed at "those who perform abortions" — *not* at "women" — that put the Republican Party on record as favoring a Human Life Amendment to the Constitution and legislation making clear that the Fourteenth Amendment's protections apply to unborn children. At the same time the tortuous Dole "tolerance" language was simply *rejected,* and a statement about "the diversity of views" in the party was included instead.

Predictably, this stirred up the "usual suspects" among proabortion governors — Weld, Whitman, and Wilson, joined by New York Governor George Patacki and Maine Senator Olympia J. Snowe — and they promptly threatened the dreaded floor fight at the convention. There remained more than a serious question, never clarified in the public reports, as to whether these people even had sufficient numbers in the delegations to mount a floor fight under the rules. Be that as it may, though, once again, it proved to be the often indulged and coddled Republican proabortion politicians who, having lost in committee, were evidently prepared to jeopardize Bob Dole's and the party's chances by an ugly public floor fight. As Henry Hyde aptly remarked, "Those who want to precipitate [a fight] are not interested in Senator Dole's well-being but in some other ideological goal."

The floor fight was averted, however, and the issue resolved by an agreement that prochoice amendments which had been proposed but defeated would be included in an appendix to the platform. This solution also had the merit that it could be effected by the sole decision of platform committee chairman: Hyde. Naturally, the proabortion side put the best face on their defeat, describing it as a victory. "We have been acknowledged in the platform as we have never before been acknowledged," said Susan Cullman, chairman of the Choice Coalition.

So the threatened floor fight never materialized, and the way was smoothed for the bland and scripted Republican National Convention that came the following week. According to syndicated columnist Robert Novak, however, candidate Dole was far from happy with the outcome. When he read in the newspapers that his aides had abandoned his pet concept of tolerance in the platform (after the platform committee had voted it out), he angrily told them to undo the deal, and was apparently only with difficulty dissuaded from precipitating an open fight with — in effect! — the whole prolife movement. Dole was perhaps understandably angry anyway because the whole new abortion brouhaha in the platform committee had eclipsed the launching of his tax-cutting proposal the same week. But the question remains: why couldn't he ever learn?

VI

So what does it all come down to? Should prolifers support the Republican ticket in November? Certainly many prolifers will accept the argument that Bob Dole and the Republicans are at the very least a "lesser evil" when compared to Bill Clinton and the

Democrats; and thus many of them will still no doubt vote Republican, and many of them may also work for the ticket as well.

A strong rational argument can even be made that, having prevailed on the platform even against the candidate's own wishes, prolifers should now work especially hard in order to demonstrate just how much their support really counts. Pat Buchanan, for example, seems to have reached this kind of conclusion and has accordingly urged his followers to support the Republican ticket as now constituted, even while perhaps waiting and hoping for a better ticket in the future. This is indisputably a legitimate way to go.

A Dole-Kemp victory would almost certainly be a net gain for the prolife movement; the candidates represent and embody much of value which prolifers would be the last to belittle. Still, it is impossible not to have some regret that this is the best "the prolife party" could do. Both Kemp and Dole had opportunities in their acceptance speeches when they could surely have admitted to the American people on national television that they did, after all, represent the prolife party. Kemp spoke feelingly of human dignity and of life as a gift of God; Dole spoke with equal feeling about families and children and doing what is right and, especially, about the need for judges to administer real justice in accordance with the law. All of these themes afforded natural openings to appeal to the American people to help end America's abortion scourge, but neither Kemp nor Dole made the connection.

Dole actually articulated the word "abortion," deploring it along with drugs, illegitimacy, and other social evils; but, again, he in no way intimated that the Republican platform actually contained a call to put an end to this particular evil.

Everything considered, while surely not wishing the Dole-Kemp ticket ill, especially in the light of the alternative, knowledgeable prolifers can nevertheless hardly have very much *enthusiasm* for them. It remains to be seen how many will work for them; surely not a few will find it hard to work their hearts out for them considering how diligently the Republican leadership has worked to marginalize the party's prolifers. It is a pity that so much prolife energy and savvy will thus in many cases not be put to work.

At a minimum Bob Dole has probably created by his misplaced priorities a state of "permanent revolution" within his own party, an instability that will surely continue whether he wins or loses: nobody can any longer be really sure whether the Republican Party is the prolife party or not.

As a result of not "getting it" about abortion, then, Bob Dole may have jeopardized his own chances of ever being president — and thereby of ever leading America's "prolife party" to victory.

Postscript

As everybody knows, the Dole-Kemp ticket went down to defeat in November, 1996. Most commentators agree that these two estimable gentlemen were simply unable to persuade sufficient numbers of the electorate that there was any good reason why they should be elected. How much effect their failure to seize upon the abortion issue, and, especially, upon Bill Clinton's veto of the Partial-Birth Abortion Ban bill, had upon the final outcome cannot easily be gauged in any exact way; certainly they did not even make any effort to persuade prolife and profamily voters why they should be elected.

What is worse for the prolife cause is that President Clinton won a majority of Catholic voters — some 53 percent of them — even while not quite managing more than a plurality of all other voters. Clinton largely carried the Northeast and West Coast states too, while Dole's major support was in the Middle West and South — areas with relatively smaller Catholic populations. What this tells us is that "the Catholic vote," in at least one important respect, is apparently no longer "Catholic," if by this term we understand "accepting of what the Church teaches." For the Catholic Church has not ceased to condemn all abortions in the strongest terms precisely during the Clinton years.

Only about 8 percent of all voters interviewed in exit polls, by the way, named "abortion" as the most important electoral issue for them; of these voters, a large majority went for Dole — a benefit for the Republicans no doubt, but not *enough* of a benefit. As long as abortion rates no higher than this on the national importance scale, it is to be feared that the politicians and candidates are going to keep trying to ignore it whenever they can, as both presidential campaigns did this time.

The 1996 elections for the House and the Senate appear to have been pretty much of a draw between the two parties as far as the actual numbers are concerned — although the fact that the Republicans retained their majority in both houses, even while their presidential candidate was going down to defeat, must be counted as a "victory" of sorts. This is especially true when we consider the huge amounts of money for anti-Republican media spots contributed by such as organized labor, the National Education Association, and the environmentalists to defeat conservative Republicans everywhere; these campaigns aimed at returning the Republicans back to minority status and unprecedented amounts of money were put up in the pursuit of this aim. Just as clearly, they failed, and may not be repeated next time around.

In the Senate, the Republicans actually increased their majority by one, the overall ratio now being 55 to 45. As far as prolife numbers are concerned, three of the new Republican senators, Wayne Allard of Colorado, Sam Brownback of Kansas, and Michael Enzi of Wyoming actually took strong prolife positions during their campaigns; and in the one case where a Republican incumbent was defeated, South Dakota even elected a prolife Democrat, Tim Johnson, in place of the "moderate" Larry Pressler.

The media had kicked off election night by wrongly predicting the defeat of strongly prolife Senator Robert Smith of New Hampshire, who, however, retained his seat; apparently, he was never even behind, which demonstrates how exit polls can be wrong. At the same time, William Weld in Massachusetts and Dick Zimmer in New Jersey, two of the kind of proabortion Republican "moderates" so favored by the media during the primary season — before the media go on to favor the Democratic candidates anyway during the general election! — these two moderates failed to win over their Democratic opponents, and, thankfully, may no longer be so prominent on the national scene. However, the "moderate" Republicans who were elected were again found to be mostly in the Northeast, where the Catholic vote should have counted more decisively against them — if only there had been a Catholic vote that was "Catholic."

In the House, the Republican majority was diminished by perhaps as many as ten votes, and the number of prolife Congressmen by perhaps as many as six. Several of the Republican losses in the House did involve strong prolife members, however, most notably that of Robert K. Dornan in California, who at this writing was alleging voter fraud in his race and demanding a recount. Some prolife members were also defeated in such states as North Carolina and

Washington. Stalwart prolife member Linda A. Smith of Washington state, however, was one of the members whom the media early singled out for electoral demise, but she apparently managed to hang on to her seat in the end.

All in all, the new Congress is likely to retain a slight prolife tilt, but it seems unlikely that there is sufficient prolife support there to overcome the inevitable Clinton vetoes of much or most prolife legislation. Thus, while prolifers should be pleased that we did not suffer any really major defeats, we must nevertheless recognize that, politically, we are still very, very far from what must inevitably remain our logical goal of restoring full constitutional and legal protection to the lives of the unborn in this country.

12

Everything You Need to Know about Partial-Birth Abortion

I

On March 20, 1997, the U.S. House of Representatives voted to ban a procedure that has come to be known as "partial-birth abortion." The house vote for this bill, HR 1122, added up to a veto-proof majority of 295 to 136.

Two months later, on May 20, 1997, the U.S. Senate approved with only slight language changes the same ban, which had been introduced into the Senate by Republican Senator Rick Santorum of Pennsylvania. The Senate approved the ban by a vote of 64 to 36 — only three votes short of the two-thirds majority required to override the veto of the bill again promised by President Bill Clinton.

A year before, in April, 1996, the president had vetoed a nearly identical bill which had been passed by both houses in 1995. On September 19, 1996, the House of Representatives had easily overridden this Clinton veto by a vote of 285 to 137. But after what amounted to one of the most intensive prolife lobbying efforts ever mounted — which included a massive rally on the Capitol steps on September 12, led in person by all of the nation's active Catholic cardinal-archbishops, joined by many other religious and secular leaders, and accompanied by the mailing of literally *millions* of individual postcards filled out in Catholic parishes — the U.S. Senate failed to override the presidential veto; the vote, on September 26, 1996, was 58 to 40 — eight votes short of the two-thirds majority necessary.

The president had dared to veto the bill even though it was known to be strongly favored by over 70 percent of all Americans,

Published in *Culture Wars*, September 1997.

according to impartial polls. Contrary to what some observers have suggested, this chameleon president does stand firm on a few issues; legalized abortion is one of them.

Thus failed in 1995-96 the first attempt to prohibit the partial-birth abortion procedure, a procedure which had sickened millions who had come to learn about it after the extensive publicity and lobbying campaigns conducted against it. The effort to ban partial-birth abortions marked the first time since the lethal practice of abortion became legalized in the United States in 1973 that large numbers of Americans had ever really been obliged to face up to what abortion itself really is.

It also marked the first time Congress had ever attempted to pass substantive and substantial legislation prohibiting any kind of abortion (as distinguished from voting to prohibit or limit government funding of it).

The momentum achieved by the effort to ban partial-birth abortions was considerable, indeed, unprecedented; and both houses in the new 105th Congress, following the November elections, promptly moved to ban the ghastly procedure a second time, as we have noted. It seemed intolerable to an increasing number of people that the first effort could have failed. If anything, the pressure on the Congress to enact, and the president to sign, a ban on partial-birth abortions became even greater after the president's veto the first time around.

Regardless of the ultimate outcome of the whole partial-birth abortion issue — whether the president finally gives in and signs the re-enacted bill, whether the Congress finds itself obliged to attempt another veto override, or whether another failure to override a presidential veto pushes the whole issue into yet another legislative session — regardless of the outcome in the short run, what has now become clear is that the partial-birth abortion controversy has now changed the terms of the debate over legalized abortion in the United States. The glacier has actually moved.

For around a quarter of a century, from the time the U.S. Supreme Court legalized abortion with its *Roe v. Wade* decision in 1973, prolifers have struggled with only limited success to get the country to focus on what abortion is: the killing of a child. In reaching its decision legalizing the practice, the Supreme Court essentially bypassed the question of the status and rights, if any, of the unborn child (dismissing with a footnote what it called "the difficult question" of when life begins). Instead, the court focused on the "woman's right" to choose whether or not to continue a pregnancy.

This whole approach, focusing on the woman instead of the child, proved to be a stroke of evil genius. With the advent of modern contraceptives, Americans had already become massively convinced that pregnancy and child bearing *were* things that people had a right to be fully in control of, in short, "to choose." In this perspective, legalizing abortion merely meant extending this control over the consequences of sexual acts and making it more effective. The whole point was to make control over sexual acts more effective; there was no longer even any argument about whether this was permissible or desirable.

The fact that abortion also just happened to take a life, however, was tacitly passed over by the votaries of legalized abortion, as it was by public opinion generally — just as it was no doubt consciously set aside by the Supreme Court as well. Few people even blinked; it was *logical*, after all, if women were to be in charge of pregnancy and child birth (and if traditional morality did not count any longer as a result of the sexual revolution) then women must enjoy *effective* control of these things. The technical means were at hand.

Everybody always understood, after all, that you cannot make an omelette without breaking eggs, as the saying goes; and abortion certainly does insure the required degree of effective control over pregnancy and child birth, even if it is after the fact. So what if we are actually killing somebody? We have to have abortion; that is the primary thing; otherwise the whole premise of the sexual revolution would be called into question; and *that* is what has now become unthinkable in our society.

Thus took over the crude utilitarianism which popular opinion often exhibits when it is a question of a goal which everybody has come to take for granted and which almost nobody can even imagine not being legitimate: "control" over the consequences of sexual intercourse. People attracted to each other desire to have this and they are inevitably going to have it, whatever outmoded "moralists" might think. Such is the current viewpoint.

The prolife movement sprang up immediately after the legalization of abortion to call attention to and defend the rights of the child, of course; but the American people generally proved reluctant to take the prolife side in what became an unpleasant public fight where being prolife was successfully presented as being "against women." Most Americans were prepared to live, however uncomfortably, with the contradiction that even if abortion is conceded to be wrong (as polls consistently show a majority of Americans believe), it can nevertheless sometimes be "necessary" (as the same polls show a majority of Americans also believe).

It quickly turned out that many of society's leaders in many fields shared these same views, if they did not view abortion as somehow even a positive good; it seemed to provide a quick answer to some otherwise seemingly intractable social problems.

So it was the prolifers who quickly became seen as tiresome by insisting that abortion wrongfully took the life of another human being, and who tried to demonstrate this irrefutably by such means as graphic color slides of dismembered fetuses or recordings of fetal heartbeats. These demonstrations reached very few people; and failed to persuade more than a very few. People reacted against *them*, in fact, and against all the aggressive and horrible accusations prolifers kept insisting on bringing forward into an otherwise supposedly calm and peaceful situation.

It was the prolifers themselves who were seen as rocking the boat; they soon became identified and stigmatized as "harsh," "judgmental," "mean-spirited," and "fanatical." In today's permissive society, they became labeled as the "extremists" merely for trying to get people to face up to an ugly reality that most people did not want to face up to, indeed, were quite determined *not* to face up to.

Having the option of legally terminating unwanted pregnancies was widely seen as simply too helpful and too expedient to allow any serious questions to be raised about it. And had not the highest legal authority in the land, the Supreme Court, decided the question anyway? And had not this decision, in effect, been "democratically" ratified by the American people by the very fact that the prolife movement, after nearly a quarter of century of agitation, had been unable to come even close to persuading a majority of Americans to outlaw abortion again? Why should anybody go on tormenting oneself and others about a question that had been "settled" at the highest level?

Then, in September, 1992, an Ohio doctor named Martin Haskell presented a paper at a "Risk Management Seminar" in Dallas, Texas, sponsored by the National Abortion Federation. In his paper the doctor described a new abortion technique he had been using. This technique, which he called a D & X (for dilation and extraction) procedure, was one expressly designed for abortions at mid- and later stages of a pregnancy. Dr. Haskell indicated that he himself had carried out the procedure more than 700 times.

Using seaweed-based dilators such as are used in other types of later-term abortions, Dr. Haskell first dilated the woman's cervix over a painful three-day period to enable the already well-developed baby to be removed intact — rather than being dismembered inside the womb and removed piece by piece, as is the case in regular D & E (dilation and evacuation) late-term abortions.

Then, guided by a sonogram, Dr. Haskell, as he explained in his Dallas paper, carefully grasped the baby's foot with forceps and pulled the entire body out with the exception of the head. At this point, he punctured the baby's skull with surgical scissors and inserted a catheter, or vacuum tube, attached to a suction machine in order to suck the brains out. The dead baby with collapsed skull was then brought out completely into the air.

Among the advantages of this procedure, as Dr. Haskell's exposition brought out, is that the abortionist does not have to collect and identify all the bloody dismembered body parts and insure that they have all been removed. Also, the procedure definitely insures a dead baby — something the saline solutions or prostaglandin drugs often used to kill the baby *in utero* in late-term abortions occasionally fail to do, to the obvious discomfort of the abortionist. The abortionist, at all costs, has to deliver a dead, not a still-living, baby.

In today's era of legalized abortion, a ghastly procedure such as this is not only resorted to by licensed practitioners, whatever the larger public may prefer to believe or imagine about abortion; it is also considered to be an entirely fit subject for discussion or publication in medical journals as just one more "medical procedure." In its issue of July 5, 1993, *American Medical News*, the official newspaper of the American Medical Association (AMA), interviewed Dr. Haskell about the procedure, along with another physician who regularly employed the same procedure — and who indeed was said to have originally developed the procedure — the late Dr. James McMahon of Los Angeles.

Dr. Haskell indicated that he performed the procedure at about 20 weeks — the mid-point of a pregnancy — up through about 26 weeks. Dr. McMahon said he performed the procedure all the way up to 40 weeks, or full term. Dr. Haskell frankly admitted that about 80 per cent or more of the abortions he performed in this manner were purely "elective," that is, they were not done for any "medical" reasons whatsoever pertaining either to the mother or the child. Dr. McMahon, who stated that he had carried out as many as 2000 of these operations, did not admit that the ones he had done were "elective." However, his definition of "non-elective" included such stated "reasons" as the mother's "youth" or her "depression." Information submitted by Dr. McMahon to a congressional committee indicated that most of the babies he aborted at 26 weeks or later were perfectly normal and healthy babies.

As public awareness grew concerning the medical procedures these physicians were resorting to, both Dr. Haskell and Dr. McMahon were invited to testify before the House Constitution Subcommittee (of the House Judiciary Committee) by the committee's chairman, Florida Republican Representative Charles Canady. The latter would continue to be one of the most important figures in Congress working against partial-birth abortions. Initially, both abortionists accepted the invitation to testify before Congress; obviously, *they* did not see anything wrong in what they were doing; they were both doing it, and they were also candidly describing what they were doing.

In the end, however, as the public controversy began to heat up, Dr. Haskell cancelled out on his date with Congress, and Dr. McMahon simply failed to appear to testify. It was left to such shills in the Congress itself as Rep. Barney Frank (D.-Mass.) or Rep. Patricia Schroeder (D.-Colo.) to argue at the Canady hearings that Congress had no business legislating about how these licensed physicians were choosing to practice medicine, or, indeed, "interfering" in the practice of medicine in any way.

This latter argument, that the government had no right to interfere in the practice of medicine, was to be a litany often repeated in the course of the subsequent debates; few pointed out how little sense such an argument makes in the era of Medicare, Medicaid, and the attempts by the Clinton Administration and, increasingly, by the Congress itself, to federalize "the practice of medicine" entirely.

Moreover, where the partial-birth abortion procedure was concerned, it turned out that the public was going to be exhibiting a somewhat greater capacity for shock and disapproval than some members of the medical profession or of Congress. The method involved in doing partial-birth abortions actually began to *get to* some people when it was brought out what it really entailed. As early as February 23, 1993, the *National Right to Life News* had published a meticulous exposé of Dr. Haskell's September, 1992, "How To" partial-birth abortion paper delivered at the National Abortion Federation's "Risk Management Seminar" in Dallas. This exposé was accompanied by a series of black-and-white, pen-and-ink drawings illustrating the procedure step by step. These drawings, from the February, 1993, issue of *Life Advocate,* were destined to play a dramatic and continuing part in the campaign against partial-birth abortions — which the NRLC had, in effect, launched with its exposé of Dr. Haskell's paper.

The drawings came to be used in countless ads sponsored by the NRLC in the course of its campaign, and they were widely reproduced. Although the accuracy of the drawings would be challenged many times in the months and years to follow, even Dr. Haskell admitted in his *American Medical News* interview that the drawings were "accurate from a medical point of view."

The drawings were very important from another point of view, one that perhaps had not been originally foreseen. For years the prolife movement has tried to get across the horror of abortion by showing pictures or slides of dismembered fetuses or those burned by saline solutions. Too often, however, these grisly slides or pictures (like fetuses in jars) have simply turned people off and caused them to react negatively against the very prolifers who were exhibiting such obviously horrible and offensive stuff in public. Those who have tried to combat pornography by themselves bringing forward graphic examples of it have similarly sometimes seen the *blame* for it boomerang back upon themselves.

The pen-and-ink drawings of the partial-birth abortion procedure, however, succeeded in graphically conveying the full horror of what was being done to a human child, but *without* turning viewers against the very ads which featured such graphic illustrations. At any rate, as it proved, most people did not react to the same extent that viewers normally react to other such graphic materials. Accidently or intentionally, the use of these black-and-white drawings by the NRLC in its ads was a stroke of genius.

Not only were the drawings to prove important in alerting the public to just what was passing as an acceptable medical procedure;

the very name "partial-birth abortion" seems to have been crucially important in garnering support for the outlawing of at least *this* barbaric abortion procedure, regardless of the fact that the Supreme Court had decreed abortion to be a "woman's right." In fact, it turned out that the name "partial-birth abortion" was going to stick, even though the proabortion people regularly went on characterizing it by such phrases as "what opponents *call* 'partial-birth abortion.'" You yourself have probably heard that phrase or similar ones on the evening news more than once by now.

However, as the *National Right to Life News* correctly pointed out (November 30, 1995): "None of the terms that the abortion practitioners prefer would be workable as a *legal definition*. The bill creates a legal definition. . .'an abortion in which the person performing the abortion *partially vaginally delivers* a living fetus before killing the fetus and completing the delivery. . ."

Whatever the reasons, then, more and more Americans evidently did become bothered by the barbarity of the method as well as, increasingly, by the dishonesty and hypocrisy resorted to in order to defend the indefensible in the case of this procedure. The idea that a doctor could deliver a baby almost completely before killing him or her in such a gruesome fashion at the very last minute did finally persuade some people that maybe America really had finally gone too far with legalized abortion.

A formerly consistent antilife legislator such as Senator Daniel P. Moynihan (D.-New York) went so far as to label the procedure "infanticide" (but as Dr. Haskell had carefully explained in his *American Medical News* interview, the *aim* of the procedure is always that "you're attempting to do an abortion." What did Senator Moynihan expect?). Another senator who had unsuccessfully tried to mount an entire presidential campaign on a proabortion platform, Senator Arlen Specter (R.-Pennsylvania), similarly came out against partial-birth abortions.

The National Right to Life Committee devised a series of newspaper ads — always employing the black-and-white line drawings — which proved to be very dramatic and effective way of getting across exactly what a partial-birth abortion consisted of. In addition to the drawings, these ads also included excerpts from the dramatic testimony before Congress of an Ohio nurse, Brenda Pratt Shafer, who had witnessed three of Dr. Haskell's "procedures" — and as a consequence had become passionately opposed to the practice. As the NRLC ads proclaimed, this is what Nurse Shafer saw:

> I stood at the doctor's side and watched him perform a partial-birth abortion on a woman who was six months pregnant. The baby's heartbeat was clearly visible on the ultrasound screen. The doctor delivered the baby's body and arms, everything but his little head. The baby's body was moving. His little fingers were clasping together. He was kicking his feet. The doctor took a pair of scissors and inserted them into the back of the baby's head, and the baby's arms jerked out in a flinch, a startled reaction, like a baby does when he thinks he might fall. Then the doctor opened the scissors up. Then he stuck the high-powered suction tube into the hole and sucked the baby's brains out. Now the baby was completely limp.
>
> I never went back to the clinic. But I am still haunted by the face of that little boy. It was the most perfect, angelic face I have ever seen."

Such was the personal testimony of Nurse Brenda Pratt Shafer. It was hard to accuse her of deliberately sensationalizing the issue (although many did anyway); she was merely describing what she had seen.

The NRLC ads also included a statement by Dr. Pamela Smith, Director of Medical Education in the Department of Obstetrics and Gynecology at Mt. Sinai Hospital in Chicago. This statement declared that "there are absolutely no obstetrical situations encountered in this country which require a partially delivered human fetus to be destroyed to preserve the health of the mother."

For the first time since abortion was legalized in America, the truth about what abortion is and what it entails was finally gotten across to significant numbers of Americans and their legislators through the publicity that was generated by the exposé of this particular procedure. In the protracted public controversy that has surrounded the whole question ever since, the proabortion forces have, finally, been mainly on the defensive — after almost a quarter of a century of legalized abortion. Subsequent frantic attempts to pretend that the baby would already have to be dead from the anesthesia before his skull was pierced, for example, had already been refuted by Dr. Haskell's own express words.

It soon became widely recognized that the proabortionists were indeed trying to defend the indefensible; even many of those engaged in doing it tacitly conceded the point; but the fact that the proabortionists could actually defend even partial-birth abortions finally brought home to an increasing number of Americans who the real "extremists" and "fanatics" on the abortion issue were.

Thus, on November 1, 1995, for the first time since *Roe v. Wade* was handed down, the House voted by a more than two-to-one margin (288 to 139) to ban this type of abortion procedure. Adding language (in reality meaningless) that the ban does not apply to a partial-birth abortion necessary to save the life of a mother, provided that no other procedure would suffice, the Senate followed suit on December 7, 1995, by a vote of 54 to 44 — 13 short of the majority of 65 needed to override a presidential veto.

The only problem for the growing number of people and their legislators now opposed to allowing partial-birth abortions, of course, was that the President of the United States was among those proabortionists still obstinately and reflexively prepared to defend the practice regardless of the growing opposition to it.

II

In order to provide some modicum of cover for his veto of the partial-birth abortion ban passed by both houses of Congress, President Bill Clinton decided to invite to his veto session at the White House on April 10, 1996, five women who were described as having undergone partial-birth abortions by Los Angeles Doctor James McMahon (who himself had died suddenly in October, 1995).

The president described these five women as representative of

> . . .a small but extremely vulnerable group of women and families in this country. . .just a few hundred a year. . .They all desperately wanted their children. They didn't want abortions. They made agonizing decisions only when it became clear that their babies would not survive. Their own lives, their health, and, in some cases, their capacity to have children in the future were in danger. . .

It all sounded so sincere; it seemed motivated by nothing but compassion for the well-being of this "vulnerable" group of women; it certainly played to the typical television audience. Yet, as far as one can judge from the state of the art in contemporary medicine, it was all nothing but a sustained and elaborate lie constructed entirely out of whole cloth. In the nature of the case, there is no evidence that partial-birth abortions were medically indicated in any of these cases, any more than abortions of any kind were medically indicated.

As the television cameras rolled, the women themselves nevertheless told stories about how they had learned late in their pregnancies that their babies were suffering from grave disorders for which Dr. McMahon's procedure supposedly provided the only remedy (it certainly could not have been much of a "remedy" for the babies, whatever their condition that had only been learned about "late in pregnancy").

And, in any case, as we have noted, none of these stories could possibly have been true; these "vulnerable" women had been suborned by the President of the United States to lend themselves to a shameless public fraud. Ample medical testimony has long since been brought forward to prove that partial-birth abortions are never necessary, whatever these poor women may have been told. It is a procedure elected by the abortionist, and, if anything, it is the procedure itself that could be harmful to the woman, since, for one thing, the abortionist has to probe blindly to find the base of the baby's skull; he could always miss, and inflict damage on the woman.

For another thing, the cervix of the woman has to be severely dilated, with possible harmful effects resulting. The television audience was never informed, for example, that one of the five women testifying at the president's veto session had had five miscarriages as a result of undergoing this procedure (perhaps the president himself was not informed about this).

Inconvenient facts such as these had nevertheless become quite well known by the time this broadcast featuring the president himself was aired. A group calling itself the Physicians' Ad Hoc Coalition for Truth (PHACT) had long since come forward with exact knowledge refuting the claim that partial-birth abortions had anything to do with "medicine" at all. The membership of PHACT quickly rose to include some 600 practicing physicians. The following excerpt was a typical PHACT answer to the proabortionist claim that partial-birth abortions could be "necessary" to protect a woman's "health":

> That claim is totally and completely false. Contrary to what abortion activists would have us believe, partial-birth abortion is never medically indicated to protect a woman's health or fertility. In fact, the opposite is true: the procedure can pose a significant and immediate threat to both the pregnant woman's health and her fertility. . .

None of this risk is ever necessary for any reason. We and many other doctors across the U.S. regularly treat women whose unborn children suffer the same conditions as those cited by the women who appeared at Mr. Clinton's veto ceremony. Never is the partial-birth procedure necessary. . .Sometimes, as in the case of hydrocephaly, it is first necessary to drain some of the fluid from the baby's head. And in some cases, when vaginal delivery is not possible, a doctor performs a Caesarean section. But in no case is it necessary to partially deliver any infant through the vagina and then kill the infant.

None of these facts appears to have affected President Clinton, however. Unfortunately, this president, by the very fact that he was still in office, had already had ample experience of how ready the American public can be to accept almost any excuse rather than face up to what America has become as a result of legalized abortion.

In his formal veto message to Congress, although he acknowledged that the bill already contained a "life exception," President Clinton declared that he would still not sign such a bill unless it also allowed partial-birth abortions to be performed for "health" reasons as well. The actual words of the President's veto message included the following:

> The procedure described in HR 1833 has troubled me deeply as it has many people. I cannot support the use of that procedure on an elective basis. . .That is why I implored Congress to add on an exception for the small number of compelling cases. . .The life exception in the current bill only covers cases where the doctor believes that the woman will die. It fails to cover cases where, absent the procedure, serious physical harm, including losing the ability to have more children, is very likely to occur.

Like the president's remarks concerning the five women who "had to have" partial-birth abortions, this veto message also seemed very sincere. However, in addition to the medically established fact that, as we have seen, there *aren't* any medical or "health" reasons for any partial-birth abortions, ever — in addition to this medically established fact, it is also true that the Supreme Court of the United States, in its 1973 *Doe v. Bolton* case, has long since in any case decided that "health," in the context of abortion, includes "all factors — physical, emotional, psychological, familial, and the woman's age — relevant to the well-being of the patient." The law thus understands "health" to be anything an abortionist decides it is — something the president surely also knows very well, since he is a graduate of the Yale Law School, after all.

In other words, a "health" exception to any abortion bill means that an abortion could be performed for any reason a woman along with her doctor decides is a "health" reason. In yet other words, an abortion can be done if a women simply decides she does not want the baby — for, in that case, being "forced" to have it would cause distress and hence affect her "mental health." In practice, a "health exception" simply nullifies anything else a law purporting to restrict or prohibit abortion says. Nobody today questions or second-guesses *anything* a medical practitioner asserts is a question of "health." Under *Doe v. Bolton*'s definition of health, abortions have effectively been and are being done for any reason or for no reason, at any stage of a pregnancy. This has been true since 1973 — the year both *Doe* and *Roe* were issued.

Anybody who has seriously looked into the contemporary abortion situation in America today knows this to be the case: abortions are being performed today on a massive scale for any reason or for no reason at any stage of pregnancy simply because the woman does not want the baby. President Clinton's assumption, however, is that the American public either does not know this or does not *want* to know it; hence he is apparently not bothered in the least by proclaiming bare-faced lies on the subject as truths; he thinks, and apparently correctly, that he is perfectly safe as far as the American people is concerned in babbling about his concern for the "health" of women. He repeated more than once his claim that all he wanted in a bill to sign was "an exception for women who would face severe physical damage." He even plaintively asked a reporter in May, 1996: "Why wouldn't [the Republicans] accept that minor amendment?"

After his re-election in November, 1996, at a press conference on December 13, 1996, Bill Clinton re-iterated that:

> I wanted to sign that legislation. When I first heard about it, I thought I would sign it. . .The problem is, I will say it again, there are a few hundred women every year who have personally agonizing situations. . .Now I pleaded and pleaded with the Congress to adopt highly restrictive language which would make it clear that there had to be a very serious health problem for the woman involved.

During the 1996 presidential campaign, Clinton had written about partial-birth abortion to the Southern Baptist Convention that "in situations where a woman's serious health interests are not at risk, I do not support [them], I do not defend them, and I would sign appropriate legislation banning them."

The reality about what the president supports and what he does turned out to be two very different things, however. Meanwhile, the national campaign against partial-birth abortions had achieved so much momentum, despite the standard lies and disinformation about abortion being parroted even by the president himself, that his veto of HR 1833 produced not more typical sorrowing prolife resignation, but rather a groundswell of further protests against both the mendacity and barbarity of it all.

The president of the Christian Life Commission of the 16-million-member Southern Baptist Convention, Richard D. Land, was compelled to say concerning Clinton's veto that "the president has now made it unmistakably clear that there is no circumstance. . .in which he will make it illegal for the mother to instruct the doctor to kill the child." The Southern Baptist Convention, of course, is the denomination to which President Clinton belongs (he seems to take his religion about as seriously as many of the Kennedys seem to take theirs).

Just as they would later lead a rally on the Capitol steps in support of a veto override, all of the active Catholic cardinal-archbishops of the United States, along with the president of the National Conference of Catholic Bishops, Bishop Anthony Pilla of Cleveland, signed a scorching letter to the president dated April 16, 1996, in which they told him: "Your veto of this bill is beyond comprehension for those who hold human life sacred." They bluntly challenged the president's reference to the "health" exception he said he wanted by reminding him that "not everyone. . .would know that 'health,' as the courts define it in the context of abortion means virtually anything that has to do with a woman's overall 'well-being." They re-iterated the point, already made many times by others, that it was the partial-birth abortion procedure itself that might constitute a danger to the health of a woman undergoing it.

And in the days following President Clinton's veto of the Partial-Birth Abortion Ban bill on April 10, 1996, dozens of Catholic bishops, not content with what the cardinals and the NCCB had said, sent in their own individual protests and/or issued their own strong statements against partial-birth abortions to their flocks. Many other religious leaders did the same. A strong statement calling for a veto override issued by the National Prolife Religious Council was signed by 29 religious leaders from the Orthodox, Presbyterian, United Methodist, Lutheran, Evangelical, Baptist, United Church of Christ, Disciples of Christ, and Episcopal Churches. This statement surely added considerable weight to what leaders of the "religious right" such as Pat Robertson and Ralph Reed had been saying all along. Similarly, the Rabbinical Alliance of America called partial-birth abortion "truly a barbaric act not far removed from infanticide."

Even the politicians found themselves able to speak more plainly than usual where partial-birth abortion was concerned. Bob Dole, well along in his presidential campaign by April, 1996, nevertheless forthrightly said that "a partial-birth abortion blurs the line between abortion and infanticide." Republican Majority Leader Dick Armey said he was "appalled that the president [was] willing to allow nearly-born children to be killed by this hideous procedure." Even President Clinton's own ambassador to the Vatican, Massachusetts Democratic politician Raymond Flynn, urged the president "in the strongest possible terms" to let the ban become law — especially after the Vatican issued a statement against Clinton's veto "about as strong as I have ever seen," Flynn remarked.

In short, there was a huge and continuous outpouring against the Clinton veto which went far beyond the usual Washington lobbying effort. This was not an issue that was easily going to be put to rest. Indeed the nation's capital had rarely seen anything like it in the memory of most knowledgeable observers.

Nevertheless, all the pressure proved insufficient in the end to overcome the president's calculated opposition to *any* restriction on legalized abortion. As we have noted, even while the House handily overrode the veto, the override effort fell short by eight votes in the Senate. Prolifers had to resign themselves to prepare for yet another legislative session — but with perhaps more grounds for hope than had been the case since abortion was first legalized in the United States.

III

The November, 1996, elections returned President William J. Clinton to the White House. Apparently it was the "economy" again (it was humming along). His veto of the Partial-Birth Abortion Ban bill evidently did not influence enough voters to put his re-election in jeopardy. Indeed, 53 per cent of Catholic voters voted for Clinton.

Meanwhile, in the House of Representatives, there was a small net loss of reliable prolife votes, while in the Senate several new prolife members were elected. Whatever the total numbers, there was no doubt that this by-now notorious abortion procedure would not fail to be seriously challenged in the new 105th Congress.

The prolife side gained an immediate and unexpected advantage in the public debate when a professional proabortion lobbyist, in a candid interview in *American Medical News*, published in February, 1997, admitted that he had "lied through his teeth" in a 1995 appearance on ABC television's *Nightline* program when he contended that women had partial-birth abortions only in the most extreme of circumstances; and that no more than about 500 of them were ever performed in any one year.

This latter figure was the figure the proabortion lobbying groups had given to Congress. However, this particular lobbyist, Ron Fitzsimmons, executive director of the National Coalition of Abortion Providers, both in his AMN interview, and in another appearance on *Nightline* to set the record straight, was now publicly owning up to an outright lie about all of this. It was not that Fitzsimmons had become converted to the prolife cause; on the contrary, he continued to believe that abortion was a woman's constitutional right; but the lies about what abortion really was, and what the abortionists were regularly doing, had apparently begun to get even to him.

The truth, as Fitzsimmons well knew because he was so heavily involved in the proaboriton cause, was that thousands of partial-birth and late-term abortions were regularly being performed each year — almost all of them on completely healthy women with completely healthy babies and with no medical indications whatsoever to justify the procedure. A single clinic in northern New Jersey, for example, had reported some 1500 partial-birth abortions for one single year. Ron Fitzsimmons observed: "When you're a doctor who does these abortions, and the leaders of your movement appear before Congress and go on network news and say these procedures are done in only the most tragic of circumstances, how do you think it makes you feel?. . .It makes you feel like a dirty little abortionist with a dirty little secret. . ."

These avowals by Ron Fitzsimmons were widely publicized in the media. Many media people, normally quite proud of what they believe is their objectivity and disinterestedness, were particularly shocked at the revelations of Ron Fitzsimmons because they had been accepting prochoice "facts" for many years pretty much at face value. Were not the prolifers the established "extremists" and "fanatics" on the "emotional issue" of abortion, after all?

But what kind of a cause is it that depends on lies? Now one of the media's favorite kinds of sources was avowing that the prochoice case was indeed based on a huge lie. The proabortion lobbying and professional lobbying organizations and associations quickly called a press conference to attempt damage control; but these same people had hardly compiled much of a record for honesty and candor — and this had suddenly become clear to some who had obstinately refused to face the truth before.

For the record shows that the proabortion people had been lying steadily from the time the whole debate over partial-birth abortion began. First, they tried to deny that any such procedure was ever used; it was supposedly a prolife fabrication. Then they tried to contend that it was only used sparingly for serious medical reasons or fetal abnormality. They even advanced the claim, against the express testimony of Dr. Haskell, that the baby was already dead from the anesthesia before his skull was ever pierced. As each of these lies was exposed, they simply retreated back to the next lie — and to other lies.

This time, however, they were obliged to try to maintain these lies in the face of all the evidence at a highly-publicized joint House-Senate Judiciary Committee hearing held on March 11, 1997. Vicki Saporta, Executive Director of the National Abortion Federation (NAF), told the committee that she could not give an accurate assessment of partial-birth abortions nationwide. When Congressman Charles T. Canady reminded her that she had testified very confidently the year before to a figure of some 450 to 500, she blustered that "no organization knows" the true number — and that the numbers question had only been raised in any case as a "tactic to distract Congress" — and that, anyway, the numbers did not matter ("Well, sure," aptly remarked syndicated columnist Charles Krauthammer, hardly a friend of the prolife movement, "now that they have been exposed as false and the new ones are inconvenient to her case").

When South Carolina Republican Representative Bob Inglis asked Renee Chelian, president of the National Coalition of Abortion Providers, to hold a plastic model of a 20-week-old fetus and a pair of surgical scissors, inquiring if she was not just a little bit uncomfortable with the procedure for which the surgical scissors were employed, she angrily responded with an overwrought account of the abortion she had had in a Detroit warehouse when she was 15, for which her father had paid $1000. "What I want for my daughters, what I want for your daughters, is that they never have to go through the humiliation, the danger, that I went through. . .before abortion was legal."

It soon became clear at the hearing that the only "argument" the proabortion people had was a naked assertion of the unfettered will, undeterred by moral considerations: we want abortion to be available, and we therefore mean to keep it legal at all costs; don't bother us with facts, arguments, or anything else. . .

When Illinois Republican Henry J. Hyde, chairman of the House Judiciary Committee, read extended excerpts from leading medical experts on anesthesiology giving the lie to the notion that the anesthesia given to the mother kills the baby before the piercing of the skull (as if that could ever justify the procedure!), Kate Michelman, head of the National Abortion and Reproductive Rights Action League, dug in her heels and stubbornly refused to retract statements she had made to this effect. She, in fact, had been primarily responsible for injecting into the national debate the Orwellian euphemism that anesthesia "causes fetal demise."

Before the committee, Michelman continued to maintain that the whole anesthesia business was still an open question, in spite of the publicized fact that one of the doctors who had been peddling this same disinformation had been obliged to admit at an earlier Senate Judiciary Committee hearing, on November 17, 1995, that she had "simplified" the whole question for the benefit of Congress. "I do not know what causes the fetus to die," this female physician had been forced to admit. The surgical scissors perhaps?

It could be asserted without fear of contradiction, of course, that the proabortion movement has been rather successfully "simplifying" the abortion issue for a rather long time. The sad thing is how frequently the proabortionists' departures from the truth have nevertheless "worked."

One discouraging note concerning these joint Senate-House hearings held in March, 1997, is the degree to which they confirmed once again how the strongest of prolife people can still remain on the defensive, even in the face of the brazen lies and shameless chutzpah of the proabortionists. At one point NARAL's Kate Michelman coolly and insultingly informed Senate Judiciary Committee Chairman Orrin Hatch of Utah and House Judiciary Committee Chairman Henry Hyde of Illinois that, since they opposed "a woman's right to choose under any circumstances, using any procedure," she would direct her remarks "to those in Congress whose minds are open."

Oh, no! Henry Hyde hastened, in effect, to assure her; he would allow an abortion to save a mother's life. Senator Hatch quickly chimed in to add that he would allow abortions also in cases of rape or incest (thus continuing to dignify these fake "indications" for abortion long past the time when any serious observer of the abortion scene should have recognized them as the fraudulent pretexts for the practice that they are).

Perhaps one of the principal reasons why even prolife people continue to be spooked by the abortion issue, in spite of the raw horror of it, and of all the lies that regularly surround it, is the desire never to be seen as anything but enlightened and respectable and mainstream. But at a time when our mainstream medical professionals are engaged in drumming up pretexts to justify abortion, or, at any rate, almost never finding any reasons to oppose it, this means that favoring abortion is itself what has become enlightened and respectable. Prolifers must consciously renounce the desire to be seen as enlightened and respectable and mainstream if this is the current price that has to be paid. House and Senate committees should justifiably have rules *denying* the right to offer testimony to anyone unwilling, like Michelman, to "address" her remarks to the committee chairman these legislative bodies have chosen.

The general problem of kowtowing to our professional elites simply because they are professional, when they are manifestly also often morally corrupt, is a serious one. Although the PHACT group has provided the true facts about partial-birth abortions in a way that amply justifies their acronym, too many of the regular medical and professional groups mechanically go on parroting the proabortion line in the face of all the true facts and arguments. The American College of Obstetricians and Gynecologists (ACOG), for example, issued a statement in January, 1997, in which it was claimed that what ACOG called "intact dilation and extraction" (a fusion of Dr. Haskell's "dilation and extraction" with Dr. McMahon's "intact dilation and evacuation") "may be the best or most appropriate procedure to save the life or preserve the health of a woman. . .and only the doctor can make this decision. . ."

This, of course, is a perfectly extraordinary statement, especially considering that ACOG itself could identify "no circumstances under which this procedure would be the only option." Critics from PHACT quickly pointed out that this ACOG statement was based upon no safety data or peer-reviewed studies whatsoever and that ACOG was violating its own professional standards in issuing it. As a result of these pointed criticisms, the president of ACOG did back off a bit in an interview with *American Medical News*. This, however, did not prevent the ideology-driven ACOG from issuing yet another statement as late as April, 1997, continuing to oppose what it called the "criminalization" of abortion and urging that, in this era of Medicare, Medicaid, and government-funded "managed care," the government should simply stay away from trying to decide "medical" questions.

In fact, the American Medical Association itself has apparently found it exceedingly difficult to take a stand against the patent abuse of the healing art represented by partial-birth abortion (or by any kind of abortion, for that matter). The AMA's Legislative Council did finally discover and announce in 1995 that partial-birth abortion was not "a bona fide medical procedure." But the AMA itself nevertheless continued its long-standing stance of taking no position on legislative questions concerning abortion. This negative AMA stance was eventually changed in rather dramatic circumstances, which we shall recount, and the AMA finally did come out against partial-birth abortions — the position any civilized person should have adopted from the moment the procedure was described. But this AMA switch was a very long time in coming.

As far as the *debate* on partial-birth abortions is concerned, though, it was clear by early 1997 that the prolife side had long since won hands down. But we must now see how this victory in the debate played out in the real-world legislative arena.

IV

President William J. Clinton had said more than once that he would sign a Partial-Birth Abortion Ban bill provided only that an exception to the ban could be made in cases of possible "serious physical harm" to the woman. As we have seen, providing for such an exception could not possibly bear any real relationship to what a partial-birth abortion consists of; the only possible serious physical harm would have to come from the performance of the operation itself.

Since the president's position is really nothing but a sham and a fabrication, then, it should not be too surprising that he has himself felt no obligation to stick with it as various legislative proposals have been discussed. On NBC television's *Meet the Press* program for December 15, 1996, for example, White House Chief of Staff Leon Panetta made it clear that the president would *not* sign a Partial-Birth Abortion Ban bill even with the "health" exception, unless the bill was also limited to third-trimester abortions (the last three months of pregnancy). The idea here was apparently that *Roe v. Wade* limited regulation of abortion to the third trimester and hence trying to regulate a particular procedure, such as partial-birth abortions, at any time, would be "unconstitutional."

Whatever the soundness of this argument, the position outlined by Panetta clearly entailed adding a new condition to what the president had said was "all" he needed in order to be able to sign a Partial-Birth Abortion Ban bill.

Another important factor here was the fact that most partial-birth abortions are performed during the fifth or sixth month, and hence a "ban" on them limited to the third trimester would not ban very many of them. This did not bother the Clinton people since nothing did, but what soon became apparent was that they had quietly left behind the "serious physical harm" business and were indeed now following a new tack. An arranged front-page story in *The Boston Globe* which appeared on March 7, 1997, signaled a new Clinton "compromise": an alternative bill that would "ban" all late-term abortions except those "required" to save a mother's life or health.

The prolife strategy of focusing on one particularly horrendous procedure, partial-birth abortions, had succeeded so dramatically in stirring up public opinion against abortion for practically the first time since the practice had been legalized that the proabortion side realized a new strategy was called for on their side. A "ban" on all abortions after viability — even though it would really not ban anything as long as the health exception was included — became the preferred new strategy. It represented an attempt to re-focus the whole issue back upon the "woman's right" which had proved so successful a strategy for so long. Of course the very fact that the proabortionists were now even talking about such things as the viability of the child meant that the debate could no longer prescind from the child — and the horror of the abortion procedure itself — entirely.

The bill containing the great new Clinton "compromise" announced in *The Boston Globe* was shortly afterwards introduced into the House by Maryland Democratic Representative Steny Hoyer and Pennsylvania prochoice Republican Representative James Greenwood. The bill contained language outlawing any abortion "after the fetus became viable." But viability, of course, is a notably elastic term. With modern life-support techniques, up to 23 per cent of babies born prematurely after as little as six months of pregnancy are capable of surviving outside the womb; and this percentage obviously rises the longer the pregnancy goes on.

One of the important questions in such a bill as this was therefore how the bill defined viability. How did the proposed Hoyer-Greenwood bill define it? It simply left it to the "attending physician" — the abortionist — to decide whether the child was viable or not. And, as if this little bit of cynicism were not enough, it was also the same "attending physician" who would be empowered under this bill to decide whether an abortion, *even one in the third trimester* — the very kinds of abortions supposedly "banned" — might be necessary "to avert serious adverse health consequences to the woman."

Asked about what "health" meant, Congressman Hoyer responded that "we're not talking about a hangnail, and we're not talking about a headache." He admitted as a matter of course that "mental health" was included — in other words, Bill Clinton's "serious physical harm" idea had indeed disappeared down the Orwellian memory hole, and we were back once again with *Doe v. Bolton*'s definition of "health" as anything affecting a woman's "well-being" as decided by the woman and the "attending physician."

Congressman Hoyer expressly defended the shift away from the president's promise to be satisfied with an exception for physical health only by asserting that modern legislators generally favor the rape and incest exceptions precisely because they cause psychological trauma, not physical harm.

What all this meant, of course, was that the famous Clinton "compromise" was yet another sham. Under it any abortionist could perform any abortion by any method at any time either by simply declaring the fetus "unviable" or by citing a "health" consideration. Since the Hoyer-Greenwood bill was submitted as an amendment to HR 1122, the Partial-Birth Abortion Ban bill, the measure was disallowed in committee and never voted on by the full House. Instead, as we have seen, it was HR 1122 which was approved on March 20, 1997, 295 to 136.

Nevertheless, the Hoyer-Greenwood proposed bill provided an important precedent for a bill soon brought forward in the Senate which received vastly greater publicity as a supposed "compromise" which the president might be able to accept. This Senate bill was introduced by Senate Democratic Minority Leader Thomas A. Daschle of South Dakota, a man who was going to prove in this instance, as he has in others, that he was no mean strategist and tactician.

The Daschle bill was brought forward in early May, 1997, precisely in order to head off the impending debate in the Senate on the new Partial-Birth Abortion Ban bill. It was, of course, brought forward with appropriate fanfare, including revised language approving its "concept" from the White House. No media reports asked what a White House "approval" on this subject could possibly *mean* at this point. A White House spokesman was able to state without fear of contradiction from the media that President Clinton had "long been an opponent of late-term abortions." (Tom Daschle was evidently somewhat worried, however, since there were also press reports that he was discouraging open support from the White House, even though the whole purpose of his bill seems to have been to save appearances for Clinton and the Democrats on the "highly emotional" abortion issue.)

The key feature of the Daschle bill was the declaration of a general prohibition of abortion by any method after viability — "unless the *physician* certifies that the continuation of the pregnancy would threaten the mother's life or risk grievous injury to her physical health" (emphasis added). At first glance, this language reads almost like a prolife victory statement; and, of course, it does represent quite a considerable psychological victory of sorts that proabortion legislators should now feel constrained even to talk about possibly banning any abortions.

More than that, Tom Daschle also apparently felt constrained to specify physical health after all of the hullabaloo over the health question that had accompanied the discussion of the Hoyer-Greenwood bill. Even then, though, White House spokesman Mike McCurry managed to muddy the waters yet again when he explained that "what Senator Daschle himself has indicated is that severe mental stress can sometimes manifest itself physically. . .The president understands that there are circumstances in which that can become physical. . ." Etc., etc.

A careful reading of the Daschle language, however, reveals that it would still empower the abortionists themselves to *decide* both about viability and about what constitutes a valid "health" indication, as was also the case in the Hoyer-Greenwood proposal. All an abortionist would have to do is "certify" that the abortion is necessary. As the famous Colorado abortionist Dr. Warren Hern candidly admitted to the media after the Daschle bill surfaced: "I will certify that *any pregnancy* is a threat to a woman's life and could cause grievous injury to her physical health" (emphasis added).

This attitude is quite typical in proabortion circles, if it is not the rule. Dr. Hern, long one of the leaders of the proabortion cause and author of a standard textbook for doing abortions, criticized the Daschle bill as an unwise stunt dreamed up merely to try to outbid prolife Republicans. Like the ill-starred Ron Fitzsimmons, apparently, Dr. Hern believes that support for abortion should be honest and above-board; proabortionists should not lie about it, as they habitually do in fact.

Those who imagine that most U.S. physicians would be too honorable to resort to such dishonesty and mendacity as to "certify" to the necessity of the abortions they perform fail to reckon with the facts that 1) some members of the medical profession have been performing virtually all of the millions of legal abortions that have been done in the United States since 1973; and that 2) in very few of these abortions is any "medical" reason even cited any longer (many reputable physicians hold that abortion, strictly speaking, is *never* "medically" necessary).

Moreover, those doctors who have engaged in abortion have never scrupled to stretch *Roe v. Wade* to the limit; and, meanwhile, virtually all of the leaders of the medical profession, like most medical associations and publications, have either actively supported legalized abortion all this time, or have done little or nothing to oppose it or protest against it — usually they have also been the leaders in stigmatizing any kind of prolife activity as unwarranted criticism of "medicine."

Douglas Johnson, legislative director of the National Right to Life Committee, and perhaps the key lobbyist in opposing partial-birth abortions, cogently explained why U.S. abortionists would readily "certify" to the necessity of abortions under a Daschle-type law —

while going on to perform all of them they wanted to perform without any restrictions whatsoever. "In their world, they're not doing anything unethical to sign those certifications," Johnson said. "They think it would be unethical not to." After all, a "woman's right" is what is at stake in their view; and their view has hardly been a secret to anybody. Johnson aptly pointed out that the Daschle bill was "like Senator Daschle supporting a ban on assault weapons if a gun dealer would sign a certification that the gun was not an assault weapon.

Or it could equally be said that the Daschle prohibition of "all" post-viability abortions would be like a law against theft that obtained unless the thief could "certify" that he "needed" the property he was taking. Thus the Daschle bill was just another sham, as it was correctly labeled by Douglas Johnson. No legislation purporting to prohibit or limit abortions can be considered serious as long as it leaves the abortion decision in the same hands as those which have been doing all the abortions since 1973. There must be objective criteria that both define what is illegal and provide penalties to deter or penalize the practitioners doing the abortions. Looked at this way, the Daschle proposal represented no real advance over *Roe v. Wade*.

Moreover, Senator Daschle was only too well aware of this. In a disingenuous article published in *The Washington Post* on May 2, 1997, this Machiavelli from the Black Hills wrote:

> The Supreme Court has clearly identified viability — the stage at which the fetus is capable of sustaining life outside the womb — as the defining point in terms of the constitutionality of restrictions on abortion. Before viability, the Constitution protects a woman's right to terminate her pregnancy. After viability, the government may restrict abortion to protect the viable fetus, but the court has consistently ruled that any ban on abortion must include an exception to protect the life and health of the mother.
>
> I believe we should prohibit the abortion of any viable fetus — by any method — unless the mother's individual circumstances require it. . .

What Senator Daschle did not say, of course, is that *Roe*'s companion *Doe* case, as we have noted, effectively defines "health" to mean anything the doctor might decide upon; and as a matter of historical fact, as everybody knows, we have effectively had abortion on demand at all stages of pregnancy since these two cases were handed down. Nor would the passage of the Daschle bill affect that situation. It would represent just one more of the lies buttressing legalizing abortion which keep on going around and coming around. The only thing that has changed is that liberals such as Senator Daschle are now merely *talking* again about what *Roe* and *Doe* already pretended to "limit" back in 1973.

However, the fact that the proabortionists are now talking about the subject again — for a very long time they went on pretending that the issue had been "settled" forever by the Supreme Court, and hence was beyond discussion — the fact that they are at least talking again seems to have led some self-declared "prolife" leaders to imagine that, somehow, great prolife gains have now been registered. Former Reagan U.S. Education Secretary and Bush Drug Czar William J. Bennett, for example, quickly injected himself into the debate as soon as the Daschle bill came up; he reportedly called Senators Trent Lott and Rick Santorum, as well as Representative Henry Hyde, to say to them: "You can't be so used to drubbing your enemy that you don't recognize it when they make some sense."

William Kristol, Bennett's former chief of staff at the Reagan Department of Education, and now editor of the Neocon *Weekly Standard* — which also professes to be "prolife" — hastened to join his former chief. "Do you want the best to be the enemy of the good even if there is a little bit of a loophole?" he was quoted as asking prolife legislators. Bennett was quoted in *The Weekly Standard* as saying: "Senator Daschle, you were dead serious about reducing the number of abortions. Let's talk."

This is not the first time that Bennett and Kristol have tried to rush up to the head of prolife ranks to counsel "moderation" at the first whiff of a possible prolife victory; they provide good conservative cover for those who continue to believe, against the evidence, that the prolifers are the "extremists" on the abortion issue in our current culture wars. The notion that there can be any serious "talk" with the proabortionists *until they stop lying about what they are doing* is itself about as serious a notion as Senator Daschle's real intention of stopping any abortions.

Moreover, the typical characterization of a Bennett or a Kristol of the goal of the prolife movement as merely "reducing the number of abortions" is surely woefully, even tragically inadequate — plain wrong, in fact: when will they realize that we simply cannot have a polity which legally covers over the killing of the innocent? It is not just a matter of reducing the number of those killed. For the short term, NRLC's Douglas Johnson's response to the Bennett-Kristol initiative was probably as apt as anything could be: "We've gotten behind enemy lines and we're blowing up ammo dumps," Johnson said, as reported by pundit Fred Barnes. "Why should we voluntarily return to the beach?"

Why indeed? The fact that the proabortionists were once again even talking about abortion measures *meant* that the prolife side had finally fought its way a bit beyond the beach. Both Senator Santorum and Congressman Hyde, while indicating that they were always ready to talk, wisely said that none of the kind of talk a Senator Daschle was evidently angling for should ever hold up movement on banning partial-birth abortions.

In the event, on May 15, 1997, the Daschle bill went down to deserved defeat by a vote of 64 to 36. Not one prolife senator voted for it. The stage was then set for the Senate vote on the Partial-Birth Abortion Ban bill itself, which, as we have noted, came five days later on May 20.

V

There was never any question but that partial-birth abortions would be banned by the Senate, as they had been by the House; the only question was whether a veto-proof majority could be achieved. Two events prior to the vote almost brought that eventuality within reach — although, in the end, it proved unreachable for the moment.

The first of these two events was the sudden and unexpected endorsement of the bill by the American Medical Association; the other event was the disclosure that Senator Tom Daschle was himself going to support the bill after the failure of his own bill.

As we have noted, the AMA Legislative Council had held since 1995 that partial-birth abortion was "not a bona fide medical procedure"; but the AMA itself had been unwilling to go farther than that until the eve of the vote on the Daschle bill, when the AMA Board of Trustees, on May 14, 1997, suddenly released a report which stated that there were no situations in which "intact dilation and extraction [partial-birth abortion] is the only appropriate procedure to induce abortion."

The AMA report went further. With regard to the life and health factors which supposedly rendered many abortions "medically" necessary, the report said:

> Except in extraordinary circumstances, maternal health factors which demand termination of pregnancy can be accomplished *without sacrificing the fetus*, and the near certainty of the independent viability of the fetus argues for ending the pregnancy *by appropriate delivery* (emphasis added).

So. Finally. Was this AMA report actually saying that abortion — killing the fetus — is not the remedy for *any* medical condition threatening the life or health of a mother-to-be? It would certainly seem to be saying something very close to this, if words mean anything. It was about time. If these AMA words mean anything, they meant that the time has now surely come to challenge the hollowness of just about everything the proabortionists have been saying about the supposed medical reasons for abortion ever since this evil first came upon us some three decades ago.

However that may be, the day before the vote on HR 1122 in the Senate, the AMA did finally come out and support the ban; it was the first time the AMA had ever taken a position on an abortion bill. Before doing so, the physicians' organization asked for some minor changes in the bill's language in order to 1) make clear that a physician intending to deliver a baby who nevertheless had to employ a procedure to save a woman's life would not be faulted; 2) define the procedure more narrowly to exclude other procedures not banned; and 3) to allow any doctor accused of violating the ban the right to a review by a state medical board before any criminal proceedings could be instituted.

Senator Rick Santorum, the sponsor of the bill, agreed to these changes; they also won immediate support from the National Right to Life Committee. The AMA then agreed to support the ban, indicating plainly in its letter to Senator Santorum that partial-birth abortions were simply not "medically indicated" — thus cutting the ground out from under all of the sob stories used up to that point.

One might have thought that this AMA endorsement would have served to turn the whole debate around. Perhaps inevitably, however, since the issue was abortion, it seems to have had little effect on the debate at all so far. When asked about the AMA endorsement, a White House spokesman gave a rote reply about how "the changes that were made in the bill today do not materially affect the president's concerns, which are to protect the woman from serious health consequences."

The egregious Kate Michelman of NARAL bitterly attacked the AMA. "It is clear," she said, "that the AMA cares more about moving their political agenda through a Republican-controlled, antichoice Congress than they do about women's health and women's rights." No sooner had the AMA announcement been made than attacks were launched on the organization itself alleging that the endorsement of the ban had been done "in exchange for" a "sweetheart deal" on some budgetary and Medicare issues currently before the Senate — if only prolife legislators *were* finally linking abortion to some other issues for a change! Proabortion Republican Senator John Chafee of Rhode Island accused the AMA of "putting doctors first"; and yet other stories appeared suggesting that the AMA's motives were entirely venal for finally deciding to tell the truth about at least one type of abortion.

Similarly, when prolifers called the offices of their senators, as this writer did, it turned out that the AMA endorsement had had little effect of any kind. In my case, the dialogue went like this:

QUESTION: Will Senator [Charles] Robb change his position and vote to ban partial-birth abortions now that the AMA has said they are not medically indicated?

ANSWER: Senator Robb cannot support the ban unless there is a provision to protect the woman's health.

QUESTION: But the AMA has now said that the question of the woman's health does not even arise as a justification for this particular procedure.

ANSWER: The Senator has not changed his position.

And so it went. Many seemed to be still frozen in the glacial ice which has covered over the reality of legalized abortion for far too long. It will no doubt be a while yet before the significance of the AMA's altered stand on abortion sinks in with many. During the debate in the Senate the proabortion side demonstrated that it had nothing to offer but the same tired — and false — rhetoric, most of which did not address the specific questions raised by partial-birth abortions at all. California Democratic Senator Barbara Boxer appeared with poster-sized photographs of women who had supposedly had to undergo the procedure in dire circumstances but then later had gone on to have children — no doubt more falsehood and sham. Her California Democratic colleague Senator Diane Feinstein listlessly said "I regret this day is upon us" — and one could well understand that she might.

Then there was Tom Daschle. Even though his proposed bill had represented no real, substantive move towards moral sanity on the abortion issue, he himself nevertheless turned out to have himself moved a little bit on the issue, especially since he actually voted to ban partial-birth abortions in the end. And he once actually referred to a fetus as a "baby" on the floor of the United States Senate. He had more than intimated that late-term abortions actually raised what he called "troubling questions."

Also, it was known that Daschle, a Catholic, had come under considerable pressure from his bishop, the Most Reverend Robert Carlson of Sioux Falls. If true, this certainly does honor to the bishop; it cannot be said, however, that the South Dakota Senator acceded to episcopal pressure, whatever it may have consisted of, with anything resembling good grace. In a highly unusual speech after the partial-birth abortion vote, he declared:

> My greatest disappointment is reserved for some officials in the Catholic Church, especially in my state, for whom I had great respect and from whom I was given initial encouragement for my effort. Their harsh rhetoric and vitriolic characterizations, usually more identified with the radical right than with thoughtful religious leadership, proved to be a consequential impediment to the decision I have made today. It was instructive.

"Harsh rhetoric and vitriolic characterizations. . .the radical right. . ." Is this to be believed, coming from the proabortion side? Bishop Carlson of Sioux Falls learned firsthand what can happen to those who think it might be worthwhile to "talk" with someone like Senator Tom Daschle: they might end up being slandered on the floor of the U.S. Senate, with the slander then given national coverage.

The good bishop could only issue his own counter-statement with as much dignity as possible, while voicing his "concern that the senator has difficulty voting against a procedure described by some of his prochoice colleagues as closer to infanticide than abortion." Needless to say, the bishop's reply did not get the same coverage as the senator's attack.

Senator Daschle had other problems as well. South Dakota happened to be one of 10 states which, by the summer of 1997, had enacted a state ban on partial-birth abortions (four more states had such bills on the governor's desk at that point). The senator could hardly move aggressively against the reigning sentiment in his own state. Thus, after his own bill failed, he announced that he was considering supporting Senator Santorum's bill. There were audible gasps in the gallery when he then did, in fact, vote with 13 other Democrats to ban partial-birth abortions.

Two other Democratic senators joined Daschle in reversing their vote from the previous year: Senators Robert C. Byrd of West Virginia and Ernest F. Hollings of South Carolina — the latter also from a state which had enacted a state ban.

However, none of these switches proved to be enough to attain a veto-proof majority. And, meanwhile, a number of Republican senators voted with the Democratic minority to continue to protect the legality of partial-birth abortions: John Chafee of Rhode Island, Susan Collins and Olympia Snowe of Maine, and James Jeffords of Vermont. (What is it about New England? The weather?)

The ultimate outcome of the long partial-birth abortion saga cannot be predicted as of this writing. Whether President Clinton relents and signs the bill, whether a veto of his can be overridden in the Senate, or whether the whole issue will be carried over into another legislative season is not clear at the moment.

What is certain, however, is that the partial-birth abortion ban effort has already achieved what is hopefully an irreversible breakthrough for the prolife cause. Legalized abortion can no longer and perhaps never again be treated as an issue that has been irrevocably been "decided" by the U.S. Supreme Court. For more than a quarter of a century, most of the elites in the United States have been quite successful in treating abortion in precisely this way; abortion was a "woman's right"; the "Constitution" must be followed. Correctly perceived as essential to the maintenance of the sexual revolution — which is currently taken for granted by all of these same elites — this supposed constitutional right of women obviously could not be abridged or made subject to any "regulation." The logic of the proabortion position on this has been abundantly clear for a long time.

By voting to ban or regulate even a single abortion technique, however, the Congress of the United States has finally broken the spell: at least one type of abortion can and must be regulated; *therefore* abortion cannot be an absolute "woman's right"!

Ironically, even the Daschle bill, although it would have continued to allow virtually unrestricted abortions in practice, would have established in law the same principle, namely, that abortion is not an absolute woman's right after all. In that limited sense, even the Daschle bill would have meant some movement on the issue (although it precisely *would not have* by itself"reduced the number of abortions," *pace* William Bennett).

But the advantage of the approach which the prolife movement actually adopted, namely, banning a particularly gruesome abortion procedure, besides its other advantages, was that it also succeeded in shifting the focus of the abortion question, for the first time since abortion was legalized, to the *child*. The cat is finally at long last out of the bag: abortion means the killing of a child. It is not going to be easy to put this particular genie back into any bottle. Never again, perhaps, can we completely close our eyes to what legalized abortion means (although given the history of legalized abortion to date, we should never underestimate the resourcefulness of those determined to have abortion as the necessary back-up for the sexual revolution).

Even so we cannot, as a civilized country affirming the rule of law, recognize that abortion is the killing of a child and then still go on just doing it anyway. No: it has to be stopped; it has to be made illegal. The only reason we have been able to go on doing it with so much abandon up to now is *because* we have never been willing or able to own up to what it was we were actually doing. We have insisted on and connived in hiding what we were doing under a cloud of lies and euphemisms. This too easy subterfuge is exactly what has now been changed — at least to some extent.

No doubt the road ahead to restoring the right to life to everybody at all stages of human development — to making abortion illegal along with euthanasia and other means of killing the innocent — will be a very rocky road. It will no doubt turn out to be a road where we will also encounter many potholes, landslides, detours, and bridges out as well. All of these obstacles will surely not fail to be encountered, if the past provides any indication.

But at least we are now back on that road. We at least have some hope that America's promise of "equal justice under law" will not go on forever being a lie as far as the unborn, the defective, the ill, the aged, and the unwanted are concerned.

13

Abortion, Family Planning, and Population Control

I

The notable prolife success on the partial-birth abortion issue has been commented on and celebrated by more than a few observers, including the present writer. To have succeeded, finally, in getting not only a significant body of the general public but a no less significant group of formerly skeptical legislators to stand up and cry "enough!" where partial-birth abortion is concerned — to have succeeded, finally, in getting the focus of the debate shifted from what happens to the woman to what happens to the child — these advances represent no mean achievement for the prolife movement.

In the end, though, what does a "victory" on the partial-birth abortion issue mean? It means that only one — admittedly a ghastly, but still only one — abortion procedure has been outlawed. Other abortion procedures still remain available to the abortionists. It means that abortion itself — the killing of a child — remains legal in the United States for any reason at any stage of pregnancy. Nor, at the moment, does there seem to be much chance that abortion will be returned to the category of the illegal any time soon, regardless of what the Constitution specifies about the equal protection of the laws.

To say this is not, of course, to belittle any victory the prolife movement can manage; the prolife movement needs all the victories it can get. Nevertheless we surely do have to revisit our prolife tactics and strategy from time to time — both to take note of where the prolife movement is going, and to remind ourselves of what the ultimate goal of the movement must be.

The fact is that, virtually since its inception, the prolife movement has concentrated so hard on stopping abortion that it has sometimes failed to take into account, much less attempt to combat,

---

Published in *Culture Wars*, October, 1997.

some of the factors which, both logically and historically, have been verifiably responsible for making abortion first morally acceptable and now widely resorted to in our society.

I refer, in particular, to contraception — birth control, family planning — whatever you want to call it. From the beginning, most prolife groups and organizations and, indeed, individuals, have agreed to "take no position" on contraception. Contraception has been seen as preventing the conception of a child while abortion certainly does kill a child already conceived; so argued Planned Parenthood itself as late as the mid-nineteen-sixties.

The prolife movement early on adopted this stance, and there has never even been very much debate about it since. Most people today, including many prolifers, would surely be hard pressed to say precisely what it is that could possibly be wrong with contraception, so widely if not near-universally is the use of it accepted today; for many it would be like saying there was something wrong with central heating or air-conditioning; it is simply an accepted "convenience" of modern life.

However, besides obscuring the fact that certain types of so-called contraceptives — in particular, some varieties of the birth control "pill" — actually function as abortifacients, that is, they prevent the implantation or cause the evacuation of embryos already conceived, the typical formulation that contraception merely prevents while abortion kills fails to take into account one immensely important fact: the fact that once effective "control" over births, over human life, has been conceded to other human beings — once it is agreed that *we* have "control" over who is, or is not, to be born — then the question becomes merely one of the most effective "method" to be used. Abortion thus quickly becomes accepted as a legitimate after-the-fact method, once the prior and primary question of who controls life, man or God, has been decided.

The logic of this progression has been historically verified in the history of the legalization of abortion in the United States. The bogus "right to privacy" which *Roe v. Wade* found in the Constitution to justify abortion went back to a legal precedent in a case concerning, precisely, contraception, *Griswold v. Connecticut*. The same logic has been abundantly borne out in other parts of the world: once birth control becomes morally acceptable, the very foolproof kind of "control" afforded by legalized abortion becomes compelling.

However, the prolife movement, in agreeing to "take no position" on contraception, has basically ignored these facts and this logic. Not only has it set aside both the logic and the actual history of the legalization of abortion, it has often resorted to the tactic of somehow trying to fight abortion by actually *promoting* government-funded family planning — taxpayer subsidized birth control. Listen to any "abortion" debate in Congress and you will hear even the prolife legislators extolling the virtues of government-funded birth control as if that were the *answer* to a myriad of problems such as poverty, welfare, family-break-up, teen-age and out-of-wedlock pregnancies, and so on — always, of course, supposedly being the answer to abortion itself as well.

And birth control *is* regularly seen as the answer to abortion. In reality, however, the acceptance of it has verifiably been one of the principal *causes* of abortion. The idea that increased federal money for birth control, here or abroad, could actually bring about a lowered abortion rate goes on mindlessly being assumed and asserted in the face of considerable data which show instead that there is a definite correlation between the acceptance of birth control and the legalization of abortion: to will the end is to will the means; it figures.

As the government sinks more and more money into family planning, more and more families are disintegrating. Indeed the very concept of "family" is being progressively lost as the message reaches more and more people that the sexual activity once thought reserved for marriage is today regarded as without serious consequences for anybody, since modern contraceptives are universally available to "prevent" any such consequences.

So why have we had a million and a half abortions every year for nearly the past quarter century? Why were these conceptions not "prevented"? (I am not implying that they should have been; I am asking a purely factual question.)

But it is a question that, generally speaking, the prolife movement rather studiously avoids ever asking. More than that, most of the mainstream prolife groups such as the National Right to Life Committee and its affiliates — like many of our outstanding prolife leaders in Congress such as Representatives Henry Hyde and Christopher Smith — have actually resorted to *promoting* increased family planning, ostensibly as a method of *fighting* abortion. This was notably the case in the first abortion-related vote in the new 105th Congress — the vote in February, 1997, on our so-called foreign "population assistance" program abroad.

This vote resulted in a significant net prolife defeat and setback in both houses of Congress, even though there were supposed to be the same prolife majorities there that were meanwhile voting to ban partial-birth abortions. More than that, the vote represented an illogical and, indeed, a ruinous strategy for the prolife movement: we are, quite simply, *not* going to succeed in fighting abortion successfully by promoting family planning, especially when some forms of family planning themselves cause abortions. Nobody who has seriously examined the modern abortion phenomenon could possibly fail to see the intimate and continuing connection between the acceptance and promotion of contraception and the acceptance and promotion of abortion; it is quite impossible to separate the two in practice: ask Planned Parenthood!

Nevertheless, the idea persists among many prolifers that only direct killing by abortion can ever be fought on the political level, never so-called mere "prevention" brought about by modern contraceptive means. This is thought to be the case even if what we are talking about are *not* merely decisions made by married couples in the privacy of their bedrooms but are rather massive taxpayer-funded government subsidies designed to provide contraceptives not only to women on welfare but even to unmarried teen-agers through school-based clinics — and not only to Americans, but to the inhabitants of countries abroad thought by some of our elites to be "overpopulated." The widespread government-induced moral corruption inherent in such a government policy and such government programs has been simply incalculable — and it continues unabatedly at the present time to be induced within the social body and the world body at large.

In spite of what one would have thought were the deleterious effects of government-sponsored family planning — they leap to the eye — the idea that it is not feasible if it is not impossible to take an open position against government-funded family planning nevertheless widely persists; it remains, for example, firmly behind the standard prolife political strategy which has obtained ever since abortion was first legalized, and which continues today, namely, that "we take no position on contraception."

It is time to take a hard look at this strategy. The best way to do this is to conduct in some detail an actual case study, namely, to look at the strategy, tactics, debates, discussions, reactions, and votes surrounding the U.S. population assistance program abroad which took place in February, 1997. As it happens, it is a very instructive case.

II

On February 13, 1997, the U.S. House of Representatives gave the Clinton Administration a victory by approving by a vote of 220 to 209 a resolution President Clinton wanted which released $385 million in so-called "population assistance" funds which the U.S. Agency for International Development (USAID) uses to support family planning organizations and programs in many countries abroad.

Although these funds were among those included in the huge omnibus consolidated appropriations bill which Congress voted and the president signed at the end of September, 1996, the release of these particular funds was held up until July 1, 1997, in an effort by the Appropriations Committee to get the House International Relations Committee to resolve several substantive issues related to U.S. support for family planning programs abroad funded as part of the current U.S. population control effort.

The Clinton resolution approved by this February 13 House vote authorized the release of these appropriated funds at a rate of some $31 million per month beginning on March 1 rather than on July 1, 1997, as originally specified in the appropriations bill; what this meant in practice was that the Clinton Administration would be able to spend during the current fiscal year some $123 million more of the $385 appropriated than would otherwise have been possible if the funds had not been released until July 1. A little more than a week after the House action, on February 25, the Senate also voted for the same Clinton resolution by a vote of 53 to 46.

Population assistance funds have been a major component of the U.S. foreign aid program for many years. After the Republicans won control of Congress in 1994, foreign aid, including these population control programs, became a favorite target for possible cuts by conservative Republicans. In the course of the Clinton years, funding for them had risen to an authorized high of over $580 million for fiscal year 1995 — a nearly 80 percent increase over the amount for fiscal year 1993. The Republicans succeeded in cutting this back down to some $356 million for fiscal year 1996.

This money for family planning programs abroad should not be confused with the money the Congress votes annually for the support of domestic family planning (or birth control) programs. The latter, mostly authorized under Title X ("Title 10") of the Public Health Service Act, and by some other legislation, amounts to around three-quarters of a billion dollars annually to subsidize birth control in this country. If we add to this huge amount the $385 million currently authorized for the overseas population control programs, it will be clear that the American tax-payer is currently being charged well over a billion dollars annually to pay for birth control services here and abroad.

Under current law, none of this money is supposed to be used to fund abortions. In programs abroad, the performance of abortions has been prohibited by the Helms Amendment to the Foreign Assistance Act since 1973, the year the Supreme Court's *Roe v. Wade* decision legalized abortion. The successive Hyde Amendments to appropriations bills, which also date back to the 1970s, similarly prohibit federal funding for most abortions (although since 1993 the government may fund abortions not only to save the life of the mother but also in cases of rape or incest). The same abortion-funding prohibition has been inserted here and there in other legislation (for example, specifically excluding abortions in military hospitals, in government-employee health-care plans, and the like).

Since the legalization of abortion in the United States, there has been a fairly consistent pattern whereby the Congress, while rarely seriously attempting to challenge the Supreme Court's legalization of the ghastly and lethal practice of abortion itself (except, notably, in the efforts both last year and this year to ban partial-birth abortions), has generally declined to support or subsidize abortions with public moneys. In addition, at the UN Population Conference held in Mexico City in 1984, the Reagan Administration successfully persuaded the international community of nations to endorse a statement urging governments to "take appropriate steps to help women avoid abortion, which in no case should be promoted as a method of family planning." President Reagan incorporated this language into an executive order withholding U.S. money from any organization performing or promoting abortion as a method of family planning.

This Mexico City language, as it came to be called, became a regular feature and condition for U.S. support of family planning abroad as part of the U.S. international population control effort. In accordance with it, organizations which used abortions as a method of family planning were not eligible for U.S. aid, and thus over 350 organizations engaged in international family planning had to certify that they would not perform or promote abortions in order to benefit from U.S. assistance. The major hold-outs, which openly refused to comply with these restrictions, were the Planned Parenthood Federation of America (PPFA); the London-based International Planned Parenthood Federation (IPPF), which, in turn, works with and through some 140 affiliates in various countries around the world; and the Pathfinder Fund, which is another significant family planning services provider abroad.

The primary effect of the Mexico City language was to deny U.S. support to these three organizations — admittedly major players — active in the international family planning field. This situation obtained between the years 1984 and 1992. In January, 1993, President Bill Clinton, in one of his very first acts as president, rescinded the Reagan executive order and replaced it with an executive order of his own allowing U.S. support to go again even to organizations which also performed or promoted abortions.

President Clinton's action was one of five separate initiatives which the new president took relaxing all the restrictions on abortion that he had the executive power to relax. These actions established Bill Clinton as a determined and aggressive champion of legalized abortion, and certainly gave the lie to the president's often quoted statement that he wanted to see abortion "safe, legal, and rare" — this turned out to be yet another example of presidential language designed to hide rather than reveal where the president really stands on the abortion issue.

The practical effect of the Clinton reversal of the Reagan Administration's policy on family planning programs abroad was to put massive amounts of U.S. money at the disposition of such entities as the IPPF and its affiliates which were admittedly engaged both in the performance and in the promotion of legal abortions. After the Republicans won control of Congress in 1994, conservative Republicans not only targeted these population assistance funds for cuts; they also attempted to restore the Mexico City language to govern their use. Not surprisingly, the president threatened to veto any legislation containing this language.

The House nevertheless included the language in foreign aid appropriations bills anyway; this has been the case, in fact, for the last two years. In the first of these two years, however, the Republican-controlled Senate, on November 15, 1995, rejected the House bill by a vote of 53 to 42. In the second year, negotiating for fiscal year 1997, the chairman of the House Appropriations Subcommittee on Foreign Operations, Export Financing, and Related Programs offered the White House a compromise: organizations refusing to abide by the Mexico City policy would be funded at only fifty percent of their 1995 level; organizations agreeing with the exclusion of abortion as a method of family planning would not have their funds capped in this manner.

It was the president's own chief of staff, Leon Panetta in person, who brought back the answer from the White House to this compromise proposal from the appropriations subcommittee chairman. The answer was no. The While House was unwilling to accept any of the abortion-related restrictions in overseas family planning programs that would have been required by a re-instatement of the Mexico City language.

By this time, the White House and the Congress were engaged in last-minute eyeball-to-eyeball negotiations on the huge omnibus consolidated spending bill which, if not enacted by the Congress and signed by the president by midnight on September 30, would have brought about another federal government shutdown for lack of legal operating funds. This was an eventuality both sides wished to avoid after the unhappy experiences with such government shutdowns the year before.

As vividly reported by syndicated columnist Robert Novak, on September 28 at 6:30 a.m., after an all-night negotiating session, Leon Panetta proposed that all international family planning programs should undergo the same thirty-five percent cut that all other foreign aid moneys were being subjected to across the board. In other words, rather than accept the restrictions on abortions which a re-instatement of the Mexico City language would have imposed, the Clinton Administration countered with its own proposal for a *cut* in total population assistance funds. The White House proved to be nothing if not consistent — proabortion ahead of any other consideration.

But faced as they were with another looming government shutdown, the Republicans believed they had no alternative but to withdraw the Mexico City language and to go along with the cuts proposed by the White House instead. (Republicans knowledgeable about this sequence of events were not happy when Hilary Rodham Clinton, in La Paz, Bolivia, on December 3, told a Conference of the Wives of Heads of State and of Governments of the Americas that "some members of the U.S. Congress have voted to limit American support for family planning initiatives. My husband's administration remains committed to encouraging a continuation of these investments." The truth was, in this instance, that it was the White House itself which proposed the cuts in order to preserve the administration's proabortion position.)

What was agreed to for fiscal year 1997 by the White House and the Congress was the $385 million amount for population assistance programs already mentioned above. However, the Republicans also succeeded in imposing further restrictions on the actual release of the money, which was to be held up until July 1, 1997, and then only released in monthly increments, unless the president in a positive finding, could certify to the Congress no later than February 1 that the hold-up of funds was "having a negative impact on the proper functioning of the population planning program."

If the Congress passed a resolution approving such a finding by the president, then the funds could begin to flow on March 1, 1997, although no more than eight percent of the total available funds could be spent in any one month; this amounted to around $31 million per month.

Imposing such restrictions on the obligation and spending of money already appropriated may seem to be one of those odd and perhaps even incomprehensible things peculiar to the U.S. Congress. However, Appropriations Committee Chairman Robert Livingston of Louisiana explained the real purpose of the hold-up: "The obligation delay," he said, "was explicitly intended to encourage the authorizing committee to address [this] issue. . .Policy issues surrounding international family planning should be addressed by the Committee on International Relations, not the Committee on Appropriations."

Chairman Livingston was pointing to an increasingly serious problem in the Congress in recent years: authorizing committees have increasingly been trying to duck the tough, controversial issues. As a result, some of the major current legislative and policy battles are being fought out in the course of the budget and appropriations processes. This is one of the reasons the battles over the "budget" have sometimes been so furious; and it has been especially true in the case of the abortion issue, as witness the successive Hyde Amendments to appropriations bills, rather than substantive congressional legislation regulating or restricting abortion.

Despite the effort of the Appropriations Committee, however, there seems to have been no movement anywhere to address any of the substantive issues concerned with U.S. support for overseas population control programs. And meanwhile, to the surprise of nobody, President Clinton on January 31 did issue a finding that the hold-up of family planning funds was having a negative effect on the population assistance program; the president declared that this hold-up was causing what he called "serious, irreversible, and avoidable harm."

The stage was thus set for the favorable February votes for the Clinton resolution in both the House and the Senate. This outcome, in turn, allowed the $385 million appropriated for fiscal year 1997 to be released and disbursed beginning on March 1 at the rate of some $31 million monthly. However, all this, as it happened, was not the whole story; it was somewhat less than half of the whole story, as a matter of fact. . .

III

The February votes in both the House and the Senate releasing population assistance funds for family planning programs abroad as part of the U.S. foreign aid program was widely perceived to be, and was in fact, an abortion-related vote. It was related to the abortion issue because the funds were released without the Mexico City restrictions which would have prohibited them from going to organizations performing or promoting abortions. The Republicans tried very hard to attach such restrictions and so, under the circumstances, this vote amounted a vote *on* the Mexico City language — and this language went down to defeat.

Thus the vote also amounted to a significant prolife setback. For the Congress, with its supposed prolife majorities in both houses, did not have to approve the Clinton resolution as it stood, making the funds available without any abortion-restrictions; the Congress had a choice; it had an alternative resolution before it all along, which would not only have released all the money, but would have removed the monthly spending limits as well, thus making yet more money available for spending during the 1997 fiscal year. This second resolution before the Congress, however, contained the Mexico City language.

This second resolution had been drafted and introduced by one of the principal prolife leaders in the U.S. Congress, Rep. Christopher H. Smith, a Republican from New Jersey and head of the Prolife Caucus. Chris Smith had been attempting to restore the Mexico City language for several years, and, in this instance, he spotted a very clear case where the Clinton Administration had actually turned down the prospect of increased family planning funding abroad rather than accept any limitations on abortion as a method of family planning.

This was, of course, entirely consistent with Clinton Administration policy. After taking office and removing the Mexico City language with his executive order, President Clinton never deviated from the course he had initially charted. The Clinton stance with respect to the 1994 UN Population Conference in Cairo, for example — and especially the actions of U.S. officials during the preparatory meetings leading up to the Cairo Conference — made it clear that it was a principal administration goal to see abortion legalized around the world. The then White House press secretary, Dee Dee Myers, openly admitted on April 1, 1993, that abortion legalization everywhere was "part of the overall approach to population control."

A month later, in May, 1993, Undersecretary of State (and former Colorado Democratic Senator) Timothy Wirth declared that the 95-odd UN member-states which still retain legal restrictions on or legally prohibit abortions were violating "basic human rights." Prior to the Cairo Conference itself, Secretary of State Warren Christopher sent a policy cable on March 16, 1994, to all U.S. embassies abroad stating that "the United States believes that access to abortion is a fundamental right."

Similarly, USAID Administrator J. Brian Atwood, who is responsible for administering population assistance program money abroad, informed a meeting of Population Cooperating Agencies in 1994 that "while obstacles cannot be removed overnight, this administration will continue to stand for the principle of reproductive choice, including abortion."

Even if the Clinton Administration had not so plainly stated its policies in this regard, these policies would have been evident from the massive funding steadily provided following the Clinton executive order to organizations which had expressly rejected the Mexico City restrictions — organizations such as the Pathfinder Fund and the International Planned Parenthood Federation in London. The

IPPF, for example, works tirelessly around the globe to undermine laws prohibiting or restricting abortion. IPPF's published *Vision 2000: A Strategic Plan* explicitly promises to "bring pressure on governments and campaign for policy and legislative change to remove restrictions against abortions."

Given this history of Clinton Administration efforts to promote the legalization of abortion around the world, the obduracy of a Leon Panetta in preferring to cut family planning funds rather than face any curtailment of proabortion activity begins to be understandable. Certainly it was instantly grasped by Representative Christopher H. Smith. "The consequences of approving Mr. Clinton's resolution," he told the House, "is a fat payday for abortion providers. The IPPF and its affiliates and allies, he added, "are acting as surrogates for the Clinton Administration in bringing down right-to-life laws."

Armed with these facts and sentiments, Chris Smith decided to call the Administration's bluff. As mentioned above, he decided to introduce an alternative resolution to the Clinton resolution. The Smith resolution, co-sponsored by Republican Congressman Henry J. Hyde of Illinois and Democratic Congressman James Oberstar of Minnesota, would have authorized the release on March 1 of the entire 1997 appropriation of $385 million. In addition, it would have removed the provision currently limiting monthly spending to eight percent of the total available; and, with carry-over funds from fiscal year 1996 (which had similarly been capped on a monthly basis), this would have made a grand total of $713 million immediately available, while the overall total under the Clinton resolution amounts to only $543 million to be spent at the rate of $31 million a month.

The kicker in the Smith resolution, of course, was that no funds could go to organizations such as the IPPF and its affiliates or allies to perform or promote abortions. With this resolution, therefore, Chris Smith and his co-sponsors and supporters, such as the National Right to Life Committee and the Christian Coalition, believed they had presented the Congress with a very clear choice to decide between:

1) *More* money *sooner* for family planning programs, provided that abortions or abortion advocacy were excluded —

versus

2) *Less* money *piecemeal* for family planning programs, but with abortions and abortion advocacy still permitted.

The idea was an obvious one. It should have had an immediate appeal for the apparently large number of those in the Congress who claim they are opposed to abortion but think family planning is just fine, indeed a modern necessity; it provided them an ideal opportunity, in fact, to vote *for* family planning while voting *against* abortion.

In the event, though, the House did not cut as cleanly as Congressmen Smith and his allies had no doubt hoped. In point of fact, the House approved *both* resolutions, the Clinton resolution *and* the Smith resolution. Having debated and then approved the first resolution providing USAID with further family planning funds on a monthly basis beginning March 1, as described above, the House them went on to debate and approve the Smith resolution two hours later by an even larger vote of 231 to 194.

This does not seem to have been the result envisioned and desired by Chris Smith and his supporters. Their idea seems to have been to get the House to *reject* the resolution releasing the funds with no restrictions on abortion, and then to *adopt* the Smith resolution that was more favorable to family planning even while it placed abortion back outside the pale. At any rate, this was how prolife telephone-tree calls instructed grass-roots activists to call in to ask their Representatives to vote.

But the fatal procedural flaw in this strategy seems to have been that, since there were two separate resolutions to be voted on, what was to prevent a House majority from passing both of them? What indeed? Whatever else the vote may have indicated, it certainly seems to have signaled that there is no House majority that necessarily even wants a clear choice to be presented between voting for family planning with abortion, or voting for family planning without abortion.

Chris Smith valiantly tried to put the best face on things under the circumstances: "There is no doubt about it that we wanted to win the first vote," he said. "But the silver lining is what we did with the second vote."

But it is not at all clear what, if anything, was really accomplished by getting the Smith resolution passed. What followed the passage of the Clinton resolution is that the measure was promptly forwarded to the Senate, where supposedly prolife Senate Majority Leader Trent Lott of Mississippi had already announced immediately following the House vote that a vote in the upper chamber would be scheduled for February 25 on "the president's request." This is exactly what happened, and the Senate too then approved the Clinton resolution, as we have already noted, so that family planning funds could begin to flow on March 1 with no restrictions on abortion or abortion advocacy.

Meanwhile, no Senate vote was ever even scheduled for the Smith resolution. If and when such a vote ever actually takes place, and the Senate passes it, a presidential veto has already been promised for it; nor is it likely that a two-thirds Senate majority could be garnered to override the veto. Thus it is probably not likely that there will ever be a Senate vote on it. It is equally probable that many of the House members who voted for it understood this all along.

What the Smith resolution chiefly seems to have accomplished, therefore, is this: it provided a prolife "cover" for not a few members who voted for both resolutions; on the one hand, the initiative to get family planning funds moving again without any abortion restrictions was hustled safely out the door; on the other hand, the vote putting the house on record against abortion will have no actual consequences in the real world.

It should be emphasized, by the way, that it was in no way the fault of Chris Smith and his allies that two different resolutions had to be introduced. The appropriations bill passed in September apparently required an up-or-down vote on a presidential finding that the population assistance program was being harmed; and there was no way under House rules to amend this resolution to get a vote on the Mexico City question. So a new resolution had to be introduced for this specific purpose. In fact, the Smith forces may have lost a few votes because of resentment that the Republican leadership was allowing a rule to be brought up authorizing a vote on the Smith resolution, while the original budget agreement had been that there would be a vote solely on the president's finding.

Thus, although the prolife intentions of Chris Smith and his allies were undoubtedly of the best, in the end their arguments failed to persuade a majority of their colleagues. The favorable vote on the first, Clinton resolution was apparently able to pass because a number of normally prolife Democrats such as Reps. Tony Hall of Ohio and Paul E. Kanjorski of Pennsylvania, were swayed by, or said they were swayed by, counterarguments such as those offered in the testimony of Secretary of State Madeleine K. Albright "that release of family-planning funds now [would] *reduce* the incidence of unintended pregnancy and abortion."

Never mind that the Smith resolution would have had the same fund-releasing effect as the Clinton resolution; it did not come with an urgent plea from a Democratic administration as far as the Democratic members were concerned; the Albright type of argument merely provided them with a pretext that they were still voting "prolife."

Never mind too the proven *fact* that increased family planning generally does *not* reduce abortion rates; rather, many studies, including some coming from Planned Parenthood related sources, have shown that the contrary is likely to be nearer the truth: once birth control becomes accepted and utilized, abortion soon comes to be seen as a necessary back-up method to make birth control one-hundred percent effective.

But this is not the main point in such a situation as the one we are dealing with here. What the actual case is not the main point; the main point is what a majority of the Congress believe the case to be. And as became evident from both the debate and the vote, a majority of the House at least claimed to be voting on the basis that family planning somehow *prevents* abortion.

"This vote is about family planning and against abortion," argued Rep. Constance A. Morella, a prochoice Republican from Maryland, echoing the same sentiments expressed by numerous other members. "To decrease abortions we must increase access to family planning services." It was the same with the debate in the Senate: the brand-new, supposedly prolife Republican Senator from Oregon, Gordon Smith, joined the proabortion Democratic Senator from Vermont, Patrick J. Leahy, in arguing that family planning helps prevent abortion. "This is a vote to support life," Senator Smith claimed, surrealistically.

In the face of such sentiments, Chris Smith and his allies proved unable to convince the requisite majority that the vote on the Clinton resolution *was* a proabortion vote. "Nobody in the Democratic party is more prolife than I am," Rep. Tony Hall declared in the course of the debate; but he said he believed that the "prolife forces have gone too far in attempting to make this a prolife issue."

The prolife side in the debate was also hampered because most of the members arguing for it spent a great part of their time arguing for the great benefits of government-sponsored family planning — something they hardly needed to convince their opponents about. In fact, not a single prolife House member spoke against family planning or population control as such; and some of them waxed so lyrically about the benefits of these things that their opponents might perhaps have been pardoned for imagining that their primary aim really was to promote family planning, after all, and not, as the prolifers maintained, to stop abortion.

Moreover, since everybody seemed so firmly agreed on the great benefits of family planning, what else was there that had to be done except to free up the family planning money forthwith? Why complicate this simple, straightforward question — for the prolifers, in effect, were admitting that support for family planning *was* a simple and straightforward affair — by bringing up the ugly, messy, and tiresome abortion issue?

If the prolife forces had somehow nevertheless succeeded in reinstating the Mexico City language by, in effect, strongly talking up family planning and population control and then adding, almost as an afterthought, "Oh, by the way, there is also this little matter of abortion," then perhaps there might have been something that could have been said for the whole effort. In view of the actual result, however, the question inevitably now has to be asked whether the strategy itself — attempting to curtail abortion by promoting more family planning — was the best — or even a viable — strategy to follow.

Another consideration irresistibly suggests itself as a result of the actual votes, namely, that many of the supporters of government-funded family planning in the Congress understand perfectly well, even if they do not admit it, that in order to be completely successful, family planning programs actually do *require* abortion as the logical back-up for failed contraception. The Clinton Administration believes this; what would be so strange, in the present climate, about a majority in Congress believing it too, even though many of them do not find it expedient to admit this?

This is the argument, after all, that organizations such as the IPPF openly and regularly advance; and it is not only possible that many supporters of family planning accept the argument; it is an established fact that they do. Prolifers, by themselves talking up and promoting increased family planning, even in the undeniably good cause of curtailing abortion, sadly, fell into a trap.

The antilifers, of course, are quite happy to accept all the support for family planning and population control they can get; in this regard they resemble the old Communist negotiators in the UN, happily accepting all the concessions anyone cares to make and then going on from there to make their demands. In this case, all the antilifers had to do, once the family planning money was freed up, was to turn right around and deny that abortion had to be curtailed as a method of achieving what everybody in any case had already agreed is the laudable aim of promoting family planning. This is no exaggeration of what actually happened in the case of these votes in Congress.

Surely, therefore, the time *has* come to take another look at the basic prolife political and legislative strategy that is currently being followed in the United States where the twin evils of government-sponsored population control and legalized abortion are concerned.

IV

Intelligent Americans are painfully and acutely aware that legalized abortion has brought unprecedented evil to our country. Both the strength and the achievements of the prolife movement over the past quarter of a century have been founded on that awareness, and on the basic moral sense of the American people.

However, it does not follow that, just because legalized abortion is so evil, everything else that is not abortion is necessarily therefore good or even always tolerable. Yet as a practical matter, since *Roe v. Wade,* the prolife movement in the United States has broadly followed the strategy that our urgent and primary aim must always be to try to stop the killing, even if it means we have to tolerate — or, as in the present case, actually promote — something else that is also verifiably evil, namely, government population control programs (even if they are theoretically shorn of an abortion component).

The truth is that the United States Government has no legitimate business whatsoever trying to tell people abroad — or at home for that matter — how many children they should be having. Nor should the American tax-payer have to bear the costs of such a dubious enterprise. This is true quite apart from the issue of abortion. No matter how they are presented, government-funded family planning programs are bound to be both intrusive and coercive. Let us stop kidding ourselves about this.

While we must surely accept the prolife premise that our urgent and primary aim must be to try to stop the killing, it does not at all follow that we also have to accept or tolerate other evils such as government-sponsored population control in order to do so. On the simplest level, of course, this is an end-justifies-the-means position anyway, a doing of evil that good may come of it. Prolifers can hardly go on honestly employing this argument against our opponents, as we so frequently do, if we end up taking the position ourselves by positively promoting population control and family planning.

In posing the whole question in this way, though, we should not for a moment doubt that the effort to re-apply the Mexico City language to U.S. population assistance programs, as long as there are such programs, was a highly desired and laudable goal; it remains a necessary goal. And Representative Christopher H. Smith of New Jersey is to be both commended and honored for his zeal in pursuing this goal so single-mindedly. In the course of his fight, Chris Smith vowed: "I will spend my time like you can't believe in making this fight on every appropriations and authorization bill in fiscal 1998."

After the first vote on the Clinton resolution resulted in the measure being passed, the New Jersey Congressman announced to his colleagues in the course of the debate on his own resolution: "Yes, the Clinton resolution passed today. That will not be the end of it, I can assure you. We will be back on the authorizing bills. We will be back on the appropriations bills when the fiscal 1998 and 1999 funds come up, and again we are going to continue with this 1997 effort as well."

Chris Smith's dedicated work is assuredly one of the very best things prolife Americans have going for them in the Congress of the United States; thank God we have him there and pray God to get 534 others like him. But even while recognizing this we must ask — especially in the light of the outcome of the February votes — whether prolife legislative strategy should ever go as far again as actual advocacy or promotion of population assistance programs. These are themselves of manifestly dubious character and utility, even if they do not include abortions.

Yes: by all means prolife legislators should try to restore the Mexico City language wherever possible; but they should not attempt to do this by throwing a sop to the population planners and birth controllers in the form of more money for the enterprises of the latter. It may be that, in the present climate of public opinion, both in the Congress and out, little or nothing can be done about cutting or curtailing these population programs themselves — which would be the ideal outcome most devoutly to be wished. But at the very least these programs should not be praised and promoted, and money actually added to them, in a vain effort to entice more "prolife" votes.

It is unfortunately true that those who serve in Congress live in a very strange and artificial world, where the moral issues involved in legislation are often very far from clear, and where straight up-or-down votes against evil are very rare. But surely the time has come for some kind of line to be drawn this side of actual prolife advocacy and support of U.S. funded population control programs abroad. (The same thing is true, of course, of the domestic family planning programs authorized under Title X and allied legislation.)

For one thing, the attempt to gain a prolife goal by such positive advocacy has now fizzled badly, very badly: been there, done that. There is surely something to be learned from this: the whole affair turned out to be nothing but a "lose-lose strategy."

For another thing, it has never been clear in practice whether contraception or birth control *can* clearly be separated from abortion in government family planning programs. Chris Smith and his allies themselves alluded to one part of this problem when they pointed to the obvious fact that money is fungible. Although the government may well place restrictions in words on the money it awards, all the awardee has to do is to put the government money in one pocket (for contraception or sterilization) while putting the money from other sources (to pay for abortions) in another pocket.

True, the point of restoring the Mexico City language was to prevent this by requiring organizations to certify that they would not perform or promote abortions; but there remains the serious question of whether this separation really can be effected or is itself real.

In the course of the debate in the House, it was regularly argued, and most of the members claimed to believe, that family planning is something that is totally distinct from abortion. Abortion kills while family planning merely prevents. Even the greatest champion among all prolife legislators in the Congress today, Henry J. Hyde, offered this same argument in the debate. "Family planning, properly defined," Henry Hyde pointed out, "is a matter of getting pregnant or not getting pregnant. *It has nothing to do with abortion*" (emphasis added).

The Illinois Congressman held that current U.S. policy regarding family planning and abortion respectively (as exemplified in the successive Hyde Amendments) had constructed a "wall" between these two distinct things, prevention and actual killing, and his plea was that this "wall between abortion and family planning should remain in place." This was the express purpose of the Smith resolution which he himself co-sponsored.

And so goes the standard argument generally. It is, of course, true that preventing the conception of a child is different from, and of lesser moral gravity, than terminating a new life that has already come into being. But it does not follow that, because contraception as such does not always involve the taking of a life, it is therefore itself morally neutral or indeed even a positive good — or that it is something that the tax-payers should be subsidizing. It also does not follow that contraception "has nothing to do with abortion."

On the contrary, what has become evident over the past thirty or forty years is that contraception and abortion go hand in hand and are generally linked quite closely together. Abortion has been legalized in the United States and around the world during precisely the same years that contraception too has become more widely, if not almost universally, employed. And once a typical "contraceptive mentality" has refused to accept the natural life-giving potential of sexual intercourse, the temptation to resort to abortion, if and when contraception fails, becomes very great.

As Pope John Paul II pointed out in his 1995 encyclical *Evangelium Vitae,* the Gospel of Life (#13): "Despite their differences of nature and moral gravity, contraception and abortion are often closely connected as fruits of the same tree." The pontiff further instanced what he called "the close connection which exists, in mentality, between the practice of contraception and that of abortion. . .It is being demonstrated in an alarming way by the development of chemical products, intrauterine devices and vaccines which, distributed with the same ease as contraceptives, really act as abortifacients. . ."

In other words, trying to distinguish between preventing conception or terminating the life already conceived is not always easy in practice; in fact, it may be impossible in practice.

Indeed, the very day the Senate voted to approve the Clinton resolution (February 25, 1997), the Federal Drug Administration

(FDA) announced its endorsement for the first time of a method of prescribing high doses of contraceptives for use as "morning after" birth control pills. When employed in this fashion, these pills do not act contraceptively at all (that is, to prevent conception); they act as abortifacients, that is, as agents which prevent an already fertilized ovum, or embryo, from implanting itself in the uterine wall.

This, of course, is a form of very early abortion. The technique of prescribing a high dosage of contraceptives for this purpose has been known since the 1970s; and doctors have been free to prescribe them since then. It is a procedure not forbidden by any law as long as abortion itself is legal. And now the FDA has specifically endorsed the technique.

Could not family planning clinic personnel in clinics abroad employ USAID-supplied contraceptives in the same way? Would the presence of the Mexico City language forbid this? Intrauterine devices (IUDs) have long been known to function in the same — abortifacient — fashion; and yet IUDs have long been a staple of U.S. funded family planning programs abroad. This was true during all the years the Mexico City restrictions were in place.

In other words, the distinction between family planning and abortion is more than a little blurred; and in some places this distinction seems to disappear entirely. The "wall" that congressional legislation has attempted to build between the two activities has been a rather porous wall at best, and in some places it appears to have been breached entirely.

Moreover, that this is, in fact, the case may be more widely known and understood than is generally admitted. In the typical rhetoric of our society on the subject, family planning is regularly represented as an indispensable benefit of modern technology which people can no longer do without. This was certainly how the debate in Congress treated the subject. At the same time, it is just conveniently *not* admitted — what nearly everyone really knows anyway — that, in our society, abortion everywhere exists in fact and is available to back up failed contraception; and indeed is counted on and employed precisely for that purpose, as the majority opinion in the Supreme Court's *Casey* decision explicitly pointed out.

In the face of this reality, prolife legislators, by conceding in advance the presumed desirability and necessity of government-sponsored family planning and population control (provided only that abortions are prohibited), have surely conceded far, far too much to the antilife forces in our society. Prolifers should be arguing, what is in fact the case, that abortion *cannot* be realistically excluded from modern family planning programs, and *therefore* these programs themselves represent an unacceptable use of tax-payer moneys.

During the debate in the House on the two resolutions, only one member, libertarian Republican Congressman Ron Paul of Texas, rose to ask the question of why the U.S. Government was funding family planning in the first place. Nevertheless, it was a very pertinent question to ask, and it is not at all clear why prolife members are not asking it. Who knows? The prolife cause might garner more support from conservative budget-cutters eager to see excised a billion dollars worth of birth control money than was attracted by the strategy of pandering to the current prejudice that government population control programs are a good thing.

How many *more* studies will have to be done before the realization finally begins to set in that massive government support for family planning is precisely *contributing* to the current breakdown of sexual morality and restraint in our society, to the steep rise in illegitimacy, to divorce and family break-up, and to the lowered current moral standards of society generally? All of these factors only fuel the demand for more abortions.

In the international arena, continued U.S. support for population control in particular makes us vulnerable (with reason) to the charge of wanting to reduce everywhere the numbers of the black, brown, and yellow races in particular. Our philanthropic and idealistic pretensions are surely reduced to absurdity when the "medical" shipments abroad under the U.S. foreign aid program turn out to consist primarily of contraceptive pills, condoms, and IUDs instead of needed medicines.

Only the prestige which birth control and family planning themselves enjoy among our elites, by the way, apparently prevents our current population control efforts from being denounced more frequently as American imperialism by today's politically correct people; these efforts do represent an American imperialism in the rawest possible form.

One thing that might have considerable effect on the whole situation would be for the Catholic bishops of the United States to begin again denouncing government funding of birth control as well as abortion. The bishops used to do this regularly, beginning back in the 1950s, and this policy was not without its effects. As things stand today, however, the U.S. Catholic bishops have not issued a statement against government-funded birth control since 1966.

Nevertheless, nobody has really forgotten, regardless of what might be said, that the Church does continue to condemn artificial birth control on moral grounds. Today, however, Pope John Paul II himself seems to be the only one in the Church still able and willing to stand up and denounce birth control openly for the evil that it is. Nearly everyone else seems to be going along, at least tacitly, with today's conventional wisdom to the effect that if birth control is not actually a modern benefit, at the very least it is not something which the Catholic Church could or should actively oppose on moral grounds. This is tragic: the moral authority of the bishops has been diminished precisely in the measure that they are perceived as politicians trying to make the best compromise "deal," rather than making plain the Church's moral teachings.

The prolife movement itself has also generally resisted opposing any of today's antilife phenomena except abortion, and, lately, euthanasia — as if any evil short of actual killing were somehow not an evil. The National Right to Life Committee, for example, sent a letter to every member of Congress urging support for the Smith resolution (and warning members that a vote for the Clinton resolution would be considered antilife on the NRLC's legislative scorecard). At the same time, the NRLC letter expressly stated that the "NRLC take no position on contraception or on federal funding of contraception services whether in the U.S. or overseas."

This position, of course, was in keeping with the policy the NRLC has followed since its founding a quarter of a century ago. Yet the NRLC, which has taken such a prominent and active role in trying to keep the abortifacient drug RU-486 out of the United States, must surely recognize that prescribing an increased dosage of contraceptive pills produces the same effect as RU-486. Why is the NRLC not opposing *this* obvious form of early chemically-induced abortions?

The world which prolife Americans now face out there today is a world in which numerous evils stemming from a fundamental antilife mentality have been steadily proliferating until they are now almost out of control. In addition to legalized abortion, we now have assisted suicide, euthanasia, experimentation with embryos, fetal tissue farming, cloning, in-vitro fertilization, surrogate mothering, withdrawal of nutrition and hydration from hospital patients, and who knows what next.

Pope John Paul II has correctly labeled our modern culture a "culture of death," and, given the fact that we are now therefore obliged to defend life across a broad front, surely the time has now come for prolife Americans to begin to recognize that our political and legislative strategies must henceforth go beyond mere opposition to abortion (and euthanasia). It is time for the prolife movement to drop the policy that "we take no position on contraception."

Moreover, among the evils that henceforth have to be combatted more directly, including especially in Congress, are surely to be numbered the population control and family planning programs, at home and abroad, which the U.S. Government is currently sponsoring. It is a fundamentally misconceived and mistaken idea that we can trade active support for these programs for additional "prolife" votes to outlaw abortion. This is the principal lesson that should emerge from the first abortion-related vote that took place in the 105th Congress in February, 1997 — if only we will prove capable, at long last, of learning it.

14

Even a "Prolife" Congress Makes Only Minimal Gains

From a prolife point of view, it appears that even a Congress that is supposed to have a decisive "prolife" majority in both houses can make only minimal gains in the present antilife atmosphere that obtains in the United States. Certainly the 1997 session of the 105th Congress, which is supposed to enjoy such a "prolife" majority, ended with a decided whimper in this regard, rather than with anything resembling a bang.

It is true that there were some gains made. However, they were minimal: the Hyde Amendment, which has restricted government funding of abortions except to save the life of the mother (since 1976), or in cases of rape or incest (since 1993), was actually beefed up by extending its restrictions beyond direct federal support programs to medical plans under Medicaid. The current ban on federal funding of any experimentation on human embryos was also extended — to forbid federal funding of any kind of human cloning experiments (in the wake of the successful cloning in Scotland of the sheep Dolly).

Similarly, the prolife majorities in both houses were able to hold the line against challenges and maintain the current bans on abortion in health plans for federal employees as well as on those abortions formerly paid for by the Bureau of Prisons.

By and large, though, this "prolife" Congress concentrated mostly on denying government funding of abortion; little was accomplished in the way of attempting to restrict or ban abortion itself. Abortion remains completely legal in the United States, as the proabortionists never tire of reminding us.

First published in *Culture Wars*, January, 1998

It is worth looking at four major issues considered by the U.S. Congress in 1997 to see how they played out from a prolife point of view. These four issues are: 1) the attempt to ban partial-birth abortions; 2) U.S. Government aid for so-called family-planning programs abroad; 3) U.S. Government support for domestic family-planning programs; and 4) the selection of another black proabortion physician as Surgeon General of the United States.

The Attempt to Ban Partial-Birth Abortions

The particularly gruesome abortion technique correctly named "partial-birth abortion," whereby the baby is partially delivered before being killed by the crushing of his skull and the sucking out of his brains, has become one of the best known — and widely opposed — "medical" techniques in use today. Both houses of Congress decisively approved a ban on this horrendous procedure in 1996. However, the President of the United States then calmly vetoed this Partial-Birth Abortion Ban Bill.

Strenuous, indeed unprecedented, efforts to persuade Congress to override the president's veto of the bill, in which millions of pieces of mail were sent to individual representatives and senators, were successful as regards the House of Representatives; but they ultimately failed as regards the U.S. Senate.

The reaction in both houses of Congress to this outcome was to re-enact the Partial-Birth Abortion Ban Bill again in 1997. The House voted to do this in March by a clear veto-proof majority and the Senate voted to do it in May; the Senate vote, however, fell three votes short of being a veto-proof majority (whereas the veto override effort had failed by eight votes the year before).

Then a long lull ensued. Neither house wanted to defy the president's standing veto threat immediately; the hope was that with the passage of time at least three more senators could be persuaded to contribute their votes to outlaw this sickening procedure. The Senate had in any case enacted its version of the bill with some minor changes included in order to secure an — again, wholly unprecedented — endorsement of the ban by the American Medical Association (AMA). The House was therefore obliged to re-enact the ban using the Senate's amended language — which it did only on October 8, by a vote of 296 in favor of banning partial-birth abortions and 132 against this.

In spite of the persistent and increasing sentiment in Congress to see this barbaric procedure banned, however, Bill Clinton, on October 10, promptly vetoed the re-enacted Partial-Birth Abortion Ban Bill, as he had vetoed the previous one; apparently he was just waiting, pen poised, to express his studied contempt for mere congressional majorities; he vetoed the bill as soon as the House acted.

No matter that a large majority of Americans had by then manifested clear opposition to partial-birth abortions. The President of the United States, for his part, evidently had no intention of allowing any such thing as the will of the people to prevail where legalized abortion was concerned.

As the Congress moved towards adjournment in November, observers noted that another vote to attempt to override the president's veto would be scheduled during 1998. Meanwhile, strenuous efforts were being revived to attempt to persuade Congress to administer to this president once and for all the rebuke he so richly deserves on this issue. Cardinal Bernard Law of Boston, for example, noted in a press conference that more than three million more postcards had been ordered by the Catholic bishops' prolife arm alone for use by Catholic parishes to generate mail to Congress. Many other groups have been similarly gearing up in an attempt to exert maximum influence on the Congress in 1998 in order to put a partial-birth abortion ban in place at long last.

At this writing there is at least an outside chance that the veto override effort will be successful this second time around: enormous pressures have been building up to outlaw this horrendous abortion procedure; even many normally proabortion legislators have voted against this one, and perhaps three more senators will be found willing to change their votes. It is a measure of President Clinton's own proabortion convictions, however, that he himself has refused to yield on the issue. The ban will have to be enacted over his veto if it is to become law at all.

U.S. Government Aid for Family-Planning Programs Abroad

As adjournment loomed, and in order to avoid a threatened presidential veto of the entire Foreign Operations appropriations bill, the Republican leadership in Congress, on November 13, agreed to drop a House-passed provision from the bill which would have restored a ban on aid to international family-planning programs performing, supporting, or promoting abortions. This House provision would have restored the Reagan Administration's former "Mexico City language" which maintained such a ban from 1984 to 1993, when President Bill Clinton, in one of his first acts in the White House, abolished this language by executive order, thus allowing U.S. Government foreign aid funds to flow unimpeded to such organizations as the International Planned Parenthood Federation (IPPF) which perform and promote abortions abroad on a massive scale as an integral part of "family planning."

The House provision in question reviving the Mexico City language was a perennial one sponsored by Rep. Christopher H. Smith (R.-NJ), head of the prolife caucus. Rep. Smith had tried but failed to attach a similar provision to last year's Foreign Operations appropriations bill; but he had promised that he would continue to offer the amendment for all relevant bills, and he and his prolife allies in the House were as good as their word on this.

However, the Senate had failed to include any Mexico City language in its version of the Foreign Operations bill. More than that, President Clinton had promised a sure veto of any bill that did contain the Mexico City language. Nevertheless, the House, with its strong prolife component, was determined to hold firm. With adjournment itself threatened by unpassed appropriations bills, the Republican leadership offered a compromise. It detached the Mexico City language from the Foreign Operations bill, thus making it possible to enact that roughly $13 billion money bill, of which some $385 million, the same amount as last year, went for the support of family-planning programs abroad. This was one of a number of bills that had to be completed before adjournment in order to keep the government operating into the next year.

Having been removed from the Foreign Operations bill to allow its passage, the Mexico City language was then added to a State Department reauthorization bill which contained, among other things, language that would have consolidated into the State Department two currently independent agencies, the Arms Control and Disarmament Agency (ACDA) and the U.S. Information Agency (USIA), as well as parts of a third agency, the Agency for International Development (AID). This consolidation plan was, as it happened, the pet project of Senator Jesse Helms (R.-NC), normally one of the strongest prolife legislators in either house.

Nevertheless, Senator Helms, Chairman of the Senate Foreign Relations Committee, had labored long and lovingly on this particular reorganization bill. Now, suddenly, its smooth enactment was threatened by the inclusion in the same bill of the Mexico City language banning aid to organizations performing or promoting abortions in international family-planning programs. Nor would the prolife House members yield on the inclusion of this language, a stance which the Republican leadership found itself obliged to support in order to keep its own base intact; the Republican leadership had wanted the Mexico City language moved out of the Foreign Operations bill so that the latter could be enacted without the threat of a veto; but the leadership was committed to standing fast on keeping that language in the State Department reauthorization bill, which did not have to be passed in order to keep the government going and allow the Congress to adjourn.

This situation produced the enormous irony of Jesse Helms himself being one of those criticizing the unyielding position on abortion of Chris Smith and his prolife House allies. Yet another complication arose from the fact that the State Department bill also contained language granting some $826 million to pay U.S. debts to the United Nations, as well as a whopping $3.5 billion dollar payment to the International Monetary Fund (IMF). These payments would be jeopardized unless the whole bill could be passed.

Moreover, President Clinton very much wanted the State Department reorganization, on which Secretary of State Madeleine Albright had been working closely with Senator Helms; the president also wanted the $3.5 billion for the IMF, principally to help stabilize Indonesia, not to speak of South Korea; and the president was equally committed with public statements to paying the nearly $1 billion U.S. debt to the U.N.

House prolifers, supported in this instance by the House leadership, actually thought they had a few bargaining chips with the White House for a change. The president wanted and needed something from them. Representative Smith, along with House Republican prolifers Rep. Jim Talent of Missouri and Rep. Steve Largent of Oklahoma, actually met with the president in order to try to get a deal. They did more than that: they agreed to modify the Mexico City language provision to limit the prohibition of U.S. foreign aid funds *only* to organizations engaged in "lobbying" abroad for the legalization of abortion; the original language had applied the prohibition to organizations performing abortions (although here the president was allowed some waiver room provided he was willing to accept a smaller amount of funds) and to countries such as China that coerce women into having abortions. But the House prolifers were quite prepared to compromise on these two latter points in order to get at least something out of the deal.

Still another factor involved in the whole affair was the pending "fast track" trade legislation that would have renewed the president's authority to negotiate trade agreements abroad without detailed congressional oversight (Congress could ratify but not amend the trade agreements made by the president). President Clinton very badly wanted this legislation too, and was reportedly making all kinds of deals in order to get the requisite votes. However, a number of prolife Republicans had made it clear that they would not support the fast-track trade legislation unless they also got the Mexico City language somewhere in one of the pending bills. Chris Smith estimated the number of House members in this category at about two dozen, which probably would have made the difference on the fast-track trade bill (assuming not too many Democratic defections as a result of any Administration agreement to allow even modified Mexico City language).

Given all these factors, it really seemed as if a prolife victory — limited, perhaps, but nevertheless very real — could be secured at the expense of our adamant proabortion president: surely Bill Clinton would have to yield and allow at least the watered-down Mexico City language in order to get his fast-track trade bill, his State Department reauthorization, his money for the IMF, and his money to pay the UN debt. All of these items were central to President Clinton's announced foreign policy — as Missouri's Rep. Jim Talent remarked at the time. Surely the president would compromise.

Nothing of the sort. The president absolutely refused to consider any compromise where unrestricted abortion was at issue. This was a president who had shown himself capable of making deals on virtually everything — but not, as it turned out, on abortion. Many observers have judged William Jefferson Clinton to be a wholly unprincipled man, but one principle he has undeviatingly upheld whatever the political cost to him, namely, his insistence that there must be no restrictions on either the advocacy or the performance of abortions by organizations funded by the U.S. Government. People in his own Administration, such as Treasury Secretary Robert Rubin,

Secretary of State Madeleine Albright, and U.S. Ambassador to the U.N. Bill Richardson, were all said to be appalled by their president's stance; from the point of view of his own Administration, the president was giving up an enormous amount merely to maintain his proabortion stance.

"The only thing I could figure out," House Speaker Newt Gingrich was quoted in the press as saying, "was that the feminist proabortion faction in the White House — which is substantial — has a rigidity on this topic that is astonishing. You'd think with Iraq and all that stuff going on, Clinton would have swallowed a compromise. It's embarrassing. . ."

Missouri's Rep. Jim Talent was quoted as saying, "When you link it up with some of Al Gore's statements like the idea that population growth causes global warming, they view abortion as an answer to environmental problems internationally. Causing abortions abroad seems to be central to this Administration's policy in a number of ways."

There were, of course, indications that some proabortion Democrats favoring the fast-track trade bill, such as Rep. Nancy Pelosi of California, let the president know that they would switch their votes if the White House ever compromised even on an attenuated version of the Mexico City language. There is no way of knowing how the vote would have come out if Clinton had been willing to compromise; but it is significant that the president was unwilling even to put the thing to a test, if it meant yielding the slightest thing on abortion. The only recourse for prolifers was therefore to deny the president the other things he wanted if he was not going to compromise with them in any way. As prolife Republican Rep. Tom Coburn from Oklahoma noted: "No give, no give. If we don't get something similar [on abortion], no IMF, no UN, and no reorganization" — not to speak of no fast-track trade bill, the thing that the president wanted most of all.

Even then, the White House was able to salvage a propaganda victory of sorts out of the whole affair; this was possible simply because, by depicting the Republican prolife House as the intransigent one in the whole affair, the White House was able to get the president off the hook; there was no hint that the president had been the one unwilling to compromise. At the same time, White House spokesman Michael McCurry was able to point out that it was "particularly ill-timed" to be snubbing the U.N. at the very time that the U.S. was seeking the support of the U.N. against Iraq's Saddam Hussein. "It is utterly bone-headed," McCurry went on, "for Congress to fail to meet the commitments that the United States has at the U.N. in terms of our arrears."

And, in fact, it is hard to see what benefits accrue to the prolife cause as such by the rejection by Republican "conservatives" of some of these foreign policy goals of the president. This whole affair appears to be yet one more instance where the prolife movement has gotten drawn into issues beyond its immediate interests — and then made to look bad because of its supposed "intransigence" and "rigidity."

No doubt it was politically necessary to inflict upon the president a political cost for his total unwillingness to compromise. That, after all, is what politics consists of in the end: you have to pay for what you decide to do. Nevertheless, it is amazing how often prolife politicians end up on the losing side in this kind of affair: themselves taxed with "intransigence" when it is the other side that has refused to yield.

As regards the failure of the fast-track trade bill, Bill Clinton was able, blandly and deftly, to turn the whole issue around so as to *blame,* once again, House prolifers for the defeat of this supposedly important legislation. "Had we been able to resolve [the Mexico City language issue]," the president declared disingenuously, "I think we could have gotten enough votes on the Republican side to pass the bill. I think we could have. But we were simply unable to do that." The president did not mention, of course, that he was the one who had refused to compromise after the other side had been prepared to compromise.

And so it was that the sustained, and even heroic, efforts of Chris Smith and his allies to put the United States out of the abortion business abroad — failed. It is hard to see how the prolife position could have been any worse if prolife House members had simply, flatly opposed all so-called family-planning programs abroad for purposes of population control. No doubt they would have garnered fewer votes from some House members opposed to abortion even while they remain convinced that family planning itself is a benefit. But what has been gained by the enormous effort expended to get language opposing abortion as a method of family planning only to fail in the end anyway? Prolifers should be opposing so-called population control programs abroad as such, not just the inclusion of abortion in these programs.

U.S. Government Aid for Domestic Family-Planning Programs

Unlike the case in some past years, prolife and conservative Republicans appear to have made no significant efforts at all in 1997 to cut government support for domestic family-planning programs — not that their previous efforts in this area have ever been crowned with more than temporary success! Given the fact that the Republican subcommittee chairman who oversees most domestic government-supported family-planning programs, including those under Title X ("Title 10") of the Public Health Service Act, as amended, is the very pro-family-planning and proabortion Republican Rep. John Edward Porter of Illinois, perhaps prolife members on this key appropriations subcommittee saw little chance in even trying to cut the funding for these programs, let alone trying to abolish the programs outright (which would certainly be a consummation devoutly to be wished in any ideal world).

Instead, the main prolife effort in the domestic family-planning area in 1977 concerned an amendment to the appropriations bill introduced by Rep. Ernest Istook (R.-OK) which would have required parental consent before minors could receive any "family-planning services" from federally funded clinics. Efforts to get this amendment inserted into the 1997 Labor and Health and Human Services appropriations bill were exerted both at the committee level and on the House floor.

In point of fact, the Istook Amendment was brought forward with a greater degree of credibility this time because of a fairly widely publicized incident in Illinois where a high school teacher had carried on an affair with a teen-ager for some eighteen months, driving her regularly to the County health department for the federally subsidized "family planning services" (birth control injections) which made this sustained affair even possible — all this without the knowledge, much less the consent, of the parents of the girl, who was, of course, a minor. In a normal world, such an incident as this would have helped render plausible what is in fact the true conclusion to be drawn from it all, namely, that government-funded birth control programs are not only a highly dubious social and personal "benefit"; they are frequently and demonstrably harmful to the public health and welfare, especially where vulnerable teen-agers are concerned.

But no: in the brave new contemporary world of the sexual revolution, such an incident as a teacher sexually exploiting a student is in no way embarrassing to the public officials who have, in effect, made it possible. No: it becomes nothing but "a very complex matter," in the words of Labor-HHS appropriations subcommittee Chairman John Edward Porter, quintessential "moderate" Republican of Illinois. Claiming that a moral issue is "complex," of course, is almost invariably the subterfuge of choice today for getting around that particular issue. It is a favorite characterization, for example, employed by those Catholic theologians who "responsibly dissent" from the teachings of the Catholic Church on matters of sexual morality. If an issue is "complex," then "simplistic" objections such as that unmarried teen-agers ought not to engage in sexual relations or that, especially, high school teachers ought not to engage in such relations with their students can easily be set aside and ignored.

"Confidential access to family-planning is critical," Rep. Porter insisted in the committee proceedings which he chaired in July; and his viewpoint apparently represented the working consensus of his subcommittee, since the Istook Amendment failed in that venue — not least, perhaps, because the normally prolife chairman of the full House Appropriations Committee, Robert C. Livingston (R.-LA), was determined to enact this year appropriations bills which were veto proof — which the president definitely would sign. No more confrontations; no more government shutdowns — the Republicans got blamed by the voters for the last round of them a couple of years back.

Appropriations Committee Chairman Bob Livingston thus had no compunctions this time around about warning his colleagues that attaching such controversial amendments as the Istook Amendment to appropriations bills could jeopardize the final passage of such bills — at the very time when the Congress was getting ready to adjourn and go home. No matter that President Clinton was quite prepared to delay the whole process by giving out vetoes wherever there was something he believed in on principle (access to abortion); no matter that the Republicans themselves are supposed to stand for something regardless of the consequences if they expect support from many of those who voted for them.

The fact remained, however, that Chairman Livingston had well before that time publicly evidenced his principled objections to including substantive amendments in appropriations bills anyway. As a principle, this position was probably completely correct. In the case at hand, however, the Istook Amendment represented a principle which the Republicans as a party could ill afford to abandon in the present permissive era if they are really going to try to hold the line on anything.

However that may be, the Istook Amendment was neatly trumped in committee by a substitute amendment offered by Subcommittee Chairman Porter himself, which simply required clinics to "encourage family participation" in decisions concerning birth control — as if it were the normal and expected thing for teen-agers who have become sexually active to involve their parents in their "decisions" — and to "counsel minors to resist attempts to engage them in sexual activities" — as if such bland and anodyne language even addressed the real issues raised by allowing government-funded clinics to provide the means of birth control to minors without parental knowledge or consent.

Rep. Istook and his allies made an attempt to revive his amendment when the Labor-HHS appropriations bill reached the House floor in September. Rep. Istook pointed out that "if you do things to make sexual activity by teens easier, there will be more out-of-wedlock births, and more abortions too." Chairman Porter blandly rejoined, however, that requiring parental notification would essentially prevent teens from dysfunctional families from getting "the kinds of services that prevent pregnancies, help to prevent sexually transmitted diseases, and in the end help to prevent abortions."

Apparently, no prolife House members stood up to challenge this assertion of Rep. Porter's — although it represents pretty nearly the opposite of the truth of the matter. The Illinois Congressman's arguments in favor of government subsidized family planning appear to have been made without notable dissent being registered from his prolife colleagues in the House. Prolife House members by and large do not appear to believe that government sponsorship and subsidies of "family planning," as such, do need to be opposed, whether on prolife or on other grounds. The necessary link between personal and social acceptance of contraception and personal and social acceptance of abortion, although it can be established beyond doubt empirically, is far from having been established in the minds of most of today's legislators. On the contrary, most of them appear to believe, against the evidence, that contraception precludes and cuts down on abortions and *therefore* must be accepted and supported — and funded by the government.

The day when our prolife legislators might begin to see that contraception in fact entails and inevitably leads to abortion — as Pope John Paul II has clearly seen and written in his encyclical *Evangelium Vitae* — still appears to be a rather distant day. The same thing is unfortunately true of most of the major prolife organizations engaged in lobbying for the prolife cause and for prolife issues on Capitol Hill: they "take no position on birth control" — and thereby they actually help perpetuate the widely perceived need to "control" births after the fact by resorting to the legalized abortion which our Supreme Court has meanwhile conveniently provided.

Introduced on the floor by Rep. Istook himself and by Rep. Donald Manzullo (R.-IL), the Istook Amendment was effectively gutted and stripped of any real, operative force. In the mysterious way that Congress sometimes proceeds, the Amendment was, technically, approved — but only after the bland Porter language merely "encouraging" family participation in birth control decisions and calling for "counseling" against engaging in sexual activities had been *substituted* for the original Istook language. This was brought about by means of another amendment introduced by Rep. Michael N. Castle (R.-DE). This Castle Amendment was approved by a vote of 220-201 on September 9; then the Istook Amendment itself — as amended by Castle! — was approved on the same day by a vote of 254 to 169. And so it was that full federal funding for domestic family-planning programs was continued without any real restrictions by the U.S. Congress for yet another year. . .

A modicum of good news did accompany the passage of the 1997 Labor-HHS appropriations bill, however: the bill also contained the perennial Hyde Amendment which, this year, was extended not only to exclude direct government funding of most abortions but also to exclude payments to managed health-care providers or health plans that provide for or allow for abortions.

What the phrase "a prolife majority" in Congress appears to mean at the present time, in other words, is that a majority of our law-makers evidently really do not want the government to be *paying* for abortions; at the same time, they appear to be doing or saying little or nothing that might ever encourage people to believe that abortion itself is wrong and should be made illegal.

Selection of Another Black, Proabortion Physician as Surgeon General of the United States

President Clinton's choices to fill the post of Surgeon General of the United States have confirmed — as strongly as anything else he has ever said or done — this president's fundamental commitment — always ahead of anything else whatever — to the abortion culture and to the sexual revolution that stands behind it. The president has consistently selected a black, proabortion physician for this post in order to preclude even the suggestion of any criticism that the Administration's proabortion and pro-sexual-license policies might somehow be aimed at black genocide or at corrupting the morals of the black community in particular. As unlikely as any such accusations might appear to be in today's decadent moral climate, a proabortion Southern president can surely never be too careful.

Thus, the president's first choice for the post of surgeon general was the inimitable Dr. Joycelyn Elders, whose radical advocacy of sexual permissiveness quickly went far beyond what anyone could previously have imagined a public official would dare to say. Dr. Elders was finally obliged to resign her post only after she had publicly advocated that masturbation should be taught to children in elementary school.

The president's second choice for surgeon general was the equally inimitable Dr. Henry W. Foster, Jr. This black physician failed to get Senate confirmation for the post not so much on account of the abortions he had steadily advocated and even himself performed; rather, his nomination failed mostly on account of the gratuitous and multiple lies he felt obliged to tell in the course of being considered for the post. Dr. Foster's record included a half dozen or more serious disabilities, any one of which, in the present climate — including instances of unethical medical experimentation — would probably have destroyed the candidacy of any candidate who was not a black. Nevertheless, Dr. Foster missed being confirmed as surgeon general only by the narrowest of margins and, indeed, on a technicality. Even a number of senators who otherwise professed prolife principles found it difficult to oppose him — or any black.

The same psychology and dynamics appear to be in play as regards President Clinton's latest nominee to be Surgeon General of the United States: he is Dr. David Satcher, currently the director of the Centers for Disease Control and Prevention (CDC) in Atlanta, whom the president nominated to the surgeon general's position on September 13, 1997.

When long drawn-out and bruising confirmation battles occur, such as the one that accompanied the confirmation of Dr. Elders, or the subsequent one that accompanied the failure to be confirmed of Dr. Foster, both sides normally draw back. Neither side wants another "controversy." For example, President Clinton simply left the surgeon general's post vacant for nearly two years following the unsuccessful battle to get Dr. Foster confirmed.

There also exists a tendency in this kind of situation to bring forward "neutral" or even "stealth" candidates for "controversial" posts — as President George Bush did when, remembering the battle over Judge Robert Bork, he named the virtual "cipher" David Souter to the Supreme Court. The latter turned out to be another unreconstructed liberal as soon as he was safely on the Court, of course; but nobody could have deduced this beforehand from his record for the simple reason that he did not have any record.

It is probably typical of President Clinton's open commitment to abortion, however, that he has been willing to name yet another black proabortion physician to the surgeon general's post following the protracted controversy over Dr. Foster — even at nearly two years' remove. For Dr. Satcher is in no way a neutral or stealth candidate. On the contrary, not only is he openly proabortion and prepared to defend even partial-birth abortions; he has also been involved in CDC research which has been challenged, apparently on pretty good grounds, as unethical — one of Dr. Foster's disabilities; and he has defended without apology, for example, CDC's controversial policy of not reporting to parents instances where HIV-positive results in infants were uncovered in the course of CDC-sponsored research.

Yet, in spite of such a known and objectionable record — which should have eliminated him from consideration from the outset — Dr. Satcher's nomination by the president failed to provoke any significant opposition, either in the prolife movement or in the medical profession. Although his disabilities would seem on the face of it to be quite serious, he has been treated in practice virtually as a stealth candidate, and has been carefully and quietly conducted through the confirmation process by Democrats such as Senator Edward M. Kennedy (D.-MA), who described the good doctor as a "respected family doctor, a respected scholar, and a leader in the public health community."

In the whole process, Dr. Satcher did encounter opposition from such consistent prolife senators as Daniel R. Coats (R.-IN), who was critical of the CDC director's partial-birth abortion stance as well as of his involvement in questionable CDC research. Similarly, Senator John Ashcroft (R.-MO) characterized as "shocking that the nominee for surgeon general. . .would associate himself with partial-birth abortion." In doing so, Senator Ashcroft pointed out, "he chooses the president over the AMA" — which now publicly favors a ban on the procedure — "and barbarity over the judgment of medicine."

Such opposition to Dr. Satcher seems to have counted for little, however. Following a hearing on nomination, the Senate Labor and Human Resources Committee voted 12 to 5 to approve Dr. Satcher's nomination and send it to the floor. A supposedly prolife senator such as Republican Bill Frist of Tennessee, himself a physician, resolved any doubts he may have had about Dr. Satcher on the basis of a simple letter from the latter claiming that he would not as surgeon general promote abortion-related issues — as if a Robert Bork could have disarmed his opposition by writing a letter stating that he would not be bound in his decisions by the language of the Constitution! Similarly, the supposedly prolife Republican Senator John Warner of Virginia stated that he was voting for Dr. Satcher's confirmation in spite of the latter's open proabortion position because, in the Virginia senator's own words, "I was deeply impressed with this man's commitment."

As Congress adjourned, Senate Majority Leader Trent Lott, ostensibly another "prolife" senator, was predicting: "I assume his nomination will be confirmed after the first of the year. . ."

And so it was as yet another black proabortion physician was nominated to be Surgeon General of the United States: there certainly did not appear to be any recognition on the part of President Clinton that nominating another proabortion physician to be surgeon general was anything he needed to steer clear of; on the contrary, the president seemed to be well on the way to the vindication of his choice by a favorable vote of the whole Senate when it reconvenes.

In the meantime, with "friends" like Senators Frist and Warner, the prolife movement scarcely seems to be in need of any enemies. . .

15

An Anniversary Comes and Goes: 25 Years of *Roe v. Wade*

I

January 22, 1998, marked the 25th anniversary of the legalization of abortion in the United States by means of the infamous 1973 *Roe v. Wade* decision of the United States Supreme Court. For 24 of those 25 years what from the start turned into an annual March for Life has brought tens of thousands of prolife demonstrators every year to the Mall in Washington to protest this evil and tragic Supreme Court decision.

Normally the participants in this annual March for Life gather on the Ellipse immediately behind the White House and, after speeches and exhortations from prolife notables on a platform erected there — notables who tend to be legislators and clergy in about equal numbers — the demonstrators then march peacefully up Constitution Avenue to the Capitol and the Supreme Court in solemn protest against this lethal court decision which has resulted in more than 37 million dead children since 1973, but which nevertheless remains "the law of the land."

At the end of the March, the demonstrators — who come from all over the country — are supposed to repair to the offices of their senators and representatives on Capitol Hill to urge an end to legalized abortion. It is now well established how both the members of Congress and the congressional staff are obliged to brace themselves every January 22 to deal with the inevitable prolife inundation.

It was no different in 1998: once again, "tens of thousands" showed up for the March. If you have ever participated in one of these Marches, you will know that you can look back down Consti-

---

This article originally appeared in the issue of *Culture Wars* for April, 1998.

tution Avenue from near the head of the March and see a solid mass of on-going marchers with their banners and signs extending all the way back to the Ellipse nearly a mile back. Senate and House office buildings are jammed for hours during and after the March. The Washington underground Metro system is pushed to its maximum capacity and beyond as the marchers use the trains to return home or to go back to the buses which brought them to Washington; these buses themselves seem to be parked everywhere, in fact.

A few years back the U.S. Park Police ceased even attempting to issue estimates of the number of people participating in this sort of mass demonstration on the Washington Mall. Their estimates, particularly those concerning the March for Life in particular, had simply become too controversial. Over the years prolife leaders constantly had occasion to protest, probably with reason, the artificially low estimates which the U.S. Park Police tended to come up with. Not even aerial photographs of the massed marchers could ever apparently convince them that some of their estimates were surely on the low side. It seemed to many observers that the Park Police just might have been under some pressure to underestimate the numbers specifically at the March for Life — while inflating the numbers for prochoice, feminist, or "gay pride" demonstrations on the Mall. At any rate so it often seemed to some who monitored both types of marches.

However that may be, the major media have certainly never given the annual January 22 March for Life anything close to its due. In the early years the Marches were scarcely reported on at all. Later, the media practice began of, yes, reporting that there was an "antiabortion demonstration" all right — with the cameras focused on the speakers rather than on the crowds — but then of "balancing" this coverage by giving "equal time" to a counter-demonstration of, say, a dozen feminists conducting a vigil in front of the Supreme Court.

"Today is the anniversary of the Supreme Court's abortion decision," the typical news item would begin, "and both sides organized demonstrations" — the proabortionists 50 to 100, and the prolifers "tens of thousands," although the actual numbers would rarely be mentioned. This has been the typical kind of media coverage accorded to the annual March for Life.

This year it was the breaking story of the dalliance of the President of the United States with a young female White House intern,

Monica Lewinsky, which crowded whatever coverage the March for Life might otherwise have rated not merely off the front pages and out of the TV evening news, but out of the news almost entirely. If it had not been for the sensational story of Bill and Monica, it would no doubt have been something else; that is how the March normally fares with the media year after year.

Yet is there any precedent in all of American history for a cause which every year never fails to bring its "tens of thousands" to the Mall in Washington to oppose the abortion "settlement" which the Supreme Court of the United States tried to impose on this country a quarter of a century ago? What more dramatic proof could there be that the abortion question is *not* going to be settled in the way our elites want and in accordance with the standards of our contemporary culture of death? Year after year, in freezing weather or even in blizzard conditions — or, as was the case this year, on what proved to be merely a cool and overcast day — the prolife demonstrators have always invariably turned out in force on January 22. The Congress knows it; the Supreme Court knows it; the media people know it too although there appears to be no easy way anybody can force them to admit it.

Nor will these Marches for Life, along with all the other continuing activities of the prolife movement, cease as long as abortion itself remains legal in this country. The prolife movement has long since and of necessity settled down for the long haul; the movement will not come to an end in this country until legalized abortion has come to an end.

This year at least a dozen prolife members of Congress such as Senator Rick Santorum of Pennsylvania and Christopher Smith of New Jersey were on hand to address the gathering. The usual contingent of clergymen were also present: Cardinal Bernard Law of Boston was able to introduce no less than 28 other Catholic prelates from around the country. The Boston cardinal also announced that a special apostolic blessing from Pope John Paul II was being accorded to several prominent American prolife leaders, including especially the founder of the March for Life, Nellie Gray, who has ably led all of the Marches since the very first one (which this writer vividly recalls). Surely few papal blessings have gone to anyone as deserving as Nellie Gray!

This 1998 March was also especially notable for the presence of a number of prominent converts to the prolife cause. These included Dr. Bernard Nathanson, who back in the 1960s was actually one of the founders of NARAL — the National Abortion and Reproductive Rights Action League. Dr. Nathanson was also a leader in the burgeoning abortion "industry" which grew up along with the legalization of the practice; he has stated that he is personally responsible for some 75,000 abortions — until his conscience finally got to him about the taking of innocent lives, and he found himself obliged to embrace not only the prolife cause, for which he has become a uniquely effective spokesman, but also the Catholic Christian faith — in order to obtain the forgiveness his soul craved for the evil of his involvement in doing abortions. Dr. Nathanson has personally traversed the road that our whole culture of death must still traverse in order that we may finally set a term to the enormous evil of legalized abortion.

The two other prominent converts to the prolife cause who were present at the 1998 March for Life were none other than the "Jane Roe" of the *Roe v. Wade* case and the "Mary Doe" of *Roe*'s companion 1973 *Doe v. Bolton* case (in which the Supreme Court ruled, in effect, that virtually any reason whatsoever why a woman might think she wanted to have an abortion was a valid "health" indication for abortion!).

"Jane Roe," whose real name is Norma McCorvey, was the woman who was used by the proabortion lawyers in getting the Texas law prohibiting abortions except to save the life of the mother thrown out by the Supreme Court in the *Roe v. Wade* case. A quarter of a century later, the same Norma McCorvey came before the participants at the March for Life to "apologize" for the role she played in the case. In testimony before a Senate Judiciary subcommittee prior to the March, she told Senator John Ashcroft of Missouri that the *Roe* case had actually been based upon what she termed "a little lie," namely, that she had been gang-raped. And hence the implication was that, as so many accepted then and still accept today, she "needed" the abortion.

But there was one major problem with this and that is that it was not true. "I think it's fair to say that the entire abortion industry is based on a lie," Norma McCorvey went on to testify to the Senate subcommittee. In 1973 she had been what she called a "willing dupe" of the proabortionists; now she was able to testify that she was "dedicated to spending the rest of my life undoing the law that bears my name."

The lies on which the legalization of abortion in the United States was originally based were brought out even more forcefully by the "Mary Doe" of the *Doe v. Bolton* case. Her real name is Sandra Cano, and she too appeared at the March for Life to recount that:

> I was poor, pregnant, uneducated, seeking assistance and getting a divorce from a man who was a convicted child molester. My only source of help was Atlanta Legal Aid. Instead of the help I sought, a feminist attorney turned my circumstances into a tool to achieve her agenda — legalizing abortion.
>
> For over 20 years now, my name has been synonymous with abortion. I was against abortion then. I am against abortion now. I never sought an abortion. I have never had an abortion. Abortion is murder. . .

Thus has the cause of abortion been based on lies and the exploitation of women from the start. Sandra Cano is only one of the women who has been used to advance this evil cause. Indeed it is fair to say that all women are exploited who think themselves obliged to abort their babies, as the culture of death has too often persuaded them is the case.

This year the proabortionists did not attempt any counter-demonstration against the March for Life, as they sometimes have in previous years. Instead, NARAL sponsored a luncheon at the Omni Shoreham Hotel. Perhaps predictably, the featured speaker at this luncheon was none other than Vice President Al Gore. Ostensibly prolife himself many years ago when he was in the House of Representatives — Gore actually once got an 80 per cent "antichoice" rating from NARAL itself — today the vice president is obligatorily antilife and has been ever since he rose up into the leadership ranks of the Democratic Party.

"The simplest way to reduce abortions is to decrease unwanted pregnancies," Gore told the NARAL gathering, repeating once again the myth that the proabortionists tirelessly propagate, namely, that abortions are done primarily because access to birth control is lacking. Has there ever been any other era in the history of the world when birth control was more available than in the United States today?

The vice president went on to tell the NARAL group: "President Clinton and I will propose a dramatic increase in family planning. . .to make abortion less necessary, all across America. To those who are anti-choice," Gore added, fatuously (and dishonestly), "I say: if you want to work together to make abortion less necessary, you will find eager, willing, partners among the people in this Administration and the people in this room" — as if the goal of those who are "antichoice" were to make abortion "less necessary." The fact is that abortion is *never* "necessary," and the goal of the prolife movement is necessarily to restore the equal protection of the laws to the innocent unborn children currently being destroyed by our court-decreed regime of legalized abortion while a man such as Albert Gore applauds. . .

II

Thus did the 25th anniversary of the *Roe v. Wade* decision legalizing abortion in the United States come and go January 22, 1998. Prolifers cannot but reflect that, although some progress has undeniably been made on the prolife front, this progress so far remains both minimal and tentative: the regime of legal and commonplace abortion remains in possession of the field.

Nevertheless, the rather surprising success of the drive to ban partial-birth abortions — a drive which currently commands large majorities in both houses of Congress, as well as in a large number of states — indicates both that the politicians are finally at long last unsure of the permanence of the abortion revolution after all, and also that they are now actually susceptible of being influenced by public opinion on the matter. Until quite recently both of these propositions would have been greeted with skepticism if not outright fatalism by most knowledgeable observers of the political scene.

In fact, recent polls do show some movement of public opinion away from the situation of legal abortion-on-demand which has obtained in this country since 1973. A Gallup poll conducted in November, 1997, for example, showed that only about 20 per cent of Americans still favored allowing abortions in all circumstances — which is exactly what the current state of our Supreme-Court-made law does allow; only two years earlier, the same Gallup Poll showed 33 per cent of Americans favoring the current abortion-on-demand situation; public support for that position has thus dropped significantly.

A *New York Times*/CBS poll conducted in January, 1998, found 70 per cent of those polled opposed to a woman getting an abortion because her career might be jeopardized by a pregnancy (up a significant amount from only 56 opposed in 1989); 48 per cent disapproved of an abortion performed to permit a teen-ager to continue her education (up from only 42 per cent disapproving of this in 1989).

At the same time, however, support for abortion for perceived or believed "health" reasons remained very high: 88 per cent, according to this NYT/CBS poll. The same thing was true of abortions performed in the case of fetal defects: 75 per cent. But the poll nevertheless showed a distinct drop in public approval of abortion for "social" reasons: 43 per cent opposed if the woman could not afford the child; 39 per cent if she simply did not want the child; 38 per cent if she did not want to marry the father.

The same NYT/CBS poll recorded a 61 per cent approval rating for abortions in the first three months of pregnancy; but this relatively high rate of approval fell drastically in the case of abortions later in the pregnancy: only 15 per cent of the respondents approved of abortions performed after the first three months of pregnancy, and this rating dropped further down to only 7 per cent in the case of abortions performed in the final three months of pregnancy. It thus seems fair to say that Americans strongly disapprove of late-term abortions. It seems equally fair to say that there has been a considerable movement of public opinion against abortion in the past few years. Although we are still apparently quite far away from any general realization that the unborn are in fact fully human and hence possess a right to life, nevertheless we undeniably have moved away from the abortion-on-demand regime which the Supreme Court saw fit to impose on the whole country back in 1973.

Perhaps paradoxically, 50 per cent of those polled by the NYT/CBS poll agreed that abortion is the "murder" of the child; only 38 per cent denied this. These results confirm something that has often been noted before, namely, that while a majority of Americans apparently agree that abortion is wrong and even "murder," a majority apparently also agrees that abortion should be a legally available option anyway. In other words, a majority is apparently prepared to accept murder as legal provided it is exercised only upon a particular class, in this case, the unborn.

The difficulty or dilemma posed by this finding — that even while Americans apparently believe abortion is murder they also believe it should be legally available anyway — should never mislead us into imagining that abortion must remain legal *because* a majority apparently favors it. This would be a serious mistake. Democracy, after all, is not a matter of "majority rule" *only*. Democracy cannot even survive on the basis of shifting and changeable majority opinions alone; democracy also, and necessarily, entails constitutional principles and the rule of law as well. Public opinion on abortion should *not*, therefore, by itself, dictate what public policy about abortion should be; nor should public opinion decide what constitutional protections should be operative in the case of the unborn.

No: law and justice need to enter in, especially where the issue is one of lethal force being used to take actual lives. In the time of Jefferson, no white jury would ever bring in a conviction for anyone accused of murdering an Indian. Up to the time of Lincoln, most people were not only content to allow the institution of slavery; they were content to see runaway slaves returned by force to their owners; abolitionists were often as marginalized and ostracized in those days as prolifers tend to be today. Such was "public opinion."

In retrospect, however, public opinion can clearly be seen to have been very wrong in denying basic human rights to Indians or blacks. Similarly, today, public opinion is wrong and implicated in injustice to the extent that it imagines that we can condone abortion even while recognizing it to be "murder." Such an inconsistency can in no way be the basis for our laws and public policies concerning abortion. These must be grounded on constitutional principles as well as upon justice and upon the rule of law, not just on what Americans happen to think at a given moment.

A recent booklet by Everett Carll Ladd and Karlyn H. Bowman, *Public Opinion about Abortion*, found that perhaps 45 per cent of Americans are basically prolife today (while some of them might allow for abortions in certain cases); another 20 per cent believe that "abortion should be available but under stricter limits than it is now"; and no more than a third of Americans approximately, according to this booklet, believe that "abortion should generally be available to those who want it." While such figures, again, cannot be the basis for decisions about something as fundamental as the right to life under the Constitution, these figures would nevertheless seem to indicate that the prolife movement at present does currently enjoy a clear political "majority" of a sort in the United States today — a majority which should be invoked and utilized in steadily trying to advance the prolife agenda by whatever incremental changes and advances prove to be feasible.

And if there really is such a prolife majority, even if only of a general nature, then the prolife movement should be more ready to assume and assert the fact of the majority that it has than it has been accustomed to do in the fairly recent past. More aggressive, less defensive tactics are called for, particularly in what is expected from politicians who declare themselves to be "prolife."

At the same time, prolife advocacy should not be limited to what the polls say the "majority" currently believes about abortion: no other basic constitutional question is ever treated only on the basis of what the majority currently believes; we need think only of freedom of speech or of the press in this regard.

In addition to measurable shifts in the polls away from public approval of abortion on demand, then, there has also been a shift in the tone of the rhetoric usually encountered on the abortion issue; this shift may indicate a growing realization that, in fact, the Supreme Court's "settlement" of the abortion question is not only not irreversible; it may and must be reversed fairly soon, at least in part. For years it was enough to invoke the mantra of the "woman's choice," and all possible counter-arguments were then supposed to fall to the ground; it wasn't *realistic* to think that what the Supreme Court had decided on this question could ever be changed. . .

This attitude has changed. Among other things there is a growing recognition, perhaps in part as a result of the recent focus on the phenomenon of partial-birth abortion, that a child as well as a woman is inevitably involved in any abortion. Today even the proabortionists are more often found admitting that abortion is a regrettable "necessity" rather than a woman's right that ought to be celebrated; we have now seen even Al Gore actually recognizing the existence of prolifers out there, while calling upon them to join the current Administration in making abortion "less necessary."

The proabortionists have surely undergone no basic change of heart, of course; they simply recognize that public opinion may be shifting rather significantly against them. What may be at least equally significant, however, is the change in tone of many who have claimed to be "friends" of the prolife movement, even while they have typically placed the issue of legalized abortion way down on their scale of priorities, certainly below such issues as tax reform, big government, preferential quotas, and the like. Some of these "friends" of the prolife movement now seem to be looking at it with new eyes, and with perhaps a new seriousness as well.

This has been notably true, for example, of the conservative journal *National Review* and the neoconservative journal *The Weekly Standard*. Both of these magazines, while claiming to be "prolife," have typically been quite minimalistic in writing about whatever the prolife movement might be thought to be capable of accomplishing at any given time. On occasion both journals have promoted causes or positions that could not but raise questions about the seriousness of their basic prolife commitment.

National Review, for example, has long been almost slavish in playing the public opinion "numbers game," that is, in severely limiting its prolife advocacy to what polls showed Americans might "believe" about abortions. The journal has consistently followed "public opinion" on abortion rather than attempting to form or lead it, as it certainly attempts without question to do if the issue concerns, for instance, the free market. *The Weekly Standard* has similarly promoted such fundamentally antilife causes as the Colin Powell for president boomlet.

As the 25th anniversary of the *Roe v. Wade* decision approached, however, both magazines evinced not only a new seriousness about abortion but not a little eloquence about how they viewed the scourge which has now afflicted our society for a quarter of a century. *National Review*'s editorial on the subject was perhaps the best and strongest the magazine has managed on this particular subject in all that time; the following is only a sample:

> "Abortion tilts the playing field toward predatory males, giving them another excuse for abandoning their offspring: She *chose* to carry the child; let her pay for her choice. Our law now says, in effect, that fatherhood has no meaning, and we are shocked that some men have learned that lesson too well. . .

National Review is still far from being integrally prolife; the magazine still favors Republican Party support for proabortion Republican candidates, for example; but no one can say it has not come a fair way with its *Roe* anniversary editorial.

Similarly, *The Weekly Standard* not only came out with a perceptive and really rather aggressive editorial focusing on how the lie of abortion inevitably undermines other freedoms as well; the magazine's editor and publisher, William Kristol, contributed to the same issue an article entitled frankly — and significantly — "*Roe* Must Go." This article declared the reversal of *Roe* to be "crucial" and otherwise focused principally on the need to get prolife judges appointed to the U.S. Supreme Court so that the reversal of *Roe* could be effected by a majority of the Court itself.

Although no prolifer is ever going to oppose the repeal of *Roe*, of course, reversing that particular decision by another court decision would still, of course, probably fall short of affirming that unborn human beings as a class must be recognized as entitled to the equal protection of the laws under the Constitution. Nevertheless William Kristol not only sees that *Roe* must go; he also recognizes the need for more definite and principled political leadership in moving forward the agenda to help bring this about. He believes, for example, that presidential candidates in 2000 are going to have to take an explicit position on *Roe*. His voice, determinedly moderate, nevertheless cannot but have influence in Republican circles as the aspirants for the Republican presidential nomination in the year 2000 begin to unveil their campaign strategies. Let us hope that the recognition becomes general among this group of Republican presidential aspirants that *Roe* indeed *must* go, and that future nominations to the Supreme Court must be pledged to be made with that end in view.

III

Further on the subject of political leadership, it has unhappily long been recognized and noted that, while the Republican Party periodically lays claim to being the "prolife party" in America, Republicans in general nevertheless rarely show much inclination to take concrete prolife stands, especially if these stands are perceived to be "controversial" (which everything about abortion is, of course). In some cases, the Republican Party even insists on taking positions which would seem to accord ill with its official "prolife" position.

The same thing is true, of course, of many individual politicians who claim to be "prolife." It may be simple realism, of course, to recognize that both parties and politicians are generally reluctant to take principled stands on any issue known to divide the electorate and thus to have a harmful effect on the electoral prospects of the parties or politicians in question.

However, for some reason this political rule of thumb seems not to apply when it is a question of the Democratic Party and the abortion issue: the Democrats today seem to be almost wholly subservient to Planned Parenthood, the feminists, and the proabortionists, even when their own apparent interests and prospects would seem to be jeopardized thereby. President Clinton would certainly not seem to be a very principled man, for example, but the fact is that he has been adamantly, obstinately consistent, whatever the cost, in supporting the principle that abortion should be available and legal and preferably paid for by the government. . .

Why can the prolife movement never seem to get the same kind and degree of support from our prolife politicians that the proabortionists seem to get as a matter of course from their proabortion politicians? There is probably no simple answer to this question, but one partial answer that has occurred to some people is that prolifers as a class tend not to sell their allegiance dearly enough; prolifers seem to be so happy to find a politician willing to be "prolife" that they tend to demand very little beyond that.

Also, prolifers tend to be the kind of people who would probably not be in politics to begin with if it were not for the compelling importance of the prolife cause itself; the idea of having to "bargain" over something that seems so transparently right would be difficult at the best of times; it should perhaps not be surprising if prolifers sometimes turn out to be not very good at it in these times. Moreover, most prolifers are not pursuing the prolife cause as a matter of *personal interest*, which is what most people involved in politics or lobbying are doing.

Where abortion is concerned it needs to be remembered too that maintaining its availability and legality is an indispensable condition for the continuation of the Sexual Revolution. Although few like to talk about it out loud, attempting to call into question the Sexual Revolution, even by implication, is something even fewer public figures could ever imagine doing. This is one of the factors that currently helps the Democrats maintain their almost monolithic commitment to legalized abortion; and it also helps explain the continuing nervousness of many of those politicians who for whatever reason have seen fit to adopt the prolife position — they almost never seem really settled in it. The net effect of all this is surely to give to the proabortionists a distinct advantage at the present time.

Whatever the validity of such considerations as these, it certainly did seem to some of the more committed prolife Republicans, as the 25th anniversary of *Roe v. Wade* approached, that greater efforts were needed to get America's prolife party to be both a little more serious and a little more consistent in working to support actual prolife initiatives — and in reducing or eschewing actions with the opposite effect (that is, actively supporting antilife initiatives or candidates).

One Republican Party action that has in fact riled many prolife Republicans recently was the party's strong support for the re-election of Christine Todd Whitman as governor of New Jersey in November, 1997. Whitman has never been anything but openly and even ostentatiously proud of being a prochoice "Rockefeller Republican," and in the course 1997 she even went so far as to veto a Partial-birth Abortion Ban bill in New Jersey. In spite of taking this action directly contrary to the Republican Party's national stand on the issue, the Republican National Committee nevertheless pumped as much as $1.5 million in national party funds into Whitman's re-election campaign. The RNC also brought in nationally prominent Republicans such as former Vice President Dan Quayle to speak in favor of Whitman's candidacy.

Whitman won re-election, although just barely — a frankly prolife candidate ran against her on a third-party ticket. Meanwhile, many prolife Republicans naturally wondered why merely being a Republican governor, even while feeling oneself wholly free to reject official party positions, should call for such a manifestly disproportionate degree of support from the RNC — using funds many of which had surely been contributed by prolife Republicans to the "prolife party." (Whitman had similarly been made one of the darlings of the 1996 Republican convention by being named a co-chairman — a decision which prolife Republicans simply had to swallow in silence out of party loyalty.)

But enough was enough. A Republican National Committeeman from Texas decided to challenge the RNC. The Committeeman in question, Tim Lambert, also a leader in the home-schooling movement, introduced a resolution to be voted on by the full 165-member RNC at its annual meeting to be held in Indian Wells, California, in January, 1998 — only one week before the *Roe v. Wade* anniversary on January 22. The purpose of this Lambert resolution was to put the party on record as denying further party financial support to Republican candidates unwilling to support a ban on partial-birth abortions.

Lambert's proposed resolution quickly succeeded in smoking out the Republican Party regulars. RNC Chairman Jim Nicholson from Colorado, who had been voted into his present position replacing Haley Barbour as a compromise "prolife" candidate for the RNC chairmanship, found it necessary to issue a statement opposing the Lambert resolution. "I adamantly oppose partial-birth abortions," Nicholson said. "The procedure is indefensible and should be banned." However, as a matter of principle, the RNC chairman added, "it is the proper role and right of Republican voters to decide who will be their standard bearer." Whitman had indisputably been the Republican candidate in New Jersey, after all.

Nicholson admitted that there were cases when a party might have to repudiate a candidate; but, according to him, "that decision ought to be reached on a case-by-case basis and should not be driven by either formulas or litmus tests." Here he seemed to have missed the very point implied by the bringing forward of the Lambert resolution: namely, that the RNC had precisely failed in the Whitman case to make an appropriate judgment in accordance with the party's official position on partial-birth abortion. Hence the need to reiterate the general principle — hence the need for the Lambert resolution itself!

As for "litmus tests," this is a term which no professed prolife Republican should ever use, since in our current political parlance it is nothing else but a pejorative code word for the position of someone opposed to abortion; and if you really *are* opposed to abortion. . .well, you get the point. . .Syndicated columnist Joseph Sobran aptly remarked about the use of the term in this particular case that "'litmus test' is one of those phrases that clog and confuse our political conversation because they seem to stand for general principles, when, in fact, they're applied to one specific topic, abortion. . ." Both parties have numerous litmus tests in fact, Sobran went on to point out, "or they wouldn't stand for anything. But the opprobrious phrase 'litmus test' is applied only to abortion to imply that opponents of abortion are uniquely 'intolerant'. . ."

And in this case it was the chairman of the Republican National Committee himself who was promoting this very implication merely by using the term. Jim Nicholson quickly enlisted in opposition to the Lambert resolution not only his immediate predecessor as RNC chairman, Haley Barbour, but the Reagan-era RNC chairman as well, Frank Fahrenkopf, and the frankly prochoice Bush-era RNC chairman, Rich Bond; he also rounded up prominent prolife leaders such as strongly prolife Representatives Henry J. Hyde of Illinois and Charles T. Canady of Florida to take positions against the Lambert resolution. Hyde wrote a letter declaring that "in politics you win by addition and we need every Republican vote we can muster to maintain our majority in the House and Senate."

Later, Hyde was flown out to California to deliver the same message to the 165 members of the RNC in person at a luncheon session. (Well and good, rank-and-file prolifers might well grant, and yet still feel compelled to ask: but when *does* the "prolife party" ever come down unambiguously on the prolife side in conflict situations?)

Michigan state Republican Chairwoman Betsy DeVos was also enlisted on Nicholson's side opposing the Lambert resolution. She declared that she was "not only opposed to partial-birth abortion, but to basically all abortions, except when the mother's life is in danger." DeVos added: "I just don't think this resolution does anything to move our ball down the field. . ." (Again, fair enough, but when *will* the national party ever get around to initiating a play or two that *does* move our ball down the field?)

It must be readily admitted that there is almost always a case to be made for party unity and solidarity. Nobody likes to be impractical or unrealistic. Nobody likes to be on the losing side. For prolifers, however, who have manifestly contributed so much to Republican victories in recent years, specific prolife initiatives sponsored by the national party continue to seem both few and far between; moreover, they almost always figure pretty far down on the list of what the party regulars consider real priorities.

Meanwhile, the real question posed by the Lambert resolution remains only too real and too insistent: when *is* the country's prolife party ever going to demonstrate that in difficult or disputed cases it is the party's official prolife position that is going to govern its decisions and actions? In 1991 the party did not hesitate to disavow and deny support to a David Duke on the grounds that he was a racist when he was running for governor of Louisiana. Why does the party expressly refuse to disavow and deny support to a Christie Whitman today when she pointedly refuses to accept the party's position on partial-birth abortions? (Because, prolife Republican prolifers inevitably have to suspect, the party is really not as seriously prolife as it is anti-racist. . .)

In the event, as was fully expected all along, the Lambert resolution denying party support to Republican proponents of partial-birth abortions was not approved by the full 165-member Republican National Committee. Instead of the Lambert resolution, the RNC members voted 114-43 for a substitute resolution condemning President Clinton for twice vetoing the federal Partial-birth Abortion Ban bill overwhelmingly passed by a Republican Congress. This vote re-affirmed the RNC's "principled opposition to partial-birth abortions"; it also put the RNC on record as committed to "banning this heinous procedure from America forever"; it commended "the congressional majority for its continuing legislative efforts to ban" the procedure; and it called on the president "to yield to the overwhelming will of the American people" in banning partial-birth abortions.

Some prolifers considered the approval of this RNC resolution a "victory." What else could they say? It is true that the RNC put itself strongly on record as opposed to partial-birth abortions, perhaps more strongly in words than the Republican Party has ever been before. In reality, however, the RNC was condemning Bill Clinton for doing exactly the same thing that Christie Whitman had done, namely, veto a Partial-birth Abortion Ban bill — and the RNC itself had nevertheless gone on to give $1.5 million to Whitman's campaign for re-election after she had shown her true colors with her veto. How serious could the RNC's strictures against Clinton appear when the same body had already rewarded Christie Whitman for exactly the same action?

Certainly we are entitled to hope that the strong language of the RNC resolution against partial-birth abortions voted in January, 1998, will discourage some Republican candidates from taking any position but one firmly opposed to this ghastly procedure. But we should also not be too surprised if some Republican candidates take note of the fact that Christine Todd Whitman's campaign treasury did not fail to be abundantly replenished by the RNC in spite of her position against the party's position. Money still does talk, as a matter of fact — probably even somewhat louder than resolutions consisting of mere words.

Moreover, the RNC resolution as actually voted, however laudably prolife it may be in words, provides no clue at all as to how the national party will actually act or react on the very next abortion-related question that arises — or on the one after that, for that matter. It apparently commits or binds the party to nothing in particular about abortion in the practical order.

This is not to say, of course, that it was a wholly useless exercise; on the contrary, it demonstrated that the Republican Party's prolife elements probably now do constitute a party majority at this point — but so far this majority has not been effectively guiding the party and its policies in any important way.

IV

Less than three weeks after the approval of the RNC resolution censuring Bill Clinton for twice vetoing the Republican-passed Partial-birth Abortion Ban bills, the U.S. Senate acted in a way that seemed to show once again that words included in resolutions, no matter how strong and clear, do not necessarily provide any clue to how a party and its leadership will act. The Senate's action seemed to confirm, in fact, that prolife considerations really do rank very far up on the priority list of very many Republican politicians, even many who claim to be prolife; certainly prolife considerations in this particular case did not turn out to be very far up on the priority list of the Senate Republican leadership itself.

On February 10, 1998, President Clinton's most recent nominee to be the Surgeon General of the United States, a 57-year-old black proabortion physician named Dr. David Satcher, was confirmed in the surgeon general position by a Senate vote of 63-35. All 44 Democratic senators voted to confirm Dr. Satcher in yet another demonstration of the Democratic Party's customary near monolithic position in favor of legalized abortion and virtually everything connected with it.

Worse, 19 Republican senators were found to vote for Dr. Satcher's confirmation as well, demonstrating how fissiparous the "prolife party" unfortunately turns out to be whenever there is any difficulty whatever in taking or maintaining a prolife stand.

More than that, these 19 Republican senators were able to vote for Dr. Satcher in the face of a brave and serious effort by some of their own prolife Republican colleagues in the Senate to prevent by means of a filibuster the acceptance of this almost insulting nomination by the president of the proabortion Dr. Satcher. Senator John D. Ashcroft of Missouri had decided to mount a filibuster effort as soon as he correctly perceived that a physician who is "indifferent to infanticide can hardly care for our children." It was surely a pertinent observation.

Senator Ashcroft also raised another question about the ethics of this particular black proabortion physician, now our surgeon general. It seems that Dr. Satcher had authorized the use of human subjects in certain experiments without their knowledge in studies sponsored by the Atlanta-based Centers for Disease Control and Prevention (CDC), which Dr. Satcher headed.

Senator Ashcroft's filibuster effort caught on, at least to some extent; it was immediately supported, for example, by such Washington lobbying groups as the Christian Coalition, Concerned Women of America, and the Family Research Council.

The position taken by these organizations provided clear evidence that there existed important Republican constituency opposition to the Satcher nomination. This fact, however, apparently had no effect on most Republican senators. No less than 31 Republican senators, some of whom nevertheless profess to be "prolife," joined the vote to end the Ashcroft filibuster; this anti-filibuster vote prevailed by a margin of 75 to 23. Voting to end the filibuster, moreover, were the current Republican Senate leaders, Majority Leader Trent Lott of Mississippi and Whip Don Nickles of Oklahoma (both of them did vote *against* the Satcher nomination itself, however, after first voting to end the filibuster).

But why did the ostensibly prolife leadership of the U.S. Senate even have to allow the Satcher nomination to come to a floor vote in the first place, much less feel obliged to help vote down a filibuster against it organized by some prominent members of their own Republican majority?

After all that has happened with respect to partial-birth abortions, could not this supposedly prolife Republican leadership in the Senate have insisted in this case that the president should begin to demonstrate "a decent respect for the opinions of mankind" before a nomination such as this could ever be considered by the Senate? Why *should* such nominations be considered by the Senate?

In the event Dr. Satcher found a Republican champion for his bid to fill the surgeon general's position; this was supposedly prolife

Republican Senator Bill Frist of Tennessee, the only physician currently serving in the U.S. Senate. And Senator Frist actually found it possible to say that he could "think of no one better qualified to be surgeon general." The Tennessee senator further remarked that he expected Dr. Satcher to honor a commitment that he would promote "abstinence" among teen-agers, as well as working to reduce the number of abortions in the United States — when shrimps whistle, as old Nikita Krushchev used to say.

Thus does the abortion issue continue to distort everything it touches; people soon cease to see anything straight once they have persuaded themselves that abortion is just one more thing on the current scene that has to be taken for granted.

If you continue to wonder why the prolife cause too so often seems to falter at crucial points today, in spite of having most of the merits of the case on its side, you perhaps need look no farther than the way the prolife cause they profess to honor is in fact treated in practice by such as Senator Frist — and by many others as well! The ink was scarcely dry on the strong RNC resolution declaring that outlawing partial-birth abortion was an overwhelming Republican imperative before the Republican leadership in the U.S. Senate was already found to be actively involved in putting in office as surgeon general a physician-advocate of — partial-birth abortions!

V

Thus did the 25th anniversary of *Roe v. Wade* come and go in the United States in 1998. Are there any political prospects for ending the mighty scourge of abortion that has afflicted us in this country for a whole quarter of a century now?

In spite of the bleakness of the current picture, there nevertheless has been some progress, and there is some hope. One of America's two major political parties now does find it necessary to pay at least lip service to the prolife cause, and, occasionally, it even goes farther than that. The controversy over partial-birth abortion truly has awakened more people, finally, to the horrible reality of what abortion itself is and of what our current abortion-on-demand regime is as well. In February, 1998, a black female Virginia Democratic state legislator became the latest former enabler of legalized abortion to switch and to become the co-sponsor of a state Partial-birth Abortion Ban bill; after years of languishing in committee in a Democratically controlled assembly, this bill has finally been reported out and passed.

This same phenomenon is repeating itself in a number of other places. By the beginning of 1998, in fact, no less than 19 states had enacted bans on partial-birth abortions, and such bans were being considered in a number of other states. The National Right to Life Committee truly managed to touch a nerve in launching its initial campaign against this horrendous and barbaric procedure. It has since been picked up on nearly everywhere, and making the procedure more widely known has proved almost uniquely capable of cancelling out the otherwise almost automatic public bias in favor of "choice."

On these grounds alone the partial-birth abortion campaign has been eminently worthwhile, and it should therefore be pursued and intensified wherever possible, even though most knowledgeable prolifers know that making a ban on this particular procedure effective represents only a beginning in the battle against legalized abortion.

Moreover, it is not yet entirely clear whether the ban *can* be made effective. Of the 19 states which have already instituted a ban, 11 states are currently tied up in litigation which has effectively suspended the bans they have instituted. Perhaps not surprisingly, given the current case law which recognizes abortion as a wholly legal procedure, abortion-rights litigators have succeeded in persuading a number of courts that partial-birth abortion ban statutes are inherently vague or — as in Michigan — "hopelessly ambiguous."

In Ohio, a judge ruled that "a post-viability abortion regulation which threatens the life or health of even a few pregnant women should be deemed unconstitutional" — no matter that, in fact, neither the life nor the health of any pregnant women would ever normally be affected one way or the other by the partial-birth abortion procedure. This case merely illustrates once again that, where abortion is concerned, the courts have from the very beginning not been ruling on the facts of given cases; rather, the courts have been ruling on the basis of a desired permissive sexual morality which validates and empowers the contemporary Sexual Revolution in our country: this is what the courts are concerned to defend. And certainly no court yet appears ready to call the Sexual Revolution into question.

It is not at all clear, indeed, whether a national Partial-birth Abortion Ban law, if Congress ever succeeds in enacting one over the president's veto, would itself hold up in a court of law, given the current legal precedents. The New York-based Center for Law and Reproductive Policy, which is involved in litigation on the subject, is quite confident, for example, that "the odds are 95 per cent that the U.S. Supreme Court will ultimately invalidate [such] legislation."

Similarly, the courts have been regularly throwing out other state legislation concerning abortion and requiring such things as parental notification or consent or mandating waiting periods. And there simply is no assurance that the U.S. Supreme Court will do anything but reaffirm in the end the abortion-on-demand regime it originally itself inaugurated if and when legislation restricting or regulating abortion in any way reaches the high court.

Thus, those who hold that it is the *Roe v. Wade* decision itself which must be reversed are surely correct. Nor can there be any question of how difficult it will be to bring about any such reversal, whether by creating a new majority on the Supreme Court — which might prove to be only a temporary measure anyway — or, preferably, by means of a constitutional amendment securing the right to life of all human beings at all stages of life through natural death.

But it must be done: that is the conclusion that imperatively imposes itself after a quarter of a century of *Roe v. Wade*.

16

Epilogue: The Political Future of the Prolife Cause

After 25 years of *Roe v. Wade*, the prolife movement still remains a "political orphan" in the United States: neither of the two major political parties is really prepared to adopt and support the prolife cause in the way in which its evident seriousness would seem to call for; one party currently rejects us out of hand, while the other party continues to do as little as possible to promote the prolife cause even while professing prolife principles and depending upon prolife votes.

If they proved nothing else, the 1996 presidential elections, for example, certainly proved that prolifers do still remain political orphans: the victorious Democratic presidential candidate frankly and proudly ran on a proabortion platform, and he took it for granted that this helped him; meanwhile the losing "prolife" Republican candidate for president consistently shied away from ever even mentioning his own prolife position or that of his party.

This is pretty much where the prolife movement still stands in the eyes of the two major parties and most of the candidates today — and no doubt for the foreseeable future — in spite of the real movement on the abortion issue which the whole partial-birth abortion business has undeniably brought about. Even the considerable pressure exerted on the Republican National Committee early in 1998 to cut off funding to Republican candidates unwilling to ban partial-birth abortion did not succeed in the end.

Nor has anything occurred during the 105th Congress to allow us to alter this estimate significantly: we still remain where we have virtually always been since abortion was first legalized in 1973, namely, in a position where government funding for most abortions can be cut off by legislative action, but where little else can be really be accomplished on the political front. Even all the progress made in the states in recent years, both in enacting partial-birth abortion bans, and in passing other restrictive abortion legislation such as parental notification or consent laws or laws requiring waiting periods, remain vulnerable to court challenges as long as *Roe v. Wade* and related Supreme Court decisions remain in place.

In view of the melancholy reality that the prolife movement still remains a political orphan in the United States today, then, what should be the strategy of the prolife movement be for the immediate, and, indeed, for the longer term, future? How do we go about getting ourselves "adopted" within the current American political system? How can we work the system to advance the prolife cause and to restore legal and constitutional rights to Americans at all stages of life?

Obviously, the most urgent need of the prolife movement today remains, as has been the case for years, getting more knowledgeable and committed prolifers to be active in the political process as it exists in the United States today. Of course, at the simplest level, we have to get more people simply to *vote* prolife than is currently the case; but an even more urgent need is to get people who are already prolife more actively into the political system where they can work at all levels for the prolife cause. The American political system can be worked; working it is quite simple, as a matter of fact; but too many prolife Americans are leaving it to others, less committed or not committed at all to the prolife cause, to work the system.

In this country anybody can work in politics at the grass roots level; and anybody who does turn out and do any real work there will soon find himself "influential" in the counsels of the parties and the candidates: most local party committees go begging for precinct or ward chairmen, for example. You can usually get yourself appointed merely by showing up.

Many prolifers have done precisely this. That many politicians now recognize the numbers and strength of the prolife movement, *and want its help,* represents a very distinct gain over the situation of a few years back. But that even many politicians claiming to be prolife and accepting the help of grass-roots prolife workers nevertheless still feel able to downplay or even abandon their prolife commitment whenever it suits them points to the degree to which the prolife movement is still not taken as seriously as its absolute numbers would already seem to warrant.

It still remains to be seen, of course, whether any of the Republican presidential aspirants for the year 2000 will be prepared to take a serious prolife position. Looking back to 1996, the Dole campaign, for example, certainly felt able to ignore the whole prolife issue pretty much across the board. The first Clinton partial-birth abortion veto should have counted heavily against the president; but Dole hardly ever even brought it up; certainly he did not *argue* the case (which he was in any case probably incapable of doing). One of the new "prolife" Republican senators, Gordon Smith of Oregon, actually moved away from his prolife position towards the "center" in the course of his campaign in 1996, declaring that, while he still opposed abortion, he would no longer vote to "criminalize" it.

The same watering-down process was evident in the attempt to get the Republican National Committee to cut off funds for Republican candidates unwilling to take a position against partial-birth abortion. The RNC was obliged to recognize the strength of prolife sentiment within the party by voting a strong resolution condemning President Clinton's vetoes of the Partial-birth Abortion Ban bills; but these strong words did not mean that the party had to be critical in the slightest of New Jersey Governor Christine Todd Whitman who did exactly the same thing the president was condemned by the party for doing.

This kind of inconsistency is going to recur until prolife numbers and influence become so formidable that the politicians can no longer afford to ignore them; this may already be true in a few places; it needs to become true in many more places before it can qualify as real clout in helping to make party policy.

So the problem really boils down to increasing the numbers and influence of prolifers actively working within the political system. And what this inevitably means, in turn, are redoubled efforts to get the prolife *message* out. Although some recent advances in the polls are heartening in this regard, they are not nearly sufficient as yet. Only as more and more people become convinced that our current abortion horror is simply intolerable in a supposedly free and democratic society can we motivate sufficient numbers of those same people to become active in the political process in order to do something about it (or, indeed, even simply to *vote* prolife consistently!).

We still have to convince many good people, unfortunately still used to thinking in clichés, that, contrary to the received so-called wisdom, they simply *have* to be "one issue voters" where abortion is concerned!

Ironically, the national debate over the Partial Birth Abortion Ban bill probably helped as much to get the prolife message out as anything that has happened for a number of years. Many people, perhaps for the first time, came to realize quite graphically just what an abortion is: the brutal killing of a child. What these people *thought* abortion was is no doubt hard for some of us to understand. Many strong and convinced prolifers have tended to underestimate the value of the campaign against partial-birth abortions: since all abortions are equally wrong, they say, why single out this one type for prohibition? Why not just work to prohibit all abortions?

The answer, in the practical order, is that if dwelling on this horrible procedure has proved to be what it takes to get some people to *see* the moral horror of abortion, then we should most decidedly continue such campaigns for what is otherwise an admittedly limited objective. Nobody on the prolife side should imagine that outlawing this particular procedure is in any way the end of the story; but it has proved to be one of the better beginnings to the story because we undeniably have succeeded in convincing a few more people that no woman can possibly have the constitutional "right" to have her child brutally executed in this manner.

The campaign against partial-birth abortions has not only converted some people to the prolife cause; it has also neutralized, at least to some extent, some of the former partisans on the other side; the proabortion people, for once, have been on the defensive on this one. Abortion is no longer just a "woman's issue"; the issue of the child has finally been brought to the fore in a way that we tried in vain to make it before.

Moreover, once we have firmly established the illegality of even one type of abortion, we have successfully breached the wall — currently buttressed by the highest court in the land no less — that abortion is an absolute "woman's right." Once this wall has been breached, other incursions can then more easily be made against legalized abortion as such. Those on the other side understand this perfectly, and that is why they still fight like tigers to defend the indefensible in the case of partial-birth abortions.

Once the prolife movement has succeeded in motivating more and more people not only to vote prolife but actively to work for the cause within the current American political system, the prolife movement then has to work a good deal harder at doing what every movement seeking political influence naturally does, whether it is the medical profession or the legal profession, the AFL-CIO, the environmentalists, the National Education Association, the American Association of Retired Persons, or whoever: the prolife movement has to be more consistent in rewarding its friends and punishing its enemies, politically speaking.

Up to now prolifers have often seemed so grateful to any politicians willing to declare themselves "prolife" that they have thereafter made few or no demands upon them; the declaration of these politicians has itself apparently been enough. Prolife support for both Bush and Dole often followed this pattern; they were the prolife presidential candidates running against a frankly proabortion opponent, after all, and hence they "automatically," it was sometimes argued, deserved prolife support.

On one level, perhaps this was even true. Nevertheless much more active and persistent efforts need to be made to remind politicians that prolife support demands something of them as well. As prolife numbers and influence in the political process increase, this "something" should be more explicitly required. Neither Bush nor Dole, for example, was ever willing to pledge, contrary to standard Democratic party practice, that no supporters of *Roe v. Wade* would be named by them to the federal courts — and just *look* at the Bush appointments to the U.S. Supreme Court! The majority opinion in the horrendous *Casey v. Planned Parenthood of Pennsylvania* case was actually crafted by three justices, Anthony Kennedy, Sandra Day O'Connor, and David Souter, all of whom were appointed by Republican, supposedly prolife presidents, Reagan and Bush!

This is unacceptable. It is unconscionable that declared "prolife" office-holders such as Tennessee Senator Bill Frist or Virginia Senator John Warner can go on imagining that a vote to confirm a pro-partial-birth-abortion nominee for surgeon general is acceptable. It is scandalous that Utah Senator Orrin Hatch could go on being considered a "prolife leader" in public life while voting to confirm declared proabortion judges to the Supreme Court (as well as voting to approve a surgeon general in favor of partial-birth abortion). It is scandalous that the Republican leaders in the Senate, Senators Trent Lott and Don Nickles, felt able to allow a floor vote on a nominee for surgeon general who had publicly announced that he was in favor of partial-birth abortions.

No other lobbying group whatever would tolerate such deviations on the part of the politicians they support. It is time the prolife movement began to demand a greater degree of commitment from the politicians it supports. To reward one's friends and punish — not just enemies, but lukewarm "friends" — this happens regularly in politics.

Two successive defeats by officially prolife Republican presidential candidates unwilling to energize their prolife base by active and vigorous advocacy of the prolife cause should finally have taught us something. Prolifers active in the political process must henceforth be actively reminding the parties and candidates, both "early and often," of how taking an active prolife position will *insure* a solid base of both votes and campaign support — while any "waffling" will *equally* insure the withdrawal of this support.

Another essential task of the prolife movement included in the future care and feeding of declared prolife politicians should be the insistence that those politicians who want prolife support and endorsement must agree to learn how to *argue* the prolife case and *answer* the media criticisms regularly launched against prolife candidates. Any waffling or even hesitancy on a prolife candidate's part has the same effect on the media people as blood in the water has on a school of sharks: prolife candidates imperatively have to learn to *defend* the prolife position; otherwise they can sometimes be more a liability to the cause than an asset.

In fact, the prolife position almost always *wins* when it is a question of the merits of the arguments; it is just that these arguments are so rarely ever made. Pat Buchanan proved one thing with his presidential candidacy in 1996, and that was that a candidate who knows the facts and arguments concerning legalized abortion can quickly reduce typical media sharks and hecklers to silence because *they* really do not know the real facts and arguments about abortion. The same goes for most of the "prochoice" political opponents any candidate will ever face: all they know is that "women" or Planned Parenthood or whoever "want" this dubious constitutional "right" (the other side, in other words, *is* rewarding its friends and punishing its enemies — and its lukewarm friends — wherever it has the power to do this.

The facts and arguments in favor of the prolife case are actually relatively few and simple, beginning with the primary argument that abortion entails the killing of a child and we simply cannot have a constitutional democracy which sanctions the legal killing of the innocent, children or anybody else for that matter. The Constitution of the United States has in effect been suspended as long as this untenable situation obtains. Abraham Lincoln invoked the Gospel's "house divided" comparison on the slavery issue of his day, and the same logic doubly applies to legalized abortion; we cannot continue to stand as a nation while it is permitted. Prolife organizations need to organize obligatory briefings and seminars for candidates seeking prolife support and endorsements in which these aspirants must be required to sit still long enough to learn to *defend* with appropriate facts and arguments the prolife position they say they favor.

The greatest single thing our current prolife efforts on the political front still unfortunately lack, however, is a solid and consistent *Catholic* vote for the prolife cause. The Christian Coalition and its allies cannot carry this effort on their own, although the Christian Coalition has already admirably and amply demonstrated how an organized political movement can exert influence all out of proportion to its total numbers simply by *being* organized and knowing what its aims and goals are.

Greater efforts need to be made to organize the Catholic vote in the same way. In view of the special gravity and solemnity with which Pope John Paul II, in his encyclical *Evangelium Vitae*, has *singled out* abortion, euthanasia, and the killing of the innocent as the principal moral problems of our time, it is time for the Catholic Church in the United States to place even greater emphasis on combatting the culture of death which the Holy Father sees as having overtaken our society.

This is not the time for the Church to be worrying about losing tax exemptions for distributing voter guides, for example; the Church should *insist* on her rights under the First Amendment to instruct her faithful about the grave moral issues which have now become part of politics. Nor is this the time to be worrying that the very political issue which the abortion is risks diverting the Church from her primarily spiritual mission and dividing Catholics; Catholics need to be bluntly told that there is only one single position on the killing of the innocent in the Church's eyes, and that is that it is a very grave sin and evil. The innocent blood that has already been spilled demands no less of us.

It is true that the Catholic bishops of the United States have regularly condemned legalized abortion in various statements of theirs ever since it became a political issue back in the late 1960s. However, more than mere statements, no matter how sound and even timely they may be, are now called for. Over many of the same years that the bishops have been denouncing abortion, the Church in the United States has also, unfortunately, been promoting the so-called "seamless garment" approach which, in practice, has prevented many good people from realizing that combatting poverty, welfare, homelessness, etc., however laudable and necessary, are hardly on the same moral level as combatting the killing of the innocent.

No one doubts that the Church is in favor of the poor and ill and homeless, and that she will continue to operate all her hospitals, hospices, homeless shelters, and the like; this should go without saying. Continuing to place too much emphasis on the "seamless garment" of all of these various current social issues that cry out for solutions, however, does tend to dilute the prolife message; nor does it help to talk about a "consistent prolife ethic" instead of a "seamless garment." Of course we want a consistent prolife ethic, but constantly talking about less-significant moral issues in the same breath as abortion *does* tend to downgrade the moral importance of abortion and of the killing of the innocent generally. It has also served as a kind of "conscience clause" for those Catholics — way too many of them! — who apparently find "prolife activism" or "one-issue voting" distasteful for some reason or other. If abortion is considered "just one issue," these Catholics can presumably go on voting in good conscience for the Kennedys and the Cuomos who are frankly proabortion, even while they zealously promote today's typical liberal panaceas for other social problems — it is all supposed to add up to the same thing for the "seamless garment" approach.

Pope John Paul II, however, in *Evangelium Vitae*, has now singled out abortion, euthanasia, and the killing of the innocent; and has placed them in a category by themselves as the most serious moral issues of our times. The Church in the United States needs to place the same kind of emphasis on these particular evils and horrors that the Holy Father has placed on them. Specifically, through all the means at her disposal — preaching, teaching, the Catholic press, etc. — the Church should no longer allow Catholics to maintain a "good conscience" while remaining even relatively indifferent to the tragedy of legalized abortion in the United States; a more active participation in the efforts of the prolife movement to protect the most innocent and vulnerable among us is imperatively called for.

While the prolife movement may still remain a political orphan in America, then, simply organizing the Catholic vote better is one thing that could already move us a long way towards remedying this situation. The Catholic Church in this country has a grave responsibility to join more fully in the active efforts which prolifers of all faiths have been carrying on now over a whole generation. We dare not contemplate the consequences for America if her legal and constitutional integrity has not been restored and the right to life guaranteed for all before another generation has passed. As none other than Thomas Jefferson once said about slavery, "I tremble for my country when I reflect that God is just."